A Zen Life in Nature

Statue of Musō Soseki at Rinsenji.

A Zen Life in Nature:
Musō Soseki in His Gardens

Keir Davidson

Center for Japanese Studies
The University of Michigan
Ann Arbor 2007

Published by the Center for Japanese Studies,
The University of Michigan
1007 E. Huron St.
Ann Arbor, MI 48104-1690

Michigan Monograph Series in Japanese Studies
Number 56

Center for Japanese Studies
The University of Michigan

Library of Congress Cataloging-in-Publication Data

Davidson, A. K. (A. Keir)
A Zen life in nature : Muso Soseki in his gardens / Keir Davidson.
p. cm. — (Michigan monograph series in Japanese studies ; 56)
ISBN-13: 978-1-929280-37-7 (cloth : alk. paper)
ISBN-10: 1-929280-37-8 (cloth : alk. paper)
ISBN-13: 978-1-929280-41-4 (paper : alk. paper)
ISBN-10: 1-929280-41-6 (paper : alk. paper)
1. Muso Soseki, 1275-1351. 2. Gardens, Japanese—Zen influences.
3. Priests, Zen—Japan—Biography. I. Title. II. Title: Muso Soseki in his gardens. III. Series.

BQ9399.M877D38 2007
294.3'927092—dc22
[B]

2007060898

This book was set in Palatino Macron.

This publication meets the ANSI/NISO Standards for Permanence of Paper for Publications and Documents in Libraries and Archives (Z39.48—1992).

Printed in the United States of America

For my wife, Linda Crockett

whose love, belief, and determination
have made this book possible.

CONTENTS

ILLUSTRATIONS

ACKNOWLEDGMENTS

Over the years that it has taken to write this book, many people have been the source of wisdom, knowledge, or encouragement, both directly and indirectly. Some, however, have been particularly important, and I would like to take this opportunity to thank them.

In Japan, I am most indebted to Usui Sachiko who, as Research Co-ordination Specialist at The International Research Center for Japanese Studies in Kyoto, provided me with the crucial introductions and materials that got this project underway, and for whose enthusiasm and generosity I will always be most grateful. I would like further to thank Professor Kamigaito Ken'nichi, also at the Research Center, for taking the time to answer as many of my questions as he could, for copies of his own studies, and, above all, for introducing me to the work of Kawase Kazuma whose book, *Musō Kokushi: Zen to teien*, provided the core material around which this present study was written. At Hanazono University in Kyoto, my thanks go to Yanagida Seizan for his patience, guidance, and frankness during a very generously long interview. Following the interview, I not only had a wealth of new material to follow up and digest but I also felt I had been challenged in return to produce something more profound, to dig deeper both personally and as a writer. It was a most important meeting. For his help in understanding the intricacies of *MA* and its pervasive influence throughout Japanese art and culture, I must thank the artist and sculptor Ida Soichi. In spite of a busy schedule, Ida-san shared his knowledge, sources, and interest in this difficult subject with me, providing examples and illustrations from his work and that of others, particularly Arata Isozaki, as well as ensuring that we ate some wonderful meals. Thanks would not be complete without acknowledging the friendship and hospitality of Bruce Harding over many years, but with particular thanks in this instance for driving on through the snowstorms and taking on the gatekeepers of Eihōji. Finally, I would like to thank Hitomi Tamura for her efforts in tracking down vital books and reference materials.

In the United States I must thank first Sharon Nakazato for her tremendous contribution to this book. Over a period of six years, Sharon not only worked on the translation of the Japanese texts with me but also provided invaluable scholarship on the meanings contained in these, the intricacies of Buddhist thought, ritual, and culture, the structures of Japanese art and literature, and many hidden facets of Japanese consciousness. In addition, Sharon brought this scholarship and sensitivity to the translation of Soseki's poetry, providing much of the material that was to prove crucial in understanding this complex person. Above all, though, Sharon's contribution lies in her enthusiastic friendship and unflagging belief and interest in the project. Similar thanks go to Ryder FitzGerald for sharing his knowledge of Chinese language and literature and for the many conversations we have had mulling these matters over. Thanks also go to Professor Dennis Crockett and his family, for their help in a number of ways over the years, Keiko Hara for her invaluable introductions, Professor Akira Takemoto for sourcing materials, and Bill Porter for his help on China's hermits and their world. Also in the United States I would like to thank Bill and Ann Ziff for their friendship and all the opportunities they have given me to understand the processes of landscaping, and David Rathbun and Anthony Archer Wills for the shared experience of working with rocks.

Finally, in the United Kingdom, thanks go to Les Staves for so many years of friendship and companionship in exploring the realms of landscape, Basil and Marion Davidson for their support and interest in the book, Tony Watson for the use of his photograph of Blea Tarn, Cumbria, Mahalo Wilbury for his photos of Saihōji, and, as always, to my wife Linda for everything else.

CHRONOLOGY OF MUSŌ SOSEKI

Year	Age	Location / Events	Major foundations temples / gardens
1275		Born in Ise	
1278	3	Family moves to Kai	
1284	9	Enters Heienji as a novice Buddhist monk, studying under Toku'a Daitoku	
1292	17	Moves to Nara to study at Tōdaiji under Jikan Rishi; takes examination to become a monk	
1294	19	Enters Kenninji (Kyoto) to study Zen under Mu-in Enban	
1299	24	Travels to Kamakura to study at Engakuji and Kenchōji under various Chinese masters, later returning to Kenninji and Mu-in Enban	
1300	25	Returns to Kamakura, studying under Issan; sets out for his first journey to the north visiting Matsushima etc.; visits Unganji for the first time on the way back	
1304	29	Studies under Bukkoku Zenji in Kamakura; leaves on second trip to the north, visiting Shiratori and Uchi-no-kusa on way back	
1305	30	Gains enlightenment at Jōshu on return journey; returns to Kamakura to meet Bukkoku and have his enlightenment confirmed; spends next couple of years traveling to Kai, visiting family and teaching in Kamakura	
1309	34	Leaves Kamakura and travels to Kai	Founds Jōkyoji
1311	36	Leaves Jōkyoji as increasing numbers of people arrive seeking instruction and retreats to Mt. Gentoku	Ryōzan-an Hermitage
1313	38	In face of growing crowds at Ryōzan-an, Soseki leaves on trip to Mino, traveling via Mt. Fuji, Dōgashima, Ōmi, and Lake Hamana. Journey takes about one year	
1314	39	Founds and builds garden at Eihōji before moving on to Myōrakuji, Tōkoji, and Shōrinji. Leaves Mino late 1316 and travels to Kyoto	Founds Eihōji (major garden)

Year	Age	Location / Events	Major foundations temples / gardens
1317	42	Leaves Kyoto early in year and travels down to Shikoku Island, settling at the Kyūko-an in Tosa.	Kyūko-an Hermitage
1319	44	Summoned to Kamakura by Kakkai Enjo Ni, Soseki lives briefly at Shōeiji before traveling to Yokosuka and settling by the sea at his Hakusen-an Hermitage	Hakusen-an Hermitage
1323	48	Leaves Yokosuka and travels to Kazusa to found the Taiko-an Hermitage.	Taiko-an Hermitage
1325	50	Summoned to Kyoto to become abbot at Nanzenji. Becomes teacher to Go-Daigo and others in the imperial family	
1326	51	Leaves Kyoto; confrontation between Go-Daigo and the Hōjō regents in Kamakura comes to a head. Travels for about eight months, visiting Ise and Kumano on the way to Kamakura	
1327	52	Stays at Jōchiji and Engakuji before moving into Zuisenji	Zuisenji (major garden)
1330	55	As the political situation deteriorates, Soseki leaves Kamakura and returns to Kai, where he founds Erinji	Erinji (major garden)
1333	58	Returns to Kyoto at request of Go-Daigo and moves into Rinsenji	
1336	61	Initiates the Ankokuji Project with Ashikaga Takauji, who has become his student once in power in Kyoto.	Ankokuji Project
1339	64	Builds major temple and gardens at Tenryūji and takes on the neglected site at Saihōji.	Tenryūji (major garden) Saihōji (major garden)
1351	76	Soseki dies at Rinsenji	
1353		Shun'noku Myōha edits the *Musō Nempu* and the *West Mountain Evening Talks*	

INTRODUCTION

April 1319: The Journey from Tosa

Spring had already brought out the cherry blossoms in many places, but in the deep river gorges of central Japan the morning still felt cold and shadowed. The tall forest trees, wreathed in mists, rose up from the clear, icy waters of the racing streams, past the steep outcrops of rock, moist and dripping in their layers of moss and ferns, up to where the strengthening sun warmed the morning air. The dense trees pressed in on the narrow trail that wound its way slowly through the steep landscape, allowing only infrequent longer views out over the forested ridges rolling away into the distance. In the quiet remoteness of the place there were only the occasional rapid alarm calls of small birds flitting away, to interrupt the steady rush of the tumbling stream and to distract the small party of monks that was making its way up the path. Moving steadily through a hushed world, they were on a journey that would take them through the mountains and on to the main road that would take them east, all the way across country to Kamakura, the bustling center of government. Usually when they were traveling they would spend as much time as possible on the lost trails and back roads of the mountains, stopping regularly to spend a few hours in contemplation of a sudden view, an ancient tree clinging to the sides of a ravine or the splash and bother of cascades of water as they banged between the rocks or fell in sheets from a rocky shelf high above them. But on this occasion the journey had some urgency, and, since it was necessary to complete it as quickly as possible, there was little time to appreciate the beauty of the landscape or the dark chill of the spring mountain morning.

Beneath the wide brims of their straw hats the monks were wearing heavy homespun traveling robes belted tight over the several underlayers necessary for the cold mountain nights, while their legs were wrapped snugly in cotton leggings and their feet protected by thick straw sandals. The frayed edges and patched places of their clothing gave witness to the many nights they had spent in simple wayside huts and to the many miles they had tramped over the preceding few years, and each moved forward with the unhurried purposefulness of those for whom this environment was almost second nature. Besides the small packs that they carried on their backs, the monks each walked with a long wooden staff, sometimes using it to help keep their balance on the steep uneven path, sometimes to push away tree branches. But mostly they moved along as one, two old traveling companions welded by long habit and many miles in each other's company into a single entity. As monks they enjoyed special privileges for traveling and, at a time when most of the population was severely limited in where they could go by the territorial boundaries of the ruling families, they were able to wander wherever their status was recognized. Although they themselves were members of a Zen school of Buddhism, when they had company on the road, their most frequent fellow companions were *yamabushi*, those "who lie down in the mountains." These wandering priests were followers of the practices of Shugendō, reclusive mountain ascetics whose beliefs, traditions, rituals, and wilderness pilgrimages dated back formally to the eighth century A.D. and informally all the way back to the shamans and spiritual world of the earliest peoples. When the opportunity arose, the monks would often share a hut for the night or a few miles of the road with these hardy, independent individuals, passing the time in debate and discussion. These opportunities provided the monks with a way to stay in touch with the deep and complex spiritual world into which they had been born, and which remained as much a part of them now as the world of Zen into which they had moved. This morning, however, they traveled alone, passing quietly through the spring landscape accompanied only by their own thoughts.

Since landing on the mainland from Shikoku island a few days before, they had been making good time and had spent the night in a small town as guests of the local temple priest. Even though the leader of the group, Musō Soseki, was still only forty-four, he was already sought after as a teacher and was, in spite of himself, sufficiently well known to be invited to stay at temples or the houses of local dignitaries that they passed. In the town, the buildings had been arranged down either side of the dirt road that ran through the middle of it; some, the shops and businesses, opened to the street, while others, the houses of the local landowners, their senior staff, the wealthier local merchants, and government officials, presented only a high mud wall to those passing. Through the elaborate gateways of these residences could be seen the open, bare, but carefully swept courtyard leading to the planked verandas that ran round the houses, while, over the walls, the stacked ridge tiles, ornate finials and swooping lines of the wide roofs could be seen. Between these larger houses and the rice fields beyond stood the smaller cottages of the village people, simple two- or three-room buildings with a vegetable patch behind a low fence. It had been in one of these smaller cottages that the monks had stayed, sleeping on the raised floor that surrounded the hard earth surface of the entranceway. The planked walls supported a thatched roof that was carefully weighed down with rocks and lengths of wood, while a narrow veranda ran around the outside at floor level under the deep eaves. They had spent many a night in such places and, often, in huts even simpler, sitting in deep meditation as the evening shadows grew longer and then, after a plain meal, curling up in their traveling cloaks to sleep on the wooden floor.

Although Soseki was traveling with the small group of his closest students and even though they were passing through this beautiful and challenging landscape on a spring morning full of promise for the day ahead, this was not reflected in his mood; rather, his thoughts matched the cold dark feel of the surrounding forests before the sun reached them. With scarcely a glance to either side of the trail, and ignoring the aches in his knees, Soseki followed his staff, his eyes taking in the path in front and guiding his feet but his mind focussed firmly on the events of the past few months. In particular, he reflected on the reasons for this journey and the effect they would have on his life in the future. As the direct successor to his teacher, Bukkoku Zenji (Kōhō Ken'nichi, 1241–1316), Soseki was expected to take up the post of abbot in one of the major Zen temples in Kamakura or Kyoto, from which position he could then both actively promote the interests of the Zen school and its networks of monasteries around the country and fulfill his role as a teacher. On the face of things there seemed to be few reasons why he would not do this, following the long traditions of succession from master to leading disciple that lay at the heart of the organization of the Zen system and the verification of his enlightenment by Bukkoku as long ago as 1305. But to Soseki, full commitment at this time to a public life of official administration and teaching within the formal world of a large monastery, with all the political, social, and educational skills and duties that this implied, still seemed premature. He accepted that at some point this was inevitably what he would have to do, but right now he still felt he had much to learn and lacked the confidence in the depth and quality of his enlightenment and understanding that such a move required. Twice now he had resisted calls to take up a formal teaching post: once, some years before, when Bukkoku himself, ailing and waiting to retire, had asked him to take over as master, and once, the year before, when he learned that a politically influential student, Kakkei Enjo Ni, was going to offer him a post in Kamakura. On both occasions, however, rather than bow to the pressure, he had managed to retreat to the mountains in search of the privacy, independence, and time he needed to pursue his search for a deeper enlightenment. On the first occasion Bukkoku, sensitive to the situation and the character of his exceptional student, had not pursued the matter, and Soseki managed to enjoy a period of relative, if not total, privacy between the years 1309 and 1318. On the second occasion, however, different forces were at work, and it was only a few months before a messenger caught up with him to deliver a message in circumstances that Soseki was unable to ignore.

The year before he had been living in seclusion in Kyoto, but, on hearing that he was going to be invited to Kamakura, he slipped away and, after traveling down the Kawakami River valley, had taken passage to Shikkoku island. Once there, he settled into a quiet life in a small hermitage he built on the cliffs above Tosa bay on the south coast. His days, and those of the few close students he kept with him, were structured around the hours dedicated to the chores of their simple life and those spent in the practice of meditation. During these Soseki concentrated on his deep ongoing contemplation of the aspects of the natural world that surrounded him, in this case the ocean. What interested him was not just the great expanses and wide horizons of the sea itself, but also the details within it: the wind across its surfaces, the swirls and endless formations of its tides, waves, and currents. And, again, he was conscious not just of the grand interface of the sea and the land, but also the sights and sounds as the sea met the shore, the water racing up and over the rocks, breaking up and seamlessly rejoining, flowing away through deep channels around the scattered and scoured pieces of the cliffs it had itself broken away during days and nights and years of pounding storms. And then, moving effortlessly in the realm of meditation, his contemplation roamed beyond these processes that animated the surfaces of this landscape to the spaces within these processes into which he could merge and his consciousness occupy. His poem "By the Sea" gives us some indication of the direction his thoughts were taking:

> Stretching into the distance
>   the sea
>   swallows a hundred rivers
> for thousands of miles
>   the spray joins the waves
>   to the sky
> What is true
>   of the time you put up
>   the old sail
> Right here
>   you come to know
>   where it is.[1]

"Right here" he identifies as that moment when you feel you are at one with the world around you.

After a few months, however, the peaceful rhythm of these days had been interrupted by the arrival of the messenger from Kamakura. Once again he had been summoned by Kakkai Enjo Ni, one of the most influential women in the capital, and avoiding her messenger a second time was going to prove impossible. Kakkai was the wife of Hōjō Sadatoki, an earlier regent of the Kamakura shogunate, and the mother of the present one, Hōjō Takatoki, a powerful social position that made it very difficult for Soseki to disregard her wishes. A few years before his death in 1316, she had become a student of Bukkoku Zenji, Soseki's teacher, and it was one of his dying wishes that she should invite Soseki back to Kamakura, hoping that with her social position and influence she could persuade him to become her teacher and take his position formally as head of the lineage. Her messenger had missed Soseki in Kyoto but was now sent after him in Tosa with the additional incentive of strict orders not to come back to Kamakura if he came without Soseki, a polite way of saying that he would be required to kill himself if he failed. It was thus a grimly determined envoy who set about methodically searching for Soseki's retreat and who, receiving no help from the locals, issued an edict declaring that anyone hiding, or helping to hide, the elusive monk, would be committing a serious crime. At this point Soseki accepted the inevitable and, being unwilling to compromise the lives of the messenger and those around him, agreed to return to Kamakura.

These were the circumstances, then, under which the present journey was being undertaken, and which made it so different from the numerous other journeys he had embarked on in the previous twenty-five years. Certainly the events of the last few months would have been going through his mind on that April morning, but as the steady, solitary routine of the journey began to take over, freeing him to think, he could start to assess the changing circumstances of his life and the new forces that were at work shaping it. Above all, he needed to understand where it all left his continuing search for a framework for his life that could reconcile, on the one hand, his need for an intensely private world of meditation lived in close, focused contact with the natural world, and, on the other, the wider world's need for him to become an accessible and active teacher and administrator, pursuing a public life fully engaged in promoting the Zen school's interests in the political, economic, social, and religious arenas of his times.

This was a problem that Soseki had been aware of for some time and one which had been of central concern to him since at least 1303. In that year, frustrated by his lack of progress towards enlightenment, he had decided to leave Kamakura and the intense environment of the monastery where he had been studying, in the hope that an extended period of travel would help to clear and refocus his mind. Bukkoku in turn had clearly sensed that this was the right way forward but was careful to provide direction for Soseki's ongoing meditative practice. Thus, as Soseki left for the remote regions of northern Japan, he was already reflecting on Bukkoku's parting words: "If a Zen student makes the slightest distinction between the secular world and priestly world, *satori* will remain unattainable." In the short term these words proved to be the critical prompt towards the understanding he had been looking for, and in a dialogue with students many years later, he spoke about their impact on his thinking and their role in his sudden enlightenment: "I spent three years in my secluded life in the mountains but I had not yet reached a final view. One day I remembered Bukkoku Zenji's parting words, [and] I realized that although I had coveted nothing at all in this secular world, my desire for the Truth had ensnared my mind and stood in the way of enlightenment. When I realized what my mistake had been, even my craving vanished, and from then on I could spend every day with my mind empty. And one night I happened to kick over the nests and dens of delusion that I had kept clinging to, and at last I saw that Bukkoku's words are true."[2]

In the longer term, however, Soseki came to understand that Bukkoku's words had much wider implications, bearing directly on the problems that faced him now, and that the deeper enlightenment that he was seeking was fundamentally tied up with bringing them to bear on his everyday life. He had spent the last twenty-five years on his "search for enlightenment," most of it focused exclusively on the effort to understand one's "true nature," but he had come to realize that this was only one part of an ongoing process. Equally important is the understanding that an "enlightened" spirit cannot exist in a vacuum, in some rarefied space separate from the outside world; it can only exist right now, right where it is, part of the greater context of Life around it. There should not, in Bukkoku's words, be the "slightest distinction" between one's priestly and secular worlds, one's public and private life, one's spiritual or physical existence. It was necessary to find, first, the context wherein these twin polarities of existence could be consistently and readily brought together and, then, the mechanisms that would enable them to interact and form a single, indistinct entity. To this end, during the preceding fourteen years since his official enlightenment, he had been trying to understand how his life connected with the natural world and how he could bring the two closer together. He had needed the time and seclusion to follow the process of discovering, and then developing, the points of contact that would enable this to happen. He sought to create a framework for his life which, wherever he was and whatever he was doing, would provide him with equal access to both; the place in the landscape where his Self and the world in which it existed became One. Barrie, in his book *Spiritual Path, Sacred Place*, helps to explain the nature and function of this "place" and its importance to all of us, in terms that take us beyond those identified just by Zen. He notes that "One's identity is contingent on the sense of belonging to a place" and that to fulfill this role "a meaningful place needs to possess an environmental identity that gives its inhabitants a sense of belonging and connection."[3] This illusory place, one of sensation as much as of fact, would be the same place that Soseki sought to come to through understanding the relationship of his enlightened consciousness and the world in which it existed.

For Soseki the search for this place appears to have found at least part of its starting point in two stories from old Chinese texts, aspects of which seem to have caught his imagination when he was still very young. These stories stayed with him, and, in time, as his understanding grew, came to represent for him the basic elements of the framework he was striving to construct. The first of these stories—and I think the more important—concerns the life of Ryo Zassu, a reclusive monk of the T'ang era (618–907) in China. Much of Ryo's life was spent as an adept and teacher of the Hanya-kyo religious tradition, but at some point he became interested in the teachings of the Ch'an school of Buddhism (Zen in Japanese) and went to study under the great Zen master Ma Tsu (709–88). Enlightenment under Ma Tsu's guidance was to prove a pivotal experience for Ryo, and, turning his back on the world in general and on his life as a teacher in particular, he headed for the West Mountains (Nishi-yama in Japanese) where he spent the rest of his life "hidden" as a total recluse. He became in time a legendary figure, revered greatly in the Zen world for his dedication and commitment to an enlightened life spent in the heart of the natural world. This reputation is confirmed in a story that Soseki seems to have read during his first years as a young trainee monk and that concerns Yushu-sai, a nobleman of the Northern Song era (960–1126).[4]

The story relates how Yushu-sai was traveling through the West Mountains and, while visiting a temple on the way, met an old acquaintance of his. They had decided to travel on together, but it was not long before they had become lost in a dark, rain-soaked valley deep in the mountains. Night was coming on, and as they looked around with increasing urgency for some indication of the right path, they became aware of another presence, what appeared to be a figure, apparently a monk, but one whose appearance seemed to suggest a different, older time. He sat on a rock a short distance away, and from what they could see he had been sitting there for a very long time; the fallen, wind-blown leaves of many autumn seasons had piled up around him, settling on his head and shoulders, lying deep on his lap, making him almost indistinguishable from the undisturbed forest around him. Something about the old man, the piercing eyes that stared out from beneath his long, white eyebrows, or maybe his worn craggy face, emanated a striking purity of heart, a sense of deep understanding and wisdom. The two travelers stood still, caught unawares by this strange, powerful presence, and Yushu-sai finally said, "Surely there are no great priests like this living nowadays." Then he remembered having been told that it was in these mountains that the old hermit Ryo Zassu used to live, but even so, how could a man who lived 300 years ago be sitting here today. Beckoning his companion to follow, Yushu-sai approached the seated man and asked, hesitantly, "Ryo Zassu, is it you?" In reply the old monk slowly stood up, the leaves falling from him, and pointed to the east. The two turned to follow the direction of the monk's gaze, and as they did so the misty rain that had been falling all day suddenly stopped, and a view into the twilight world opened up. Surprised and wondering, they turned back to the monk only to discover that he had disappeared. There was no trace of him among the scattered leaves, except that the rock on which he had been sitting a moment earlier was still warm and dry.

There is much of great interest in this story, other aspects of which we will be looking at later, but for the moment there are two images in particular within it that we need to register since they appear to have been central to Soseki's inner world. In the first place, and in a general sense, he appears to have looked on Ryo Zassu's life as a kind of benchmark against which he could measure his own, both in terms of his depth of enlightenment and of the kind of life he was leading. There is no doubt that he saw Ryo's life as a kind of ideal existence in which one is able to renounce the world and retreat to a "hidden" place in the mountains where one is able to concentrate exclusively on the pursuit of total understanding, the point at which one's physical and spiritual worlds become an undefined whole. In this way Soseki saw Ryo's life as representative of the wider tradition of hermits and monks from both China and Japan who, since the earliest of times, had renounced the everyday world with all its demands and distractions in favor of a solitary, simple life that provided them the freedom to shape and reshape their existence in the light of the continuing revelations thrown up by the hours they spent in meditation. The crucial point about this way of life was that it enabled them to maintain a consistent, interactive bond between the physical and spiritual polarities of their existence—an accessible bridge by means of which they could pass back and forth between the two as the need arose.

In this general sense of looking back for inspiration to the lives of the well-known hermit monks of T'ang China, Soseki was following in a well-established tradition, but the second image concerning Ryo Zassu relates to something much more personal and private, and he seems to have taken it specifically from the story of Yushu-sai's experience in the mountains. For Soseki, the description of the old monk nestled on his rock among the leaves, in other words, totally connected with and absorbed into the landscape around him and yet maintaining his individuality, provided the crucial image for how his life should be lived. It represented a nonspecific but sharply focused sense of what he was looking for, of what this integration of his worlds might look and feel like. This was Ryo Zassu's place in the landscape, the place where Self and Place merged, where an individual fitted into the greater context and belonged, the place that Soseki had to find if he was going to meet the challenge implicit in Bukkoku's words of advice and construct a life where no distinction existed between his priestly and secular selves.

The second story relates to events in the life of Nan'yo Echū (Nan-yang Hui-chung, 675?–775?), a Zen master who had been a student of the strange and brilliant Sixth Patriarch, Hui-neng.[5] Following in the footsteps of his eccentric teacher, Nan'yo led an unorthodox life and, like Ryo Zassu, became better known the longer he spent in seclusion. Having attained enlightenment and been confirmed as Hui-neng's successor, Nan'yo chose to retreat from the public world of teaching and spent the next forty years in "retirement" on Mt. Pai-ya in Nang-yang. His stated intention was to avoid what he saw as the divisive world of monastic life and drop from sight, eventually to fade away in the mountains "as a leaf falls and rots." Inevitably for such a well-known figure, his reputation grew with the passing of the years, and instead of fading away, he became increasingly sought after as a teacher. Eventually, in 761, after he had turned people away for many years, he received a summons from the emperor Su-tsung to become the Zen master at the imperial court. Feeling unable to turn this request down, he finally left his beloved Mt. Pai-ya and became teacher to both Su-tsung and his successor Tai-tsung, but it was clear from the start that the old monk was far from happy in the world of the court and that he missed his life on the mountain. The emperor, however, was determined to keep him there, and to this end he worked hard to please Nan'yo, taking care to anticipate his needs and to follow his suggestions to ensure the continued promotion of the Zen school.

As one aspect of this effort the emperor asked at one point what he could offer in return for Nan'yo having left his mountain to become his teacher, and he is told by the master to build him a "seamless tower" as a memorial and to ensure that it is maintained. The emperor, being concerned as to the form that such a "tower" should take, consults with one of Nan'yo's close disciples and receives an equally enigmatic reply in the form of a poem:

> South of Shō, north of T'an;
> In between there's a land filled with gold.
> Beneath the shadowless tree, there is a ferryboat;
> Within the crystal palace there is no one who knows.[6]

We will be looking at the implications of Nan'yo's seamless tower and the form it took in a later chapter. For the moment it is sufficient to say that what Nan'yo and his disciple were trying to tell the emperor was that, rather than worrying about what Nan'yo might need, it should be his mission as emperor to establish the Law of Buddha here on earth and ensure that it has everything it needs to survive and flourish. For our purposes at the moment, however, it is important to see the parallels between Nan'yo's and Soseki's lives. There are immediate similarities between them: in particular, the fact that both of them were exceptional students who were handpicked by well-known teachers to succeed them as the heads of their lineage. In addition, they both felt that at that time they were not prepared to take on the duties and responsibilities of that position. For Nan'yo, retreat to the mountains meant that he had been able to put off that aspect of his life for a good number of years, but that in the end he had been unable to resist the demands that the position put on him. Now that Soseki found himself in a very similar position, what he seems to have been particularly interested in is how Nan'yo coped with life once he had left Mt. Pai-ya, and how he managed to create a personal space for himself within the wider context of his public life.

Through these stories of the old Zen masters we are able to gain a little insight into the direction that Soseki's thoughts may have been taking during his journey back to Kamakura, how he saw himself being able to fulfil the roles he was going to take on and, at the same time, stay in touch with his solitary, meditative life of the last ten years or so. Although the framework of his life in the future was not clear, we can be certain that the image of Ryo Zassu, deep in his mountain place, was in Soseki's mind at this time and that it was to provide the starting point for him to construct a vision for his future. As he made his way through the mountains that April in 1319 he knew that his life was about to change forever, but, rather than fearing this, he would no doubt have seen this as a challenge. As he was to write later, "It is a characteristic tendency of human beings to indulge in emotions such as happiness, grief, or anger in response to present conditions, failing to balance these feelings with the awareness that present conditions are the results of past causes. It is illogical to face the present only as an object of enjoyment or tolerance, neglecting to use it as the opportunity to create the future."[7]

Using this opportunity to assess his position, he could clearly identify the achievements of his life since the day that as a precocious nine-year-old he first entered a temple to start his training to become a monk. He had, after a long and often tortuous process, eventually achieved enlightenment under Bukkoku's guidance, one of the most esteemed teachers of his day, and had been deemed exceptional enough to be named as his successor. Since that time he had built steadily on the understanding attained at his enlightenment and had been teacher to a growing number of students. He was a well-respected poet and calligrapher, with a growing body of work in each of those arts, had founded a number of temples during the course of his travels, and had built gardens at both the temples and his private retreats. His health was good, although as a younger man his legs and knees had caused him a great deal of pain, perhaps the inevitable result of the endless hours he had spent sitting cross-legged in meditation. In recent years, however, he had been largely able to control the problem, and now, in spite of what lay at the end of it, he was no doubt enjoying the rigorous physical challenge of the journey and the chance contacts and sights that it threw up. On the face of things, then, he seemed well equipped to hold his own in the competitive and unforgiving world of Kamakura once he got there, but he was experienced enough to know that things would not be easy and that he would have to be very careful not to lose his way.

In spite of these circumstances it is clear that he could sense the opportunities offered by his present situation, and he could draw immediately on two sources of inspiration to help guide him. As a starting point he had the image of Ryo Zassu, someone who had managed to retain an individual presence while also being deeply absorbed in the world around him. Looking at Soseki's creative and artistic endeavors for personal expression throughout his life, we can see that all his imaginative vision and his artistic talents were directed exclusively towards the realization in his own life of this critical image. It was the guiding impulse behind the routes he chose to travel, the places he chose to live in, the gardens he started to build, and a lot of the poetry he was writing throughout all this activity. Following on from this starting point, the second source that Soseki knew he should draw upon were the mountain landscapes that he had grown up in, and later traveled through, and with which he had developed such a deep affinity. These would provide him with the raw materials from which he could start to frame his own version of Ryo Zassu's place. The challenge he faced at this moment was how to bring these two together to establish that crucial point of contact that could be used to remove the distinctions between the different elements of his life that Bukkoku had been so careful to warn him about.

Uncertain of the immediate future, but no doubt bolstered by his clear vision of what he wanted to achieve, Soseki completed his journey to Kamakura and a whole new phase of his life began. He had long suspected that it was not going to be simple or straightforward for him once he became accessible to the larger world, and so it proved. With the continuing distractions of public life making a difficult quest even more complicated, it was not until 1339, some twenty years later, that he felt he had everything in place and had achieved his purpose. Once it had happened, however, he entered the most influential and active period of his life. During this time he had a substantial and lasting effect not just on those immediately around him but also on the quality and organization of the Zen school itself, on those who administered the country, and, in a number of ways, on the development of Japan's spiritual and cultural life. He had finally been able to construct the framework within which he could bring together the different aspects of his life, drawing on the image sources he had nurtured for so long, and when it came, the crucial element in making it happen turned out to be: *a garden*.

It is the purpose of this book to find out how and why this garden, at the Kyoto temple Saihōji, could play such an important role for Soseki, and in the course of finding these things out, I hope also to be able to bring into focus the wider, more universal applications this role may have above and beyond his time and place. To these ends, then, we will be looking at Soseki's life and times in some detail to discover the influences, both direct and indirect, on the evolution of his perception of a sense of place, and then, beyond that, how the garden came to express this and in so doing provide the point of contact with the landscape he had been searching for.

By looking at his life before 1319 we will try to find out who he was, how he found his way towards Zen enlightenment, and why he was considered to be such an exceptional monk. In these years too we will learn of his complex reaction to achieving enlightenment, where this took him, of the increasing demands that his growing reputation made on him, and the strategies he developed to deal with them. Following this we will examine various aspects of the times in which he lived, to provide some context for the events of his life and to discover the cultural influences which shaped his spiritual and artistic worlds and provided him with the tools to explore them. Here we will be looking at influences from religion, art, and aesthetics, both Japanese and Chinese, to gain some insight into how Soseki saw the world and expressed his comprehension of it.

In his life after the journey of April 1319 we can follow his attempts to gradually merge his private life as a monk with his new life as an administrator—needing to shape his school of Zen and find patronage for it—and teacher—needing to find a method of teaching that would explain his "way" to understanding. Initially he found it very hard, but circumstances were somewhat on his side as the confused and fractious political life of Japan during these critical years provided him with enough time to find a workable answer to Bukkoku's conundrum. With this achieved, Soseki was able, in the last twelve years of his life, to become a monk, abbot, poet, architect, garden designer, teacher, administrator, fund raiser, arbitrator, advisor, and mentor with responsibilities both within the Zen organization itself and on the larger stage of national politics and government.

Against this background we will then look at some examples of the gardens he built or developed. In some cases these were specific places laid out in association with temples he founded or took over. Others were the more general environments that surrounded his retreats and to which he added various elements, and a few were built for small temples, and in one case a private residence that had associations with his ancestral families. By looking in detail at the locations he chose for his temples and retreats we can start to build up a picture of his developing consciousness of the landscape. We can see how he methodically identified the elements of the natural world to which he particularly responded and then how he repeatedly used them in different combinations to provide the focal points from which he could meditate and view the world. From this it is possible to trace the repetition both of the criteria that Soseki used to locate the gardens he built and the natural elements he included in his designs. The whole process enables us to follow the development of his ability to take control of his environment and to be able to take with him those essential aspects of the natural world that made up his place within the landscape. We can see, in short, the processes that led up to the creation of the garden at Saihōji, processes that it seems to me have great significance for designers whatever tradition they may be building in.

In this section of the book I am particularly indebted to the work of Kawase Kazuma from whose book *Musō Kokushi: Zen and Gardens* many of the descriptions, anecdotes, and historical notes are taken. In the late 1960s Kawase sensei traveled all over Japan with the intention of visiting and recording all the sites known to have been associated with Soseki. In some cases there was still much to see, in others time and neglect had taken their toll, and in others again progress and development had left little more than faint ghosts and traces. Only occasionally discouraged, Kawase provides not only wonderful descriptions of the sites, and the landscapes they overlook, but also an informed commentary on what Soseki's thoughts about the sites may have been, and of the experience of following in Soseki's footsteps up into remote parts of the mountains and river valleys to the places he chose as his sites for meditation. Without these descriptions the present book could not have been written and a great deal of Soseki's work would have remained intriguing but inaccessible. It seems a great loss to the wider literature of Zen, garden design, and self-realization that this book has never been translated from the Japanese.

The final part of the book will bring all these themes together in a detailed history and description of the garden at Saihōji. Equally well known as the "Kokedera," or Moss Garden, Saihōji remains today one of the most exquisite examples of Japanese gardening. Yet even the most carefully taken photographs of it struggle to capture more than a glimpse of its ethereal beauty and fascinating complexity. Access to the garden is now by appointment only, with the result that it is one of the most pleasant to visit. In spite of its turbulent history and the demands of modern tourism, it is still possible to find in its remoter corners some hint of the special qualities that drew Soseki to the site, and of the deep calm that will have pervaded his hours of meditation in its midst. It is possible to get some sense of how he saw his place in the landscape.

NOTES

1. Musō Soseki, *Sun at Midnight: Poems and Sermons,* trans. W. S. Merwin and Sōiku Shigematsu (San Francisco: North Point Press, 1989), p. 104.

2. Ibid., p. 109.

3. Thomas Barrie, *Spiritual Path, Sacred Place: Myth, Ritual, and Meaning in Architecture* (Boston: Shambhala, 1996), pp. 51, 52.

4. This version of the story is taken from Yoshikawa Motome, *Karesansui no niwa,* Nihon no Bijutsu 61 (Tokyo: Shibundo, 1960) and from Yanagida Seizan, "Musō Soseki," *NHK "Reading the Heart" Series* (Tokyo: Japan Broadcasting Publishing Association, 1992).

5. Story taken from *The Blue Cliff Record,* trans. from the Chinese Pi yen lu by Thomas and J. C. Cleary, foreword by Taizan Maezumi Roshi (Boulder, Colo.: Shambhala, 1977) and Yanagida, "Musō Soseki."

6. Translation based on *The Blue Cliff Record.*

7. Musō Kokushi, *Dream Conversations: On Buddhism and Zen,* trans. and ed. Thomas Cleary (Boston: Shambhala 1994), p. 2.

CHAPTER ONE

The Dream Window—Early Life, 1275–1319

When he was seventeen Musō Soseki (1275–1351) went to study Buddhism in Japan's old capital city of Nara, a move which first introduced him to the experience of a large city or town. Before this time, his life and the influences on it had been almost exclusively to do with the landscapes, communities, and age-old traditions of rural thirteenth-century Japan. Born and brought up in the present-day prefectures of Mie and Yamanashi, his early world was one shared with the ancient spirits of the mountains, forests, and streams, and the particular atmosphere of the great shrines at Ise, the potent focal point of Japan's mythical and spiritual consciousness. Additional texture was given to this background by the comings and goings of the secretive *yamabushi* priests and the cults and magical rituals formed by the integration of local traditions and deities with those of the Buddhist world. This rural world and the beliefs that sustained it were in turn shaped and dominated by the landscapes that provided both a physical and spiritual context.

Filling Soseki's young life were the landscapes described so vividly in the eighth-century *Nihongi*, the ancient chronicles of Japan, as "a land of high mountains and profound valleys. Verdant summits are piled up ten thousandfold . . . The cliffs are precipitous . . . and many thousand are the hill ranges." Amid these, isolated communities found a home among the cypress, pines, and maples that filled the narrow valleys, dotted along the banks of the fast-flowing and rock-filled rivers. The valleys were lit in spring by the bright greens of new leaves, while the deep shade of summer by day twinkled with bright azalea flowers and by night reverberated with the rasping buzz and hum of countless cicadas. In autumn they lit up again in a vivid blaze of reds and yellows as the early frosts touched down on the forest leaves, and, after the leaves fell, came the deep frozen snows, with ice on every puddle, pool, and bucket. It was a cold quiet world, yet one in which here and there the winter sun would pick out the dull green of the pine needles to remind people of the seasons to come. And always, like a constant companion, there was the moss lying gently throughout the villages and forests on anything that stood still. During the rainy season monsoons of early summer the air was filled with flying rain, battering everything in its way, streaming off roofs, flooding roads, and turning streams into impassable torrents. Passing on, the storms left a dripping world shrouded in mist, and as this curled gently up out of the valleys, the temple bells tolled slowly and the little shrines deep in the woods filled again with the hush of the forest and the scent of sandalwood. Beyond all this, on occasions when the forests permitted a glimpse, or on a special trip, Soseki would also be able to see the sea stretching away from the broad Ise Peninsula, dotted first with small islands and then beyond these a clear, vast plain laid out, leading away, open and empty.

These places of Soseki's childhood were well removed from the immediate events of contemporary Japanese history, the great battles on the distant seashores of Kyūshū against the Mongol attacks of 1274 and 1281, the day-to-day intrigue and treachery of the power struggles in Kyoto, and the often violent hostilities between the more powerful schools of Buddhism. Yet they were inevitably pervaded by something of the troubled atmosphere of the country at large. On the one hand, the Hōjō Regency, in power by the late thirteenth century for over one hundred years, was becoming increasingly unpopular and out of touch with the mood of the nation. Isolated as it was in its power base in Kamakura, it had succeeded in alienating both the agricultural and merchant communities, as well as many of the warrior families on which it depended for support. On the other hand, the increasing uncertainty about the stability of the political system was dramatically underlined by the unprecedented danger of the Mongol invasion, a specter that haunted the country for more than ten years. The situation was then further destabilized by the feuding that had broken out among the various schools of Buddhism. This occurred as the traditional and long-established schools fought to retain their privileged position of power and influence in both Kyoto and Kamakura in the face of challenges from newer, more recently introduced schools, such as the rapidly growing Zen sect. It was into this landscape and national mood that Soseki was born in 1275.

His family was living at the time in the small village of Miyake on the Ise Peninsula, and, even though they soon moved way, the village has continuing associations with him. Above the village on the slopes of Mt. Ōnzoshi, now called Mt. Kokushi after the honorific title Soseki was to receive later in life, a small temple containing a Kannon statue stands on or near the site where he founded Zennoji, a temple dedicated to his ancestors. The link between Soseki and the site lies in the statue of Kannon, a figure who was central to Soseki's spiritual world throughout his life and whose presence was in many cases a sure sign of his connection with a place. To this day, as Kawase tells us, the slopes of Mt. Kokushi and the site of the temple provide long views out across the valley to the mountain ranges beyond.[1]

Although not very much is known about them, it appears that Soseki's parents lived the lives of minor officials, not independent or wealthy in their own right, but living in areas within familial spheres of influence where they were protected and provided for to some extent by family connections. His father came from the Genji family, a part of the powerful Minamoto clan who had been victors in the Gempei Wars some one hundred and fifty years before. Through this connection it is recorded that Soseki was a ninth generation descendant of the emperor Uda (867–931); a distant but nonetheless very important connection in a country where family lineage and the webs of mutual obligation run very deep and are of enormous importance.

His mother, on the other hand, was from the Heike family, historically connected to the Taira clan who had been so soundly beaten by the Minamoto warriors at Dan-no-ura in 1185, the decisive battle of the Gempei Wars. Although that battle settled forever the question of supremacy between the two clans, they nevertheless remained longstanding rivals, and a legacy of hostility was passed on from one generation to the next. The early medieval period of open warfare between the various clans that were vying to replace the Fujiwara regents had in theory ended with the establishment of the Kamakura *bakufu* and the overall supremacy of the Hōjō clan, but undercurrents of conflict continued unabated in the jockeying for position and influence within the new order. An enduring and murky legacy of clan loyalties and the settling of old scores was very much a part of the world into which Soseki was born, and, as a result of his parents somewhat unusual marriage, it all directly affected his family.[2] From an early age on Soseki was required to "choose" sides between his ancestral families at a number of important points in his life, accepting the patronage or assistance of one at the cost of thereby, tacitly at least, rejecting the other.

Apart from the fact that they were relatively comfortable on his father's income as some kind of a local official, and the possible family backgrounds of his parents, little else is known about the circumstances of Soseki's family. They would certainly have considered themselves to be a Buddhist family, but this practice overlay older affiliations, creating a rich and diverse spiritual background to the family's beliefs. The powerful families from the provinces who came to power with the rise of the Fujiwara regents after the Heian period all retained strong links with their local Shintō traditions. These then became integrated with the prevailing Buddhist practices and cosmologies. In this way "the Taira clan proclaimed its loyalty to the goddess Itsukushima, and the Minamoto clan worshiped Hachiman, the god of war." Hachiman, whom the Minamoto later enshrined in Kamakura, was "considered as a manifestation of Amida Buddha, while Itsukushima was the 'manifest trace' of Kannon (known in India and China as the bodhisattva Avalokiteshvara)."[3]

Some details of the kind of people they were, however, emerge from the writings of his students and friends, especially the work of Shun'oku Myōha (1311–88), who was not only one of Soseki's major students but also his nephew. It was to Myōha that the task fell of editing Soseki's writings, which he produced some years after Soseki's death as the *West Mountain Evening Talks*, a collection of his sermons and conversations, and the *Musō Nempu*, the biography of his life. In particular, anecdotes about his mother reveal a warm, religious woman whose spiritual life largely revolved around the figure of Kannon and the rituals associated with the Taira clan's traditional faith. While Kannon is linked with the Shingon school of Buddhism, in rural Japan at this time Shingon practices were closely intermingled with many of the older rituals of Shintō and shamanism, creating rich localized blends of belief that were often largely "Buddhist" in name only. Whatever the exact nature of his mother's beliefs, however, it seems apparent that their central focus was the wise and all-embracing compassion of Kannon, particularly after the birth of her son. The story is told that his parents had particularly wanted a boy and that his mother, while praying to Kannon, had suddenly seen a shaft of light come out of the west, where lay the Buddhist paradise, and that thirteen months later she gave birth to a baby boy.[4] His life thus started surrounded by miraculous associations. It seems clear that he was from the beginning considered a special child whose life promised great things to come, while this close connection with the figure of Kannon developed into one of the central features of his spiritual life.

At the age of three, things changed rapidly for the young Soseki. First, in the early part of 1278 his family moved from Ise to the Koshu area of Kai, now known as Yamanashi Prefecture, settling near Kofu. Second, in August of the same year his mother died. Nothing specific is known about the circumstances of either event, but the combination of the two must have completely altered his life, introducing him to a new home and influences as well as facing life without his mother. It must have been a very difficult year. There are suggestions that the move was connected to problems within the Heike family, but whatever the immediate reasons the family started anew in a region that lay firmly within the influence of his father's family and where, as he grew up, those connections were able to help considerably with his career. Koshu itself is another mountainous area, and the family's arrival there marks the beginning of Soseki's association with a landscape that was to be a key influence in his life and to which he would repeatedly return, spending more than twenty-three years there overall. The central point of the landscape in this part of Koshu is the huge bulk of Mt. Gentoku, which rises up out of a wide sprawl of foothills to dominate the region, and as such it represents one of the central locations of Soseki's consciousness, a place that constituted "home" in both a physical and spiritual sense. Living in its shadow as a child and then meditating on its slopes as a young novice, Soseki also returned to it later in life during his long search for a deeper enlightenment. Here he was to build two temples, Jōkyoji and Erinji, and a hermitage, the Ryōzan-an, the latter tucked away somewhere among the small valleys of the swift streams that rush down from the highlands.

The death of his mother soon revealed in the young child an intense religious sensibility that surprised even his family. She was buried at Heienji, and Soseki, already a precocious child, broke all precedent by spending seven days after the official memorial service was over chanting the *Lotus Sutra* to ensure in his mind the safe deliverance of her spirit. It was a very early indication of the dogged perseverance with which he conducted his religious practice throughout his life, and it must have helped his father decide that he should as early as possible start a formal religious training. Although the death of his mother clearly affected him very deeply, the overall rhythm of his family life does not appear to have been upset for long. His father rapidly remarried, this time to a member of the Takeda family, a locally powerful member of the Minamoto clan network and one closely allied to the Genji. From now on the family was firmly positioned amid a strong and stable interrelationship of extended family loyalties, a situation that was to give Soseki access to influential patrons and supporters throughout his life.

By 1278, after all these changes in his family's circumstances, Soseki was four years old, a child heavily influenced by his mysterious connection to Kannon, by the death of his mother and the arrival of his new stepmother, by the tensions inherent within his family background, tensions paralleled to some degree by those affecting the country at large, and by the forms and atmosphere of the places where he was being brought up. It is hard to overemphasize the importance of this last influence on him, and his subsequent life revolved to a large extent around his continuing quest to understand and express the effect that these landscapes had had on his developing consciousness. As he grew up amid the mountains and streams of Kai, it became clear that he was indeed an exceptional child. He appears to have had a photographic memory, which enabled him to learn and recite long passages of Buddhist text and prayers in *Sanskrit,* which he then used in prolonged periods of solitary prayer. He also seems to have displayed unusual independence and self-assurance. Rather than playing with other children and taking part in games, he set himself to study texts and to understand the intricacies of calligraphy.

At some point during this time his family decided that he should enter formal Buddhist training; the family's bewilderment concerning their strange precocious child is hinted at in his father's comment, recorded in the *Musō Nempu*, to the priest at Heienji: "This child does not seem suited to the secular world, please do what you can with him." Buddhism had become established in Japan during the fifth century A.D., flourishing in an assortment of schools, each one emphasizing a different combination of study, prayer, and meditation depending on their view of the Buddha's teachings. Behind them all, however, lay a perception of the physical and spiritual worlds, and the links between them, which when combined with the traditional beliefs of Japan formed the consciousness that lay at the heart of Soseki's world and, in a larger sense, as we will see in the next chapter, that of medieval Japan itself.

For Soseki formal training in the "way of the Buddha" began in 1284, at age nine, when he entered the world of the Buddhist temple as a novitiate monk. His father took him to Heienji, a place already full of associations for him since his mother had been buried there some six years before, and this became his home and the center of his world for the next eight years. The temple records credit its foundation to Gyōki Bosatsu (668–749), the itinerant monk on whose practices the Shugendō order was based, but it was later to become an important center of the Shingon school of Buddhism, with an extensive network of subtemples and agricultural lands to support it. It had also at some point in its history belonged to the Tendai school, but it is unnecessary to make too much of these distinctions since many of these practices came under the wider definition of Mikkyō, a Japanese word that meant literally the "secret teachings." This covered the mystical or tantric aspects of Buddhist practice that came to Japan as part of the teachings of Saichō, the founder of the Tendai school, and Kūkai, the founder of Shingon. In most of these mountain areas during the medieval period perhaps the strongest tradition was still that of the *yamabushi* shaman/priests, and at the rural temples there tended to be a mix of Tendai-Shingon-Yamabushi ritual and practice, while the buddhas, bodhisattvas, and native deities were all largely interchangeable, the emphasis depending on the particular background and interests of the presiding priest. Thus, when Soseki entered Heienji, he met the esoteric tantric tradition of Shingon overlaid with strong influences from Gyōki and the *yamabushi*. He combined these with his faith in Kannon, his long-time companion. For an eager young apprentice priest the ritual and texts that he met at Heienji must have been very attractive, bringing him into direct contact with the mysterious and ancient traditions of religion.

Clearly the move to Heienji suited Soseki since behind his drive to become a priest lay a deep curiosity about the world and how it worked, and the temple represented one of the few opportunities open to him to satisfy this. His teacher, Toku'a Daitoku, himself a member of the Takeda family, seems to have taken immediately to his eager young apprentice and to have recognized his special qualities from the start. This recognition is reflected in the Buddhist name Daitoku gave him, Chikaku or "clear knowledge." It appears that Daitoku sensed from the start that Soseki was capable of becoming a major Shingon priest, and he treated him accordingly. Although this was not to be, none of the training he received at Heienji was to be wasted.[5]

Once Soseki started training at Heienji, his life took on the basic structure that was to dominate it for the next fifty years or so; a life where side by side he pursued an "official" path, of study followed by priesthood, and a private path, his own interior search for understanding of self and its place in the world. For the moment, though, the young apprentice's life was dominated by lessons with his teacher, long hours of prayer and practice, and the daily round of chores the monks had to carry out. During his practice, a lot of his time at this point will have been taken up with learning long passages of text and prayers at which he was as obsessively determined to be as fast and faultless as he had been as a child. His biography, the *Musō Nempu*, relates that he was a continually curious student, reading and memorizing the sutras while questioning his teacher on their meanings and on a precociously wide range of religious and secular matters. He also appears to have read widely on a number of disciplines beyond Buddhism, including the works of the great Chinese philosophers Confucius, Lao Tzu, and Mencius. Indeed, he appears to have become well versed during this time on a wide range of China's literary and artistic traditions, their forms and images, its history, stories, and mythologies, as well as reading as much of its poetry as he could find at Heienji. Perhaps most important of all, however, he would have started the formal practice of *zazen*, sitting in meditation in the austere and potent atmosphere of the Meditation Hall, the key discipline that lay at the heart of his training.

One story in particular that he came across at this time seems to have had a major influence on how he saw his life ahead, and perhaps he identified with it so strongly because it too concerned a young boy in search of enlightenment. The story, found in the *Ganda-vyūha* sutra, tells of the journeys of young novice Sudhana seeking out those who could guide him towards understanding. On his way to find Manjushri, the bodhisattva of wisdom, he meets fifty-three other people, ranging from the future Buddha, Maitreya, to soldiers, fishermen, merchants, and prostitutes, all of whom in some way teach him about life or give him advice. What is interesting here is that in the end he gained enlightenment primarily from his own experience of the world and its people, rather than from a single teacher in a monastic setting. Sudhana had met the Buddha-nature permeating everywhere, everything, and everyone and had found enlightenment through experience of this. As Soseki's search for enlightenment unfolded, it becomes clear that this story had influenced him deeply, and that he saw himself from a young age as following in Sudhana's footsteps, always traveling on to gain sufficient experience to be able to understand the Truth.[6]

Alongside these official studies the *Musō Nempu* also records that he was practicing calligraphy and may even have helped with the construction of a pond at Heienji, activities that along with his reading indicate that he was already pursuing as many ways as possible for expressing his growing consciousness through artistic means. Certainly we can be sure that in terms of landscape, the country around Heienji, the views that spread before it, and the central presence of Mt. Gentoku were beginning to influence the landscapes of his interior life. He was becoming a priest but he was also becoming an individual, a unique soul defined by his inner consciousness, its sensibilities, and the experiences that had shaped them; and stories of his life at this time begin to give some clue as to the kind of person he was becoming. Although Daitoku will have kept his students very busy within the structured framework of temple life, the *Nempu* makes it clear that Soseki was a regular visitor at home, seeing his family at least once every ten days. The image of him that emerges at this time is of a gregarious outgoing person, who routinely took his fellow students home with him from the temple to share in large family meals that his stepmother prepared. They enjoyed a warm hospitality at his home, and one forms a vivid and endearing picture that helps us animate the written records of his life, even if it lacks specific details. One story in particular illustrates this. On his journeys to and from the temple he had witnessed people eating sumptuous meals while their servants ate leftover food and scraps. Deeply shocked by this, and by the plight of the poor he saw around him, he vowed never to treat in such a way those with whom he would later come into contact. It was evidently an aspect of life that disturbed and preoccupied him at this time, something that seemed so unnecessary and senseless.

His individual responses to the world he met begin to chart this enduring preoccupation. At fourteen he drew a personal interpretation of the "Nine Worlds of Suffering," a well-known Buddhist artistic image, but instead of creating the standard generalized cosmological image, he related it directly to the people he saw around him. His version of it evidently illustrated the lives of the illiterate, rural population of the mountains, people with whose destiny he already felt deeply connected. The picture represented the unique vision of the world that his Buddhist sensibilities were fashioning and illustrated the caring and involved sense of compassion that lay at its heart; and, as always, over his shoulder we sense the presence of the Kannon figure patiently occupying a secluded spot in the dark recesses of the Kannon Hall. The *Nempu* leaves us in no doubt that during this time Soseki became increasingly disturbed by the inequalities and suffering he saw around him—not simply the clear divisions between the privileged and the underprivileged, but the apparent and inexplicable randomness of trouble and misfortune and of whom and when it struck.

During this time, perhaps in an increasingly urgent attempt to understand these seemingly unavoidable, everyday circumstances of life, he began to seek solace away from temple life at Heienji by walking out into the mountain forests around it. Here, in familiar surroundings, he was in clearer contact with the mysteries of life, in a place where he could concentrate on his meditation. Passing freely among the Takeda lands, he appears to have spent a lot of time during this period on the upper reaches of the Fuefuki River, where its waters tumble over successions of falls and the forests press in on the river's twisting path. After trekking up into the hills, he chose particular trees to sit under while meditating, purposefully following the Buddha's example, trying to come to terms with the world as it unfolded around him. With his back to a tree, the mountainside rising steeply behind him, and the river tumbling past in front, he found a clearer head in the calm rhythms of the undifferentiated forest, where everything was equal, unselfconscious, living with unintentional intent: just being. "Sitting under trees," or on a mossy rock, for *zazen* practice, rather than in a meditation hall, was part of a long tradition that ran back all the way to the early shamans and hermits of both China and Japan. It was a particular focus of the Shingon school, seeking to emphasize the "Buddha-nature" in everything, and was a vital form of access to the power of meditation for the *yamabushi* who had long inhabited these places. In short, Soseki's particular sensitivities led him outside strict Buddhist orthodoxy even at this early age.

Other than these details and developments not much more is known about Soseki's life until 1292, when at the age of seventeen he left Kai and traveled to Nara to officially become a priest. Daitoku had taken his young protégé as far as he could, and Soseki was not to return to Kai for a number of years, years he spent concentrating on the "official" pursuit of enlightenment through a program of study and practice in several of the major teaching temples. After the relative freedom and independence of life at Heienji, he appears to have needed the focus and discipline of these temples, and of the rigorous formal practice he would undergo there, to move his studies along.

On leaving Heienji, he entered Tōdaiji in Nara to take his test, a kind of national entrance examination that was required of those wishing to become a Shingon priest. Having passed this test, and one can imagine just how prepared he was for it, Soseki then "shaved his head," a Buddhist expression for becoming a priest, and duly entered the demanding and strictly disciplined world of a major urban temple. Apart from official duties and the daily chores associated with temple life, he received instruction from the well-known teacher Gyōren (Jikan Rishi) in a broad range of Shingon and Tendai teachings and practice brought together under the umbrella of the Mikkyō school. While at Tōdaiji it seems that any spare time he had was taken up with studying and memorizing Buddhist texts and that he gave up all his peripheral studies, his secular reading and interests, and concentrated solely on the Buddhist Canon, focussing all his attention on the "One Path."

For the next two years Soseki settled into this routine of duties and studies; few details emerge but he does seem to have found a teacher from whom he could learn and under whose direction he felt he was moving steadily forward. But the chronicles then record a sobering event. Gyōren died after a short but very distressing illness, and the circumstances surrounding his death seem to have seriously shaken Soseki's faith in the Mikkyō teachings, throwing him back once again on his own resources. As Gyōren's illness progressed rapidly towards its increasingly painful end, there was a proscribed sequence of rituals available to him specifically designed to help ensure a serene and untroubled death, freed by transcendence from physical and spiritual pain. Soseki was very disturbed to see, however, that his teacher was in such pain and despair that, as his condition worsened, he was unable to follow the ritual sequence, dying in the end with no comfort from his faith. He was evidently deeply shaken by the depths of his teacher's suffering, something that even his wisdom and knowledge could not alleviate, and he had great difficulty coming to terms with what had happened. He became very unsettled. His whole path ahead, his training and beliefs, seemed to have been brought into question, since through the processes of enlightenment this was not supposed to happen.

Very disturbed, he took it upon himself to conduct the ritual cleaning of his teacher's death room, and on the completion of this he embarked on a one-hundred-day period of solitary prayer. Reaching back to the rituals that had served him since he was a young child, he set up a Shingon-style altar, and, sitting directly in front of the Buddha image, he set about trying to find some renewed calm and understanding of what had happened. We can only imagine what a strange and tense time this must have been at Tōdaiji, as the temple as a whole tried to use the liminal period immediately following the teacher's death to settle the spirits and regain the atmosphere necessary for it to conduct its business. For Soseki at least, this extended period of prayer proved to be one of the pivotal moments in his life as his intuitive wisdom, accessed through intense meditation, began slowly to correct the balance between his inner and outer selves, his intuitive consciousness and his intellectual thoughts, between himself and his training. The format and disciplines of the Mikkyō studies had taken him too far in one direction, emphasizing the general at the expense of his personal inner self. It had failed to address who he actually was and had let him down, just as it had apparently failed Gyōren. Soseki seems to have known instinctively that something was wrong, and during his extended period of prayer, as he focussed on the beliefs that had formed his consciousness, a new way forward suggested itself through the "dreams" that came to him.

Over the course of the hundred days of prayer and meditation he seems to have gone back to the times before he became a priest at Tōdaiji to draw on the sources of strength and understanding that he had accessed during his apprenticeship in Kai. He was effectively "sitting under a tree" again, his mind roaming in the landscapes that had comforted and calmed him when he felt confused or overwhelmed by the suffering in the world around him. He was intuitively drawn toward the situation and contexts that reflected this part of his life, calling on everything that his personal experiences could offer. The purpose of this prolonged solitary prayer was to go out beyond the orthodoxies of the temple religions he had been exposed to and which, at this time at least, seemed so wanting.

As the days passed and he drifted further and further away from the world of the intellect, he found his mind running on from his present existence "under his tree" to the stories of people who had found their enlightenment in similar places, and in particular those of the "Ancients," the hermits and Buddhist masters of old China. Drawing on his own experiences of meditating in the hills and on the insights that had been prompted by the natural world, he appears to have reflected deeply on the world of the T'ang era hermit sages and the Buddhist masters who had found alternative ways to enlightenment than those provided by the mainstream temple system. Toward the end of the hundred days he found himself reflecting specifically on the stories concerning two Zen monks from this era who had both taken their names from the mountains on which they lived, Sōzan and Sekitozan. Given the extent of his studies, he certainly would have known all about the Zen school, although at this moment it seems that it was these persons' approach to life generally rather than their Zen Buddhism specifically that he was thinking about.

Three days before his self-imposed hundred days were up, Soseki appears to have been struck by a vivid image, a sudden sharpening of focus that brought together the content of his long days of meditation.[7] His mind's eye suddenly started to pierce through the hazy gloom, and in his meditative dream he saw an image of himself following in the footsteps of the two monks Sōzan and Sekitozan as they "climbed" their mountains to enlightenment. He seemed to be sharing their existence, free of doubts, worries, and dogmas, just himself and the "climb" up his personal mountain. Realizing that his intuition had pointed him towards these people and their particular situation for a reason and recognizing that in this lay the way ahead for him, he determined to fix this moment and the image it contained at the very center of his world, fix it as the point from which he would restart his search for the Way. To this end he took the first character from the names of the two mountains, "So" (meaning dispersed, isolated, separate) and "Seki" (meaning stone, rock), and combined them into the name Soseki, an image of the isolated rocky landscape over which he would travel toward enlightenment. To this he added "Mu" (dream) and a different character that was also read "So," but which in this case meant "window," creating the name Musō. For him this name expressed the state of mind, the "dream window," with which he had been able to initially penetrate the confusion surrounding him and through which he would be able to continue his search. At the moment he took the name Musō Soseki, as Yanagida Seizan puts it, "the Shingon priest Chikaku died and the Zen priest was born."[8]

Through the experience of his prolonged prayers Soseki seems to have realized that meditation was the vehicle that would carry him forward, even if he did not specifically recognize the Zen school as the meditative discipline he was looking for. The important point was that this intense period of contemplation had put him back in touch with himself. It had redirected his life, making it more in tune with his natural inclinations, his personality, and his individual experience, and it was redirected in a way that would draw on his strengths, not ignore them. This moment in fact launches the real purpose of his life, his search for his enlightened self and the "mountain" on which he will find it, that is, his place in the landscape.

Following the events at Tōdaiji, Soseki decided to leave Nara and go to Ise where he would pursue his practice of meditation, but this time under the auspices of a Tendai temple. Fate, however, was not done with him yet and intervened straightaway to redirect his steps. As he traveled to Ise he met a friend on the road who had become a Zen priest and who persuaded him that the best course for him was to pursue the Zen path to enlightenment, the path that went "beyond the scriptures," being based fully on the practice of meditation. It was crucial advice at a time when he was very open to suggestions, and it must have fitted well with his frame of mind since he turned round immediately and, at the age of nineteen and with a new sense of purpose, traveled instead to Kyoto and entered the Zen temple of Kenninji.

This decision cannot have been made without considerable trepidation, since taking it meant not only turning his back on ten years of training as a Shingon priest but also leaving the places he knew and entering the uncertain world of Kyoto, the center of much religious controversy. On top of all this, he was passing into the hard and demanding world of Chinese Zen (Ch'an in Chinese) and the Chinese Zen masters, many of whom had survived great hardship and danger in Yuan Dynasty China, and who were now determined to establish a new, vigorous form of Zen in Japan in spite of unrelenting hostility that was both political and religious. Once Soseki had made his decision, however, two things were in his favor. First, Kenninji was under the patronage of the Minamoto family, and so he had no difficulty with enrolling, and, second, Kenninji's founder Eisai had included elements of the other schools in the temple practice. Thus Soseki would have had some access to the familiar amid the new world of Zen to which he was introduced by his new teacher Mu-in Enban. Whether or not these factors eased the transition for him, Soseki appears to have had no second thoughts, and he took to the new discipline with all the enthusiasm of a new convert. He gave up all his other interests and studies and, inspired by the energizing clarity of the Zen teachings, dedicated himself to long hours in the Zendō, or meditation hall, starting the long and difficult path up "Mt. Soseki." Much later in life he said of this period, "When I was twenty I became a novice at Kenninji. I never left the Zendō at all but gave myself up completely to my practice."[9] For the next three or four years this total immersion in the disciplined, uncompromising world of Zen seems to have suited him.

Life at Kenninji would have reflected what Collcutt describes as Eisai's "full-scale adoption of Ch'an monastic life," a very different world from the one Soseki would have experienced at Heienji or in Nara. Eisai had stressed the importance of the "four hours of meditation," encouraged frugality and strict monastic discipline, and insisted on the full workday for everyone. The four hours of communal meditation took place in the Monk's Hall where "Meditation platforms should be built [along the sides of the hall]. . . . When resting, monks should lay their headrests at an angle to the lip of the platform and lie down on their right sides with their hands supporting their heads. . . . They rest only briefly even though the meditation sessions have been long. This should not be thought of as sleep but as reclining meditation." The four hours of communal meditation were held at 8 to 9 p.m., 3 to 4 a.m., 9 to 10 a.m. and 3 to 4 p.m., and these would be followed up by private talks with the abbot in his room and public debate at gatherings of the community.

We get an interesting glimpse of Soseki's life at this time in Collcutt's description of the Monk's Hall itself:

> The platforms were just deep enough to allow monks to stretch out and sleep. Against the rear walls were shallow cupboards into which were put bedding, under-robes, the blade used for shaving and a few other possessions. Each monk's set of bowls used for eating and taking tea was placed on a ledge above this cupboard and his spare outer-robe on a rail running the length of the back wall. The outer edge of the platform was made of a length of polished, but untreated, timber about twelve inches wide running the length of the platform. This lip was treated with great respect. During meditation, the monk's *kesa*, or coarse wool shawl, rested on this lip. It was also used as a meal table and as a headrest at night. All Ch'an codes stress that monks should be careful not to set foot on this 'pure place' when getting up or down from their places. During meditation, monks sat on cushions facing the back wall, while for meals they turned and faced the body of the hall.[10]

In addition to the formal round of work and meditation the monks will have taken every opportunity to meditate on their own and in their own places as they pushed on toward understanding. As to falling asleep on a platform during meditation, Dōgen quotes the head of a monastery in China who explained to him: "Formerly I used to hit sleeping monks so hard that my fist just about broke. Now I am old and weak, so I can't hit them hard enough. Therefore, it is difficult to produce good monks. . . . The more you hit them the better."[11]

For Soseki, however, the search for enlightenment was to take another ten years from the time he entered Kenninji, and they were to be years full of doubt, confusion, and frustration. Enlightenment certainly did not come easily for him, and from the moment he had decided to follow the Zen path, those qualities that had served him so well as a young apprentice—his prodigious memory, his facility for learning, his curiosity, and his compassion—were only of limited use to him. Indeed, there are ways in which his past precociousness and strong self-image would have actively blocked his attempts to reveal his "true self"; it is as though he had to unlearn a lot of what his youthful enthusiasm had taught him and start again from scratch. Looking back at his experience it seems as though it was not until the context of his meditation changed a number of times, as he restlessly moved around searching for the key, that he was able to connect the Zen experience with his own consciousness. Without that connection, impossible in these early days in Kyoto, he would not be able to make significant progress. He seems, however, never to have doubted the validity of the Zen approach, and he followed it for the rest of his life.

After the initial years spent at Kenninji, we see him start a pattern of wandering, determinedly changing the circumstances of his meditation and studying under new masters, which was to become the basis of his life until 1305. Traveling back and forth between Kyoto and Kamakura, he studied for the next few years under various Chinese teachers. It is clear from these circumstances that it was not the essential teaching that he sought to change but rather the context, hoping that something would jog or jar him into a deeper understanding. There can be little doubt that Kamakura provided a very different atmosphere and conditions from Kyoto since Zen thrived there under the encouraging patronage of the Hōjōs, freed from the hostility of the long-established schools in Kyoto. In addition to this, although the masters he met were very different individuals and each had their own approach and techniques, they were all determined to reestablish all that had been best about Zen in Song China. All of this meant that Soseki had access to the best and most motivated teachers of his time. The Chinese émigrés in turn believed the Japanese to be very capable of responding to Zen, but that they needed an uncompromising style of teaching to jolt them out of their academic and orthodox state of mind. Bukkō Zenji (Wu-hsüeh Tsu-yüan, 1226–86), who had arrived in Japan in 1278, summed up the general attitude when he commented, "I doubt that many students in Japan will attain *satori* in their lifetimes," adding that "some students in this country tend to admire intellectual understanding instead of trying to attain *satori*."[12]

In all probability something like this is what delayed Soseki during his initial years of Zen training, but it must be said that this style of Zen was new and it must have taken a while for those who had undergone orthodox training to understand what was required of them. In addition, Zen training was based firmly on the master-student relationship, and it took some years for this system to become fully established. In the new monasteries the teaching regimes tended to revolve around a strictly ordered day of chores, prayer, and meditation, but within this structure the students were left to a large extent without guidance or overt "teaching"; prompted by their masters, they were expected to seek enlightenment on their own terms. Whatever the immediate reasons, Soseki clearly found the early years of his Zen training much more confusing than enlightening, and the experience he relates about one of his teachers points up just how vague Zen instruction appeared to those more used to orthodox methods. In the *West Mountain Evening Talks* he tells how an old priest at Kenchōji advised him to study the records of the old Zen masters, saying, ". . . in this degenerate latter day of the *Dharma* it is very hard to find true teachers. But if we read the records in order to encourage our own earnest aspiration, we will come to see that the forerunners' *satori* experiences are really our own here and now. Where in the world, then, is the difference between past and present?"[13] It is not clear just how specific this advice was intended to be, what exactly the priest meant for Soseki to understand, but left to his own devices he interpreted the advice to mean that he should look for understanding not from a teacher but from the written records. Accordingly, Soseki relates that for the next three years he spent every available hour away from the Zendō, reading all the books he had recently turned his back on. For all this he found himself no nearer understanding and, if anything, more frustrated since he could make few connections between his experiences and those of the old masters from a different time and place. His chances of attaining *satori* seemed slimmer than ever.

Yet however frustrated he must have felt during the years between 1295 and the turn of the century, things were slowly moving forward, since he was increasingly benefiting from the long and consistent practice of meditation. We can catch a tantalizing glimpse of him during this time when he left Engakuji to return to Kyoto in 1298. Restlessly moving on and drawing on the Zen tradition of continually seeking out alternative experiences, he returned to his old master Mu-in Enban. As he did so, however, he left a parting poem with his teacher:

> From beyond 10,000 rivers and from behind 1,000 mountains, the wanderer comes
> And again to the 1,000 mountains and the 10,000 rivers he returns
> This time there is another true message:
> The wind disturbs the forests in the mountain valleys and the fallen leaves fly.[14]

When this poem was shown to Bukkoku Zenji, the successor of Bukkō Zenji, he is reported to have been deeply impressed by Soseki's talent and understanding and to have predicted a great future for him. Bukkoku, who spent much of his time outside Kamakura at his temple Unganji in Nasu (Tochigi Prefecture), was apparently impressed in particular by Soseki's "poetic soul" and with the skill and knowledge with which he used the Chinese characters. It is clear, then, that although Soseki may have felt that things were moving at a frustratingly slow pace, when his Zen practice and understanding were channeled and expressed by his personal experience, his talents were starting to emerge in their "Zen" forms, and he was beginning to stand out from those around him.

To break out of the apparent impasse his studies had reached, in the autumn of 1300 Soseki decided to leave the temples of Kyoto and Kamakura and return once again to the mountain landscapes that had provided him with so much inspiration in the past; it was time to concentrate within and to draw on the strengths and insights provided by his own experiences. Urged on by his instincts to return to the physical landscapes away from the intense interaction of the temples, Soseki decided to follow one of the most important of the ancient pilgrimage routes used by the *yamabushi* ascetics. This route would take him up into the isolated mountains and quiet forests of the "deep north" of Dewa and Mutsu (the modern prefectures of Miyagi and Yamagata), those lands in medieval Japan north of the Kanto Plain that stretched up into territories only tenuously under imperial control. His intention on this trip was to call on his experience of the mountain worlds in which his spiritual consciousness was securely based to help him move on. He was profoundly drawn to the spiritually powerful places of these landscapes, and he visited not just the mountains in a general sense but specific valleys, waterfalls, rivers, and islands that had been visited since time immemorial by shamans, hermits, and wandering priests seeking contact with the spirits of the mountains. In these places Soseki sought the insight to help him along the road to self-understanding and enlightenment.

On this first trip he eventually made it all the way up to Ryūshakuji on the slopes of Mt. Haguro, penetrating as he did so into one of the most significant and powerful centers of the world of the *yamabushi*. This was a place where insight and wisdom were gained by intense secret practices of the most demanding nature, practices that were still shrouded in mystery over three hundred years later when Bashō, passing through the same mountains, was "forbidden to betray the holy secrets."[15] During this trip, two stops he made seem to have been of critical importance. Early on Soseki had visited Zuiganji, where he attended a series of lectures on the esoteric Tendai school Tendai Shikan, the practices of the mountain monks. As Kawase points out, this school saw enlightenment as the result of perception gained by intense sensitivity to one's experiences. In this process intellectual knowledge, logic, and thought became a positive hindrance, causing a person to lose sight of the "True Self." Kawase believes that Soseki's hearing this series of lectures at this moment in his life was a very clarifying experience for him, helping him to gain some perspective on his practice up to now. Things must have seemed much clearer and more direct up there, reconnecting him with the world of the *yamabushi* and "sitting under trees."

Over the next six months Soseki slowly made his way back south, stopping for weeks at a time to meet fellow priests and visit sites of particular interest, and as he passed through the Ōkita River region he made the second crucial stop of this journey. He had heard that Bukkoku Zenji was in

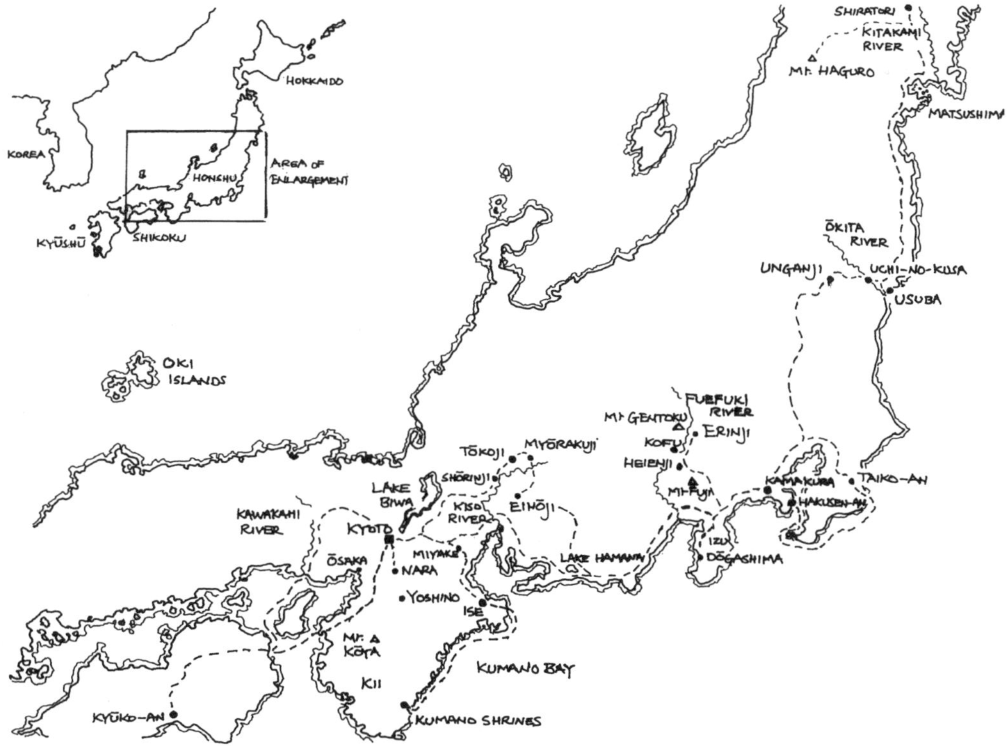

Figure 1. Map of Soseki's journeys and places mentioned in the text.

residence at Unganji, and, in the true Zen tradition, on the spur of the moment he decided to pay him a visit. Arriving at Unganji, Soseki found that official duties had called Bukkoku back to Kamakura, but since it was now very late in the year, he decided to stay until the spring thaw made traveling easier. In addition to the weather he was also experiencing increasing pain in his legs and needed an extended period of rest. Whether his legs were beginning to suffer from the long years of sitting in meditation or from the hard walking of the last year is not clear, but by the winter of 1301 it had become a real problem. Kawase indicates that at this time Soseki believed that as much as anything the pains in his legs were a symptom of physical attachments, one of numerous barriers preventing him from seeing his "real self," in this case the constant presence of the physical body obscuring what lay within. He determined to stay at Unganji until he overcame this problem. As he would do throughout his life, he set out to do this by combining the practices that had underpinned his spiritual life since childhood: he set up an altar to Kannon to conduct a seventeen-day "purification" ritual. During the course of this ritual of prayer and meditation he found himself beset by a number of strange images and voices speaking to him, vivid enough for him to remember clearly at the end of the practice. Looking back at the experience, he asked himself why they had appeared and what the "demon" voices and images had to do with who he really was, and, in that instant, he realized that the answer was *nothing*. They, like all other matters over which he had puzzled, were all forms of external illusions, not part of the deep matters of process that were all that actually lay at the heart of life, existence, and consciousness.

Apart from the continuing insights such as these that Soseki gained during his stay at Unganji, his time there seems also to have marked an important step forward in his sense of how the enlightened soul might relate to the physical world around it. Visiting the places that for generations had drawn the *yamabushi* ascetics, he was exposed once again to the power of the natural world and the ability of places within it to create a connection between the inner spiritual world and the physical reality in which it existed. During his prolonged winter stay at Unganji this sense of connection seems to have been particularly strong. In this context we should remember the image of Ryo Zassu sitting on his rock, since it gives us a glimpse of what Soseki was looking for here in the mountains and his image of himself in the landscape. The picture of the old monk almost lost from sight in the forest, barely perceptible beneath the fallen leaves, formed for Soseki a precise image of what he needed to achieve: such a deep and intuitive connection between self and place that the person and place are essentially merged into one. Existence is no more or less than him, then, in that place, at that moment, and that moment recognized and consciously acknowledged in the continuing process of life. For Soseki his trip to the north seems to have initiated a slow redefinition of those connections he had felt so strongly as a child and had perhaps lost track of during the years of formal training.

Part of the importance of this stay at Unganji was that the temple and the immediate landscape that surrounded it had been created by Bukkoku, a Japanese master, and not, as was the case in the Kamakura temples, by Chinese masters. Rankei Dōryū's (Lan-ch'i Tao-lung, 1213–78) standing stone garden at Tōkoji, for example, was firmly in the Southern Song Chinese style, however much that might have been adapted to the Japanese setting. At Unganji, however, the setting for the temple had emerged from a Japanese consciousness, using the natural landscape itself to provide the theme and content. Since we do not know exactly how this garden looked in 1301, it is dangerous to draw too many specific conclusions about it, but from what we do know, from what Bukkoku seems to have done there, it seems likely that this was one of the first that Soseki had experienced where the intention was that it remain "natural." Bukkoku seems to have intended to focus on the natural setting itself rather than using it as the backdrop for a group of standing stones or a meandering stream. If so, this represents a radical new departure in Japanese garden design.

Unganji had been founded, at least the version that Soseki knew, by Bukkoku in 1264 when he was twenty-three, a fact that in itself indicates something of his great talents. Having studied under various Chinese masters, he achieved enlightenment early on and left Kamakura for a long period of isolation at Unganji. Eventually he returned sometime around 1280 and, after becoming a student of the newly arrived Bukkō Zenji, succeeded his master as the head of the lineage in 1286. The temple at Unganji stands, as Rankei Dōryū's Tōkoji had done, at the foot of a steep section of the mountain that rises up and away behind it. Behind the temple the setting was made even more special by a waterfall, known as the Ido no Take, the "Waterfall of the Well," which springs from the rock face out of the tangle of clinging forest, falling in a long stream into a pool at the foot of the cliff.[16] To one side of this, the setting is completed by the opening to a small cave. Kawase believes that Bukkoku will have initially built up the pool to act as the water source for the temple, hence the reference to a well in the name of the fall, but soon also made it and the fall the focal point of a small garden, adding a few rocks to complete the site.

Over the winter of 1301–2 Soseki apparently spent more and more time meditating at the mouth of the small cave, "sitting under the cliff," looking out over the pool. It became, in fact, his chief place of practice, and he clearly felt an increasing sense of connection tucked away at the foot of the cliff with the great mass of the mountain at his back, an encompassing presence wrapped around, above, and behind him like Ryo Zassu's pile of leaves, and a view in front out over the world. As Kawase puts it, "This place, with the thin, flying waterfall, was particularly suited for clearing the heart. This pristinely beautiful and mysterious setting performed the function of creating a single point around which, through nature, he could focus his thoughts."[17] On this trip he had visited many other places of great beauty, but here at Unganji he found a new situation, a unique combination of the natural and the man-made, which acted as a contact point between the two. From this time on Soseki consistently established a private space for meditating outside in the landscape beyond the public spaces of the temple or hermitage in which he was living. Following again the lead of Ryo Zassu, he created a place that often took the form of a *zazen-seki*, "meditation rock," set out in the forest.

Returning the next spring to Kamakura, Soseki reentered Kenchōji and resumed his studies, but this time he seems to have immediately sensed that something was not right. After thinking about it, he suddenly saw that in following earlier advice to read and study the records of the old masters he had, in his own words, "left Buddhist theory only to lose myself in Zen scholarship," that both were equally based on an intellectual understanding. Once he realized this, he goes on to say, "I gathered up all the odds and ends that I had treasured up until then and put them in my satchel, and without a moment's hesitation threw them into the fire."[18] Up in flames went his books and collected papers and his long years of studying first one kind of text and then another. All this came to a sudden end with his dramatic and intuitive gesture. Once and for all his search for enlightenment would be concentrated on meditation alone. A conversation with his teacher at the time, Issan (I-shan I-ning, 1247–1317), in which we get some indication of the frustration he still felt in spite of the progress he had made, is recorded as follows:

> Soseki: I cannot attain enlightenment. Show it to me.
> Issan: There is no word in our school. There is no rule to transmit.
> Soseki: Show me your compassion and your Way.
> Issan: There is no compassion. And there is not any Way.[19]

Answering Soseki point by point, Issan tries to make him forget all those differentiated concepts, "schools," "rules," "transmissions," "ways," and look only at what lies within himself, but as yet Soseki cannot follow him. At this moment he could not go beyond "enlightenment" and the "way," and even his sense of compassion, his lifelong companion and to him the key quality of Buddha's teachings, had become a concept that now blocked his way forward. Thus his clear, precocious insights that had propelled his early career were now part of the problem. Frustrated by this exchange with Issan, but determined not to lose the momentum of the last few months, he straightaway decided to leave and seek out Bukkoku, drawn instinctively to the teacher he had missed a year or so before but whose temple had had such an effect on him. Bukkoku in turn passed on some advice that his own teacher had given him many years before: "*satori* is something you must arrive at without help from anyone." Soseki seems to have taken this advice immediately to heart, and he informed Bukkoku there and then that he would leave on his search "without help from anyone" and not return unless he had gained enlightenment. Encouraged by his experiences of a few years before, by his sense that things may be coming to a head and by Bukkoku's specific and clear advice, he set off at once on a second, critical trip to the north.

Traveling first right up to Shiratori, he eventually made his way back down again to the Ōkita River region, where he built a small hut at Uchi-no-kusa. In the *West Mountain Evening Talks* Soseki later spoke about this period, and it is quite clear that he was reaching some kind of a make-or-break point. He seems to have realized that he held all the keys to enlightenment in his hands if only he could understand how to use them, and he outlined his intentions with great clarity: "I left Engakuji and went to the Deep North to build a hut far out in the mountains. . . . I made a vow to myself. I said, 'I will either come to see my Original Self or I will die among the grass and trees.'"[20] And so, with nothing but the wilderness of mountains around him, he settled down to meditate, attempting to lose himself on his meditation rock among the falling leaves as the year turned toward winter.

Things progressed slowly until one evening when, after he had completed his meditation for the day, he sat in prayer in front of his Kannon statue. During this routine practice, in other words at a time when he was no longer thinking specifically about enlightenment, but with his mind free-wheeling within the space provided by familiar, almost subconscious, ritual, he made another significant breakthrough in understanding. As Kawase relates the story, Soseki was "sitting" one evening at his Kannon altar when he began to fall asleep. He was awakened suddenly by the setting sun shining on his face, and his first reaction was to be ashamed that he had fallen asleep, but on further reflection he realized that he was supposed to be someone for whom "sleeping" and "waking" were no different; if there was no differentiation, except that of language, then it did not matter in what state he sat in front of the altar. This abrupt, clarifying realization made him feel that he was suddenly much closer to his goal, and this persuaded him to travel south again to talk to Bukkoku and perhaps turn this leap in comprehension into enlightenment itself.

Thus, in February 1305 he left for Kamakura, but, while passing through Jōshu, he was caught up in a quickening sense that understanding was very close at hand, and it was there, one evening in May, that everything was to change forever. On this evening, during a break from meditating in front of his Kannon statue, he stepped out into the garden of the house in which he was staying for some fresh air. Very tired after hours spent in *zazen*, he soon fell asleep in the cool evening air only to awake some time later to discover it was pitch dark. No doubt annoyed at himself for once again falling asleep, he rose to go inside to continue his meditation. Unfocussed for a moment as he got up, his mind empty, he leaned back to support himself on the wall he assumed to be right behind him, but there was nothing there, and he fell over backwards. Springing to his feet, he laughed out loud into the empty black night; at the moment of falling over he had gained enlightenment.

In one unguarded moment all the assumptions he had been making about what existed and what did not evaporated, and the nature of his Original Self became clear. Laughing with relief and excitement, Soseki shrugged off all the long years of frustration, and he "realized that although I coveted nothing at all in this secular world, my desire for the Dharma [Truth] had ensnared my mind and stood in the way of enlightenment." Once this became clear, "my craving vanished and from then on I could spend everyday with my mind empty." The balance had been restored. Not coveting things in the secular world but not turning his back on them either, he could finally see and accept Life for what it was. On the one hand, Shingon-Buddhist practice had confused him with the concepts of "schools" and "ways," and, on the other, Song Zen had been too severe, too extreme, and dislocated from his experience. For too many years it had become for him a practice without a context. Slowly, however, under the influence of his native landscapes, the roots of his experience and consciousness, he had learned to moderate it, and this, in conjunction with his Kannon practice, had provided it with a vital context of place, both physical and psychological. His enlightenment thus came eventually through a complex mix of Zen and Shingon practice rooted in the shamanistic past of the mountain landscapes. It had arrived once he was able to bring together his experience and consciousness, without the intervention of a master, with the physical world. Not in a meditation hall but among the "grass and trees," in direct connection with his roots.

At this point, in accordance with the Zen tradition, he was required to write a poem that would express his enlightened understanding, a poem by which Bukkoku could gauge whether enlightenment had occurred. The moment represented for Soseki the culmination of a thirty-year search, from his early practice with his mother, through his years as a Shingon priest, to this complex experience among the hills. The poem he wrote he called "Sitting in Solitude":

> For many years
> I have dug in the ground,
> seeking the blue skies.
> Time after time
> gaining only obstructions
> in my heart.
> One night
> in the midst of the darkness
> I kicked up a piece of tile.
> Just letting go
> I realized the already empty bones
> are struck into bits.[21]

It is in many ways a conventional poem, yet its structure underlines the nature of what happened in the juxtaposition of "For many years" with "One night" and "Time after time" with "Just letting go," summing up what was so different about this particular experience. The two key phrases "one night" and "just letting go" both indicate that no matter how hard you try, logic and the intellect engaged in thinking and studying will not help; enlightenment comes when it is ready, at sudden, unpredictable, and uncontrollable moments of intuitive comprehension. The ideas captured in these two phrases trigger the rushing action, "kicking up," that smashes through the repeated weight of the "many years" and "time after time." "One night" expresses the randomness of the moment, not this night or that night, but a time that could not be planned, anticipated, or manipulated. It happened at a moment beyond his control, catching him and his habitual processes of thought off guard, in an instant when his intellectual knowledge and life experiences were suddenly balanced and given context by an intuitive understanding of reality. And why did it happen that night and not on any other night before? Because this was a random, unlooked for event. For the first time he had suddenly "just let go," and a moment of involuntary, intuitive action took place. In Chinese, *tokan*, and in modern Japanese, *iikagen*, the meaning of "letting go" here is qualified with the sense of the action being involuntary, not the use of the will but rather the opposite. This "one night" was different because everything happened without a thought, precisely what failed to happen so far. As he was to put it later in another poem, "The light of awakening appears when it has been forgotten."

Because on this evening these criteria were in place "in the midst of the darkness," associated in Zen imagery with the realm of non-duality when differentiation slips away, the whole conceptual superstructure, "the empty bones," that his intellect had constructed was smashed to pieces and his Original Self was revealed. All that he had learned, digested, and experienced was condensed and expressed in these two phrases, giving this strange little event in the darkened garden a massive significance. On his return to Kamakura, Soseki met with Bukkoku at Jōchiji, and after a further series of questions and answers, in which his master sought to confirm that a real shift in understanding had occurred, Bukkoku gave his poem the seal of approval, confirmation that to his master's satisfaction Soseki had achieved enlightenment.

Over the next four years Soseki remained at Jōchiji fulfilling his obligations to Bukkoku "in the work" of teaching and running the temple system. At this point the patronage of Kakkai Enjo Ni, who was the mother of the present regent Hōjō Takatoki and who was to figure so prominently in the events of 1319, provided Soseki with rapid access to various posts in the Kamakura monastic system and helped ensure his acceptance as Bukkoku's successor. During this period, Soseki briefly returned to Kai, staying at Heienji to visit his family and his old teacher and to take his place as a senior monk in the family affairs. On his return to Kamakura, Bukkoku appointed Soseki as his official successor, on his death handing over to Soseki responsibility for what had become the most influential lineage of the time. Between them during this period Bukkoku and Soseki defined the style and content of Japanese Zen in Kamakura, as the Chinese masters had done earlier and as Soseki and Daitō would do later on in Kyoto. By this time, however, it seems that Bukkoku was beginning to feel the strain of the long years of teaching and decided to retire. Thus, in 1309 the partnership broke up and the old master's students all transferred their allegiance to Soseki. Unwelcome as all this responsibility may have been for Soseki, Bukkoku formalized the new arrangement by passing on to him Bukkō Zenji's book of teachings, and he insisted that Soseki must repay his debt to Buddha by carrying on the teaching work. Although he must have been fully aware that Soseki would have preferred to return to the peace and quiet of the mountains, he reminded him that "the teacher does not fight what is ordained in heaven," and with that Bukkoku took his leave of Kamakura, returning to Unganji for the last seven years of his life. Throughout the years that followed, until Bukkoku's death in 1316, the two corresponded frequently, maintaining a close relationship that was clearly based on a deep mutual respect and affection. Soseki we know attributed his enlightenment to Bukkoku's caring and compassionate teaching and was very fond of his old master, while Bukkoku said of Soseki at this time, "There's no knowing how far Soseki will go; this old priest cannot match him."[22] Clearly, he was still as impressed by the potential of his student as he had been on reading his poem many years before.

Although he accepted that he would eventually become master of the lineage and everything that went with this, Soseki was not yet ready to stay in Kamakura and become involved in its day-to-day administration. Even though his responsibilities were growing fast and students were coming to him in increasing numbers, in himself he felt that he had not yet fully "realized that which had no limitations" or that he had fully understood the implications and subtleties of his enlightenment. He felt that there was still much more to grasp before he could usefully commit himself to becoming a full-time teacher.

It seems evident from his actions up to this point in his career that he still saw himself as following in the footsteps of Sudhana, journeying on to seek wider experiences. His route to enlightenment had taken him out of the monasteries and into contact with the world, and now he seemed determined to keep the independence he needed to continue this course. Bukkoku seems to have understood this and was content to let him go. Soseki's choices at this point were also influenced by the life of Chung-feng Ming-pen (1263–1323), the Chinese monk "prized [in Japan] for his reclusive life and his blend of Pure Land and Zen."[23] Soseki seems to have followed closely the life of this influential and charismatic recluse who was, as Parker points out, "known for having refused numerous requests of his contemporaries, including the emperor, to serve as abbot of Five Mountain temples. Instead he spent several years living a mendicant existence." It is remarkable how quickly Chung-feng's reputation spread to Japan, and, even though Soseki was later against too much direct influence from China, he seems to have found in Chung-feng's life a precedent that validated his own reluctance to "enter the world" and to have followed his example closely. It is interesting to note Parker's further comment, "Beginning in 1298 [Chung-feng Ming-pen] also resided in small hermitages for periods lasting a few years at a time, until moving on after the number of students who had taken up residence with him became too large."[24] As we will see, this is very much the pattern of Soseki's life over the next sixteen years, continually moving on when places got crowded and avoiding requests from Bukkoku, the emperor, and the *bakufu* to take up temple positions.

Thus, with these influences at work on him, in 1309, he once again left Kamakura and set out for Kai, where he hoped to begin the process of deepening his enlightenment and understanding better the relationship between his inner need to continue his meditation practice and the increasing demands of his public life. He seems to have felt at this point that he needed to understand his experience of enlightenment, to find out where he fitted into it, in the same way that he had found his place as a child in the landscapes of Kai, and in the same way that he had found a place in the psychological space of the Kannon altar. Now he needed to know where his enlightened self fitted into the everyday world. The initial journey to Kai may have been short enough, but it marked the start of another period of extended journeys that was to last until 1319.

As a starting point for this trip he seems to have had an idea of the kind of place he was looking for, those places, or rather those types of places, where, sitting in meditation, he felt instinctively connected to the world around him. These were the places where he chose a rock to be his *zazen-seki* (meditation rock). In official practice one took one's place in the Zendō with its images and calm atmosphere, but outside there were no such officially prepared places, only those chosen by individuals. For Ryo Zassu this had been a rock on West Mountain, a point of total integration between person and place, where his presence lingered after he was gone. Soseki built on this idea in his search for a contact point, incorporating into the places where he sat a *zazen-seki* that connected him not just with the spot, but also with Ryo Zassu and all the enlightened people who had found their places, where they had become covered in leaves and integrated with their surroundings. Speaking of this period in later life Soseki told his students that he "spent the next twenty years doing nothing" but that he "never let my back or sides rest on the bed." In short, he was making sure that he remained totally free from the comforting support of a set framework of existence, and that he gave himself up to an intuitive search for the way ahead.

It is hard to trace a clear orderly pattern by which this search progressed, but retracing his journeys, noting the kind of places where he chose to stop and the temples and huts that he built, one can see a progression that finds an echo later in his exposition on landscape gardening, and this seems to provide us with a useful background against which we can set an account of the journeys. In the early 1340s, when the material for the *Muchū Mondō*, a record of the questions and answers that passed between him and a leading student, was being assembled, he outlined his thoughts on "gardening," and in these he lists the levels of understanding with which different people approach this. He grades these from the shallowest to the most profound, and in so doing provides us with a kind of retrospective record of the stages he will have passed through as he sought to understand his own connection with the natural world. In the *Muchū Mondō* they are listed in four categories:

> 1. "Those who practice the art of gardening out of vanity and a passion for display, with no interest whatever in their own true

> nature," these are people who will never get beyond the surface forms.
> 2. There are those "who love mountains and rivers," who see them as friends, as something from which they can learn about themselves and life. These people "raise their spirits by reciting poems in the presence of waterfalls or rocks." They are starting to react to an intuitive connection between themselves and the landscape, gaining spiritual insight and comfort. Soseki sees this as a fundamental step forward, as the "root of transformation" to a more enlightened person.
> 3. When this understanding starts to manifest itself, there is "a spirit that comes awake in the presence of these mountains and rivers"; more than just a comfort, or a setting, the landscape becomes a channel for understanding, it becomes a part of the "practice of the Way." But even at this level people have not fully realized the extent of the connection because there is still "a distinction between mountains and rivers and the practice of the Way," a distinction between landscape and one's sense of consciousness.
> 4. Finally, there are those who can "see the mountains, the rivers, the earth, the grass, the trees, the tile, the pebble, as their own essential nature. . . . Their minds are one with the atmosphere of the waterfall, the stones, the grass, and trees, changing through the four seasons."[25]

At this point there is no distinction between "self" and "place," as at Ryo Zassu's rock, and this was the level of understanding that Soseki was looking for as he set out to Kai in 1309, a search that we now need to follow.

After leaving Kamakura, Soseki stayed again at Heienji until, under the patronage of the Nikkaido family, he founded a new temple, Jōkyoji, as a major regional center for the worship of the Genji family ancestors. He then spent about three years at the new temple until the continual arrival of those seeking instruction from him, many of them encouraged by Bukkoku, drove him even further up into the mountains around Mt. Gentoku. In so doing he returned right back to the beginning, to the place he had left as a teenager and to the time before he began to study Buddhist theory. To access again the places where he had sat under the trees, he walked up into the upper reaches of the Fuefuki River and built a small hut he called the Ryōzan-an, the "Dragon Mountain Hermitage." A clue to his frame of mind at this time comes from the fact that an alternative reading to the Chinese characters he used for the name is Inzan, "Hidden Mountain," the name of another T'ang era Zen monk who, like Ryo Zassu, had been a great influence on the young Soseki. At this point it seems as though Soseki was looking to invoke the image of the hidden mountain, the "isolated rocks" that made up his name, to escape the growing crowd at Jōkyoji and in particular to meditate on a key story from Inzan's life. As Yanagida Seizan relates it,[26] a traveling monk got lost in the mountains but came eventually to a river beside which he found Inzan's hut. Meeting with the old monk, he asked him how long he had been there, to which Inzan, not eager to talk, replied briefly that he did not know. Persisting, the monk asked him where he came from and Inzan told him, "From a place where the trees change color from green to yellow, yellow to green." Implicit in Inzan's reply is the understanding that "self" and "place" are the same thing. The monk has not realized that his questions are based on false distinctions: "How long have you been here?" assumes that some time different existed before, and "Where did you come from?" assumes some place different existed before, and the questions also assume that Inzan is somehow a separate entity from both. In his reply Inzan tries to point out that no time before exists, just right now, and that no other places exist, just the great never-ending processes of Life. For Soseki there must have been a particular attraction to the idea of coming "from a place where the trees change color from green to yellow, yellow to green," a place, in short, at the very heart of the processes of Nature.

Initially life at the Ryōzan-an seems to have fulfilled Soseki's expectations. A *waka* poem he wrote during this period reflects the deep peace and quiet that seems to have pervaded both the place and his mood:

> Though no one comes seeking
> my lowly hut,
> Yet spring has come and left its mark
> in the melting of my garden snow.[27]

For Soseki, however, the peace and quiet at the Ryōzan-an was not to last long. As increasing numbers of those left behind at Jōkyoji found out where he was, the isolated hut became steadily surrounded by new ones springing up along the river. In addition to this pressure, in the course of their regular correspondence, a message arrived from Bukkoku asking him to come and help with the teaching. One can imagine just how close Soseki would have felt to Chung-feng Ming-pen at this difficult time. Increasingly distracted and feeling responsible for all the activity which he felt must be disturbing the spirits of the mountain, Soseki suddenly left one night in the autumn of 1312, taking with him his long-time friend Gen'nō Hongen (1281–1332), who had joined him at the Ryōzan-an, and seven or eight of his closest students, leaving no more than a poem pinned to his hut. They traveled for over a year, moving first south through the mountains, past Mt. Fuji, and then west along the coast around the foothills of Mt. Ie to Lake Hamana. Here they turned north, traveling up to Mino and the range of hills around

Mt. Kokei. In this region the Kiso River runs through its wide meandering flood plain on its way west and then south to Ise Bay, and along its route it is joined by fast-flowing streams and rivers cutting their way down from the surrounding mountains. In late 1313 Soseki and his little group made their way up one of these rivers, the Tōki River, and soon found the kind of place they were looking for, a place that provided that unique combination of cliffs, river, and views, to establish a new hermitage.

The new site looked very promising high up the Tōki River at a point where it enters a series of steep-sided gorges that wind around Mt. Nagase, and it had a distinct flavor of the settings for many of the old stories of Zen hermits in T'ang China. Above all, however, it seemed as if its very remoteness offered them some hope of a respite from the demands of students and the monasteries. That first winter they built a small hermitage at Old Kokei (*ko* meaning "old" and *kei* meaning "deep mountain valley") at a point where the Tōki gathered itself together to twist its way down over a series of falls. In this spot, now in his fortieth year, Soseki settled down for a winter of meditation, his frame of mind reflected perhaps in the lines of a poem he wrote a little later:

Steep mountains
    deep valley
no one finds the way there . . .[28]

The next year, after they had explored the area a little more, they found what seemed to be an even better site slightly further upstream. Old Kokei had served them well for the first winter, but Kawase feels that it was probably a little too closed in, lacking the wider views that had been a feature of so many of Soseki's earlier sites. The new one provided these and room for more buildings since the landscape opened up a little as the river swung round a sharp bend in the gorge. The river was wider here, and the broken line of cliffs on one side ran back away from the water, leaving a substantial level area from which one could see not just the fast-flowing river as it ran into the bend, but also, a wide view back up the valley. With the cooperation of the local landlord they set about building a new temple as a focal point for their huts and gave it the name Kokei, but this time Soseki made an interesting alteration to the characters. He changed the *ko* character so that it sounded the same but referred this time to Tiger Mountain, one of the peaks of the Lushan mountain range in southern China, a place steeped in the legends of early Zen recluses. Through this change of name Soseki was deliberately associating his new temple with the traditions of Lushan and the matter of the Chinese Zen cultural tradition.

Figure 2. The waterfall at Eihōji. The waterfall spilling over the cliff into the Sleeping Dragon Pond gives a strong impression of the rugged setting of the garden, a setting which invoked for Soseki the atmosphere of the landscapes around Mt. Lu in southern China, home to many Zen monks and hermits during the T'ang era. The Tengu Cliff, on top of which Soseki had his *zazen-seki,* was located in the tangled woods beyond the pond. The pavilion and lantern at the top of the falls are both modern and have much reduced the scale of the cliff. Photo by the author.

The temple is now known as Eihōji, and we will be looking at it in considerable detail in chapter 5 because it was here, during his three-year stay, that Soseki constructed one of his first major gardens. On first arriving at the site, Soseki had exclaimed, "The pure and pristine heart, this is it!" and certainly for over a year it seems that few people managed to find the way there. They proceeded with a rapid building schedule during 1314, completing the beautiful Kannon Hall, which stands to this day, and the main features of the garden, much of which is also largely extant. Later that year Soseki was rejoined by his *dharma* brother (one who had also been a student of Bukkoku Zenji) and long-time friend Gen'nō Hongen, and the proximity of Eihōji to Gen'nō's home perhaps suggests a reason why they came to the Mino region in the first place. Gen'nō was one of a group of people with whom Soseki had a long and very close friendship, but their time together in this pure and pristine place was to be of a short duration. People had discovered where Soseki was, and the community at Eihōji rapidly expanded throughout that year. In the face of the increasing numbers, Soseki's original group of monks returned to the relative seclusion of Old Kokei, and at some point during 1315 he joined them there, turning over the running of the main temple to Gen'nō. In the Foundation Hall at Eihōji today one can see Soseki and Gen'nō sitting quietly side by side, looking out toward the Tōki River as it flows by beneath the wooded cliffs, the colorful wooden statues radiating something of the deep calm that must have marked their initial days together there.

By 1316, apart from the ever-growing number of students arriving at Eihōji, Soseki also had other sobering news to digest. Early that year word had reached him that Bukkoku had died, aged seventy-six, at Unganji. This news, in addition to personal sense of loss, meant that he was now the head of Bukkō's Zen lineage. He would now have to be even more determined in his pursuit of privacy since many influential and powerful people would be looking for him to return to Kamakura to take up Bukkoku's mantle as teacher and administrator. As Soseki and Gen'nō held a memorial service for their old teacher, one has a keen sense of the lineage moving on and evolving: Soseki leading on from Bukkoku, and Eihōji leading on from Unganji, the people and the places moving on in step.

With all these developments going on, things rapidly reached a head at Eihōji during what was clearly a difficult moment for Soseki. The tone of one poem he wrote at the time gives us a sense of how he was feeling:

How many times
    have I tried to live in hiding
Only to leave again the dwelling
    I have fashioned in this uncertain world.[29]

and his growing frustration shows when he exclaimed, "I came to live here in retreat. Students, please go and find an esteemed lodging somewhere else." He had invested a lot in the temple and its gardens and had yet to fully exploit the potential of what he had created, but he must also have concluded that it was time for him to leave if he was to continue his personal search and if he was to avoid "the swarming visitors" as he referred to them in one poem.[30] As Kawase points out, Soseki must also have realized that since he had created such a magical place, he can hardly have blamed all the people who wanted to come there to pursue their practice, and, in spite of his apparent frustration, he seems to acknowledge this when he wrote,

> Living in the middle of the mountains in Kokei
> where the path is unclear
> But still those who wish to learn come
> and I look after them.[31]

In the end it seemed clear that he would have to leave. This he finally decided to do; leaving the temple in the care of Gen'nō and with the sounds of the Tōki River in his ears, he left in the late summer of 1317, having, in addition, just heard the news of his old master Issan's death at Nanzenji in Kyoto.

In the years that followed Soseki stayed initially in the hills to the north of the Kiso River, spending time in particular at three small temples, two he founded, Myōrakuji and Shōrinji, and one he adopted, Tōkoji, before making his way to Kyoto, his first recorded visit there for some twenty-two years. He made sure not to repeat the experience of Eihōji, keeping his stops at these temples short and constructing little more than his "grass" hut, while using his time to take advantage of the sweeping landscapes for his continuing meditation. None of the three sites have any substantial records of Soseki having built gardens, but their locations give us an idea about how Soseki's sense of landscape was continuing to develop, something that we will be able to follow in chapter 5. What is worth noting now is that he had clearly decided to focus on finding the right setting for his meditation, rather than the right setting for a temple or garden. His emphasis during this period was on finding places of outstanding natural beauty that were the right place for practice, the right setting for the *zazen-seki*. At Myōrakuji and, especially, Tōkoji he took advantage of high, exposed mountain ridges to meditate in places where the views spread out for miles in front of him, the landscape of mountain ranges filling the view to the horizon. His aim at this time was to stay unattached and, as Kawase puts it, "to gaze into nature."

Interestingly enough the third of these sites, Shōrinji, shows a marked change in direction in his choice of location, and it must demonstrate that he was beginning to make substantial progress in his quest for understanding. From the mountain fastness of Tōkoji he moved down to Shōrinji, the first of three important sites where he would subsequently immerse himself in long views not of mountains but of water. The site is on the Kiso River as it flows away from the mountains and out into open country, at a point where it had already become a wide, braided waterway winding slowly back and forth across its expansive, level floodplain. The small temple was at a remote spot out on one of the low islands that dotted the river, and the slight rise in elevation that this provided gave it wide views out across the river and plain to a panorama of mountains in the background; it is a kind of view that is quite rare in Japan, clearly a carefully chosen spot. In his account of his visit there, and on which this description is based, Kawase notes his astonishment at just how much the view opened up when he reached the site and walked up to the low mound where Soseki's temple had stood. Now all traces of the building are gone and just a few pines occupy the rise in the ground that was once the island. The river has been contained between concrete revetments, its numerous channels tidied into one, and the strings of marshy islands long turned into fields; a place once alive with water and wildfowl now lies quiet but for the wind in the pines.

By the end of 1317 Soseki had left the Mino region, his stops at Myōrakuji, Tōkoji, and Shōrinji having been short and concentrated. Traveling out of Gifu over the high mountain pass at Sekigahara down to Lake Biwa, he made his way to Kyoto. Nothing more of this visit to Kyoto or the specific reasons for it is known other than the fact that he seems to have stayed well away from the center and the temples where he was well known, living quietly in a small lodging house in the northern suburb of Kita-yama. As is so often the case, the fullest record of the visit and the reasons he made it can be found in a poem he wrote at the time:

> Right among the people coming and going
> I have a place to stay.
> I shut the gate even in the daytime
> and feel as though I had bought
> Wo-chou the great mountain
> and had it with me in town.
> Never since I was born
> have I liked to argue
> and now my mouth is quiet
> Suspended between
> heaven and earth
> and the universe is still.[32]

The poem contains a number of things that are of interest to us, not least those concerning Wo-chou, a reference that we will be looking at in some detail in the next chapter, and it gives us a snapshot of his life and preoccupations at the time. "Argue" is the closest we can come in translation to the word Soseki uses, but it should be seen in the context of this poem as having a wide meaning that covers a range of interactions from a quiet conversation to heated debate. It should be seen as falling into the general worldly "busyness" that he records in the opening lines. The introduction to the poem records that his lodging house was in the middle of the market area of Kitayama, and in the poem he is using the image of the comings and goings of the market to express those daily, often subconscious activities, which occupy one's time and which often get mistaken for Life itself. Included in these activities are the kinds of debate, discussion, and discourse that are involved in the life of temples and teaching. The practice of meditation must penetrate through the distractions of this "superficial" activity, this time occupying busyness, and for it to do this he needs to create an internal space, a "place to stay," a quietness of nonactivity where he can concentrate. In the mountains, of course, this is not hard to do, but in the middle of town or at the center of the temple organization it is another matter, and it was a problem which, as we will see in the next chapter, had been addressed many years before by the hermits of China. This was the nature of the challenge he is addressing in the poem and one aspect of the wider questions he was trying to answer before events forced him to return to Kamakura.

As we already know, pressure to return to Kamakura was not long in coming, this time in the form of an "invitation" to Soseki from Kakkai Enjo Ni to become her teacher. Receiving a direct invitation such as this from a person in her position would have been impossible for Soseki to turn down, and so, on hearing that it was coming, he left Kyoto and could thus be said not to have received it. It is not clear whether he had already selected Shikkoku Island as his final destination or whether it was simply the place to which his journey from Kyoto eventually led him. Either way, it was here that he landed during 1318 and where he established himself at the Kyūko-an near Tosa. By 1319, however, even in this remote dwelling place he was unable to "shut the gate even in the daytime," and Kakkai's determined messenger made sure that Soseki did not slip through his hands one more time. The period of relative peace and quiet that Soseki had been able to create for himself thus came to an abrupt end some ten years after he had left Bukkoku and Kamakura behind in the immediate aftermath of his initial enlightenment. Spring 1319 found him on his way back to the busyness of public life, and only time would tell whether the years he had snatched for himself had been sufficient to provide him with the understanding he needed to survive the tasks ahead.

NOTES

1. Kawase Kazuma. *Musō Kokushi: Zen to teien* (Musō Kokushi: Zen and Gardens) (Tokyo: Kōdansha, 1968). Details describing what remains at the various sites and the countryside surrounding them are based on Kawase's accounts taken from this book.

2. See in particular Yanagida Seizan, "Musō Soseki," *NHK "Reading the Heart" Series* (Tokyo: Japan Broadcasting Publishing Association, 1992).

3. Tsunoda Ryūsaku, Wm. Theodore de Bary, and Donald Keene, comp., *Sources of Japanese Tradition,* vol.1 (New York: Columbia University Press, 1958), p. 264.

4. See Kawase, *Musō Kokushi,* p. 130.

5. It is worth noting here that although I am referring to "Chikaku" as Musō Soseki, this latter was in fact a name he gave himself later in life. At this point Chikaku is the first name by which we know him since his actual birth name is not recorded.

6. Yanagida, "Musō Soseki," p. 38.

7. Much of the detail and flavor of this is taken from Yanagida, "Musō Soseki."

8. Yanagida, "Musō Soseki," p. 114.

9. Musō Soseki, *Sun at Midnight: Poems and Sermons,* trans. W. S. Merwin and Sōiku Shigematsu (San Francisco: North Point Press, 1989), p. 147.

10. Martin Collcutt. *Five Mountains* (Cambridge, Mass.: Harvard University Press, 1981), p.139, 147.

11. Tsunoda, de Bary, and Keene, *Sources of Japanese Tradition,* vol. 1, p. 248.

12. Musō Soseki, *Sun at Midnight,* p. 150.

13. Ibid., p. 147.

14. Nakamura Bunpo and Inoue Hakudo, *Musō Kokushi no fuko* (Tokyo: Shinjūsha, 1998), p. 18.

15. Matsuo Bashō, *The Narrow Road to the Deep North, and Other Travel Sketches,* trans. from the Japanese with an introduction by Nobuyuki Yuasa (Harmondsworth: Penguin Classics, 1966), p. 127.

16. Description based on Kawase, *Musō Kokushi,* p.137.

17. Ibid., p. 137.

18. Musō Soseki, *Sun at Midnight,* p. 148.

19. Ibid., "Introduction."

20. Ibid., p. 149.

21. I am very grateful to Sharon Nakazato for this translation.

22. Nakamura and Inoue, *Musō Kokushi no fuko,* p. 50.

23. Collcutt, *Five Mountains,* p. 129.

24. Joseph D. Parker, *Zen Buddhist Landscape Arts of Early Muromachi Japan (1336–1573)* (Albany, N.Y.: SUNY Press, 1999), p. 167, 168.

25. Musō Soseki, *Sun at Midnight,* p.162 ff.

26. Yanagida, "Musō Soseki," p. 106.

27. Nakamura and Inoue, *Musō Kokushi no fuko,* p. 18. The introduction to this poem records that the patterns of the melting snow that spring looked in places like footsteps across the garden, hence Soseki's choice of image.

28. Musō Soseki, *Sun at Midnight,* poem #109, "Tiger Valley," p. 119.

29. Kawase, *Musō Kokushi,* p. 153.

30. Musō Soseki, *Sun at Midnight,* poem #115, "On the Wall of Cloud-Friend Hut," p. 125.

31. Nakamura and Inoue, *Musō Kokushi no fuko,* p. 57.

32. First eight lines of this translation from Musō Soseki, *Sun at Midnight,* p. 6, poem #2, "A Lodging House in Town." The last four are translated by Sharon Nakazato, and I feel that those four are much closer to the sense of the original.

CHAPTER TWO

MA and the Five Mountains: Sources of Creative Expression

By the summer of 1319 Soseki was back in Kamakura, his ten years of relative privacy at an end, and he was preparing to take on the duties and the responsibilities of teaching and administration. As we will see in the next chapter, however, political events were moving at such a pace during these years that things did not work out quite as simply as that. The circumstances of the times meant that he was in fact soon able to slip away again, and when we next catch up with him, we find him comfortably secluded in a hut overlooking the sea, and as he wrote in a poem at that time "All on my own I'm happy."[1] Yet his mood in 1319 was very different, and, as his party approached Kamakura on the long walk from Shikkoku, he must have had in place some plan as to how he was going to deal with the new realities of his life, since, as far as he knew, for the foreseeable future he was going to be anything but alone. Some idea of both his mood and his plan is, I think, to be found in an exchange of poems he had at this time with one of his new students. Interestingly enough, the other poet was none other than Kakkai Enjo Ni herself, and it is clear that, in spite of her role in persuading Soseki to return to Kamakura and the manner in which this was done, they had a long-term on-and-off relationship as master and student. The first poem was Kakkai's,

> There are endless storms in the mountains
> I am not attempting to fight them.
> I live instead in the world of a dream.

to which Soseki replied,

> As I think of the world of dreams
> I am even more inclined to abandon the world
> and hide myself in the mountain that is not in the mountains.[2]

Kakkai's poem opens by outlining the challenges that she faced, the "storm in the mountains" image referring not just to the difficulties of fighting one's way through to enlightenment, but also to the storms, political and military, that were sweeping through their lives at this time. The poem then goes on to tell us how she had determined to cope with both sets of circumstances, not fighting against them but retreating instead into the "world of a dream." This image refers to Soseki, the "dream window" of his name, and, therefore, Kakkei tells us that she proposes immersing herself in the pursuit of enlightenment as his student. Soseki's poem in turn gives us a clear indication of how he intended to handle the circumstances he was in, and his inclination to abandon the world and hide tells us much of his mood at this time. Whatever plans others had for him, he seems to have arrived in Kamakura more determined than ever to continue following the reclusive Chung-feng Ming-pen's example.

Of real interest to us in his poem, however, is this image of the "world of dreams," which Soseki repeats, and his subsequent image of the "mountain that is not in the mountains." What exactly did the image of "dreams" mean to these people and why does Soseki talk of hiding in what appears to be an illusory world where mountains are not in the mountains? What role can we suppose these images of dreams and illusion played in Soseki's interior world? Where do they fit into the wider cultural and religious influences that made up his consciousness, and the forms in which, through this, he saw the world? Indeed, what were these wider influences that shaped his interior world and that of the culture of which he was a part?

Since Soseki first looked through his "dream window" and saw the way ahead, we have been following his long and difficult spiritual journey as he made his way up the *soseki*, the "isolated rocks" of his mountain toward, and then beyond, enlightenment. But now, before we continue tracing the developments in his life after 1319, we need to understand the answers to these questions. Specifically we need to understand how he "saw" the mountain itself, how his life so far and the culture in which he lived had shaped his view of the physical landscape, what meanings it held for him, and how he had begun to give his place in this landscape some form and context. Where was this "mountain that is not in the mountains" in which he intended to hide as his bleak mood in Kamakura inclined him to abandon the world? In the following chapters we will be tracing his life and the development of his garden building as he steadily moved towards his ultimate expression of his place in the landscape at Saihōji, but, as essential background to this, we need first to understand something of why he built what he did. What were the influences at work on him, and what was behind the images and ideas that formed his interior world and which provided the tools for his creative expression as he developed the forms and themes in his gardens?

His spiritual consciousness we know to have been an individualistic combination of a wide variety of influences gained throughout his early life that were finally focused and brought together by his Zen training and eventual enlightenment. Here was an individual who had been brought up in the close world of the extended networks of one of medieval Japan's most important family groups, the Minamoto. His early life appears to have been dominated by the religious fervor of his mother's faith in the figure of Kannon and the major Shintō shrines at Ise, and, following this, his adolescence was spent in the mountains of Kai, a deeply rural area through which the *yamabushi* priests often passed. His early training to become a priest exposed him to the teachings of both the Tendai and Shingon schools of Buddhism, and it was during this time that he began to spend as many hours as he could in the mountainous landscape around the temple developing his skills of meditation. On entering Kenninji he became in turn part of the world of Zen Buddhism, a whole new world to explore and one which, without doubt, represented the seminal influence of his life.

Through his long years of temple training and his subsequent immersion in the cultural world of elite Kamakura society, he would have been introduced to the full range of China's massive cultural and religious heritage. He would have been as familiar with the philosophers, moralists, historians, artists, poets, and politicians from the earliest Chinese dynasties to the establishment of the Mongol dynasty in 1271 as he would have been with the events and figures of Japan's history. He would have known about the great achievements and the individuals involved in the flowerings of Chinese culture during the T'ang and the Southern Song Dynasties, and above all he would have known about the great figures of China's spiritual and religious traditions. His young imagination would have been full of the lives and legends, the poems and paintings, the sermons, the outbursts, and the eccentricities of the Taoist and Zen hermits and priests who roamed at will, as the various dynasties came and went, through China's physical and spiritual landscapes. And as they did so they created an enormously rich and influential cultural tradition.

These wide and powerful influences not only shaped the way Soseki's artistic sensibilities saw the physical world but also determined the meanings that the details and different aspects of this world had for him. We need to understand, therefore, what these cultural and spiritual influences were and some of the allusive meanings they in turn wove into Soseki's perception of the world around him and which he then drew on to create his gardens. Essentially these influences break down into two main areas: first, those which arose through the Japanese religious and cultural traditions that he was exposed to from early childhood and, second, those from

China that he came into contact with through his life as a student and then as a Zen Buddhist priest.

As a basis for understanding the first of these areas of influence it is necessary to visit briefly those distant early times when people began to settle permanently on the islands of the Japanese archipelago. First, as rising sea levels cut the islands off from the mainland, people began to arrive from the north, moving south and east down and across the islands from a central Siberian homeland, and sometime later these early populations were joined by people migrating up from southern China. Initially these populations found a good living exploiting the rich marine life of the coastal zone. The religious and cultural traditions of the mainland also adapted to the new circumstances to create a new synthesis.

Making up the basis for this synthesis were the Altaic traditions arriving through China and Korea, and equally through Manchuria, the Sakhalin islands, and Hokkaido, which "brought with them a vertical cosmology according to which deities descended from a higher realm on to trees, mountains and pillars."[3] These traditions appear to have developed in the general area of central and southern Siberia and, more specifically, are now associated with cultures that developed among the pasturalist peoples of the Altay Mountains of southern Siberia. The high plateau of this mountainous area is known to this day as the "pastures of heaven," revered since time immemorial as the resting place for the spirits of the dead, where even now it is forbidden to shout or raise your voice for fear of disturbing these spirits. Present-day tradition from this area gives us at least a suggestion of the vertical ordering of the cosmos that developed there long ago and is clearly still in use since "the name [of this place] local people tell me means 'the end of everything.' They believe these pastures lie within the second layer of heaven, a step above ordinary people and events. . . it is as close as their world comes to the great beyond."[4]

Thus we see indicated here a view of the world whereby everyday life and existence is lived on one level. Below this is a nether world of darkness, while above are various layers of heaven, built up and vanishing beyond sight and comprehension into the blue. The spirits of the dead can rise up into these higher planes, and, most critically, these spirits, and the energies and powers of the deities can also descend down through them to interact with the level of human existence. Of central importance to this tradition were the mountains that dominated these peoples' lives and gave visible evidence of the structures that supported this vertical world, separating everyday existence from the heavens above. Besides, and in contrast to these, came the traditions of people who had colonized coastal Asia, sea-faring, fishing people whose view of the cosmos was very different. Theirs was a world that saw life existing in that place where the mountains meet the sea, in which the spirits settle far off over the horizon on mythical islands.

Although apparently in complete contradiction, these two traditions fused in Japan over time, complementary yet distinct, setting up a multidimensional psychological space for the population's spiritual consciousness. This fusion has created a sophisticated and subtle cosmology and spiritual awareness that had profound implications for the way Japanese culture developed. At the same time, the tension inherent in Japanese culture between the vertical and horizontal, water and air, and so on, promoted a unique aesthetic sensibility. As part of this there also developed a unique recognition of place, where one's location is identified by the intersection of things. These can be as mundane as street layout, where, as Hall has pointed out, "the Japanese treat the intersecting points [of their grid street system] technically and forget about the lines. In Japan it is the intersections but not the streets that are named."[5] Directions are given to the nearest named intersection rather than a location along a street. At the other extreme, the point where the mountains and the sea meet is seen as the "place" where people first settled, where the nation's life began in the "space" created at the intersection of the vertical and horizontal cosmologies.

This fusion of traditions was made possible, at least in part, because, in common with many early populations all over the world, both groups of people accessed their spiritual world by means of the person and practices of shamans. While their vision of the cosmos may have envisioned two different models, they shared the shamanistic approach to accessing it, and at the heart of this approach lay the perception of two distinct states in which this cosmos was inhabited. These two states lay on either side of the moment at which the physical body died.

One of these states was that of the spirit occupying the body and living in the physical, everyday world, and the other was the spirit, released by the "death" of the body from this world into that which lay over the horizon or up in the higher levels. It was in this latter state that all the generations of ancestors and all the spirits of those who had created the world, the deities who had made life possible, dwelt. There were two worlds, one physical and one spiritual, inseparably linked and mutually dependent. The one needed access to the experienced guidance and energies of the spirit world; the other needed sustenance and recognition from the physical world to exist "because, from time to time, the spirits are in need of human warmth for a little while."[6] Between these two worlds clear and generally insurmountable barriers were recognized that defined the distinct but inseparable forms of existence. In addition, these barriers defined the difference between the states of ignorance and understanding, between those people who could perceive the means by which the barriers might be crossed and those who could not. These barriers brought the two worlds into contact and hence enabled the flow of mutually beneficial energies between the two worlds. Specifically, it was recognized that what those people, known as shamans, could do was identify, and then exploit, those few and special places where the barriers between the two worlds were thin enough to be crossed. They could see where useful access between the two worlds was possible and then create the means by which this access might be achieved.[7] The places the shamans chose were the crucial points of contact that enabled life to be lived, contact points that provided people with access to the powers of the gods. These contact points thus provided the means of establishing the critical balance between the two worlds that sustained life on both an individual and a community level.

Brought together by the common use of shamanism as the mechanism by which the different worlds were accessed, the two cosmologies of the northern and southern traditions were thus blended into a unique mix of images and ideas. This led in turn to an understanding of space and time that prompted an entirely different view of the relationship between the spiritual and physical worlds from that of the western cultures and even that of the eastern mainland. As Carmen Blacker puts it, "by the late [Japanese] prehistoric period, the fifth and sixth centuries A.D., shortly before the coming of Buddhism and Chinese ethics and institutions and the system of writing by which they were recorded, Japanese Shamanism was already a complex intermingling of two broadly different streams—northern and vertical with southern and horizontal,"[8] and at the center of this intermingling lay the implications of the moment of death. Death was the critical event that lay at the heart of the interrelationships of this cosmological structure, and it is of great importance for understanding the Japanese perception of its process and the potential they saw in the moment when the spirit leaves the body. In particular, it is important to understand the conventions they developed to handle the process of the spirit leaving since they had an important influence on the methods Soseki was to employ to express the presence of the spirit in the garden at Saihōji.

We begin with the perception of the processes of existence in terms of two states, one on either side of the moment of death. The spiritual world was seen as existing just beyond bridgeable barriers, which meant that dying or passing into it was not in any way seen as a dread, final extinction since there was no permanent or insurmountable break between the worlds. There is a sense here that the spirits of the dead do not completely "vanish" or pass completely beyond the reach of the living. They clearly pass beyond defined barriers, but they can be recalled by suitable ritual, ceremony, or prayer. The importance of this is that death is not perceived as a total termination, a complete and utter loss; death is seen rather as a step through certain barriers, and this gives it a lightness, a sad but not depressing connotation. In other words, by using the conventions of ritual and creating the right ritual spaces for the spirit of the deceased, beneficial mutual contact can be maintained. Death was in this way just another stage in the ongoing process of existence. Once having accepted the existence of the spiritual world, the next step was to identify its location in relation to the physical world and, hence, the most efficacious places for making contact with it.

A particularly useful section of Ebersole's book[9] helps us to understand how the early Japanese perceived this passing of the spirit and the steps they took to remain in touch. As he notes, many of the poems of the early *Man'yōshū* collection (eighth century A.D.) suggest that "rather than having died . . . the nobility are often said to have gone somewhere, be it to another land or distant place or somewhere beyond the clouds." He quotes the following verses to illustrate this:

> The Prince who crossed the sleeves
> of his evening robe with hers
> has passed beyond the jewel-trailed
> fields of Ochi. . . . (MYS 2:195)
>
> At the Nakisawa Shrine
> I offer sacred wine
> and pray, but
> you, my Lord,
> now rule in the High Heavens. (MYS 2:202)

(And he also notes how these two in turn suggest first a horizontal and then a vertical sense of cosmology.) Yet the situation is complicated by the fact that the rituals and forms that had been developed by this time to handle death also allowed for the spirits to remain concealed in our immediate world. Another verse from a *Man'yōshū* poem illustrates this idea:

> Our Lord,
> who, while we trembled,
> fixed the far and heavenly
> halls of his shrine
> on the field of Makami in Asuka
> and, god like, has secluded himself
> in the rocks there. . . . (MYS 2:199)

Known as *kofun*, these "rock tombs" were megalithic burial chambers that represented a marked change in burial practice around A.D. 300 and remained in use until about the seventh century, and in this case the spirit has remained concealed within the shrine rather than journeying to some distant place. In short, one way in which the spirits remain accessible to the world is to conceal themselves in the landscape and structures of the physical world. As Ebersole then explains, the key ritual behind this idea was that of "double burial." This practice emerges from the texts, such as the *Kojiki* and the *Nihongi*, historical texts written in A.D. 712 and A.D. 720, respectively, and the poems in the *Man'yōshū*, as one of the pivotal developments in the Japanese perception of death and the dead. During the early periods of the texts, "double burial" was the focus of the burial practices of the imperial court and was concerned specifically with a period of temporary internment, a kind of lying in state, before the body was removed to its final resting place. It was during this otherworldly liminal period before burial that there was an opportunity to establish a link between the worlds by which the spirit could still be accessed, and, in the case of the imperial family, help to ensure the succession. This liminal, bridging state came to be seen as a period that expressed a continuity of life in death, or the arrival of death in life. It was a moment when through death the barriers between the worlds were particularly thin, thin enough to be crossed both ways. As such, it represented a moment of great potential for interaction. For us the importance of this tradition lay in the idea behind it, in the possibility of a state of life in death whereby a spirit can still interact with and guide those left behind, the idea that a spirit can, temporarily at least, lie concealed yet active in this world before leaving for the next.

If the moment of death, and the rituals of the liminal period of temporary enshrinement that became associated with it, was one of the times and places when the barriers between the worlds were thin enough to be bridged, two other bridging points are represented by the figures of the shamans themselves and by the mountain landscapes in which they traveled. The shaman/priests were the most direct contact that most people had with the spiritual world and were recognized as people who, through some gift or knowledge, were able to cross the barriers, visit the other world, and return. While the barriers between worlds were seen to exclude human access back and forth, the spirits could cross at will, as could the shamans who were able to gain access over the bridges they created by spell, chant, ritual action, or a trance state, either self- or drug-induced. For thousands of years from far back in prehistory right up into the historic period, the shaman figures were central to every aspect of spiritual life. Steady changes, however, in the structure of society eventually led to their marginalization as the central point of access beyond the barriers.

In the cases of China and Japan, as increasingly large centralized states emerged, albeit at different times, temporal and spiritual power became focused on the divine emperor figure. The inevitable result of this was that the notion of shamans exercising individual access to the deities and using this on behalf of other people came to conflict increasingly with the concept of divine imperial power through which the emperor, and the emperor alone, interceded with the gods on behalf of the nation. Pushed steadily from the center the shamans became over time associated with the hermit sages, the wise men of the mountains, secretive and shadowy figures who had to be sought out in the wild places of the mountains or invited in as they passed by on their solitary pilgrimages. They became part of the large body of itinerant priests who came by each year to conduct the critical rituals and ceremonies for the village, to purify the wells and springs, contact ancestors, or ensure a good crop. In Japan they became the *yamabushi*, the "mountain-priests" who followed the "Way of Austere Practices" or Shugendō sect, and in these ways became part of the hermit traditions that in both Japan and China ran back deep into prehistory.

"No explanation has ever been offered or demanded for the admiration the Chinese have had for hermits. Hermits are simply there. . . . As far back as records go, there were always hermits in China."[10] And much the same can be said for Japan, and for similar reasons. In both places, hermits and the landscape they inhabited have always been understood, in spite of the onrush of civilization, to represent a prime repository of ancient wisdom and knowledge, and as such came to be identified with the role of the shamans. Their very aloofness from the doings of the everyday world has meant that historically most people, from the emperors down, have revered the hermits and respected their freewheeling existence. They were acknowledged as the successors and spiritual descendants of the mythic deities who created the worlds, of the sages and kings who had flown freely and at will to heaven and back and who knew the secrets of a long and healthy life. The hermits filled popular imagination and populated the mist-shrouded mountains, keeping open the crucial points of contact between the spirit world and the difficult, often dark and dreadful, everyday world. In this way the actual landscape itself became an enduring image, one "of spiritual freedom, religious power, moral purity, and a political position outside ordinary life."[11]

So powerful and subtle did the hermit tradition and this image of landscape become that they formed one of the most important influences on the Zen monks of medieval Japan, who referred to them consistently in their lifestyle, poetry, and art. Originally the aims and functions of reclusion were exclusively part of the religious system, a way of making contact with the spirits by sharing the mountain landscapes they "occupied." Gradually, however, the idea came to serve an increasingly broader purpose, and of particular interest to us are the developments that occurred in China during the late fourth century.

Foremost among those people who were driving these developments was the poet T'ao Yuan-ming (365–427), who believed both in the value of reclusion and in the Confucian necessity for one's life to include participation in the affairs of the world. He gave poetic expression to an important new alternative to a totally reclusive life in the line "when the mind is distant" from his poem "Drinking Wine, No. 5," part of which reads,

> I build a hut in the world of men,
> yet I hear no noise of carriages and horses.
> Ask me how can I be like this?
> When the mind is distant, the place sets itself apart.[12]

In short, he realized that what was important was not so much the location of one's reclusion but the frame of mind in which one approached it. If one can free the mind of everyday and conventional concerns, then one can be as free in a small urban garden as one can in the mountains. As Shuen-Fu Lin writes, "Freedom and self-contentment were recognized as a matter of mind," and we are clearly seeing here one aspect of the impact that Buddhism was beginning to have on Chinese thought. This shift in emphasis reflected the Buddhist idea of "going within" to find one's real self, finding answers and contentment in who you are and where you are right now. With the widening influence of Buddhism, the more extreme hermetic lifestyle was giving way to the realization that the need to live a life physically apart had subtly changed to the need to live a life where the spiritual consciousness of the mind set it apart—where the mind, not the body, is distant.

It is in this way that we should understand Soseki's reference to bringing Wo-chou with him to town in the poem "A Lodging House in Town" that we looked at in the last chapter. The poem tells us that although Soseki is living "right among the people coming and going," his mind is wandering freely through the landscapes of Mt. Wo-chou. The poem shows quite clearly the immediate and continuing influence of these early Chinese poets on medieval Japanese life. Soseki's lines, "I shut the gate even in the daytime / and feel as though I had bought / Wo-chou the great mountain / and had it with me in town," directly reflects those of T'ao Yuan-ming written some nine hundred years earlier. Thus, the Zen monks used the mechanism of "distant mind" to bring the greater "landscape" into their lives in town and draw directly on the influence of the hermit world. Parker has summed this up usefully as follows: "By interpreting the natural landscape in terms of their lives in the busy world of the capital, the monks laid claim to its religious values and spiritual authority for themselves" and in so doing developed "new directions for discovering meaning in city life in a way that remained responsible and attentive to religious, moral, and even political insights derived from a life of reclusion in the natural world."[13] There is no doubt that in understanding this idea of reclusion, and the kind of language in which it is expressed, we can begin to answer the questions that were thrown up by Soseki's poem and the image of the "mountain that is not in the mountains."

Yet, as we have seen, these mountain landscapes were not only the homes of the hermits, and the subject of Chinese traditions, they also formed the basis of the old vertical cosmology, and had long been associated with the spiritual world, forming a critical connection by projecting up from our world into the lower levels of the heavens. But they were important places not just for this reason, or because they were home to the hermits, but also because they represented in Japan "another world even older than the Buddhist heavens and hells, for it was from these wooded slopes . . . that the ancestral dead were believed to return for their annual visit to their old homes. In yet other holy hills the supernatural denizens were not the dead but the mysterious numina known as *kami*."[14] Thus, in Japanese tradition the mountain ranges held a particularly important place in the perception of the spiritual world, forming a contact point with the realms above as well as playing host to the hermits, the spirits of the ancestors, and the *kami*.

Predating the arrival of Buddhism and other religious and cultural influences from the mainland, the *kami* lay at the center of an indigenous spiritual consciousness that formed the roots of the Japanese native religious practice, and in the late prehistoric and early historic phases this was based on a loose integration of shamanistic traditions that addressed the needs of fishing and early agricultural communities. With the steady consolidation of the Imperial Yamato state through the seventh century A.D., however, came the need for identifiable, centralized forms of ritual, offices, festivals, and regalia that could focus the nation's larger spiritual life around the imperial court and concentrate the organization of religious rituals and the calendar of events in the hands of those appointed by the court to do so. The arrival of Buddhism around this time coincided with these new needs and priorities, and its formalized ritual, use of texts, ordered cosmology, and sense of a compassionate moral consciousness had an enormous influence on the organization of Japan's loose integration of beliefs into a national "religion" that became known as Shintō (The Way of the Gods). It was as the representatives of the spiritual world in the Shintō system that the *kami* played a central role in Japanese beliefs, a role that remains essentially unchanged even now as the twenty-first century begins.

In the widest sense, the *kami* are the energies and powers that define life and the natural world. They are the animating forces that the shaman knew and that the Taoists and Buddhists identified as *ch'i*, the energies that fill the hollows of the rocks and the trees. They flow through the mountains, seas, and rivers, passing back and forth, from the heavens and clouds down through mountain peaks and out across the countryside. The word *kami* literally means "above," with the idea that these are something out of the ordinary. They are manifestations of a power outside the everyday world, and thus "the emperor, dragons, the echo, foxes, mountains, rocks and the sea . . . are all *kami* because they are mysterious, full of strangeness and power. The *kami* may thus be descried in certain people, in certain trees and stones, mountains and islands, in the excellence which overshadows the practice of certain crafts, in the continuity and protection which attends a family stemming from a remembered ancestor . . . In all these things there shows through, as though through a thin place, an incomprehensible otherness which betokens power."[15] This power is manifest in all these numerous ways, and certain aspects of the natural world indicate their occupation by the *kami* by their size or unusual shape. This occupation is acknowledged in turn by the act of tying a straw rope, or *shimenawa*, around the particular rock or tree. The rope thus fixes the place, identifying a specific projection of the spirit world into ours, and making the *kami* accessible. Thus the *shimenawa*, along with other special objects and places, forms the connection or bridge between the worlds.

The immediacy and accessibility of this spiritual world just beyond, but projecting in many places into, our own created an interesting spiritual atmosphere in Japan. The Japanese did not live fearful, trembling lives in a superstitious world beset by forces beyond their control. They accepted natural disaster when it occurred as a regular part of life, with the frank acceptance of any people whose lives are lived alongside volcanoes, earthquakes, and typhoons. Death, as we have seen, was not feared, and the dead were seen not as permanently departed or set aside outside everyday life. Graveyards, for example, are considered places of beauty, places for visiting and for enjoying the trees and blossoms, places to share some peace and quiet and perhaps a meal with the departed. The places of the dead were not filled with sadness and loss but rather were powerful contact points where wisdom and knowledge could be accessed. In this tradition the spiritual world is another, different, but parallel experience to physical life, but it is not essentially "other-worldly." The Japanese perceived the boundaries between the two but saw that they could be stepped through, in either direction. It was a close relationship free of a sense of dread. The spirits were not hungrily demanding endless, painful sacrifice, but rather, they were looking for a mutual recognition and the sustenance that flowed from this closeness. It was a deep, almost casual, relationship, largely free of images or iconography, in which the spirits were notified of prayer or offerings by a clap of the hands, or by an arrow shot from a bow, or by the scent of incense wafting through the shrine and out on the breeze.

In creating the physical space where the contact with the other world could occur, the key factor was to provide the kind of atmosphere and associations that would enable it to also become a psychological space—a space where the mind, the intuitive, spiritual side, could associate freely and move beyond the immediate world. This was achieved in a number of ways, and these in turn lie at the heart of what Soseki was trying to build into his gardens.

The starting point for creating one of these spaces was to mark it off in someway, to separate it from the world around it, and then to purify it for occupation by spirits. In what seems to be their earliest surviving form in Japan, these spaces, whose "boundaries" were usually more implied than actual, consisted of small stone circles with a central pillar stone. These first seem to appear around 500 B.C., and their similarity in layout to the domestic architecture of the times is very interesting. It marks a continuing tradition in Japanese culture whereby sacred and domestic spaces share a common form. This idea is a useful clue to the perception of the relationship between the sacred and the secular that lay behind it, a perception where the two were equal and balanced. This idea reflects the view we have already defined where the physical (domestic world) was paralleled and equated to the spiritual (sacred world). Around A.D. 200 domestic architecture in Japan changed over from round pit dwellings with a central post to the square or rectangular style where an overhanging roof was supported by four corner posts. The four corner posts and those employed to define interior divisions became the key components in the Japanese definition of space, both sacred and domestic, after this time. Their use may date back to the introduction with wet-rice cultivation of rectangular rice granaries sometime in the third century B.C.

Alongside these open, accessible kinds of spaces, where the spirits are contacted and celebrated, the Chinese and Japanese traditions also include another kind of space, one that is dark and enclosed, one that serves the same kind of purpose that caves and tunnels did for the early shamans. This was focused on accessing the powers of the spiritual world by going back to the original dark space where, in the darkness, sacred power and energy "gestates and grows, until eventually it bursts its covering and emerges into the world."[16] Here is the old connection with the interior flowing energies, and the vessels or interior spaces that have this quality of containing supernatural power are known in Japanese as *utsubo*. These containers can range from the "hollows" within rocks or caves, to gourds and *stupas*, and the idea extends to such structures as the "Komori-dō," or seclusion hut, a windowless retreat where pilgrims traveling to sacred waterfalls or mountains could pause to meditate in the energized dark space within. The other important kinds of enclosed space designed in much the same way were the passage tombs of the *Kofun* era. These were conceived of as connected projections into both worlds, into the vertical worlds by the height of their mounds and the horizontal by the length of their passages and tomb space. Within this matrix they provided a place where the spirits of the dead could be at rest and yet remain accessible. The tombs enclosed a space that embodied the quality of *utsubo*, the space where spirits could reside and, most critical of all, be contacted in the space of the entrance tunnel, which thus became the bridge or passageway connecting the two worlds. This was the critical point of contact that then made the whole concept work.

While all these forms of interaction with the spirit world stemmed from the native culture that shaped Soseki's consciousness, one other important form of psychological space created for the same purpose that deeply influenced Soseki's spiritual life was that utilized in the Tantric practices of the Shingon school of Buddhism. We have seen how, on a number of occasions alongside his practice of meditation, Soseki also set up a Kannon altar. We have also seen how he constructed Kannon Halls as important features of the temples he built. His continuation of these practices throughout his life emphasizes just how important they were to him. If we are to better understand how he finally came to create his place in the landscape, we must understand something of these practices.

The teachings of the Shingon school were brought back from China in 806 by the monk Kūkai (774–835), who established his temple on Mt. Kōya in 816. The school's practices were based on secret teachings that were passed down from master to pupil, ensuring, in effect, that only those who were vigorously initiated had access to them. In this way the teachings and the practices retained their potency, since their occult powers would have been weakened or lost if written down or otherwise revealed to the uninitiated. The central aim of these practices was to make contact with the spirit world, accessing the spirit energies to assist with the revelation of the truth, and helping the monks gain and harness the powers of enlightenment. In this, Shingon shared with the wider shamanistic tradition a perception of spiritual and physical worlds needing to be brought together and reconciled, as well as the kind of practices which made this possible.

The practices of Shingon are "predicated on the idea that there is a transcendent and all embracing Buddha named Dainichi . . . and that all other Buddhas and Bodhisattvas are transformations of him." Thus, everything, all realities physical and spiritual, all sentient beings, and all the "ten thousand" things of the natural world, emanate from and are One within this Buddha. This being so, one can gain Enlightenment and attain buddhahood by utilizing the access points provided by the figure of Dainichi and using him as a way to connect with the Greater Reality. Shingon practice in fact identifies three areas of access, corresponding to Dainichi's body and its actions, his speech and its sounds, and his thoughts and the energies that animate them. Utilization of these, a process "regarded as Dainichi's thoughts, sounds, and actions emanating through the believer,"[17] leads to a frame of mind, a physical and psychic participation in Dainichi's activities, that in turn generates the energies necessary to reach an understanding of the true nature of buddhahood. Specifically, access to his thoughts and energies is provided by contemplation of the two mandala, the "Womb" or *Taizokai* mandala and the "Diamond" or *Kongokai* mandala. These were stylized diagrams of the cosmos in which cosmic energies were represented by the various deities, centering on the figure of Dainichi. These energies were then progressively accessed and harnessed by the monks as they "moved" through the mandala during meditation. The mandala were hung prominently in every temple, while his sounds and actions are contained, respectively, in the chanting of secret incantations (*mantras*) and the ritual hand movements (*mudra*) and handling of objects that take place during the services. The mandala themselves were seen as representations of these thoughts and energies in two- or three-dimensional form, and were used not only to present the chaos and complexity of these in an approachable form but also to provide a route to be followed during seated meditation and also during night walking meditation and pilgrimage. The mandala thus had both an interior and an exterior function, both spiritual and physical.

One important function of the mandala was its use as part of a group of the ritual objects that were utilized to create the physical and psychic space inside the temple within which the priest, sitting and facing the image of Dainichi, carried out the ritual practices. While the priest was thus paired with the Buddha statue, on the wall to his left hung the Diamond mandala and on his right hung the Womb mandala. Thus were formed two sets of related yet opposing polarities, priest and Buddha and the two mandala, creating the boundaries of a location within which the energies of the universe could be accessed. In the center of this space between these two sets of polarities stood a low altar, in front of the priest, and on which was laid a kind of three-dimensional mandala of ritual objects that acted as the focusing and locating point for the energies that were being released. Thus, within the physical space of the layout, a psychic space was also created in which the energies were gathered. The specific ritual performed in front of the altar at the beginning of the service, and which starts the whole process in motion, is known as *kekkai*, "fixing the world" or "fixing the boundaries of the world." In this the priest focuses the psychic space, fixing it within the three-dimensional mandala, purifies it, and then uses this fixed, purified space to raise the consciousness of the monks, battling with all the energies good and bad that swirl within it and snap like arcs of electricity across the purified air between the opposed polarities. He is using physical representations of the universe to create a psychological representation of it to bring together through the connecting energies, just as the shamans had done, the physical and spiritual worlds to demonstrate their Oneness, their participation in a greater whole. In this highly charged atmosphere the monks then go through the exercises of *mantra* and *mudra*, creating the energies that will propel them out of themselves, break through all the barriers that block the way to understanding, and help them see their "Original Self," "no-body," "no-thing."

Perhaps the most easily recognized manifestation of this three-dimensional space that the Shingon ritual utilizes can be seen in the architecture of the pagoda, first introduced to China from India in the fifth century A.D. and arriving in Japan with the earliest temple architects a short while later. Here, built into the physical shape itself, are manifestations of the psychic connections that were recognized as existing between the worlds. The ritual of climbing round and round up the pagoda was an accumulative raising of the consciousness, similar to other Shingon practices, and, by the time one reached the top, he or she had penetrated up into and become psychically one with the spirit world. At the same time, the climber is physically connected to the relics buried below, the spirit of the pagoda, by the central pillar that runs right down through the center of the building. The climb displaces a person in conventional time and space and puts him or her in touch with another level of consciousness, as well as strongly reaffirming the vertical cosmos. Again, there is behind this a conceptualization of intertwined real and psychic space that had its origins in the art of the mandala.

One other aspect of the use of the mandala we need to look at concerns the way in which they were used as guides for pilgrimages since this forms an important part of Soseki's gardens. The pilgrimage hinges on the religious experience of process, that of arriving at a sacred site, but also that of the journey itself; the route, the settings, the time taken, and the frame of mind all join together to create a transformation of consciousness. As the vehicle for this process the routes and often the areas they passed through became sacred in themselves. It is unknown when these kinds of routes were first laid out through the mountains of Japan—certainly well before the arrival of Buddhism—but it was following the introduction of Shingon and the establishment of Kūkai's temple on Mt. Kōya that the system became formalized, with many of the new routes inevitably following those of older local traditions.

With Kūkai came the steady "mandalization" of the landscape of Japan for Buddhist purposes, and this started initially along the tracks through the tangled mountains that spread out from Mt. Kōya across the Kii Peninsula. This process involved the laying out of pilgrimage routes following patterns taken from ritual progress through a manadala. Thus, the Diamond mandala was overlaid on the mountains north of Mt. Ōmine, around Yoshino, while the Womb mandala corresponded to the Kumano area to the south, the abode of Kannon the bodhisattva of Compassion. In this arrangement Mt. Ōmine thus took on an enormous significance as the pivotal point of interface between the two. These are large areas, and, for those up to the task, long difficult trails of pilgrimage wound through the valleys, along steep ridges, down cliff faces, across rivers and streams, up towering mountain peaks, and past important stopping places at caves, waterfalls, and other points of natural significance. As this sacred geography spread, and older aspects of it were formalized into the new, three main categories of space were defined: sacred sites, sacred areas, and the nation as a whole, the sacred nation.

The first of these, the sites, were mainly from Shintō and pre-Shintō traditions. They were places either naturally occurring and recognized as being occupied by spirits or places that had the potential for occupation after some preparation. In the second case, it follows that if more than one of these places then became joined by a pilgrimage route, the whole area in which they occurred became sacred, particularly after the interaction between Buddhism and native traditions. As Grapard has pointed out, these areas covered by pilgrims which had a mandala projected onto them then became, rather than a residence of spirits, a place where buddhahood could be realized. As he notes, unlike "other schools of Buddhism, which maintained buddhahood could only be realized in a space that was not of this world, esoteric Buddhism proposed that buddhahood could be realized in this body, in this life, and in this world."[18] The concept of the sacred nation was the logical step after seeing pilgrimage paths stretching out across the whole country, paths that joined these sacred areas into a whole. Part of imperial thinking since the writing down of the *Nihongi* and *Kojiki* foundation myths, this idea only really came into sharp focus when it was suddenly given meaning by the threat of Mongol invasions and is not of the same importance to gardens as the first two, which were seen as an integral part of the patterns of movement that were built into a garden's design.

In the preceding pages we have looked briefly at some aspects of how the Japanese traditions of accessing the spiritual world worked and at some of the ways that the contact points of sacred or psychic space were created. If, however, we are to really understand how the Japanese "saw" this intertwined world and organized the forms this took, the physical and spiritual associations these had, and the ways these forms deeply interpenetrated with their lives, domestic architecture, environment, and culture, then we need to go a few steps further and identify what it was that underpinned all of this and welded it into a cohesive culture. This is especially true if we are going to come to some understanding of how these forms and their "occupation" by the spirits gave rise to a unique sense of aesthetics and how the artists and designers like Soseki approached their work and created, in turn, one of the world's uniquely original and instantly recognizable artistic cultures.

Once we do this, of course, things start to get more complicated and we need to refer back to the ancient spiritual consciousness of the shamans and their perception of the distinct but interconnected worlds; of the movement back and forth of the *kami*, or spirits; of the active occupation of the spaces or contact points in our world from where they could be accessed and approached; and of the bridges that reach across the barriers and make communication back and forth with the spirit world possible. In addition, we have to imagine again the nature of the flexible boundaries between the two worlds that at certain points, and in certain circumstances, are thin enough for this penetration to occur. We must be able to identify those special spine-tingling moments when we are aware that this has happened and when we sense in a space or an object the manifestation of something recognizably not of our everyday world. Above all, though, we have to be conscious of and understand the mysterious liminal moments of half-light, of the shadowed transition zone between the bright "day" of our physical world and the dark "night" of the world of the spirits, at which point the communication is made and the spirit world manifests itself. This is the moment when for an instant everything shares the same unseparated world, when we exist at one with our intellect and intuition, our body and soul, our mind and spirit.

In referring back to this consciousness, in imaging its structures and understanding its manifestations, we can find our way back, beyond the immediate work of Soseki and Japan's other designers, artists, and craftsmen, back into the thousands of years of traditions that grew up in the long prehistory of the islands as the peoples experienced their world and as they struggled to create a place for themselves in the great processes they felt swirling through it. These are the traditions that come down to us today as *MA*, an ephemeral will-o'-the-wisp that is sensed rather than seen, a complex and subtle framework within which their consciousness could be manifested. *MA* is more than simply a conceptualization of space and time, although this may be the most precise way it can be described in western terms. It encompasses not just the apparent structures of their world but also the qualities by which they recognize them and introduce them into their everyday lives. *MA* is an idea that even the Japanese have difficulty in explaining although they acknowledge it and feel it expressed all around them in the contexts they have developed for their physical and spiritual lives.

More than anything else *MA* is the reason why the products of Japanese culture, including of course the gardens, are immediately recognizable from any others. It provides these products with that dimension beyond the immediate surface forms, which indicates that they can only be Japanese and nothing else. It represents the Japanese sense of their active, ongoing occupation of space, and in its variety of expressions lie the origins of not just their architecture, but also the aesthetic qualities, later known as *sabi*, *wabi*, *aware*, and *yūgen*, that lie at the heart of Japanese art and taste. By such aesthetic qualities the fourteenth-century culture of the *Gozan* Zen monasteries and the sixteenth-century culture of the tea masters are defined. Those aesthetic qualities of remoteness, age, the mysterious and ephemeral, the unadorned and uncontrived, have their origins in an ancient consciousness defined by the "meanings" of *MA*, and these qualities are the expression of these meanings in action. So, at the risk of losing sight of the essential nature of *MA* in an attempt to define it, of obscuring its mercurial forms in the language we use to describe them, we need to gain some awareness of it, if we are to fully appreciate Soseki's work.[19]

At the heart of the Japanese consciousness lies a recognition of the fundamental part played by PROCESS, the incremental mechanisms by which life develops in the physical world around us, in our spiritual world, and in the culture with which we surround ourselves. From this starting point, if we are then to be able to provide the inner workings of our physical and spiritual lives with sufficient shape or order to be able to access and interact with them, we need some way of first identifying and then defining "process" in action. That is to say, we need some method by which to extract a definition. In Japan this definition has been based on a recognition and exploitation of the intervals that mark the workings, or progression, of process in action and, specifically, the recognition of the things that indicate the existence of these intervals. On a universal level in cultures around the world, these things are recognized by such things as day and night, the intervals of the appearance of the sun and moon, but in Japan the entire vertical and horizontal cosmologies that give a structure to their consciousness are expressed through these intervals and the things that mark them. This is the meaning that we can understand behind a remark like that of Sobin Yamada, the abbot of Shisendō-in, Kyoto, "We don't divide things simply into good and bad, right and left; there is a vagueness, a sense of *MA,* or space between things; that's how the universe itself is constructed."[20]

In fact the Japanese language does not have a single word that would be the equivalent of the abstract entity conveyed by the word "space" in English. The closest thing would be *MA,* and that is by definition "a space between things." In other words, space cannot exist without being associated with the things that define it, and this "space" is then the point of interaction between these things and therefore a dynamic place where there is the potential for things to happen. It cannot be simply an empty place of no fixed abode; it is an interval in or between the things that define it and is filled with the particular activities of the processes happening between them. This aspect of the meaning of *MA* is emphasized by the characters with which this word is written: 間. Here the 門 part of the character has the meaning of "gate," or shutters, and the 日 part represents moonlight. Thus, the moon shines through half-opened shutters conveying the idea of something that occupies or flows into and fills the space between two objects. Space is never simply empty. The Japanese language has no equivalent word for it since "space" only occurs in the sense of a break or gap in a sequence, a point of entry or access, a leading on from one place or condition to another: something is always going on in it. There is an impression here that it is not so much the length of wall or fence that interests the Japanese but the breaks in it that define it and enable us to pass through and beyond.[21]

The Chinese, perhaps from their shared traditions of shamanistic consciousness, also recognized the importance of these intervals in the structure of things and placed the positive potential of them right at the center of the framework of their spiritual world. In defining the Taoist vision of the world, Lao Tzu acknowledges these "between" zones, and one example of this occurs in his chapter 5,

> the space between Heaven and Earth - is it not like
> a bellows?
> It is empty yet not depleted. . . .

In other words, the space is empty yet filled with the potential for creation. It is exactly in these spaces, formed at the point of interaction between the polarities of Ying and Yang, and between all the other opposed polarities that make up our world, that the Taoists see Life and all its potential at work; and it is in these spaces, like those we saw created in Shingon temple ritual, that the processes of Life can be accessed and exploited. *MA* too should be seen as an expression of this vision, an understanding that the actual reality of Life exists in the potent spaces of interaction between all the inseparable opposites: between body and spirit, between me and my world, my nature and Nature, life and death, day and night. These intervals, or spaces in-between, have no simple explanation; they are where life occurs, the catalytic "gates" in the interpenetrating processes that flow between the apparent boundaries of phenomena. Thus, in defining, or marking, the manifestations of process, these intervals come close to indicating what in the West are seen as space and time, but, of course, like them, "in practical experience there is no time without space and vice versa. . . . they are interpenetrating."[22] And so the manifestations of *MA* make no attempt to establish them as distinct entities.

In his book Hall makes the following comment: "In the West we are taught to perceive and react to the arrangements of objects and to think of space as 'empty.' The meaning of this becomes clear only when it is contrasted with the Japanese, who are trained to give meaning to spaces—to perceive the shape and arrangement of spaces; for this they have a word, *ma*. The *ma*, or interval, is a basic building block in all Japanese spatial experience." This is a helpful explanation and serves to emphasize the idea that these spaces are positive and dynamic places where the individual enters, creates a catalytic interaction by active participation, and in so doing "discovers something as an individual." Active participation is inevitable since the Japanese "believe that memory and imagination should always participate in perceptions."[23]

With these general thoughts in mind we need to look now at how *MA* is perceived and recognized. The architect Arata Isozaki uses Iwanami's *Dictionary of Ancient Things* in his essay on *MA* to help define it further in relation to space and time, and I pass the definition on. *MA* is "the natural distance between two or more things existing in a continuity or a space delineated by posts and screens (rooms) or the natural pause or interval between two or more phenomena occurring continuously."[24]

The "two things" are thus fundamentally interrelated but can be recognized and measured by the intervals in the processes or structures by which they are defined. Given these objects, and the spaces associated with them, their place in the ongoing processes were the moments of occupation, the arrival and departure of the spirits, since "space was also identified with the events or phenomena occupying it." Time is thus inferred from these sequential intervals as much as space, but it is not perceived as a regulated homogeneous flow but rather exists "only in relation to movements or spaces." Since Time only exists at these moments of continual manifestation, the Western concepts of past, present, and future, of a flow of time, cannot be discerned. Put in different terms, but nevertheless describing the same idea, the Buddhist consciousness of Time helps explain this. For Buddhists "the three worlds of past, present, and future are not stretched out to inaccessible distances. . . . All time exists here in this Buddha body: the past exists in its memory, the future exists in its anticipations, and both of these are Now."[25]

Having reached this point we need now to understand the wider implications of all this through illustrations of the way in which these intervals are recognized and, then, how they have impacted on Japanese culture. Sobin Yamada has already given us some indication of this when he says "there is a sense of *MA* or space between things," and another writer, Jun'ichirō Tanazaki, also points the way when he identifies the key indicators of Japanese culture as "reticence and atmosphere. . . . but most important of all are the pauses."[26] The pauses, or intervals, in this understanding are not dead moments of silence or negative spaces of inaction or emptiness, but, as we have seen, the spacings that define the moments of interaction, the active bridge between elements, pauses pregnant with potential and life. In the different arts these pauses have different significance. In music they relate to rhythm, and in particular to the appreciation and enjoyment of intervals of silence amid the sounds. In the theater they are dramatic breaks in the action, while in dance the pauses are recorded as the time or spaces between movement. In all of them, however, activity defines a silent, still moment that in itself then becomes the subject of aesthetic qualities and thus evaluation. Performance skill is judged as much by how these pauses are handled, how emphasis and definition are provided by the buildup and then the "hold," as much as by anything else. Amid the rush and color of Kabuki theater, for example, the sudden emphatic "frozen" moment in the action can elicit cries of admiration and spontaneous applause if handled particularly well.

To further illustrate the presence of *MA,* I have chosen a few of the definitions that Isozaki included in his exhibition, that is, the examples that seem most immediately relevant to our area of interest. It is important to realize, however, that this is a selection and that *MA* extends across the whole framework with which the Japanese have defined their consciousness. Having looked at these, we will see how they relate to the way architecture and landscaping have developed.

First we have the idea of *Himorogi* which Isozaki defines as "*MA* as a way of situating the place where *kami* descend." This term initially applied to the creation of a shrine, defining a sacred space by setting up four poles, at the center of which was placed the *yonshiro*, or column that the *kami* occupied. Definition of this space was completed by stringing the *shimenawa*, or hemp rope, between the poles to enclose the purified space. In time, as we have seen, domestic architectural space came to be defined in the same way, with four corner poles and a central column being augmented by a roof and then walls. In both cases the shrine or the house was recognized as the intervals that were defined by the edges of the posts, ropes, or walls rather than these structures in themselves. The places that the spirits occupied were in "the natural pauses between two or more phenomena occurring continuously."

Following on closely behind *Himorogi* is the idea of *Utsuroi*, "*MA* as the way of sensing the moment of movement," the critical moment of occupation that animates the space. "Later it came to signify the moment when the shadow of the spirit emerged from the void . . . the moment when nature is transformed, the passage from one state to another." *Utsuroi* provides the crucial element of *MA* that signifies the process of life in action, manifestations that carry the full implications of the Western idea of time and the passing of time. Of the utmost importance here was sensing these intervals of occupation, sensing when the spirits arrived and departed, since being able to know the *MA* of this process "lay at the heart of the Japanese concept of consciousness."

Another important definition is *MA* as *Hashi*, the boundaries between the worlds that also provide bridges between them. By its occupation of the intervals, *Hashi* has the meaning of "both edge and bridge, and in ancient times [it] also meant a ladder." This last meaning specifically refers to the stepped ladders or staircases that led up to the spirit houses in early shrines, forming the bridge between worlds. Generally, however, *Hashi* does not refer to specific things but rather to the idea of the bridging of *MA*, the space or pauses between two or more things. In the sense of a boundary, *Hashi* is seen as the edge of something, the limit of one world "that assumes the existence of another world beyond." Anything that "crossed, filled, or projected into the chasm of *MA* was designated *Hashi*," and in this we get a strong sense of the old objects and methods of contact of the shamans. An important form of *MA* in this sense is the use of the bow and arrow for initiating a ritual or ceremony. The arrow magically joins the two worlds as it flies into the air, penetrating beyond the edge of one world and into another. In another sense, this zone of an interval, separating yet joining two worlds, can be seen permeating right through Japanese culture in the form of the *temenos*. It literally means the land adjacent to or surrounding a shrine, temple, or sacred site, and it comes to take on the sense of a sacred precinct. As such, it forms the crucial defining buffer between the sacred and the secular which one must pass through to approach the temple. This acts as both a physical and spiritual layer of protection for the sacred site and as a preparation zone for those crossing it. In this way the meaning of *Hashi* covers a wide range from, for example, the forests and mountains around a shrine, the *roji* garden around a teahouse, or the moats around the larger, imperial *kofun* tombs.

To ensure that these boundaries could serve as both edge and bridge they had to be handled very carefully, primarily to ensure that they were never totally exclusionary, since a crucial part of their function was that they should be penetrable and even interpenetrating. They were often implied rather than actual. A good example of how this works is the architectural space known as the *gen-kan*, the subtle function of which has been summed up well as "a bridge like threshold space."[27] The *gen-kan* space is used as the entrance to both sacred and secular structures, the temples and houses, and provides the crucial separation between the outside, everyday world and the living spaces for people and spirits. The *gen-kan* is "an entrance that extends deeply into the heart of a house," not in the form of a regular room but as a piece of the outside that penetrates the inside. It is thus a liminal space that helps to bridge the two but which marks the interval needed to pass from one to the other. Partly to ensure that people using it stop and acknowledge the transition, and partly to maintain the purity of the inside space, the *gen-kan* is the place where the ritual of removing outdoor shoes takes place.

Barrie goes on to describe other such bridging boundaries, this time at Daisen-in in Kyoto: "A wide veranda surrounds the building, forming one of a number of volumetric edges. On its southern edge, steps descend to the garden [where] tile and granite paving form an additional edge." Here we have a design that builds up a sense of boundaries pressed up against each other, pressed thin and therefore penetrable, at the edges of the building space. "The *Hōjō* is experienced as a series of compressed volumes, and there is a distinct edge formed between the edge of the building and the surrounding garden," an edge that is a bridge rather than a barrier. Compressed, squeezed, pressed together, the traditional designs thin out the barriers around those sitting in meditation in the temple, making it easier to pass through to other worlds of consciousness. This is reflected too in the spaces provided within the structure of the Monk's Hall where so much of their living and meditating was done. Inside the hall the monks ate, slept, and, above all, meditated on lines of knee-high platforms arranged down the middle and along the walls. Collcutt's description of these platforms that we saw in chapter 1 shows the monk's space to have been carefully set apart behind a wooden lip, which was "treated with the greatest respect."

He goes on to add, "All Ch'an codes stress that monks should be careful not to set foot on this 'pure area' getting up or down from their places." As a threshold between two areas and states of mind, this lip was a manifestation of *MA*.

But there is still more. In another manifestation, "*MA* coordinates movement from one place to another." Known as *Michiyuki*, this aspect recognizes the intervals into which space is divided as one travels through it, the sequential processes of "one's movement and breathing" as one passes through. Most typically this can be illustrated by the stones of a stepping-stone path in which "spaces between stones—*MA*—regulate the walker's rhythm." In this way, whenever one enters a garden or indeed a temple, one's progress is manipulated by the use of *MA*, and the path along which one walks relates to the presentation of process, creating awareness of the changing moment. This process of moving expresses "space as time-flow," with space defined by the ongoing experience of movement.

Moving on to the world of aesthetics, we come to those aspects of *MA* known as *yami* and *sabi*. To start with, we find the idea of *yami*, in which "*MA* is maintained by absolute darkness." Originating in the understanding that we exist in alternating intervals of night and day, light and dark periods created by the appearance of the sun, spirits were considered to occupy the mysteriousness of the dark or *yami*, the world of shadows, and to initiate the powerful magic of twilight. There was particular emphasis put on this liminal interval during which both worlds were manifest and could therefore interact, but, in addition, darkness was a quality that was greatly valued for its expression of the sacred at work. It was a quality that the Japanese sought always to keep close at hand in their lives, and whereas in the West, where the revelation of the frameworks of consciousness has always been by light and the banishment of the dark, in Japan the reverse is true.

Sabi, "*MA* . . . filled with signs of the ephemeral," expresses another extremely important quality like shadowy light. "*Sabi* . . . refers to the tips of things and also the precise moment when something moves. *Hi* [altered to *bi* when combined into the word *sabi*] means the activity of the soul. Thus *sabi* expresses the feelings of one who recognizes the spirit moving toward the tip of something [in preparation for leaving]." It is the recognition of process at work, of the transmutation toward destruction, the passage of time reflected in the changing surfaces of things. It reflects the "beauty of fading colors," and at its root is the sense of the dissolution of all things, the processes of erosion. All phenomena exist in temporary stages in the approach to extinction. That is the fleeting, lonely sense of *sabi*.

Apart from these general aspects of *MA*, its presence is also felt in much more practical and direct ways, and in particular in the architectural vocabulary. In the first place, architectural floor plans are known as *ma-dori* (this literally means "acquiring *MA*"), and, as Isozaki points out, "This word makes explicit the fact that architectural spaces in Japan were believed to include *MA*." It appears that *MA* may have originally expressed the interval between two points, but it seems in time to have come to refer to the empty space defined by four points, as in the corner posts of a shrine. From this developed the living spaces of domestic architecture and the floor plans associated with them, defined in their turn by the walls between the posts. Second, although the basic measuring units were based on the proportions of the human body, the standard measurements for domestic architecture in Japan once again explicitly include *MA*. While the Chinese ideograph *ken* indicates that the measurement refers to the distance or interval between posts, the Japanese names for the two sets of standards for house measurement, one for urban and one for rural houses, are, in the first case, *kyo-ma ken* and, in the second, *inaka-ma ken*.

The great importance of this sense of *MA* at the center of Japanese consciousness is indicated by the fact that a standardized cohesion of domestic architecture developed from very early on and remained almost completely unaffected by incoming continental influences. This cohesion was provided by the *ken* measurement in its role as the basic tool for the expression of consciousness. It provided the ability to repeatedly capture the spaces of process in such a way that they could be related to human existence and experience. Its "correctness" as a tool is illustrated by its age and its unchallenged role and validity. While imperial and Buddhist influences from China set the standard for Japan's cities, palaces, and temples, alongside these, even fitted into the new grid system of streets, the *kyo-ma ken* remained the same, an unchanging constant throughout Japanese history. There were some changes in the styles by which space was organized, but the basic units of measurement stayed constant. Equally, the design and architecture of the Shintō shrines remained indigenous, although some sense of Chinese layout for the buildings is detectable in later shrines.

There is not room in this book to cover any more of the manifestations of *MA* in Japanese culture, but whereever one looks, whether it be in poetry, painting, ceramics, calligraphy, or the various forms of Japanese theater, there one sees the various forms of *MA* at work. One other important observation needs to be made, however, and this relates to the way in which the Japanese perceive their occupation of these spaces. As Hall points out, the Japanese are particularly aware of the center of spaces, both physically and psychologically, and it is here that they locate focal points of their lives, whether it is placing the communal hibachi in the middle of the room or sensing the presence of Mt. Fuji at the psychological center of the nation.[28]

In the case of the former, the heater or the table which covers the heater (the *kotatsu*) is located in the center of the room and becomes the central location of domestic activity. Life focuses toward this center, not to the sides or peripheries of the room as it does in Western living rooms where the fire around which people gather is usually located against one wall. There is a sense in Japan that it is important that this center can be approached from all sides. Similarly, although it is not strictly true geographically, Mt. Fuji is felt to be the spiritual center of the nation, the place from where spiritual power radiates out in all directions to touch lives all around it no matter how distant. Again, there is the sense of a central hub, focusing the activity of the country and accessible from all corners. Following Soseki on his travels, one gets the impression that he was very aware of Mt. Fuji's central place in the nation's life, and whereever it was possible, he would choose a spot to live or meditate that provided him with a view of the mountain, no matter how distant. Whether in Kai or Mino or, later, in Kamakura or Miura, Fuji was the fixed point in the universe around which his personal search revolved. It was the central unifying presence in the country, much as he hoped that Zen and the *Gozan* monasteries would become in the divisive years ahead.

It will be clear from all this that the influences on Soseki of Japan's cultural traditions were part of a complex and powerful body of ideas that provided him with a number of tools that helped him perceive and express his consciousness of the world. But these influences form only a part of the picture, and to complete it we need to look at the impact of Zen Buddhism on his artistic sensibilities and his ability to reconcile and bring together the polarities of his private and professional lives through artistic expression.

The arrival of Zen from Song China in the latter half of the thirteenth century had such a deep influence on the subsequent culture of Japan that it is almost impossible to overstate it. Every aspect of Japanese civilization felt its influence to some degree or another, and to a large extent those aspects of its culture that make it distinctive and recognizable today are products of the fusion that occurred at this time. As D.T. Suzuki has put it, "What we now regard as particularly Japanese was in the process of hatching during these periods." It seems that the impact of Zen and of its associated arts was so powerful because they were able to touch the deepest parts of the national consciousness and help give new and dynamic forms to the loosely defined ideas that we have met as *MA*. If this is so, then the key factor in them being able to do this was that by their very nature Zen arts aim to transcend their origins, to actually lose any self-conscious definition in a greater matrix of expression. Thus, they did not need or try to reinvent Japanese cultural forms, but rather to encourage what existed to better and more precisely express the consciousness that lay behind them. In any event, it was Zen's flexibility that enabled it to succeed, since, as Collcutt has made clear, "popular diffusion of Zen . . . was only achieved by the dilution of traditional Zen teaching and monastic practice with more readily comprehensible elements of traditional Japanese religious belief."[29] The key element here was that it was a popular diffusion, a mutually beneficial integration of cultures and traditions, not the colonializing imposition of a culture. It was a unique opportunity in a nation's history to set aside those traditional cultural conventions that may have become moribund and to look again at how its art might be expressed and how this might interact with the other aspects of national life.

Although the detached, solitary nature of the Zen experience provides it with an endearing romanticism, its real attraction is that it palpably expresses something very profound, something that is accessed by means that transcend superficial technique or knowledge. Perhaps the critical ingredient in the Zen outlook was the acceptance of the transcendent equality of all the components of an integrated world, of the existence of the Buddha-nature in everything, and its search for an understanding of Life based on this. The human and all other aspects of life contribute as equals, not one manipulating the other, and through this the Japanese were able to express their ancient accommodation of the natural world and their understanding of an essentially shared experience. For the Japanese, Zen art became a liberating expressionistic medium, and because of this they were able to approach their consciousness and perceptions of the world free from divisions and structural conventions.

Apart from the fact that Zen was able to modify itself to suit the Japanese situation, it is not easy to pinpoint just why it was able to connect so deeply with Japanese culture, but perhaps the words of an old Japanese folk song give us some idea: "The brushwood we gather—stack it together, it makes a hut, pull it apart, a field once more."[30] Zen it seems caught exactly the mood expressed in this simple lyric, the recognition of the temporary nature of things amid the processes of Life, and insisted on an artistic expression of things that, like the song, provides a view of life as a series of incidents, temporary combinations of elements. Crucially, however, Zen Buddhism and the arts associated with it did not arrive in Japan with preconceived ideas of how all this should be expressed, what forms art and artistic expression should take. It sought merely to find the best ways of providing its students with an enlightened understanding of the reality of the processes of Life that the Japanese already acknowledged in their own terms as the manifestations of *MA*.

If Zen came to be a dominant influence on Japanese medieval culture then the instrument that made this possible was the Five Mountains monastic system, known in Japan as the *Gozan.* Although the Japanese monks Esai and Dōgen had returned from China to found their Zen monasteries as early as 1191 and 1227, respectively, it was not until the arrival of such Chinese Zen masters as Rankei Dōryū in 1246 that a Zen monastic system, based on that of the Five Mountains in Hangchou, started to take shape. Rankei found the means, the patronage of the Hōjō regents, and the place, the new capital of Kamakura, to found a lineage of temples that was able to develop and grow, safely removed from the hostility of the traditional Buddhist schools in Kyoto. His job was ironically made easier in this by the very people who had caused him to leave China, the Mongols. One reason the Hōjō started to patronize the Zen monks at this time was that the "Mongol conquest of China and Korea in the thirteenth century suddenly posed a threat for the Japanese themselves, and when the Hōjō regency had to make momentous decisions, Zen monks were chosen as its advisers because they were considered to have first-hand knowledge of China."[31] This helped the network of monasteries get a rapid start and, from this time on, they grew steadily, reaching a zenith of national power and influence under Ashikaga patronage between the 1330s and 1460s.

The establishment of the *Gozan* network began officially in 1246 with the building of Rankei's temple Kenchōji in Kamakura. This was followed by the founding of Rinsenji (Kyoto, 1249), and then Nanzenji (Kyoto, 1264) and Engakuji (Kamakura, 1279). Both cities, the respective power bases of the imperial court and the *bakufu* government, rival factions for the control of the country, were well aware of the importance of gaining some influence over this rapidly expanding and important network. The subtle power plays of this rivalry meant that the location of the leading temple passed regularly from one to the other. It was not until 1386 that Nanzenji was established as the head monastery, when Ashikaga ascendancy in Kyoto finally put an end to the matter. By this time the *Gozan* had developed into an enormous organization of interrelated monasteries, temples, and subtemples with extensive holdings in rural areas that provided food, building materials, and income. The *Gozan* represented a substantial concentration of power, wealth, and influence. By the time the Ōnin Wars (1467–77) brought destruction to most of those temples in the Kyoto area and ended forever their ascendancy, there were some 300 officially registered temples and monasteries within the central network, with many more closely associated auxiliary foundations spread across the Kansai and Kanto regions. These had come to represent what Collcutt describes as "the major nodes in the medieval cultural fabric,"[32] largely because the *Gozan* monks played such an active part in the cultural and social life of the times. As Parker has put it, because the Zen monks worked hard to explore the "Buddhist significance of seemingly secular circumstances, ideals and aesthetics," they spent much time outside the immediate master/student relationship living "lives of considerable social interaction and debate about the meaning of Zen Buddhism, of artistic and literary study and practice, of social relations and political theory and of natural landscape and its applicability to their lifestyles in the busy capitals." All this activity not only affirmed their ideas of the positive role everyday experience plays in gaining enlightenment, but it also placed them at the very center of elite Japanese life and its cultural fabric.[33]

From the very start these temples were broad and inclusive places, a situation due mainly to the way in which they had developed originally in China. The Mongol invasion of northern China in the early twelfth century had driven the Song emperors, and with them most of the leading philosophers, artists, and poets, south to the Yangtze River basin. This sudden move south and the consequent intermingling of people brought together a variety of disparate cultural influences at a time of change and dislocation. The result of this was a period of extraordinary flowering of Chinese culture during the Southern Song Dynasty. The unique and dynamic intermingling of spiritual and cultural life created new movements in the arts and literature, and at the center of all this were the monks of the Five Mountain monasteries. The open structure of the monasteries, places full of life and visitors, where the resident Zen masters were easily accessible, provided an ideal focal point for Song culture following the loss of traditional centers of culture in the north. The émigré monks who came over to Japan in the face of further Mongol expansion in the late thirteenth century brought with them this dynamic Zen and the arts it had thrown up. From this a new aesthetic sense began to emerge in the *Gozan* monasteries that they founded. Shaped by the Zen recognition of the universality of buddhahood and the insights that were gained into the workings of this through meditation, this new aesthetic "was so powerful and attractive it infused the cultural style of the medieval age."[34]

This emphasis on the universality of buddhahood lay at the very heart of what Zen had to offer, and it meant that everything and everyone was recognized as having an equal potential to express or demonstrate the characteristics by which the state of buddhahood was identified. It was a revolutionary attitude, and it had enormous implications for a broad range of people and things that had traditionally been disenfranchised from participation in the nation's culture. From now on the entire range of form and life experience, from the most meager bowl or scrap of leaf blown by an autumn wind, to the finest china or plant specimens, from the poorest life to the richest, was relevant and had a role to play in expressing the mysteries of existence.

Instead of making use of existing conventions of art, the Zen arts looked inward to find cultural forms that arose simply from the expression of enlightened consciousness, or from the workings of enlightenment expressed through artistic forms. At the heart of this lay a relationship in which "that which is expressing itself, and that which is expressed are identical,"[35] where there was no separation or externally imposed rules, where everything was generated from within. Drawn as they were out of the heart of the Japanese consciousness, these forms were the subtle refinements of the traditional consciousness of *MA*, itself the purest expression of Japan's perception of reality. For the Zen masters, gauging a pupil's progress along the way to enlightenment meant identifying in their art or utterances certain benchmark characteristics or qualities of that reality that had to be present if any artistic expression of it were to be deemed valid. Thus, it was the presence of these characteristics and the degree of their inclusion that was important, rather than any specific outward forms. Following from this, it was the clarity with which these were expressed that enabled the master to judge his pupil.

We have already met these basic characteristics in their role as indicators of the presence of *MA* and we now see them again, this time given a sharp redefinition by the clear light of Zen. In this context these qualities were found in the combinations of three aspects of a piece of art or poem. The first is concerned with the artist or designer's approach to the piece of work, in which it is important that the viewer senses a contemplative attitude, one that reflects qualities defined as *Tranquillity* and *Freedom from Attachment*. Second, *Naturalness, Simplicity,* and *Asymmetry* should be apparent in the attention paid to the natural form of the material or image, and, third, the work should contain some palpable expression of the reality of process in action, an expression definable by *Sublime Austerity* and *Subtle Profundity*.[36] The aim, then, is that artistic expression should contain a sense that it is informed by a deep and concentrated contemplation of the natural world in which an unblinking and unsentimental eye is looking below the surface form of things and identifying the greater shared experience behind them all. In turn, this identification should project a sense of sympathy that reflects the Buddhist sense of compassion for the things observed. Further, in the artist's attention to natural form, there has to be a sense that this contemplation has produced a piece of art or a poem that has captured a "frozen" moment, intuitively recognized as an internal or momentary manifestation picked out of the wider ongoing processes; it is a moment that is not only expressive of itself, without manipulation by external conventions, but in which the processes at work beyond, of which it is a fleeting component, are also apparent. Having established the general principles, we now need to give some explanation of the terms.

The quality of *Tranquillity* has a long history as part of the meditative state of mind of the old hermits, sages, and shamans. The term indicates "a quiet calm . . . an inwardly orientated composure," the crucial component of concentration that can take us beyond the superficial. In this state of "No Stirring," the True Self beyond a superficial form can be awakened and can immediately influence everything around it. Hisamatsu goes on to suggest that "in the times and places this awakening occurs the entire society comes under the influence of its expression in culture . . . because this 'Self without Form' is our true and ultimate manner of being." In addition to *Tranquillity* the artist's approach must reflect an acceptance of the impermanence of things, a recognition of their existence not as fixed, permanent objects, but as the changing manifestations of process in action. In this approach to art there must be evidence of a perception of the world that is completely at home in the shadowy, changing world of process, and one that does not need to see it through a set of fixed forms. This quality is known as *Freedom from Attachment*. Beauty is found in the transient moments beyond conventional rules, moments that capture and illustrate the process in action: a fish jumping, a mayfly rising on a summer's evening, a snowflake passing, or frost on a twig. The approach reflects an appreciation of the things that are here and gone, with no attachment to any one of them in particular. Zen activity is perceived as happening at lightening speed, and if there are any lingering attachments, this cannot occur.

Naturalness in artistic expression means the production of something without ulterior motives, with "no mind" and "no intent" involved. This stems from the understanding that since everything was seen as being originally One, the art must reflect this consciousness with no apparent separation between artist and materials evidenced by technique or attitude. Thus, artistic form should not appear to be used for the artist's own ends, and, in particular, it should not be used as a symbolic form, a situation that requires it represent something other than what it is. When things are thus manipulated, they no longer appear in their natural state, the only form in which they have any value in the pursuit of understanding. A further key element of natural form is the quality of *Simplicity*, an idea summed up by Hisamatsu as follows: "When the simple self—nothingness—manifests itself in something, the being or form of that something else is also simple [but] this is not simple in the sense of plainness." It is, rather, a simplicity that transcends detail, since an object may be complicated yet still contain it. Tearoom architecture, for example, "looks very complex in the ordinary sense of the term . . . yet its complexity has a kind of serene simplicity that is not to be found even in such simple structures as the Ise Shrine."

Following the qualities required in the approach and the handling of natural form come those that manifest the effects of Process at work. It is not enough that the approach of the artist be seen to be tranquil and "free," or that form be presented with a natural and simple asymmetry; there must also be evidence of the process of life present: a demonstration of the place of process at the heart of "Reality." We have in fact already met this evidence in the traditional Japanese aesthetic qualities of *sabi* and *yami*, but the expressive scope of these were further refined by Zen sensibilities to become what Hisamatsu defines as *Sublime Austerity* and *Subtle Profundity*. In the quality of *sabi* we saw *MA* expressed in the ephemeral images of time passing and in the effects of time and process working. Here was the steady emergence of essential essence over time as the confusing surface layers are peeled away. It was the expression of process in the fading of flowers, the truth emerging after the superficial, sensuous beauty has passed on. Also involved in this, of course, was the movement of the spirit, *michiyuki,* that is implied by the arrival, occupation, and departure of life in this physical form.

In the tightly focused world of Zen, aspects of *sabi* and *michiyuki* became refined to a recognition of *Sublime Austerity* in the defining characteristics of the natural world. In the first place, the workings of process become identified by the characteristics that result from it, and some of these are valued as particularly potent expressions of this activity. Part of what Zen artists look for, then, are "astringent—or dried—or sublime—or lofty—being, in short, advanced in years or life, being seasoned . . . Roughly speaking, it means the disappearance of the sensuous—of the skin or flesh—and becoming bony." These are the fleeting images, like those of *sabi,* that indicate that in the object or person displaying them "weakness has ceased . . . since it is only then that true freedom from insecurity occurs. Hence this implies the meaning of advancing years, or becoming aeons old." In the "seasoned sturdiness" that results, there is a quality beyond beauty or any such term that the Zen artists called *Sublime Austerity*.

In the second quality related to the revelation of process in art, we find ourselves revisiting the shadowy world of *yami*, *MA* expressed as absolute darkness, focusing in particular on the interaction with the spirit world that occurs there. Specifically, we are interested in that aspect of it that indicates the sense of the depth of things, down beyond the immediate surfaces of the natural world, to where those qualities of it that we respond to intuitively lie. In Zen terms these qualities are summed up as that of *Subtle Profundity*, an idea that Hisamatsu defines as including "profundity, darkness, reverberation, a *Deep Reserve*." He goes on to add "here infinity, depth of content within, something far beyond the actual painted form is expressed. In this unstated, unpainted content lies the quality of *Deep Reserve*." Behind this is the same darkness that Tanizaki talked of, the darkness and deep reserve of the teahouse, the meditation halls and the *tokonoma*, a kind of darkness that heightens awareness, bridging the boundaries between this world and that, this shore and the other shore, bringing them together.

In recognizing the characteristics of reality that needed to be reflected in art, Zen steadily refocused the content and application of the traditional aesthetic qualities of *sabi*, *yūgen*, and *aware*, and identified another one, *wabi*, giving them a wider, more universal, application. In the case of *sabi*, the quality of the ephemeral, of decay, and process moving on past a given moment, it came to emphasize the last point, the existence of spirit moving behind the surface image, of a transcending and passing outside the immediate. Hence, *sabi* came to imply in Zen art and poetry the quality of solitariness, isolation, and detachment as a condition of existence in the intervals of process. A well-known example of the quality of *sabi* in poetry comes from Fujiwara Sadaiye (1162–1241) who wrote,

> Looking about
> I see no cherry blossoms
> And no crimson leaves:
> A straw thatched hut by the bay
> In the autumn dusk.[37]

The poet senses the year moving on. Gone are the blossoms of spring and the bright maple leaves of fall and with them all the sensations and events of the past year. Standing at dusk, wrapped against the cold breeze, the poet has a fleeting sense of loneliness and regret pass through him as the sight of the solitary hut of a fisherman's family by the bay catches his eye. The sight calls attention to the moment, stops his life long enough to register these thoughts before the moment passes and is gone. But, because it happened, one long ago moment is caught forever.

For its part, *yūgen*, which we have met before as expressing the mysterious depths of things, came to emphasize the tranquil "stillness" to be found in those depths when, through a deep communion with the natural world, one recognizes the Oneness of everything in Life. A wonderfully clear image of this quality is found in the following poem,

> This slowly drifting cloud is pitiful
> What dreamwalkers men become.
> Awakened I hear the one true thing—
> Black rain on the roof of Fukakusa Temple.
> Dōgen (1200–1253)[38]

Dōgen compares the pitiful worries and difficulties people encounter when striving towards enlightenment, just as Soseki had done, to the almost unbelievable simplicity that is revealed at the moment of awakening. This moment in his life is filled with the quality of *yūgen*. It is the point of recognition that rain falling on the temple roof at night is, as much as anything else, the "one true thing," the universal Buddha nature in everything,

A similar sense of refocusing was also applied to the quality of *aware*, that fleeting sensation of loss and compassion one feels when witnessing the results of change, while nevertheless accepting the processes of change as inevitable. It had begun life as an expression of surprise at the sudden beauty or pleasantness of a moment in life; in the eighth-century poetry collection the *Man'yōshū*, *aware* was evoked in poets by such things as the melancholy call of birds. By the time of Lady Murasaki's *Tale of Genji*, written in the early eleventh century, *aware* had come to express a gentle sorrow, conveying the poet's awareness of the beauty and perishability of a sight or sound.[39] By the fourteenth century, and under the influence of Zen, this had become extended to the conscious acknowledgment of something gone, still sensing the reverberation of its passing, while in the act of moving on to the next phase; it was the sudden, piercing perception, and then acceptance, of the impermanence at the root of life. Buson's poem that follows illustrates this quality.

> I feel a sudden chill—
> In our bedroom, my dead wife's comb,
> Underfoot.[40]

If *sabi*, *yūgen*, and *aware* were moods or qualities that were redefined by Zen aesthetics, *wabi* was actually identified by it, focusing attention not so much on the description of the objects perceived, or the subjective reaction of the viewer, but acknowledging the active process by which one ensures that one encounters these things. Thus, while *wabi* centers on the recognition of the universal nature of *sabi*, *yūgen*, and *aware*, that is, that things are passing even as we contemplate them, it emphasizes the viewer's active role in creating and participating in an environment that is designed to awaken this sensation. Hence, the quality of *wabi* reflects the life of an enlightened person that is "associated with poverty, insufficiency, and imperfection."[41] That person gains in this way an appreciation from the situation of the commonplace and the humble. In doing this, one may suddenly see the beauty of an everyday object that one would otherwise overlook, and one may understand through its humbleness and acceptance of circumstances something important about one's own existence, as in the following poem,

Why, it's but the motion of eyes and brows!
And here I've been seeking it far and wide.
Awakened at last, I find the moon
Above the pines, the river surging high.
Yuishu (sixteen century)

Thus, the aim of the *Gozan* artists was to reveal the true nature of things in art not by use of conventional forms but through the presence of these distinctive qualities and moods outlined above. They were the tools by which Zen art was created, and the degree of their inclusion in a work of art was a measure of just how much an individual understood. Equally important, however, was just how these were given form, what exactly was the nature of the images, whether in poetry, art, landscape, or any other "way," that were used to express these aesthetic characteristics. We have just been looking at a few examples of how some of the poets expressed them in poetry and the kind of images they came up with to do so, but we need now to focus on how Soseki visualized his understanding of the nature of existence and the world in which it existed; we need to answer a few more of the questions raised by his reply to Kakkai Enjo Ni. Investigating this critical piece of the puzzle, we bring together all the sources of his creative expression that we have looked at in this chapter and focus on the results that they produced. Staying close to those things we know to have been of particular importance to Soseki, we need to start by revisiting the story of Ryo Zassu, the mysterious hermit of the West Mountains.

We have already seen that the story seems to have provided Soseki with a powerful image of that critical place in the landscape where an enlightened soul becomes one with the greater matrix of Life within which it exists: the place at which the nonduality fundamental to the Buddhist perception of existence is expressed. But an aspect of the story that is equally important to us is the way in which it is presented as the travelers are led inexorably out of their everyday lives into the other-worldly, rain-soaked mountains, the ancient locations of the spirit world. Once there they become increasingly lost, displaced in a world where all certainties start to fade with the approach of the misty, rain-soaked evening, and a sense of unreality starts to take over. The dreamlike qualities of the story become stronger when the pair come across the figure sitting on his rock, a figure who appears to be an old monk but also, in his covering of leaves, seems to be part of the forest itself. This atmosphere is then reinforced when Yushusai senses that this was a monk sitting before them who actually lived some three hundred years before. The dreamlike story then takes on a sense of magic as the monk vanishes, leaving only the warm, dry rock behind as evidence that he had been there. This sense is compounded when at the end Yushu-sai comments, "Although we met, it was as though we hadn't."[42] As the experience unfolded even he is not sure exactly what happened, and we are left with the understanding that it was as much as anything the illusory nature of the story that appealed to Soseki and which played such an important part in the way in which his creative expression developed. This role of illusion at the center of his art is confirmed implicitly in a poem he wrote around the time he was constructing the garden at Saihōji, and it helps to form a much clearer picture of the sources of inspiration for Zen art.

Called *Poem on an Artificial Mountain,* it includes references to a number of important themes in Zen art, starting with that of illusion:

> Without a speck of dust
> a high peak rises
> Without a drop of water
> a loud waterfall plunges.
> On one or two evenings
> the wind and the full moon
> have enabled the right person
> to create and play within the scene.[43]

In the original Japanese, Soseki emphasizes in the first four lines that not a speck of dust or a drop of water is present, not simply implying that, for example, "no water is falling here," but that neither phenomena exists, with the clear implication that this is an illusory landscape. Thus the scene created is an illusion of reality and occasionally, when the right elements (especially those of an illusory nature such as wind and moonlight) combine at the right moment (especially a slightly unreal, liminal period such as evening), contemplation of this can result in an enlightening experience for a person in the right frame of mind. In other words, the experience is enlightening for a person who, through studying the way of Zen, has learned to "play" and for whom, therefore, this set of circumstances has some meaning.

We will be revisiting this important poem in a later chapter, but, for now, certain aspects of it are of great interest. First, the whole content of the poem explicitly refers to an illusory landscape, and, further, to one that is best appreciated in illusory circumstances. Second, the scene for this is set by the title where Soseki specifically uses the word "artificial" to ensure that readers understand that this is not a poem about a "reality." Rather, it concerns the results that occur when the Zen mind roams freely through the whole range of manifestations of Life and Process at work.[44] As Parker has pointed out, the word artificial actually carried an important double meaning for the Zen monks. In one sense, things were "artificial" because the world is "illusory and evanescent" and only "exists in a net of causal relations." Thus, the world we perceive is impermanent, unreal, or artificial. On the other hand, "artificial" also refers to the fact that the landscape, in the context of this poem, is produced by human effort and is therefore not "natural." Parker also suggests that by means of the poem Soseki "points out the seeming paradox in such an artistic creation as an image of advanced spiritual practice" and that "in playing on the double significance of the term [he is] suggesting that human artistic creation is a subjective projection into the world of an artificial reality."[45] In addition, Soseki is careful to point out that as the viewers contemplate the scene they not only "create" the scene by their participation in it, but, having done this, they should "play" in it.

Right here we are given the closest thing to an "explanation" or guide book to the Zen arts as we are ever likely to find. The themes and aesthetic qualities of Zen art that we have looked at in this chapter were to be given form by the use of illusion, a use of illusion that contains many of the elements of the "vagueness" that we have seen as a component of the way *MA* is expressed. They were not to be pinned down in conventions of subjects and style but rather were to be specific glimpses of the intuitive world at work presented in unspecific terms. They are flexible, uncircumscribed images of the integrated physical and spiritual worlds in process. It is important to remember at this point that fundamental to the Zen vision was the understanding that Life existed in an entirely undifferentiated state, and that there was therefore no difference between reality and illusion. What Zen art was interested in, then, was how best to instructively approach and express this truth. Thus, artists developed a vision that was full of potential: as Hisamatsu says, full of content "far beyond the actual form," and which expressed "the illusory and dreamlike quality of reality" that could be accessed through "the unimpeded play of the enlightened being roaming, free of attachment, in the realm of nondualism."

As Parker goes on to point out, both illusion and play were fundamental to the Buddhist vision since they "refused in their very constitution the production of a stable world that might provide the basis for delusion and attachment" and "entail[ed] an intrinsic sense of movement and transformation that erodes or breaks" the rigid world of convention. They were powerful tools in the hands of Zen masters as they strove to break down the preconceptions of their students. If the images were to be based on illusion, then play was a critical element in the contemplation of these images. Through its very nature, the idea of play helped to break down the intense seriousness of the students' search for enlightenment, removing some of its preciousness and the self-importance of the search itself. As Soseki had pointed out in his enlightenment poem, the truth will emerge only when you can "just let go." Play was an ideal vehicle to help people to do this since "through its imaginative, wandering, and transformative aspects 'play' disrupts the settled attachments of deluded perception."

The place, then, that Zen found for itself was one that existed within illusory images; it thrived in the unspecific descriptions of landscape found in the poetry of the T'ang poets, landscapes which the monks of medieval Japan had not seen and indeed could never actually *see*, and yet with which they deeply identified and felt at home in. Their art, poems, and gardens are full of references to this illusory, ideal land of Zen. It was where the tales in the *Blue Cliff Records* and the *Mumonkan* took place, where famous teachers like Hui-neng, the Sixth Patriarch, lived out their eccentric lives, and it was where the poets and artists, such as Han-shan on Cold Mountain, lived precarious lives among the mists, crags, and chasms of wild mountain wildernesses; all of these were as much the places of enlightened consciousness as actual landscape, and were the places that Dōgen reached when he wrote in a poem, "The village I finally reach / deeper than the deep mountains."[46] The Zen masters in the classical stories are not just historical figures, but also represent some aspect of Zen. The incidents that are related, and the locations in which they happen, become part of the illusory world of images built up around a Zen understanding that invests our physical world with extra dimensions beyond the immediate surface, a place where the spirit is free to play.

The images of the Ryo Zassu story and the poem of Nan'yo's disciple were part of that illusory world, and, fleeting and undetailed though they were, Soseki saw them clearly enough to understand that within them he could find his place and create from them the garden at Saihōji. Once he had decided this, he was able to call on all the native and mainland traditions that we have examined in this chapter to give form to his place in the landscape.

NOTES

1. Musō Soseki, *Sun at Midnight: Poems and Sermons*, trans. W. S. Merwin and Sōiku Shigematsu (San Francisco: North Point Press, 1989), poem # 17, p. 21.

2. Kawase Kazuma, *Musō Kokushi: Zen to teien* (Musō Kokushi: Zen and Gardens) (Tokyo: Kōdansha, 1968), p. 159.

3. Carmen Blacker, *The Catalpa Bow: A Study of Shamanistic Practices in Japan*, 2nd ed. (London: G. Allen and Unwin, 1986). I am very much indebted to Blacker for a number of the ideas that appear in this chapter, and I have drawn extensively on her very useful book that covers the historic and current practices of shamans in Japan.

4. Natalya Polosmak. "Siberian Mummy Unearthed," *National Geographic*, vol. 186, no. 4 (October 1994).

5. Edward T. Hall, *The Hidden Dimension* (Garden City, N.Y.: Doubleday, 1966), p. 106.

6. Norman Hallendy, *Inuksuit. Silent Messengers of the Arctic* (Vancouver: Douglas & McIntyre; Seattle: University of Washington Press, 2000), p. 114.

7. See Blacker, *The Catalpa Bow*, ch. 1, "The Bridge" for further discussion of this in the Japanese context.

8. Blacker, *The Catalpa Bow*, p. 29.

9. Gary L. Ebersole, *Ritual Poetry, and the Politics of Death in Early Japan* (Princeton: Princeton University Press, 1989), ch. 3.

10. Bill Porter, *Road to Heaven: Encounters with Chinese Hermits* (San Francisco: Mercury House, 1993), p. 1.

11. Joseph D. Parker, *Zen Buddhist Landscape Arts of Early Muromachi Japan (1336–1573)* (Albany, N.Y.: SUNY Press, 1999), p. 18.

12. Shuen-Fu Lin, *The Transformation of the Chinese Lyrical Tradition* (Princeton: Princeton University Press, 1978), p. 21.

13. Parker. *Zen Buddhist Landscape Arts of Early Muromachi Japan*, p. 109.

14. Blacker, *The Catalpa Bow*, p. 9.

15. Ibid. p. 34.

16. Ibid. p. 98.

17. James C. Dobbins in Seattle Art Museum, *A Thousand Cranes: Treasures of Japanese Art* (Seattle: Seattle Art Museum; San Francisco: Chronicle Books, 1987), p. 32.

18. Allen G. Grapard, "Flying Mountains and Walkers of Emptiness: Toward a Definition of Sacred Space in Japanese Religions," *History of Religions*, vol. 20, no. 3 (1982), p. 202.

19. Although describing *MA* is a daunting task, it has been made considerably easier for me by, among others, the work of the architect Arata Isozaki and the artist and sculptor Soichi Ida. The definitions of *MA* around which my account is based come from Isozaki's catalog for his exhibition at the Cooper-Hewitt Museum, New York. I am equally indebted to Soichi Ida for answering my many questions and his patient explanations of his understanding of *MA*, its role in the creative process, and its expression through art. For examples and discussion of his work see *Paper Works 1978-1982* and *Paper Works 1983-1988*, vol. 2, both published by Shikosha Publishing Company Ltd. in Kyoto.

20. From an interview shown as part of the film documentary *Dream Window: Reflections on the Japanese Garden*, Smithsonian Institute.

21. When looking for a Chinese character to express the idea of *MA*, the Japanese settled for this one as being the closest approximation. In Chinese, this character as a noun has the meaning of a partition, opening, room, or space; as a preposition, among, meanwhile, between, in the midst of; and as a verb, to set apart, separate, or interrupt. All of these senses have some relevance to the meaning of *MA*. I am very grateful to Ryder FitzGerald for his help on this specifically and for his interest in the subject matter of this book in general.

22. Marie-Luise von Franz, *Time: Rhythm and Repose* (New York: Thames and Hudson, 1978), p. 5.

23. Hall, *The Hidden Dimension*, p. 153.

24. From the Cooper-Hewitt catalog, p. 5. All the following quotations are also taken from this catalog unless indicated otherwise.

25. Alan Watts, *The Way of Zen* (New York: Pantheon, 1957), p. 159.

26. Tanizaki Jun'ichirō, *In Praise of Shadows*, trans. Thomas J. Harper and Edward G. Seidensticker (New Haven, Conn.: Leete's Island Books, 1977).

27. Thomas Barrie, *Spiritual Path, Sacred Place: Myth, Ritual, and Meaning in Architecture* (Boston: Shambhala, 1996), p. 57, while the following quotes are from p. 132.

28. Hall, *The Hidden Dimension*, pp. 149, 150.

29. Martin Collcutt. *Five Mountains* (Cambridge, Mass.: Harvard University Press, 1981), p. 294.

30. Tanizaki, *In Praise of Shadows*, p. 29.

31. Tsunoda Ryūsaku, Wm. Theodore de Bary, and Donald Keene, comp., *Sources of Japanese Tradition*, vol.1 (New York: Columbia University Press, 1958), p. 255.

32. Martin Collcutt in Seattle Art Museum, *A Thousand Cranes*, p. 57.

33. Parker, *Zen Buddhist Landscape Arts of Early Muromachi Japan*, p. 16.

34. Martin Collcutt, in Seattle Art Museum, *A Thousand Cranes*, p. 57.

35. Hisamatsu Shin'ichi, *Zen and the Fine Arts*, trans. Gishin Tokiwa (Tokyo and New York: Kodansha International, 1982), p. 16.

36. These descriptive names for the qualities sought in Zen art are taken from Hisamatsu's invaluable book, *Zen and the Fine Arts*, as are the quotations that follow. For these see pp. 31, 36, 54–57, and 59.

37. Martin Collcutt, Marius Jansen, and Isao Kumakura, *Cultural Atlas of Japan* (Oxford: Phaidon, 1988), p. 118.

38. Lucien Stryk and Ikemoto Takashi, trans., *The Crane's Bill: Zen Poems of China and Japan* (New York: Grove Press, 1973). This and the next two poems are taken from the introduction to this collection.

39. Summary based on that in Tsunoda, de Bary, and Keene, *Sources of Japanese Tradition*, vol. 1, p. 172.

40. A direct translation of the characters of this poem gives an indication of the sudden, stabbing sense that is so much a part of the way these aesthetic qualities are experienced and which is lost in the more wordy conventions of Western poetic convention: "Body-in-pierce: Dead-wife's comb / bedroom in / tread-on." They were not afraid to approach these things directly, in a way that often seems insensitive to Western readers.

41. D.T. Suzuki, *Zen and Japanese Culture*, 2nd ed. rev. and enlarged (New York: Pantheon Books, 1959), p. 284.

42. Nakamura Bunpo and Inoue Hakudo, *Musō Kokushi no fuko* (The artistic sensibility of Musō Kokushi) (Tokyo: Shunjusha, 1998). This additional piece of the story comes from the version related in this book.

43. Translated by Sharon Nakazato, who also helped explain the intricacies of the meanings interwoven into the Chinese characters.

44. At the time Soseki wrote this poem, the word *Karesansui*, which now has the meaning of Dry (*Kare*) Landscape (*Sansui*), carried the sense of "made" or "artificial" (*Kare*) Landscape (*Sansui*).

45. Parker, *Zen Buddhist Landscape Arts of Early Muromachi Japan*. In understanding these aspects of Soseki's work I have found the wider discussions of illu-

sion and play in Parker's book very useful.

46. Dōgen, *Moon in a Dewdrop: Writings of Zen Master Dōgen*, ed. Kazuaki Tanahashi, trans. Robert Aitken (San Francisco: North Point Press, 1985), p. 214.

CHAPTER THREE

Mountain Villages and Harbor Towns: Travels, 1319–33

After leaving the mountain paths and walking east for some two weeks along the "sea-coast" road, Soseki and his group of monks arrived back in Kamakura in 1319, their years of wandering seemingly at an end. In accepting Kakkai Enjo Ni's invitation to return, they were aware that they faced a future of changed circumstances, but for the moment the sights and sounds of the town would perhaps have been reassuringly familiar to Soseki and the monks who had spent long years studying there. Kamakura was still essentially a garrison town, full of the troops required to protect the Hōjō *bakufu*. Formerly a small fishing village on lands owned by the Minamoto lords who first brought the *bakufu* here from Kyoto, it was now a major military stronghold, home to the feudal lords who supported the government, their families, retainers, and troops. Also in the crowded streets lived the merchants who fed these armies, the artisans, the sword and armor-makers, who armed them, the dealers who supplied their horses, and the entrepreneurs who entertained them. Stables, teahouses, inns, and shops stood side by side with the shrines dedicated to the gods of all these different people. The river and the main road ran up through the town from the sea into the wooded hills that surrounded it on three sides, while on the fourth the view stretched out over the wide expanses of Sagami bay. Nestled in these hills were the five great Zen temples (Jōmyōji, Jufukuji, Kenchōji, Engakuji, and Jōchiji) founded by Chinese monks for the Hōjō regents, with their large grounds and clusters of administrative buildings and subtemples. Built to the specifications of the Song Zen masters, these were an exotic presence among the vernacular architecture of the government buildings, shops, and houses below.

The main street leads up through town straight toward the Tsurugaoka-Hachiman shrine, founded in 1063 by the Minamoto family for their patron god, Hachiman, the god of war. Up behind this, the hillsides were full of caves, many of which had been burial places since long before the Minamoto arrived. The streets now were filled with troops dressed in the rich costumes of the ruling families, their banners fluttering as they jostled among the crowds, while guards stood outside the gatehouses of the larger compounds as groups of armed horsemen rode in and out. As they got closer to the town, Soseki's group will have passed the calming presence of the Daibutsu, or Great Buddha, before entering the bustling world that Soseki had last met some ten years before when he had lived briefly at Jōchiji in 1308.

But if this world was familiar to Soseki it was like a foreign land to many of those who lived in the disengaged, refined atmosphere of the imperial court in Kyoto. Just how deep the gulf between the two had become is illustrated by a court lady's diary entry on her reaction to seeing troops from Kamakura for the first time: "To see savages so close at hand made me think I was in a different country."[1] Lady Hino Nako's horror at the sight of troops sent to Kyoto to protect government interests is symptomatic of the serious splits that had developed in the country and that were to make the next decades so disruptive. A breakdown in communication and understanding between these two centers of Japanese life had slowly developed, and so much of what was to happen in the immediate future stemmed from this lack of mutual appreciation between the twin worlds of court and warriors that formed the governing elite of the country. In this fragile situation new forces were at work, pulling at the fabric of Japanese society, and the combination was to bring great changes, not only to Soseki's life, but to the nation as a whole.

One event that was to create part of these new forces had in fact occurred the year before when, in 1318, the emperor Go-Daigo ascended the throne. Destined to play a very large part in Soseki's life for the next twenty years, Go-Daigo was a complex man who was very much a product of the circumstances that surrounded his position, having grown up and ascended the throne during very strange times for the imperial families. Mainly this was because they had inherited a situation whereby two lines of the family succeeded to the throne alternately, a situation imposed on them by the Hōjō regents and one which was to prove unacceptable for the ambitious and driven Go-Daigo. Unlike many of his predecessors, he did not ascend the throne as a compliant child but as a man of thirty, and during his long wait to become emperor he had become increasingly determined to return the Imperial family to what he saw as its rightful place as the very center of power, not an institution to be manipulated at will by the regents in Kamakura.

The emperors had been forced to share power with regents since early in the seventh century, but the balance that had been established meant that nominally at least the Imperial family maintained control over their own affairs. This all changed in 1221 when emperor Go-Toba, feeling he had the support of the leading noble families, the powerful temples, and many of those within the structures of the regency, raised an army against the Hōjō and attempted to reestablish full imperial power. It was a cause doomed from the start, far too much had changed to put the clock back 600 years, and, in the event, Go-Toba's forces were easily crushed by the Hōjō armies. His cause collapsed and he was allowed to retire in exile. From now on, though, the Hōjō were in a position where they could dictate terms to the imperial family, and, above all, that meant determining who succeeded to the throne. In 1290 the Kamakura government formalized an arrangement whereby princes descended from the two main imperial lineages succeeded alternately. Thus things proceeded until in April 1318. Go-Daigo then took the throne, a man who looked to the example of China's Southern Song era as a model for how Japan might be if he could restore the imperial authority of his predecessors when they were still absolute rulers. By the time he ascended the throne, Go-Daigo saw the problems that were arising from an increasingly weak Hōjō regency, particularly with the great threat of the Mongol invasions, a sign that the country was ready for a return to direct imperial rule.

Like his father Go-Uda, who had studied under the Chinese monk Issan, Go-Daigo was a strong supporter of Zen for itself, but also, it seems, because, as Collcutt puts it, "He was attracted by the vistas Zen offered into Chinese culture."[2] In addition to this, he saw the future stability of Japan as based around a politically strong, centralized Imperial government supported by the religious and cultural influence of a Zen monastic system based on the Five Mountain monasteries of China. This combination had already proven very successful in the face of adversity in China where, in spite of having been forced to retreat to the southern half of the country by the invading Mongols, the Song emperors harnessed the dynamic energies of the Zen monasteries and presided over the greatest flowering of mainland culture since the distant days of the T'ang. As he waited for the throne Go-Daigo followed the development of the *Gozan* system in Kamakura and knew that to succeed in his plans he would have to relocate its center of power to monasteries in Kyoto. This would also mean relocating its most influential monks, and this meant, in particular, Musō Soseki. Once on the throne, Go-Daigo moved forward steadily with his plans and, through the first five years of his reign, his court became the focal point for all those who for one reason or another were disaffected with the Hōjō government. But in the end, perhaps inevitably, he proved no more successful than Go-Toba. Go-Daigo's anachronistic, inexperienced court lacked almost everything, from the assets of patronage, money and lands, to the military power it would need to impose its will on the powerful feudal families whose armies had kept the Hōjō in power for the last 120 years. In the end, not enough of these people were willing to gamble their positions on supporting him, and not enough was known about them by those close to the court in Kyoto to engage them fully with the imperial cause. Most seriously of all, however, Go-Daigo and his advisors lacked the political instincts that would have told them when and how to compromise and build on the opportunities that did come their way.

Go-Daigo like Go-Toba had misjudged, and he was to die in exile from Kyoto, his most loyal followers all lost in the vicious military campaigns, leaving a country divisively split and fighting within itself for the next fifty years. The fighting, by the time of his death in 1339, had led to widespread neglect and destruction in the country at large and the five or six major battles to take or retake Kyoto had left the city in ruins, with many of the certainties of life in the capital gone with the buildings. Beyond this, the consequences of Go-Daigo's attempt to take on the power of the feudal lords, and their fierce resistance to his ambitions, dominated every aspect of life from 1331 onwards and created the circumstances in which Soseki lived for the last thirty-two years of his life. They had a direct bearing on the course of his career as a monk and were responsible for the atmosphere in which his greatest artistic achievements were produced, inevitably influencing both their forms and content.

Many other figures were to play their parts in the unfolding drama of these years but none more so than a young warrior from a powerful branch of the Minamoto clan whose family had for a long time provided much of the muscle that kept the Hōjō government together. Ashikaga Takauji was just fourteen when Go-Daigo came to the throne but in the few short years between then and Go-Daigo's bid for power he had become one of Kamakura's most ruthless and successful generals. As such, and as an ambitious man, he was to be the other leading player in the events that followed and thus another important factor in Soseki's life during this period.

As spring turned to summer in 1319, however, and Soseki completed his journey back to Kamakura, these things were all in the future and there was little reason for anyone to suspect just how much everything was going to change. Initially he settled at the small temple of Shōeji in quarters provided for him by Kakkai Enjo Ni. The temple itself appears to have been abandoned at some later date and the site of it is now lost, but at the time it seems to have been just what Soseki was looking for. He did not want to get involved in life in one of the larger temples he had lived in before and so a temporary place in a small, out of the way temple suited his plans. He may have returned at Kakkai's request, and even taken advantage of her hospitality, but it was clear from the moment he arrived that he had no intention of entering Kamakura life or, indeed, of staying very long.

Settled behind closed doors at Shōeji, he turned down repeated offers of posts at the big Zen monasteries and even refused to meet directly with Kakkai, although he may have begun indirectly overseeing her studies. Everybody was waiting to see what he would do, it being beyond any one individual's authority to order him to meet with visitors or take a particular job. He even refused to see his old friend and fellow student of Bukkoku Zenji, Taihei Myōjun, when he arrived to appeal on Kakkai's behalf for him to become her teacher. In his appeal, in the form of a poem, Taihei argued that now he was back, Soseki should engage in the "work" and that people thought it very strange that he should have come so far just to hide himself away. Soseki's reply to this was another poem:

> I won't let even the Buddha
> and Patriarchs through my gate,
> so I never thought to welcome
> some guests and roll my eyes at others.
> I open the gate a little
> to thank you for your visit,
> and at once the mountains and the rivers
> stand up and start the famous dance.

In this poem, in Kawase's interpretation of Soseki's mood and intentions, Musō laughs and replies "I don't know why people should think it so strange . . . even a simpleton knows that there is a right place and time for everything. Besides, if I were to meet with throngs of people who have no eyes to see, what would that achieve?"[3] In the battle of wills that ensued in the next few weeks, it became clear that Soseki was determined to maintain a large degree of independence, even if he had accepted that it was necessary for him to settle near Kamakura and to be on hand. These events took place just three years after the death of Bukkoku Zenji, and Soseki's senior position in the lineage meant that he had to take some responsibility in ensuring it had strong leadership and that its affairs were being taken care of. Thus, although he was against taking on the full time job of running a large monastery and he wanted to stay clear of the infighting that arose over monastic positions, it seems clear that he was involved in some aspects of organization and teaching.

Being in touch was one thing but the mounting pressure on him to "open his gate" wider soon became a major distraction, and, in the autumn of 1319, he left Kamakura, traveling down the nearby Miura Peninsula to Yokosuka, where he founded a small hermitage he called the Hakusen-an. The name translates as "Harbor where the boat is moored," reflecting both the quiet place he had found to settle and a new interest in including human activity in his practice. Whereas at Kyūko-an and previous hermitages the name he gave them referred to places in the world of Zen, at Hakusen-an it referred to the place he actually was and the life that is going on around him in the fishing community. In the peace of his thatched hut, with its wide views out over the ocean, he settled down to a reclusive life once again, but this time he was only a short journey from the capital, and in this situation he was able to remain undisturbed for the next four years. The years at Hakusen-an seem to have been especially rewarding and fulfilling for him, representing a crucial period of reflection during which he finally had the time to come to terms with everything he had learned and understood in the preceding years of traveling. In fact, the four years that he spent at the Hakusen-an represented his longest stay in any one place since he first entered a Zen temple at nineteen, some twenty-five years before.

In his discussion of these years Kawase emphasizes his belief that this was a particularly critical period for Soseki, and that one should pay very close attention to what he was up to here if one is to understand the events and activities of his later life. In this spirit, perhaps nothing is more important than the poem he wrote on arrival and which he posted on his door with an accompanying note. The note told any potential visitors that he had dashed this poem off to explain his frame of mind and that, at the moment, he had nothing more to say; in short, please leave me in peace. The poem reads:

> A mere handful of thatch
>   the roof of my hut is a vast expanse
> The mountains form a rough fence around me
>   the sea becomes my garden.
> Countless people seek me out
>   only to leave again unsuccessful,
> All of them complaining about finding my gate
>   firmly closed in the broad daylight.

At this point, he seems to be saying, he is unable to help those who cannot see that it is not him as a person, or his hut as a place, that is important. To the enlightened mind neither exists, but rather, by looming so large in peoples' minds, these things are actually blocking out the real truth. Those who have become fixated on reaching his hut and on having an interview with him are missing the point: they have "no eyes to see," and he is not in a position change this. In the *Musō Nempu*, the biography complied by his disciples after his death and published in 1353, the final two lines of this poem are amended to read "There is no covering /over my life inside this hut / Yet those who come insist on complaining / that my bamboo door is closed."[4] Whether this version is closer to what he originally wrote or whether he later rewrote them, these lines make the point even more forcefully. He was not willing to take on people who sought him out because of his position or fame, but who were not serious students. He had no time for all this; he was too busy finding out the Truth for himself.

That this was indeed what was happening is illustrated by another aspect of this important poem. In the opening lines Soseki introduces one of the very few "artistic" images to be found in his written works. In these lines he suggests that although he may physically be in a small hut, he is actually occupying the limitless spaces of enlightenment. The hut itself is an illusion and the enlightened soul roams freely in "vast expanses" that are defined only by the places where his soul makes contact with the landscape, the mountains, and the sea. Thus, the "hut," roofed by endless spaces of the heavens and defined by the entirety of the natural world, is not understood to be a physical place but a contact point between his worlds much like the individual spaces in the monks' hall at the temples or the *zazen-seki* out in the forest. It is to those who do not perceive this and see the "closed door" of the hut as a barrier to their further enlightenment that the poem is directed. Forced to provide some suggestion of how the hut should be perceived, Soseki articulates the alternative "image" of the roofless hut defined by its position in the landscape and this is of great important for us, since it provides some indication of the way his thoughts were progressing during this period. From this point on this image reappears often in his work and can be seen as the basis for understanding how he "saw" the landscapes of his garden projects.

Hakusen-an without doubt represented an important place for Soseki, and he would have picked it with care. Perhaps he had found it as a young man when studying in Kamakura, or perhaps he found it on his return. Either way Kawase suggests that he will have had a number of these places tucked away in the back of his mind, places that he had passed or visited on his travels, and noted down as places that would be suitable retreats should the need arise. To a large extent Hakusen-an seems to have served its purpose. He managed to find the degree of seclusion that he was looking for, while at the same time being close enough to Kamakura to remain in touch with those friends whose company he valued and to conduct any temple business that might arise. While being a solitary figure in search of deeper understanding, he was also a Zen monk, and that meant he enjoyed participating in the cultural pursuits of the time such as exchanging poems, drinking tea, and holding long conversations on matters of common interest. Thus, his seclusion at Yokosuka did not imply total isolation, and his meditative life there needs to be seen against a background of many comings and goings, visits by him to see friends and colleagues in Kamakura to stay in touch with affairs, and return visits by them to sit with him looking out over the sea and writing poems. Those known to have made the trip to see him include two old friends from student days, Taihei Myōjun and Daisen Dōtsū, the latter to ask once again that he formally take over the succession. Others included Reizan Dōin (Ling-shan Tao-yin,1255–1325), the recently arrived Chinese Zen master, and, perhaps, all the way from Kyoto, Lord Tamekata, a well-known poet.

The hermitage itself appears to have been built on the slopes of Mt. Hakusen, one of the two or three small mountains that made up this part of the peninsula, and to have had wide views out over the sea and a long view west, all the way to Mt. Fuji.[5] His time at the hermitage seems to have been divided between daily chores, his hours of practice on his meditation mat, walks down to and along the shore, and time spent meditating on the view from a small cave up on the slopes of the mountain. The fact that his time here was a happy and productive one can be sensed time and again in the poems he produced there, and this is typified perhaps by these light hearted opening lines: "All on my own I'm happy. . . . My only friend is this wisteria cane / Last night / we stayed up talking." One senses in his life a quickening of activity such as was so noticeable just before his enlightenment in Jōshu, and we can picture him walking along the sand, enervated by the sea air, "Staff thrust out, I hum like mad."[6]

Certainly he is at peace with his decision to come here and is beginning to fall under the spell of the sea at his door,

> I leave to the highborn
> all the honors
> of this dissolving world
> a life of poverty
> has taught me to love
> haze and mist.

and is happy to share this with old friends who visit,

> Today in the spring
> the friendship between us
> adds warmth to the sunlight.

It is clear, though, that what becomes increasingly important is the dissolving world of haze and mist that has begun to preoccupy his thoughts. In another poem he invokes the sights and sounds of the seashore to present an image of life that is increasingly illusory,

> The sound of the waves
>   as the tide recedes from the shore
> The drying shore after the waves have left
>   cannot be seen for the rising mists.

It seems that the crucial aspect of this time by the sea was that it gave rise to this new series of images, which were based on the dissolving world of water, sea mists, haze, and spray. Throughout the poems the endless variety of this world and its different manifestations are explored alongside glimpses of the ways in which he spent his days. In one poem he writes: "My mind is weightless / and without color / like the lingering fog. . . ."; "The sound of the waves / wake me / from my afternoon nap. . . ."; and "Day after day / watching the sea. . . . " In another, he vanishes into the shadows, "Leaving my footprints / nowhere / north or south / I go into hiding / here by the bay full of moonlight / and the misty hill. . . . ," while in a third, different images arise: "The sun reflected on the green waters / The mist swirls / Like in China." Seas, strands, mists, rain, fog, and the drying sand as the waves pull back, all these fleeting images of metamorphosis build into an illusionary world "like China," which, of course, he had never seen but which nevertheless had formed a vivid impression in his mind from the stories and images of Chinese art and poetry. These illusory impressions now became central not only to his deepening understanding but also to the artistic palette he was to use to express it.

Finally, at Hakusen-an, he had the time to bring into focus the thoughts he had been pursuing since he left the mountains for Shōrinji on the floodplains of the Kiso River and continued as he settled by the sea at the Kyūko-an in Tosa. The importance of this period was that he was able to bring to his practice something to balance the years he had spent since childhood solely in the mountains. Through this an artistic aesthetic began to evolve around images that emerged wrapped in the illusory forms of the liminal zone between the land and the sea.

It is also clear, however, that Soseki had more than just meditation and poetry on his mind during this time, and that living by the sea had begun to open up a lot of new experiences for him. He seems in particular to have thoroughly enjoyed the company and communities of the fishing people among whom he had come to live. These were people very different from the farmers of the mountains where he had grown up and spent most of his life, very different from those who studied with him as a young monk, and very different from the kind of person whom he met in the administrative worlds of Kamakura and Kyoto, or, indeed, at the large temples. One senses that as he spent time on the fringes of the fishing villages he will have become increasingly aware of their lives, aware of the unique hardships and pleasures that go with a life shared with the sea; a life that produced no-nonsense, independent people whose everyday problems made the concerns of Kamakura seem trivial and who seemed to have come to terms with the sudden uncertainties of the world. In some of the poems one gets a sense of the loneliness and isolation of their life, a sense of *sabi* that we met in the lines "A straw thatched hut by the bay / In the autumn dusk," and then in others the sheer enjoyment of their robust communal company,

> In these mountain villages and harbor towns
> I'm happy to have found
> good company
> A crowd of fishermen
> in and out of my hut
> the whole time.

He finds a chance to "play," to take a refreshing break from his everyday concerns and practices by joining in with the different rhythms of their everyday world, laughing at himself as he relaxes,

> East of the strait
> beside my hut
> I fish in silence
> no more chatter about
> pure land
> impure land.

and he begins to see in this pared-down, straightforward existence parallels to that which should be lived by a Zen monk. I think that in this he saw how the Zen experience could be brought into touch with all those people outside the monastic system, beyond all those people who sought out the teachings themselves and were able to enter the life of a monk or nun. It seems as though, through the example of the people he met here, he was beginning to look beyond the immediate concerns of those already involved in the Zen experience toward ways in which this could be brought to bear on the life of the nation as a whole. Something of all this is reflected in the following poem written at the time in which, among the many layers of reference, the unwanted and unloved "crooked tree" finds a use in the fishermen's world, a use that goes on to suggest how the Zen experience could be integrated into everyday lives. On another level this "use" in turn gives it, the form or image itself, an aesthetic significance that anticipates the later developments of the teahouse culture and much of what was to make up the aesthetic palette of the artistic output associated with the *Gozan* monasteries.

From the beginning
the crooked tree
was no good for a lordly dwelling
how could anyone
expect the nobles
to use it for their gates
Now it's been thrown out
onto the shore
of this harbor village
handy for the fishermen
to sit on
while they're fishing.[7]

In recognition of his growing awareness of the importance of these people, Soseki's next project was to erect a three-storied pagoda on a hill above Hakusen-an. Called the "Kai-in Fuza" (*The Mudra Floating in the Sea*); the tower was built high up on a headland, Kite Nose Point, that runs out into the sea. Many ships passed this point, particularly those of the fishing fleets on their way in and out, and the tower became a well-known landmark.[8] Soseki introduced a number of Buddhist references in both the structure and the name of the tower, hoping not only to protect the fleets when they were out at sea but also perhaps to "open the eyes" of some of those who saw it as they passed by on the waters beneath the cliffs. For Soseki this was clearly a way of continuing the "work" even while he was in seclusion, but it also seems to mark a recognition of the changes in his practice that the time spent at Hakusen-an and the time spent with the fishing people who had been instrumental in this had brought. This time spent by the sea had brought a new balance to his perception and broadened his horizons. It made possible a transition in his life that marks the end of his long period of relative seclusion since his enlightenment and the beginning of the part of his life when he reenters public life. Attached though he may have been to the fishing communities among which he lived and to the hut that had enabled him to share their lives for a while, it was not his world, and he had to move on.

Takahashi has searched in vain and, even with the help of the U.S. Navy, was unable to find any real traces of Soseki's time at Mt. Hakusen. He tells us that all remains of the hut are gone and that even its location on the peninsula is lost, as is the cave on the hillside that he used for meditation. Everything has been overtaken by the subsequent development of the area, first as a steelworks and then as a major base for, in turn, the Imperial

Japanese Army and now the U.S. Navy. To create these facilities Mt. Hakusen was leveled and the bay filled in; Takahashi's best guess for the location of the hut is under the present-day Dock #1. The loss of the exact sites notwithstanding, it seems clear that Soseki would have roamed widely over the whole area, "sitting" in different places as the mood caught him, and that it was the proximity of the hut to the sea and the lives of the fishing community that was of key importance. It is interesting to note, however, that although his focus may have been on the sea and its world, he chose a place to live where a short walk up the hill gave him a view of Mt. Fuji, forever in touch with that central place.

We cannot know how many years Soseki expected to stay at Hakusen-an, but he would clearly have been delighted that circumstances made it possible for him to stay there as long as he did. In the larger sense the circumstances that enabled him to go there in the first place, the lack of real authority at the center of power in either Kamakura or Kyoto, remained in place, but, as so often in his life up to now, it was the slow and steady accumulation of people wanting to be his students that forced him in the end to abandon his hut and travel further afield. Thus, in 1324 we see Soseki leaving Miura for the more distant province that is now present-day Chiba Prefecture. He must have left, however, with a particular sense of regret, since it is clear that he was particularly fond of Hakusen-an and considered the time he spent there as a seminal moment in his life. In later years he seems to have traveled out there again before leaving the Kamakura area for good, and the poems that he wrote then about that earlier time reflect something of that regret.

In part of one such poem he can still barely contain his delight and awe at the beauty of the place,

> On the blue waves
> the sun glitters
> as the mist is burned away
> Then the mountains appear
> soaring close to the shore
> each one the most beautiful.
> Already I have loaded the boat
> to sinking point
> with the joy of the passing spring.

Already it is clear that the images of the Miura Peninsula are passing from real experience into the illusory, suggestive forms of Zen art. They have taken on properties of the steep, towering mountains in which the hermits of T'ang China lived, confirming for us that the critical shift in consciousness had taken place for Soseki whereby the physical environment had been removed from the everyday world of perception and placed in a context where it was accessible to the realm of artistic and aesthetic expression; this was now how he "saw" the landscape around him. In a second poem we catch a glimpse of the attachment and sense of connection that remains as strong as ever, even though he is now only a visitor,

> It is some time now since I lived here on this coast
> But today brought a special pleasure to this visitor:
> I shall never forget the setting around my hut
> and the fresh green among the flowers offers me
> once again a glimpse of the departing spring.

Both poems show his delight at seeing the place again, but both end on a wistful note with the reference to the passing or departing spring; he cannot go back but still remembers that earlier time, a time that he sees now as the creative springtime of his endeavors. Others, too, were aware of how important this place had been to Soseki and many visited over the years. His leading disciple and prime mover in the *Gozan* arts as they developed after his death, Gidō Shūshin, records having visited there in 1371 to remember Soseki at a place he had been particularly fond of. All of this adds to the sense that during his stay there, something of particular importance was achieved, and that, looking back, he and those closely associated with him recognized that. Some lines from a poem he wrote many years later in old age seem to sum up what had been achieved at Hakusen-an,

> Beyond the point where the rivers
> end and the mountains vanish
> you have kept on walking.[9]

By 1323, however, it was time for Soseki to move on and his four years at Yokosuka came to an end. True to the spirit of the place, though, when he did go it was by boat, sailing from one of the fishing villages he had come to know so well, past Kite Nose Point, and out toward the mass of the Chiba Peninsula. Kai-in Fuza marked for all to see the place where Soseki had spent so much time meditating on this very ocean.

For his next stopping point he was to choose somewhere entirely different again. The boat trip took him round the bottom of what was then Awa province and up the Pacific coast to Kasuza. Here he left the world of the fishermen and headed inland to found the Taiko-an hermitage among the farming community of Nojitsu. Kawase notes that the area is characterized by its warm, mild climate and its valleys of farming villages enclosed by low mountains. Nojitsu was one of these villages, one particularly noted for the fertility of its soils and dependability of its harvests, and Soseki would have found there a thriving, well-ordered landscape that reflected the predictable, steady turning of the agricultural year. In this way the move to Taiko-an marked a considerable change in circumstances of the community in which he now lived, and, in turn, a change in the tone of Soseki's poetry, which loses its exuberance and light-heartedness and becomes more deliberate and less personal in its tone and themes. Its tone is more "official," and this gives us a strong indication of the things that were on his mind now. An example of this change of tone may be found in a poem called "Gem Mountain,"

It towers
    from the beginning
    without a flaw
The rain beats upon it
    the wind cuts it
    it only shines brighter
Even the fog and cloud
    cannot hide the path
    to the summit
Lin Hsiang-ru was wrong
    running his errand
    to the Ch'in castle.[10]

Gone are the snippets of life, views from his hut and crowds of fishermen that filled the Hakusen-an poems; here instead are the mainstream images of formal Buddhist poetry couched in the literary references of Chinese literature. We no longer get the sense of Soseki striding along, staff thrust out and humming like mad; instead, he seems to be reestablishing his credentials as Bukkoku's successor, preparing to leave the world of Ryo Zassu and enter that of Nan'yo once he accepted a position at court. Certainly this is what Kawase feels was happening during Soseki's stay at Taiko-an.

The site of the hermitage is believed to have been near the present-day temple of Daikoji. The temple is not in itself very old, but the main hall is dedicated to Kannon and contains an old statue.[11] The exact location of the hut is uncertain, but an existing hermitage, the Gyō-an, may be on the same site, particularly because it sits next to a spring, brook, and pond. The scene reminds Kawase of one of the small streams that enters the pond at Saihōji, and although the spring and brook are now filled in, the area around the pond still very much has the feel of a garden, leading both him and Takahashi to feel that this was where the Taiko-an stood. In the *Musō Nempu* there is an entry about the Taiko-an that notes, "above and to the west of the hall there is a cave with a grave marker." It is in this cave that

Soseki appears to have done much of his meditating, and on the wall he carved three characters that read Kinmo-kutsu (Golden Thread Cave). The *Nempu* note is also very interesting because it seems to indicate that at some time the cave had been used as a place of burial, or at least for the rituals of burial, and thus marks the beginning of a series of places that Soseki chose for meditation that had traditional connections with the spiritual world beyond death—places that brought the two worlds together.

In the case of the Golden Thread Cave there are clear signs that this had been worked on, extant grooves cut in the roof indicate that at one time beams had been put in, and a leveled area in front provided a place where Soseki, having walked up to the cave, could "sit." Kawase says of the view from the mouth of the cave: "If you sit and look out from the cave you see the rice fields and the hills beyond. The gentle mountains flow down into a landscape of cultivated fields dotted with groves of trees." How different all this was from the wind and waves of Yokosuka. He had moved on to a place devoted to the cultivation of the land, to drawing from its fertile soils all the things necessary for food and shelter, a place that, when worked on diligently, would promote life and community.

Looking beyond the cycles of history that drove the transitory elite world where individual emperors and other figures with political power came and went, he appears now to be focusing on the communities that he saw as the enduring basis of the national social structure: the lives of the fishing, farming, and artisan families that held this structure together, providing consistent moral values as well as the enduring social stability on which the Zen monastic system depended for sustenance and income. These communities were the contact points through which he could draw on the positive, sustaining energies that flowed just below the surface of an apparently troubled nation in which the ruling elite had lost their cohesion, direction and, therefore, much of their authority. Similarly, in the rapidly changing circumstances of the medieval world, there were other social classes emerging who also looked to these traditional sources for guidance. Most notable among these were the warrior families who steadily gained power as the ruling families of the *bakufu* and the court lost their grip on government and the control of land, especially in the provinces. In addition to these were the merchants and entrepreneurs who became the lynchpins of the new national economy as money-based trade expanded.

Thus Soseki was not alone as he pondered the new realities of the world he was about to rejoin. His attempts to understand the issues can be seen as part of a larger cultural movement that saw, around the world, the transformation of many medieval societies into essentially modern ones that, for the first time, were able to act also as national cultures, breaking down the old regionalisms and involving the traditional ways of life and their beliefs in the new economic and social realities. Yet even as they looked back to traditional lifestyles for structure and values, those in Japan looking to the future at this time were swept along by a new, creative dynamism, that of Zen Buddhism, a force that was to reenergize and change forever the spiritual and cultural forms of that traditional society. As part of all this, and in a way different from before, it was now necessary for Soseki to confront the realities and difficulties of the relationship between the spiritual and secular worlds. Zen and the *Gozan* culture had to be integrated at the most fundamental level into the secular world of work, trade, and government if they were to be more than a passing phase in Japan's religious life. If he was to reenter the world and succeed with this integration, Soseki had to understand how this could be done without compromising either, how an enlightened consciousness could play a useful role in a secular world driven and manifested by powerful forces of its own.

It is significant that at this time of reassessment Soseki was back in touch with developments in China through a new friend, Reizan Dōin, himself recently arrived from there, since many of the problems he faced were similar to those the Chinese Zen masters had been wrestling with since the beginning of the Southern Song era.[12] Between meditation practice and poetic exchanges one can imagine that Soseki will have been eager to hear Reizan's news and views on recent developments in the Five Mountain monasteries in China and of the ideas and solutions that had taken shape there since the rise of Zen a century earlier. Of the fundamental questions that the Song masters (and those following), had tackled, one was of particular importance to Soseki at this point of this life: "How [could he] remain true to Buddhist insight while building social and cultural relationships both with fellow Five Mountain monks and with non-ordained and political elites?"[13] As Parker goes on to explain, the Zen monks saw the way forward as extensive participation in the social and cultural activities of society at large, but the problem of how to balance these with Buddhist insight remained as "they forged socio-political alliances and rivalries, promoted the economic interests of their monastic complexes, enjoyed the privileges of considerable wealth, education and other manifestations of great social influence and prestige, and otherwise remained active in the elite circles of mundane Japanese society." A further complication was concerned with maintaining moral credibility, and with establishing oneself "in the present as morally autonomous from political authority—yet remaining responsible to the whole of society."[14]

That Soseki recognized all these problems is clear from his later writings. In the *Muchū Mondō* he is very specific about the clear distinctions that have to be made and the balances that must be maintained. In one section he says, "Religious institutions might be supported for secular ends, while secular institutions might be supported for spiritual ends. It is important to discern the distinction in reference to both types of institution." Later he warns of the dangers of losing sight of the ultimate goal of seamlessly combining the spiritual and secular: "People meditating on the fundamental carry out their ordinary tasks and activities in the midst of meditation and carry out meditation in the midst of ordinary tasks and activities. There is no disparity between meditation and activity. . . . Yet even this is still in the sphere of accomplishment and is not true merging with the source of Zen."[15]

Seen in this context it was a logical step that Soseki should move from Yokosuka to Nojitsu. At the Hakusen-an he had watched fishermen make a living from the sea, but now the emphasis was switched to the world of cultivation, and to the associations between cultivation of the land and that of people. He was, in short, preparing to engage actively in the "work" as Bukkoku had wanted him to do all those years before, and become a teacher. Kawase is certain of this and describes the Taiko-an as "the bridge between Soseki's previous life of isolation and his preparation to reenter the world."

In a poem written at the time, Soseki gives us a clear indication of the reasons and the context in which he saw his stay at Taiko-an, and that after the insights gained during his years at Hakusen-an, he was using this time to review his situation and make a decision,

> I have cultivated a piece of overgrown wasteland
> All the soil is now beginning to shed light
> Autumn is the time of harvest and each grain gathered
> has the value of several castles.[16]

He has spent all his life so far cultivating the "overgrown wasteland" of un-enlightenment, and now, some thirty years after his "enlightenment" was officially acknowledged by Bukkoku, he feels that the long years of practice are starting to pay off, to shed some light for him; he is "beginning" to understand what enlightenment can mean. He senses that as he approaches fifty, the autumn rather than the spring of his life, everything is starting to come together, and he can see what it is that he is able to offer those who wish to follow.

While all these events were taking place in Soseki's life, others in the country at large were bringing the simmering political and social tensions to a head. In 1324, as Soseki looked out over the peaceful fields of Nojitsu, a plot to attack the *bakufu* forces in Kyoto was uncovered by government agents and quickly disposed of. Go-Daigo's claim of total ignorance of the attempt was accepted by the Hōjō, but everybody was now on guard. The tension between the two forces in Kyoto, coupled with an increasingly difficult economic situation, led to a number of demonstrations of dissatisfaction in the city. Anonymous wall posters began to appear attacking the government in Kamakura and criticizing local lords and priests for failing to react to the fall in the quality of life and to attend to the needs of the people.[17] Clearly it was in a number of people's interest to stir up controversy and destabilize the situation in Kyoto as much as possible.

By 1325 Go-Daigo must have felt that things were starting to go his way. His cause had survived the suppression of the uprising the year before and public opinion seemed to be blaming the government in Kamakura for the state of the country and the general uncertainty of the times. Whatever the immediate reasons, he seems to have felt that the time was right for a significant challenge to the authority of the Hōjō, and one which if successful would help establish a new balance of power between the Imperial Court and the *bakufu*. Thus, in the spring of 1325 he sent a messenger to Soseki at the Taiko-an "requesting" him to return to Kyoto to take up the abbacy of the large urban monastery of Nanzenji. Collcutt characterizes Go-Daigo's request as follows: "This move precipitated a tug-of-war, with Go-Daigo seeking to keep the influential monk in Kyoto, the Hōjō trying to entice him back to Kamakura, and Soseki himself striving to maintain neutrality, although sensing, perhaps, that the Hōjō were losing their grip. Go-Daigo's attempt to detach Soseki from his erstwhile warrior patrons may be seen as one small but significant part of the emperor's anti-*bakufu* maneuvering."[18]

Soseki's initial reaction was to stall the emperor, and he recorded his reply to the messenger in a poem,

> The affairs of the world
> are nothing to me.
> I am tired of coming and going.
> This poor hut is perfect for me
> the one possession
> of a monk who does nothing.[19]

But this may only have been to give himself time to assess the situation. It was in fact the opportunity he had been preparing himself for at Taiko-an, the chance to join the mainstream teaching efforts of a major *Gozan* monastery, and it was not long before he agreed to go. This was a very critical moment for Soseki because he had to decide where the best interests of the *Gozan* movement lay at this time, in its traditional power base in Kamakura where the big monasteries of the Chinese Zen masters were, or in Kyoto, a place historically very hostile to the Zen movement, but where it seemed more influential patronage may lie in the future. As Collcutt suggests, he may well have sensed that the Hōjō were a spent force and could not see where future patronage in Kamakura might come from. He may also have wanted to distance himself from the uncompromising nature of the continental Song Zen that dominated there as he prepared to take an active role in Bukkoku's lineage, which had a distinctly Japanese flavor, something that mirrored his personal style and that he wished to emphasize. Whatever the immediate reasons, and there were many other factors that could have influenced his decision, in himself he was ready to go and by the summer he had started on his journey west.

As he set out for Kyoto in August of 1325, Soseki must have felt as uncertain about the future as he had in arriving in Kamakura from Tosa some six years before. He had clearly made a number of important decisions, ones that would decide the fate of Bukkoku's Zen lineage for some time to come. These decisions had to be made at a time of unrest and uncertainty in the country at large. He may well have had less choice in these matters than one supposes but this was clearly a key moment for both himself and the *Gozan* monastic system and the best course of action would have been far from clear. Perhaps it is a reflection of this that the route he chose to take was not along the more direct coast road but up through Koshu instead, thus prolonging the journey and taking him through the places of his childhood home and down the Kiso River valley past the places of practice he had used some twelve years before. One senses that it was a reflective journey, his thoughts firmly on the tasks ahead, and, perhaps to help him go over the many issues and questions on his mind, he stopped by at Eihōji to pick up his old friend and dharma brother Gen'nō Hongen. Together they traveled down to Kyoto and entered Nanzenji in the autumn. Gen'nō was to remain with Soseki for a while as they worked to establish their Zen lineage and authority at the center of the Kyoto *Gozan*, and he was to play a major role in the question and answer sessions that went to make up the bulk of the *West Mountain Evening Talks* before returning eventually to the seclusion of Eihōji.

One of Soseki's first actions as abbot was to rename the temple Taiheikuokoku Nanzenji, an act that Yanagida sees as a clear statement of his agenda at this time. The idea of *Taihei*, or Great Peace, went back to the early Song dynasty when the emperors of the newly reunited country set about reinventing the nation after the extended years of civil war that had followed the collapse of the T'ang. They sought to initiate a period of peace during which the government administrators and all the others at court, religious leaders, scholars, philosophers, artists and poets would actively seek to reestablish the social and cultural fabric of the country. It would be an attempt to end war and division, bringing people and factions back together again to create a newly invigorated and stronger nation. Nanzenji already had a strong connection with Song China, having been founded by Issan, and Soseki can be seen to be building on these associations as he looks for ways to set up the mechanisms by which such a healing period of unity and peace could be promoted. Encouraged by Go-Daigo's enthusiasm for the institutions of the Southern Song renaissance, Soseki was seeking to position the *Gozan* monasteries at the center of this effort, to look beyond the present uncertainty to the kind of nation that they wanted to see in the future. The renaming of the temple, associating it with the "great peace," was an important part of this effort.[20] The central importance of the reinvigorated Nanzenji in the *Gozan* organization, and its importance as the keystone in Soseki's plans, is indicated by the fact that it was the only temple in either Kyoto or Kamakura to attain the highest ranking of *Gozan-no-Jo* (Superior *Gozan*), and, from the beginning of 1334 through the next fifty years, the heyday of the *Gozan* system, it was never ranked below *Gozan* 1.[21]

This flurry of activity continued throughout 1325 as Soseki worked together with Go-Daigo, although their motives may have differed, to put the institutions they both felt were necessary into place. In the summer of that year, encouraged by Soseki, Go-Daigo authorized the first official mission to China for almost five hundred years in the form of a trading ship. The "Kenchōji Ship" was sent ostensibly to raise funds through trade for building work at Kenchōji, but it was also used to send priests and envoys to make contacts in China with the Imperial court and the leading monasteries. For Go-Daigo this was a chance to further his agenda of establishing his credentials as statesman and diplomat, while Soseki was concerned to establish strong contacts with the Five Mountain monasteries, and in particular with those monks who had been studying under the charismatic Chung-jen Ming-pen until his death a few years before.

Matters continued thus for about a year until, in late summer 1326, Soseki suddenly left Nanzenji, traveling initially to remote areas south of Nara and then on to Kamakura, and not returning to Kyoto for some seven years. That something serious had happened is reflected by the fact that both he and Gen'nō left Kyoto at this time, and the tone of a parting poem he sent his friend on leaving seems to suggest that he is worried about the future,

You climb
    Mount Hiei
    On ladders of cloud

I walk
out of Kyoto
with a wisteria cane
A thousand miles apart
like the stars of the east
and the stars of the north
and this is our one chance
to remind each other
that we are friends.[22]

There is something ominous in the line, "and this is our one chance," as if Soseki is really not sure what is going to happen next, but he has clearly felt it important that he leave Kyoto and needs time to decide on the next course of action. As so often in the past, his proven method of dealing with uncertainty was to travel and revisit the places he felt at home in. For the next six months or so this is what he did, but before following him we need to understand something of what had happened to precipitate his departure from Nanzenji at a time when so much important work was being done.

It appears as though three factors came together to create a situation that made it personally difficult and professionally unwise to stay so closely involved in things in Kyoto. Kawase suggests that the sheer pace of life at Nanzenji had taken Soseki by surprise. In the month of August alone he had been summoned three times to the palace to instruct Go-Daigo and other members of his family and he must have felt a growing unease at becoming so closely identified with the imperial family. In addition to these commitments, the sheer volume of people arriving at Nanzenji to become his students was threatening to overwhelm the temple's limited resources. It is reported that the community ran out of food and supplies on a number of occasions as they attempted to feed and house all those who turned up at the door, and it rapidly proved impossible for Soseki to be able to organize instruction or accommodation for such large numbers of people.[23]

Among these general concerns the catalyst to his suddenly deciding to leave may well have been Go-Daigo's continuing machinations in his struggle with the *bakufu*. In a direct challenge to the authority of the government in Kamakura he named his own son as his heir-apparent, refusing to continue the arrangement of 1290 whereby the succession should have reverted to the alternate branch of the Imperial family. Whereas in the anti-*bakufu* plots of the past, Go-Daigo had remained in the background and avoided any overt responsibility, this action brought him into direct personal confrontation with the Hōjō, a potentially dangerous situation that could prove difficult for those perceived to be his allies or supporters. On top of this development, Soseki had also received an invitation from his old patron Hōjō Takatoki to take up the post of abbot at Jufukuji in Kamakura.

One can understand if Soseki felt at this point that things were starting to get out of hand, that his life was drifting beyond his control to a degree that he could not have possibly imagined as he weighed the odds of reentering public life back at the Taiko-an. He will have made allowance for the fact that a large number of people would be attracted to Nanzenji while he was there, but Go-Daigo's actions will have been a major worry. Up to this time it was possible to be in Kyoto and to be part of the emperor's plans for expanding the *Gozan* system and so on, without overtly taking sides against the *bakufu*. Now, however, everything was changed, and those who did not actively distance themselves from the emperor would have been perceived as tacitly supporting him. This was not a position that Soseki had looked for, not one in which he would have felt comfortable, nor could he possibly have felt such a position would be advantageous for Zen or the *Gozan* monasteries. On the other hand, it would have been difficult for him to have immediately taken up Takatoki's offer and moved to Kamakura, since this would clearly have put the gains of the Kyoto *Gozan* in jeopardy. It seems that in the end, seeing no other way out of the accumulating problems, Soseki decided to head for some neutral, secluded area for a cooling off period, distancing himself from Go-Daigo for the time being and giving events time to work themselves out.

There is no doubt, however, as the poem already quoted indicates, that Soseki took the present situation very seriously, and as he set off to his birthplace near Ise, Gen'nō left Kyoto to make his way back to Eihōji. In Kawase's account of these events, the decision to leave came suddenly and probably caused great consternation for those outside his immediate circle and who were not privy to his plans. He refers to the *Nanzenji Goroku* ("Living in Nanzenji"), which records the events of the time and describes how Soseki prepared a parting poem,

> Even a peaceful wisp of cloud
> goes through many great changes
> Following the dragon
> it rested for a while in these mountains.
> But by its nature
> it cannot be nailed in one place
> Blown by the autumn winds it travels to other lands.

After gathering the community, he sat holding his fly-whisk, flicked it, read the poem, threw the whisk away, got up, and walked out. He was gone.[24] Seeking further explanation for this, Kawase also points out that Soseki had just celebrated an important birthday, his fifty-first, one of the most significant in the Confucian tradition. Following a fiftieth birthday one is allowed the freedom to pursue personal interests and to take time out from the network of familial and professional obligations which up to this point in a person's life will have taken precedence over any self interest. Soseki may well have used this, in part at least, to justify his actions.

In any event, the autumn winds would have been rustling the bright red leaves of the maples as Soseki left the city. "It was still dark when I left the capital. The light of the daybreak moon was reflected in the waves of the eastern river, and lingering cockcrows could be heard even after I had passed some distant villages. The sky, completely misted over, looked extremely beautiful."[25] We can imagine that Soseki, for all his preoccupations, would have felt good to be setting out on a journey again and, invigorated by the cold morning, would have been looking forward to the whatever lay ahead, doing once again those things he enjoyed best.

The journey he set out on now is interesting since the places he chose to visit give us some idea, first, of how he was reacting to the events of the past year and, second, of what it was he felt he needed if he was to recover some peace of mind. Since we had last seen him sitting in the mouth of the cave at Taiko-an calmly contemplating his return to the world, his belief in this course of action must have been shaken by the way things had turned out. The worries about the everyday running of the temples in Kyoto, how to cope in the long run with the large numbers of people arriving at Nanzenji, would have made it very difficult for him to concentrate on the very serious decisions that he needed to make in the light of the rapidly deteriorating political situation; his course of action now would seal the fate, one way or another, of his lineage of Zen and possibly the whole *Gozan* system for the foreseeable future. He needed to find a place where he could sit in meditation and regain the clarity of mind he had felt at Nojitsu. No doubt, at this important moment in his career, the example of those monks who had been such positive influences on his life, monks like Ryo Zassu and Chung-jen Ming-pen, came into sharp focus and he set off to get in touch with them once again.

He first visited Ise, and, having taken part in the purification ceremonies that were such an important part of pilgrimages to the great shrines, he set off by boat down the coast of the Kii Peninsula towards the ancient shrines of Kumano. The seas of Kumano Bay sweeping in from the Pacific Ocean meet a rugged coastline of cliffs that lifts steadily up into tangles of remote mountain ranges behind. In these steep-sided, inaccessible mountains lay the peaks, caves, gorges and waterfalls that marked some of the oldest sacred places in Japan and the network of old pilgrimage routes that joined these places together. Here too stood Mt. Omine, the focus of ritual climbs since the eighth century when the ascetic Gyōki Bosatsu made it the center of practices that became the basis for the Shugendō Order, the "hard practices" of the *yamabushi*. Further west lay Mt. Kōya, the secluded peak where Kukai had founded Shingon Buddhism, in the heart of the landscapes long sacred to the *yamabushi* rituals and practices to which it was closely affiliated. To the north lay Yoshino where the twists and turns of the mountain landscape provided safe haven for a while in 1185 for the tragic figure of Minamoto Yoshitsune as he was hunted down by his brother Yoritomo, and where, on his journeys through them, the monk Saigyō (1118–90) had immortalized the transient beauty of the cherry tree blossoms in sad poems as he fought with the demons of loneliness the landscape inspired.

The geography of the peninsula, aligned northeast / southwest and pointing generally towards India, led to early associations with the origins of Buddhism and in particular with the promised land of Kannon, and pilgrimage to the shrine at Nachi helped ensure entry there in the afterlife. The shrine at Nachi is one of three that make up the shrines of Kumano and was a major objective of Soseki's visit. Since at least the tenth century the Kumano shrines had been a very important pilgrimage route for everyone from the emperors, their families, and leading figures at court to the general populace, anyone in need of healing at the hot springs to those seeking the wisdom and compassion of Kannon. The Hongu, or Main Shrine, is situated in the mountains close to the springs and is connected back in myths to Katsumiko no Omikami, the god of the forests, while the shrine at Shingu down on the coast, is associated with Hayatami Omikami who had "arrived there on a ship borne along on an 'ocean current' that also brought mild weather and rich schools of fish."[26] The third shrine, dedicated to Kannon, is situated on the Nachi River as it makes its way down through the mountains at a point where the waters plunge 130 meters in spectacular falls. The Nachi Falls, one of the greatest in Japan, had long been a focal point for *yamabushi* practice, and were considered to be a special center of spiritual power. The towering column of water fills the rock basin with noise and spray as it free falls down and down to crash at the bottom on a series of ledges, a place where great forces hurl tremendous energy out from one world to another.

This trip marked Soseki's first visit back to the coast since leaving Hakusen-an and he must have relished the chance to reconnect with the rhythms of the sea. How long this trip and its particular destinations had been in his mind is impossible to tell, but it is significant that to put the problems of Kyoto behind him and regain some perspective on his life, he chose to visit a place that was full of associations not just with the mountains and their history of *yamabushi* activity, but also with the ocean, the deep and mysterious inner workings of its currents and its interplay with the land.

On top of this, of course, it was also a place that had long been a center of practice connected with Kannon, a very important focus for his beliefs since childhood. Just how long he stayed in the Kumano area is not clear, but one of his poems records his visit to the Kannon Hall at the Nachi Falls. This hall, at the Seigantoji temple, not only overlooks the falls but is also the starting point for the long pilgrimage trail that takes in the thirty-three temples in the western provinces of Japan that are dedicated to Kannon. Perhaps the poem marks the end of his visit because in it, speaking directly to Kannon, Soseki gives thanks for the compassionate peace of mind he has been granted, enabling him to shut out the turmoil of life in Kyoto where the human cascade had filled his world with noise and confusion similar to the falls below him now,

> Heaven's river bursts forth
> a human cascade,
> The cold roar of the plunging waters
> echoes in the blue sky.
> Greatly Treasured Compassionate One,
> the Free and Ubiquitous Kannon,
> Fortunate am I to have no ears to hear it.[27]

This was what he had come for. During his stay, as he walked in the mountains, climbed through the deep forests up steep paths around Mt. Nachi, looked down over the sea twinkling far below, or sat at his practice in the cool, spray-filled updrafts that swirled above the falls, he had found some resolution to his problems and comfort for his soul in the compassionate care of Kannon. As he prepared to leave Kumano and make his way back up to Ise, one cannot help but reflect how torn he must have felt to be leaving this place he had so carefully sought out and how quickly he might have responded to Saigyō's plea of a hundred or so years before, as the drenching rains and blasts of winter winds threatened to overwhelm him with sadness,

> If only there were
> someone else
> willing to bear this loneliness—
> side by side we'd build our huts
> for winter in a mountain village.[28]

For Soseki, however, there was a boat waiting to take him back up to Ise. His brief respite from the world was over, but he had had time to think and with his usual deliberation had come up with a course of action, a plan as to how best to proceed given the circumstances in Kyoto and the tensions in the country at large. On reaching Ise he took time to deal with some personal family business, founding Fuoji temple and conducting ceremonies there for his family ancestors, but then, rather than returning to Kyoto, he set off once more for Kamakura.

This journey to Kamakura was different from the one seven years before because this time he was going there on his own volition; no one had sent for him, and, possibly, no one was actually expecting him. Thus, toward the end of 1326 he quietly entered Kamakura and set himself up in a small hermitage, no doubt another of those special places that Kawase believes he had earmarked for just such contingencies. His course of action can only mean that he felt it necessary to distance himself at this difficult time from Go-Daigo and the direction in which his ambitions were taking him, and, in addition to this, he may have felt it was better for Nanzenji and the *Gozan* to go on developing quietly without the additional attention that his presence there would inevitably draw. On the other hand, he was not prepared to accept Hōjō Takatoki's offer of Jofukuji just yet either, and he appears to have decided to pursue a neutral middle course for a while and to see how things were going to develop.

Apart from the problems associated with the weaknesses within the Hōjō *bakufu* and the sense that the country may be in for some problems ahead, it seems that this would have been quite a stimulating time for Soseki. The question of rules and regulations for the monastic institutions would have been uppermost in his mind as he tried to organize the *Gozan* temples into a cohesive whole and just then in Kamakura these issues were under debate. The big temples had all been founded by Chinese Zen masters brought up in the strict regimes of the Five Mountain monasteries, and little or no allowance had been made for the differences between monastic practice in China and Japan. To increase membership and boost the position of the Zen temples, they had to be made more accommodating to Japanese style and traditions of practice and more responsive to Japanese sensibilities. To this end a review of monastic practice was being attempted by the recently arrived Chinese master Seisetsu Shōchō (Ch'ing-cho Cheng-ch'eng, 1274–1339), who had been installed at Kenchōji. His idea was to modify the monastic regulations that he had brought over from China to better suit Japanese conditions, and since Soseki would soon have to issue regulations himself, he would have been very interested in these developments.

These may indeed even have encouraged Soseki when he finally agreed, the following year, to enter Jōchiji at Takatoki's invitation, a decision perhaps prompted by the news of Taihei Myōjun's death at Unganji. Apart from being one of Soseki's closest friends, Taihei had been an important figure in the continuing work of Bukkoku's school, taking over Unganji on

Bukkoku's death when Soseki was far away in Eihōji and, with it, many of the responsibilities of successor. He had on a number of occasions appealed to Soseki to return and take over, the last time seven years before when Soseki had refused to see him and left for Hakusen-an. But now, with his passing, Soseki was on his own. Lines from Soseki's poem "For the Death of a Monk" seem to provide a touching farewell,

> Now a spring wind
> is playing for you the tune
> "Return to the Origin"
> and even the Buddha's hands
> cannot interfere
> with your homecoming.[29]

After a brief stay at Jōchiji, in August of 1327 he moved across Kamakura to take over Zuisenji up in the hills to the north of town, a place that will have suited him much better and where he could create a more personal atmosphere away from the continental style at Jōchiji. It was not only more remote; it also had a cave in the hillside beside it and from the mountain above there were panoramic views of the country around. Here was the kind of place where he particularly liked to practice, and, sensing its potential, he began to add to it the next year, planning to stay for some time.

For the next three years, between 1327 and 1330, it appears as though that was Soseki's intention. He developed Zuisenji as the focal point for his practice and the administration of the lineage and began to participate in the social and cultural world of the *Gozan* monasteries, no doubt participating in the debate about monastic rules, but also encouraging the arts and artistic discussion. At Zuisenji he added a Kannon Hall and built a small pavilion, the "Ichiran-tei" (Whole-World Viewing Pavilion) on the mountain above the temple. The pavilion's name reflects the fact that the view from it was not just down over Kamakura and out to the sea beyond, but, also, looking west, one could see the cone of Mt. Fuji rising above the mountain ridges, the view that Soseki had sought out time and time again in the past. What is significant this time, however, is that this hut does not appear to have been conceived primarily as a hermitage, a place of retreat reserved solely for meditation, as so many of his earlier huts in such places had been, but rather as a gathering place that could act as a catalyst to interaction. The Ichiran-tei soon became a favorite meeting place for Soseki and his friends, especially the Chinese masters such as Seisetsu Shōchō, who gathered there to exchange poems, to discuss and comment on art and other matters of common interest. At the same time Soseki also started to develop the garden at Zuisenji, perhaps the first large-scale project he had worked on since

Eihōji, thirteen or fourteen years before.

For us the garden at Zuisenji marks an important moment. It was the first in the sequence of gardens that Soseki built after reentering the world that represent his attempt to bring into his immediate environment all the things that he had identified over the preceding thirty years as the key points of connection between him and the greater reality of Life. His life as a free-roaming monk, when he could travel at will to the places where he felt these connections, had come to an end, and, from now on, he would have to bring these critical elements of the landscape into the temple spaces he occupied. He had provided himself with the tools and was now starting to experiment with creating these elements in the form of his temple gardens, places where the monk, abbot, teacher, administrator, all his public personas could vanish and merge seamlessly with the landscape around. The sequence runs from a starting point in the garden at Zuisenji to a conclusion at Saihōji some ten years later, where he finally seems to have achieved his goal, and the development of this sequence through six or seven gardens is the subject of the final chapters in this book. Of importance now is the need to understand the general circumstances in which it began.

Partly the time was right. The deepening understanding that had come to him during the years since his initial enlightenment seems to have suddenly taken on a sharper focus, particularly in the years he spent at Hakusen-an, and this focus had in turn made the content of that understanding more immediately accessible. Thus, as Soseki started to participate actively in the cultural world of the *Gozan*, both in Kyoto and then in Kamakura, he was able to make use of this content to express his enlightenment in the social activities of calligraphy, poetry, and tea, and also in the wider forms of architecture and, more particularly, garden building. Having taken on the role of teacher he now needed to participate in all the "Ways" that provided opportunities for the Truth to be passed on. The crucial thing underpinning all this, however, was that by this time he had developed a crystal clear vision of the "place" the enlightened soul inhabits, the nature of the contact points that can bring the worlds we inhabit together as one, eliminating the dualities of conventional reality, and the shift in consciousness necessary for this place to be accessed. In a poem he identifies this place quite specifically,

> Living secluded
>   above the cloud
>   at the top of Mount Su
> abiding in your origin
>   you demonstrate
>   the truth of Zen. . . .
> You have moved far from town

from now on you renew
the Way of Bodhidharma.[30]

"Moving far from town," shifting consciousness, brings one to the place where enlightenment comes and the enlightened soul dwells. The poem then describes this place in the illusory terms of Zen, a place that is not a "physical" reality but rather a combination of differing elements, or images, that make up the "right" place for each individual, "above the clouds at the top of Mt. Su." Soseki's strength of feeling about the importance of this is demonstrated in the consistent frustration he displays with those who travel to study in China, not realizing that the truth lies "below their feet," right where and who they are. In two examples of this he writes poems to mark the embarkation of his students for China and tells them in no uncertain terms that they are wasting their time. In one he could not be more specific,

Setting out over the sea to the south
looking for the truth—
but it's too late
Sailing all that way
what do you hope to find
over the ocean.
Right here and now
I'll spare you thirty blows
for a while
and wait for you to come back
some day
in brocade robes.

Soseki is telling him that it is too late, he has already missed the point. He will come back some day in "brocade robes," but these will only be the exterior trappings of Chinese Zen, and that what he needs to find is in fact "right here, right now." In the other poem he is just as frustrated,

Whale billows
thousands of miles
all the way to the end of the sky
don't betray
the boundless clear wind
and the bright moon
When you have
worn out
your straw sandals
you will be back
leaping free
of the pit of Nang-yang.

It does not matter how far you travel, even to the "end of the sky," or how many wonderful and exotic things you see. Truth lies in the boundless clear wind and the bright moon, and these things are all around you now. All you will do is wear out your sandals, and, coming home, freed from the trappings of Zen, you will find that the Truth was here all along. Even when his close friend Kosen Ingen, a person whose understanding he deeply respected, leaves for China, he can only hope that "the original sail," the guiding truth of Zen, will soon "bring you / east again to this land."[31] While he values Chinese Zen for providing the essential, illusory "location" and "matter" of Zen enlightenment in the events of the lives of its masters and the landscapes in which they occurred, as well as for its monastic organization, he still believes that enlightenment can only come from within the context of one's unique consciousness and the locations in which it formed. He himself had failed to find his "place" within the world of Chinese masters even though they were in Japan, and, while he was not for a moment doubting the depth and validity of their enlightenment, it was not until he found a shared context with Bukkoku and his temple at Unganji that he began to make real progress.

Such were the times, however, that even though he was actively involved with the temples in Kamakura, he was still sought after to head up one of the major temples, and his relative peace at Zuisenji came to an end the next year. Hōjō Takatoki had kept up an unrelenting pressure on Soseki, and, in the end, in 1329, he entered Engakuji as abbot. At the time, Engakuji like a number of other monasteries was going through a very difficult period. Like the country as a whole, they were suffering from a particularly widespread famine that is recorded as having lasted until the end of 1330. Times were hard everywhere, but the temples, reliant as they were on alms for much of their food, would have been particularly helpless. To begin with it cannot have seemed like a good thing that Soseki should be on his way for the community of Engakuji, since he would inevitably bring large numbers of extra people with him, but as it turned out his arrival proved very beneficial. As the famine continued through 1330, the temple was actually spared its worst effects by a rich merchant who, on becoming Soseki's student, donated to it a large sum of money. Although he may have helped with the short-term survival of the temple, Soseki was also very wary about becoming too closely associated with the Hōjō at this time; too much was in flux, and he had to be very careful to remain uncompromised by either side.

So, it is not surprising that in September of 1330 he quietly slipped out of Engakuji and, after returning briefly to Zuisenji, he left Kamakura altogether, setting out for his home base in Koshu. By making an appearance in Kamakura, he had kept all his options open, but even Zuisenji on the outskirts of town was too closely associated with the *bakufu* cause for him to remain long. It seems that his actions at this time were driven not so much by any desire to actively manipulate the principal players in each center of power, as by a firm resolve to stay uninvolved in the maneuvering. He had to keep his attention focused mainly on what would be best for the future of the Zen temples and on his own fortunes only when they would have an effect on these. His decision to leave Kamakura and base himself somewhere politically neutral is entirely in keeping with this, but he would no doubt have welcomed the chance to spend some time in Koshu again, his first visit for some twenty years.

Once in Koshu he founded Erinji (Forest of Wisdom Temple), a place of importance for us because it was here that he built the next in the series of gardens leading up to Saihōji, and the first in a series that he would build from scratch. Previously, the gardens had been attached to hermitages or temples in tucked-away locations where he still hoped for privacy, or, as at Zuisenji, where he had added to already existing gardens. Erinji thus marks a significant important new development, and it cannot be purely coincidental that he chose a location so close to where he grew up to start the process. The temple was built on land donated by Nikkaido Sadafuji (b. 1267), who was a leading member of the local Takeda family and a senior official in Kamakura and who had introduced Soseki to a number of important figures, including Ashikaga Takauji. Once established, the temple became the focus for Takeda family ceremonies and burials. It was situated close to the well-known Mt. Enzan, in the center of prosperous farmland, with long views over the countryside toward Mt. Gentoku. Kawase reports that it was a spacious temple precinct in what then would have been a heavily wooded area, and that behind it is an area where "the white clouds leap up and the cliffs are sheer."[32] He adds that, looking straight out from the middle gate of the temple, you can see the peak of Mt. Gentoku, but that as you climb the mountain behind and reach a place now called "Musō's Field," the whole of the distant mountain becomes visible. Most importantly, however, behind the temple there is a garden laid out with "many stones," and Kawase believes that, although damaged, it is Soseki's original work.

Erinji seems to have had a special place in Soseki's heart, and even when he eventually had to leave, it was one place with which he kept in touch, taking an interest in its affairs. His poems over the subsequent years seem to reflect this, recording at least three occasions when friends, Kosen Ingen and Daido Myōtetsu, and a disciple, Kasan Sōshō, became head priest there, and it was in one of these poems that Soseki records an image of Erinji that seems to reflect how he saw the temple and its role in the continuing uncertainty of the times,

Actions to save the world
have their ups and downs
depending on circumstances
You have to be careful
as though you were dragging half a ton
by a hair
Spare no efforts
to bring the Dharma rain
to this countryside
The Forest of Wisdom
will grow dense
and cover the world.[33]

Certainly, as 1330 drew to a close, the situation in the country was becoming increasingly tense. It had been four years since Go-Daigo had declared his own son to be his successor and thereby openly challenged the authority of the Kamakura government, and since widespread famine had further destabilized the country. Rumors abounded in Kyoto of plots and counterplots as the emperor continued to push for the reestablishment of full imperial power. No doubt the seeming hesitancy of the Hōjō to take action against him served to encourage Go-Daigo's ambitions and almost certainly lulled him into a false sense of optimism about his chances of success should he declare war. As the months of the apparently peaceful stand off went by, no one seemed ready to make a move until, late in the year, the government got wind of another major plot against them and sent a number of troops to reinforce their garrisons in Kyoto. At Erinji, Soseki would have been fully aware of the course events were taking and may even have received direct appeals from both sides to support their cause. Knowing as much as he did about the protagonists and being fully aware of the vulnerability of the *Gozan* monasteries should they lose the patronage of one or the other, or be perceived to have backed one against the other, this must have been a worrying winter for him.

In a move perhaps symptomatic of the nervous times, Soseki returned to Zuisenji in early 1331 where he would no doubt be in a better position to help protect the interests of the monasteries. As soon as he returned, Hōjō Takatoki offered him the abbacy of Kenchōji, a post Soseki declined but for which he recommended instead his old friend Kengai Kōan. Now was certainly not the time to accept direct patronage from anyone, Erinji having been an exception since the land and money came from his family, and he knew as well as anyone that "You have to be careful . . . depending on circumstances." The incident is interesting, however, as an indication of just how much the balances of power had already been altered by events. Twelve years or so before, Soseki would have had difficulty turning down an offer such as this, but now he has emerged as a figure free enough from political control to do so. And things were about to change again. After the apparent calm of the previous three or four years, things suddenly started to happen very quickly and soon everyone had a lot more than temple abbacies to worry about.

In August of 1331 Go-Daigo, no doubt feeling that he should move before the government further reinforced their armies, indicated that their garrisons in Kyoto should be attacked. Warrior families loyal to the imperial family, waiting impatiently for just such a gesture, lost no time and fighting broke out. The war this attack led to was to last for the next five years, seeing rapidly changing fortunes for both sides, but in the end it proved to be a fight that nobody could win outright. The protracted, periodically brutal war, dragged on relentlessly in increasingly desperate campaigns that caused tremendous destruction, not just in Kyoto and Kamakura, but throughout the country as a whole, and, when it ended indecisively, the stage was set for years of similar actions. It was for all sides the worst possible result and weakened the social and political structures of the country to such an extent that it was to be almost three hundred years before any one faction was able to exert the kind of authority over the whole country that the Hōjō regents of the early fourteenth century had done; emperors and shoguns came and went but their power was limited and the country at large was effectively governed on a local level by whichever powerful family could impose its will.

The fighting in 1331, however, was soon over. If Go-Daigo had been counting on the troops of the government forces to change sides and support their newly emergent emperor, then he misjudged the situation. His small force was easily defeated, and the emperor was captured. Given the option to abdicate and "retire," he refused, and after being stripped of the imperial regalia, the key symbols of legitimate succession, he was exiled to the Oki Islands in the Japan Sea. All this had been very sudden, and many people seem to have been unprepared for the rapid reversals in fortune as a diary entry from that time reveals: "The report that His Majesty [Go-Daigo] had disappeared on the night of the 24th day of the 8th month reached our ears at dawn on the following day, causing immense confusion."[34] Indeed, although the immediate fighting had ended, the confusion was only to grow, and, for many, things were never to be the same again.

At Zuisenji that winter, a poem Soseki wrote reflects his reaction to events and his sense that this was the start of a bleak season for everyone, a time when much would be obscured and when the impermanence of what had seemed certain in life would be apparent. The introduction to the poem indicates that it was written on a day when he was watching the snow fall on the Ichiran-tei,

> Waiting in my little hut
>   the pines overlap pines
>   and mountains overlap each other,
> The white snow continues
>   to fall on the tips
>   of the branches in my garden.[35]

In 1332 the situation in Kyoto stabilized for a while. The Kamakura government moved swiftly into action and established an alternative court with the coronation of Kōgon, the successor Go-Daigo had passed over in favor of his son, and the power vacuum in Kyoto was filled. Court officials and administrators adjusted to the new realities and life seemed set to get back to normal, even though Go-Daigo's son and the many warriors still loyal to the exiled emperor moved south to the safety of the mountains around Yoshino to establish a center of opposition. That spring Soseki returned to Erinji determined to get on with all the projects he had postponed the year before, and this is probably when he started work on the garden there.

In spite of everything that must have been on his mind, Soseki seems to have been in a positive and determined state of mind. Between this time and August of 1333, he undertook the major garden project at Erinji and a second garden, for other members of the Takeda family, at the Nishikawa residence nearby. He also traveled across the valley to the foot of Mt. Gentoku where, in the village of Tokuwa, he built the "Yaemon" guesthouse, and in so doing appears to have repaid an old debt. As Kawase recounts the story, when Soseki was a young monk finding his way around the mountain for the first time, a local farmer called Yaemon had been particularly helpful, allowing him to stay in his house and possibly acting as his guide in the mountains.. It seems that Soseki never forgot this kindness, or the frank open-heartedness that lay behind it, and to express his enduring gratitude he now returned and built a guesthouse, naming it after his old friend. Tokuwa, where Yaemon had lived, represented for Soseki the "way in" or gateway to the mysterious world of Mt. Gentoku and was therefore of great importance to him. Yaemon had played an important role in those days, and in the difficult times of the present, Soseki went out of his way to emphasize the importance and virtue of people such as these and thus indirectly passed judgment on those above who were tearing the country apart.

On his arrival back at Erinji, Soseki was visited by his old dharma brother Tengan Ekō (1273–1335) who had just returned from studying in China, and it seems that the visit, during which they walked in the mountains and wrote poetry together, cheered Soseki up and reinforced his positive state of mind. In part of one of these poems he writes,

> Lovely! Our hearts are open
>   Not a grain of sand
> in our friendship
> May it go on just like this!
> The memory of this visit
>   should be handed down forever
> There is something beyond happiness
>   inside the gate
>   of this mountain.[36]

Other poems written during this visit also reflect this mood and his apparent acceptance of the degree and quality of his enlightenment, and, as he looks back over the events of the past years, he seems to be coming to terms with what has happened and to be ready to move on. It is almost as though he realizes that this may be his last chance to roam freely in the mountains as he had done for so long and he is saying goodbye. In one he notes,

> Thirty years,
>   so many events
> have come and gone
> Now I let them all go
>   and sit in stillness
> and am still.

Thirty years have passed since Bukkoku acknowledged his enlightenment, and he knows that he has achieved a deep understanding—"Already I have attained the essence"—but he still cannot think of anywhere that he would rather be,

> Is there anything better
>   than to stay at the foot
> of this misty cliff
> watching in meditation
>   the calm clouds
> on their way home to the cave.

But he has to get on, and, in another poem, he looks forward to the projects he has ahead of him. In this poem the third and fourth lines should be seen to refer to how he sees his "realization of Self." It is an image of his enlightened Self blowing free and unattached through the world,

> After wandering for a long time
>   I had a realization of Self

The wind blows freely
    through the house
Not seeking the unusual
    My offerings are
These white stones and this pure spring.[37]

The stones and spring seem to refer to the garden project he was engaged on when Tengan came to visit him, the details of which we will be looking at in a later chapter.

For all the pleasant ways he was spending his time, however, it was not possible for him to forget the events going on elsewhere in the country, and he acknowledges this in a couple of particularly foreboding lines,

Waking up my dream
    is suddenly interrupted
and I return to the darker world.

Another translator gives the last line additional menace,

. . . and I see shadows moving in the afternoon.[38]

It is a very interesting group of poems, reminiscent of those written at Hakusen-an, a frank and, in places, lighthearted exchange of ideas with a friend he was particularly happy to see again after such a long time. One of the shadows, however, that moved through his life at this time was the news from Eihōji that his other old friend and companion on many of those wanderings in the past thirty years, Gen'nō Hongen, had died at the age of fifty-one. He had now lost three of his oldest and closest friends from the days when he was a student of Bukkoku's in Kamakura, and he had good reason to feel that he had returned to a darker world as the year drew to a close. 1332 had seen an increasing amount of small-scale fighting in many rural areas as the Hōjō sent out troops to reestablish *bakufu* authority. Local warrior families in many places had risen in Go-Daigo's cause, and the authorities could not let this pass unpunished. This low key and widespread campaign continued into a new year, which seemed to offer very little respite.

NOTES

1. Donald Keene, *Travelers of a Hundred Ages* (New York: H. Hold and Co., 1989), p. 167.
2. Martin Collcutt. *Five Mountains* (Cambridge, Mass.: Harvard University Press, 1981), p.85.

3. Musō Soseki, *Sun at Midnight: Poems and Sermons,* trans. W. S. Merwin and Sōiku Shigematsu (San Francisco: North Point Press, 1989), poem #4, p. 8. The "famous dance" refers to that of the "Three Stars" in the constellation Ursa Major. In short, although the geography of the poem is based on earth, an enlightened visitor like Taihei Myōjun releases the context of their exchanges into the infinity of the universe.

4. The texts used for these translations are from Yanagida and Kawase. Working with Sharon Nakazato, I have given here what I believe is the closest reading of Soseki's intent in these poems without using the more "poetic" forms in English that some translations, aiming to present poetry rather than records of Soseki's thoughts, have produced.

5. Kawase Kazuma, *Musō Kokushi: Zen to teien* (Musō Kokushi: Zen and Gardens) (Tokyo: Kōdansha, 1968),; Takahashi Kyōichi, *Sites Associated with Musō Soseki* (in Japanese). These descriptions of the sites at both Hakusen-an and his next hermitage, the Taiko-an, are taken from Kawase and Takahashi, the latter exhaustively searching the Yokosuka area for traces of Soseki, both in the records and on the ground.

6. Lucien Stryk and Ikemoto Takashi, trans., *The Crane's Bill: Zen Poems of China and Japan* (New York: Grove Press, 1973), p. 43. The lines of poetry that follow are taken from Kawase, *Musō Kokushi,* and Takahashi, *Sites Associated with Musō Soseki,* translated by Sharon Nakazato, and Musō Soseki, *Sun at Midnight,* poems #5, 8, 12, and 17.

7. Musō Soseki, *Sun at Midnight,* poems #13, 14, 15, pp. 17–19.

8. See particularly Takahashi, *Sites Associated with Musō Soseki.*

9. First and third poems from Musō Soseki, *Sun at Midnight,* poems #38 and 66, pp. 42, 76. Second poem from Takahashi, *Sites Associated with Musō Soseki,* p. 6.

10. Musō Soseki, *Sun at Midnight.* poem #19, p. 23. The poem note explains the reference to a Chinese tale in which Lin is tempted to trade a flawless gem [enlightenment] for earthly gain.

11. This account is once again based on the work of Kawase and Takahashi, who both visited and explored the area forming their best guesses as to where things were. Takahashi in turn refers back to Kawase's account for much of his interpretation of Soseki's stay there.

12. For further discussion of this and, in particular, the changes in Song China, see Kidder Smith, Jr. et al., *Sung Dynasty Uses of the I-Ching* (Princeton: Princeton University Press, 1990).

13. Joseph D. Parker, *Zen Buddhist Landscape Arts of Early Muromachi Japan (1336–1573)* (Albany, N.Y.: SUNY Press, 1999), p. 6. This book also contains a very useful discussion of the relationship between Zen and the changing society of medieval Japan.

14. Smith et al., *Sung Dynasty Uses of the I-Ching,* p. 5.

15. Musō Kokushi, *Dream Conversations: On Buddhism and Zen,* trans. Thomas Cleary (Boston: Shambhala, 1994), pp. 6, 53.

16. Musō Soseki, *Sun at Midnight,* poem #62, p. 69.

17. Yanagida Seizan, "Musō Soseki," *NHK "Reading the Heart" Series* (Tokyo: Japan Broadcasting Publishing Association, 1992). p. 102.

18. Collcutt, *Five Mountains.* p. 92.

19. Musō Soseki, *Sun at Midnight,* excerpt from poem #22, p. 26.

20. Yanagida, "Musō Soseki," pp. 97, 98 for a detailed discussion of this side of Soseki's work.

21. Collcutt, *Five Mountains*, Gozan Ranking Chart, p. 110.

22. Musō Soseki, *Sun at Midnight*, poem #31, p. 35.

23. Kawase, *Musō Kokushi*, pp. 164, 165.

24. Ibid., p. 164. In the poem the "dragon" refers to the emperor.

25. Keene, *Travelers of a Hundred Ages*, p. 184. Passage taken from Sokyu's diary entry of 1350 in which he describes setting out on a journey from Kyoto.

26. Mary Sutherland and Dorothy Britton, *National Parks of Japan* (Tokyo and New York: Kodansha International, 1980), p. 97. The authors identify this current as the Pacific Ocean's "Black Current." Otherwise known as the "Kuroshio" (The Black Stream) or the Japan Current, this warm, northward flowing ocean current sweeps close to the southeastern shores of Japan where it mingles with colder water coming down from the north, moderating the coastal climate and providing unusually rich fishing grounds.

27. Kawase, *Musō Kokushi*, p. 165.

28. Hiroaki Sato and Burton Watson, ed. and trans., *From the Country of Eight Islands: An Anthology of Japanese Poetry* (New York: Columbia University Press, 1986), p. 177.

29. Musō Soseki, *Sun at Midnight*, poem #32, p. 36.

30. Ibid., part of poem #41, "Cloud Mountain," p. 45.

31. Ibid., extracts from poems #43, 44, and 42, pp. 47, 48, 46.

32. Kawase, *Musō Kokushi*. The following descriptions of Erinji are taken from pp. 167, 168.

33. Musō Soseki, *Sun at Midnight*, poem #83, p. 90.

34. Keene, *Travelers of a Hundred Ages*, p. 164.

35. Nakamura Bunpo and Inoue Hakudo, *Musō Kokushi no fuko* (The artistic sensibility of Musō Kokushi) (Tokyo: Shunjūsha, 1998), p. 100.

36. Musō Soseki, *Sun at Midnight*, poem #49, p. 53. The extracts that follow are from poems #56, 50, and 59, pp. 63, 57, 66.

37. Kawase, *Musō Kokushi*, p. 168.

38. Ibid., translated by Sharon Nakazato. Musō Soseki, *Sun at Midnight*, poem #56, p. 63.

CHAPTER FOUR

Musō Kokushi: Life in Kyoto, 1333–51

The year 1333 started ominously for Soseki when messengers arrived at Erinji from Hōjō Takatoki, once again offering him the abbacy of Kenchōji. It seems that the Hōjō, fresh from their victory over Go-Daigo, were anxious to consolidate their new supremacy and align Soseki once and for all with their cause. Soseki's immediate reaction was to excuse himself on the grounds of illness, and in the end no further action was necessary since events soon overtook everyone. The first indication of what a momentous year it was going to be came with the news not only that Go-Daigo had escaped from exile, but that he had managed to make his way back to the Kyoto area and was now, with a large army raised by loyal supporters, poised to retake the capital. In the city great confusion reigned, with crowds of people milling around in the streets outside the court trying to find out what was going on, while inside the palace the courtiers and officials were particularly worried since they had participated in the coronation and administration of the emperor Kōgon. Things became even more alarming when, in March, Kōgon and the court left Kyoto for the relative safety of Rokuhara, the longtime stronghold of the Kamakura authorities in the Kyoto area, to await the arrival of the *bakufu* army that would defend the capital from Go-Daigo's forces.[1]

By spring of 1333, this army was well on its way, and, however confident Go-Daigo's generals might have been, they would have been well aware of who commanded it and that when it arrived there was going to be a desperate fight. Equally, those in the beleaguered city loyal to Kamakura and the ousted court waiting for news in Rokuhara would have taken comfort in the fact that the relief force was under the command of Ashikaga Takauji, a young man recently promoted to the top ranks of the Hōjō armies and one whose fierce reputation proceeded him.

Takauji (1305–58) was one of the country's brightest military stars and just twenty-eight when he was sent to secure Kyoto for the government. On the face of it his life appears to be a straightforward success story, a local warrior rising to become a major player in the history of his time. But there are few figures in Japanese history who are so controversial or who have been so vilified by future generations. He was later seen as the person who not only crushed the dream of full imperial restoration and then, by changing sides, bought down the Hōjō Regency, but he was also, by his actions, responsible for weakening the political institutions and the court, and leaving the country divided and at war with itself. During the Tokugawa period, and particularly after the Meiji Restoration of the 1860s, he was heavily criticized and attacked for his actions, to the point where his grave was desecrated by outraged scholars and his statue at Tōji-in was beheaded by imperial sympathizers. Soseki's reputation has seen equal changes of fortune, by association with Takauji, and in both cases the truth is a much more complicated matter. In the case of Takauji, however, untangling fact from fiction is much harder since very little is known about his thoughts and personal life. We do not have diaries, records kept by close associates, or personal writings, and the few poems we do have were written at public gatherings, covering general topics such as blossom viewing and so on. He remains enigmatic and a difficult person to judge dispassionately.

What is undisputed, however, is that he came from a powerful family, the Seiwa Genji branch of the Minamoto clan, who held extensive lands near Kamakura and who had been close allies of the Hōjō since they assumed leadership of the *bakufu* by marriage on the death of Minamoto Yoritomo in 1199. Takauji first enters history as part of the Kamakura forces that initially captured and exiled Go-Daigo in 1331, but his reputation as a military commander had been growing for some time. His chance to actually lead an army came with the campaign of 1333, when the *bakufu* armies had to be split up, the main force having already headed south to take on Go-Daigo's son and his supporters in Yoshino. Another force was needed to cover the sudden developments that resulted from Go-Daigo's escape from Oki and his march on Kyoto. Takauji's reputation as a heroic and brilliant commander meant that the task fell to him to raise troops and head for Kyoto to recapture the exiled emperor and secure the city for the emperor Kōgon. He was already known to be totally ruthless in war—estimates of the number of people killed as a result of his campaigns over the next twenty years range as high as sixty thousand, and he certainly showed no apparent hesitation in ordering the death of two of his brothers when they later challenged him for power. None of this has done his reputation any good.

While he was clearly an ambitious man, it is not clear how much of this was purely personal or how much wider his motives were. What does seem apparent, however, is that, as he set out for Kyoto, this ambitious young general, with a large army loyal primarily to the Ashikaga family, was already deeply disaffected with what he saw as an increasingly ineffective Hōjō leadership in Kamakura. And there was another problem. From his position in a leading branch of the Minamoto clan, he had inherited a deep resentment of his family's subordination to the Hōjō whose assumption of *bakufu* leadership was seen as having been opportunistic and whose continued control increasingly lacked legitimacy or reason. Given all this, the Hōjō may well have mistrusted their young general but, indicative of their lack of options at this difficult time, they appear to have had little choice but to rely on him. We have no way of knowing what Takauji's real intentions were at this time, but history has always assumed the worst. Soseki, however, was to come to a different conclusion about these events, and, as we will see, it is one which perhaps helps to get closer to the truth.

It appears, though, that as Takauji set out for Kyoto he received a letter from Go-Daigo inviting him to support the restoration, to turn on the Hōjō and, by so doing, once and for all return legitimate rule to the country. It was, no doubt from necessity, a vague letter and one that did not offer Takauji any specific rewards, but one can probably assume that from its content he would have taken for granted that appointment as shogun would follow should he take up the imperial cause. For Go-Daigo this was a major power play that, if successful, would virtually have guaranteed his restoration, and he may well have been encouraged to try it because of rumors of Takauji's dissatisfaction with Kamakura. Exactly what he expected from his potential ally or what role he saw for him in the future is not so clear, and it is by these uncertainties that the seeds of later problems were sown.

If Takauji had already been thinking along these lines, then the letter from Go-Daigo may well have been the decisive factor in making up his mind, since an invitation to fight the enemies of the emperor would have provided his actions with a legitimacy that they would otherwise have lacked, and would have given him realistic expectations of a senior position in the new imperial administration. Certainly his actions from the time that he received orders to leave Kamakura suggest that he, if not already thinking along these lines, was at the very least keen on keeping his options open and strengthening his own hand for whatever lay ahead. Instead of taking one of the main roads west and arriving in Kyoto as fast as possible, he took a meandering course, through family lands in Koshu and the Kiso River valley, to Tamba, north of the capital, where he then waited as his people ascertained the situation in town and the strength of Go-Daigo's forces. Along the way he had been collecting troops from families loyal to the Ashikaga and strengthening his family's alliances. He was certainly not taking anything for granted.

Assessing the situation as it stood in early summer of 1333, it is hard to tell exactly what Go-Daigo and Takauji expected of each other, but it was not long before both were disappointed and they were at war. From Takauji's point of view, given that he was from the somewhat isolated world of warrior families and politics in Kamakura, it is quite possible that had he known more about court life, Kyoto, and the full extent of Go-Daigo's ambitions, he may well have been more cautious in his approach to the situation, but it seems that both of them may have taken too much for granted about each other's world. What Takauji saw as a chance for the Ashikaga family to wrest control of the *bakufu* from the Hōjō, Go-Daigo saw as a chance to destroy the institution altogether, and he seems to have assumed that Takauji's sense of loyalty was a traditional one, that assisting the imperial cause as a field general was reward enough in itself. He would also have been listening to those around him, many of whom would not have been Takauji's friends. It seems likely that the leading cause of the tragedy that was to follow was the mutual ignorance of the two centers of power of each other and the different perspectives, lifestyles, and aspirations that had grown up over the years of separation during the Kamakura *bakufu*.

Whatever Takauji's private calculations may have been, he seems to have been impressed by the strength and morale of Go-Daigo's forces, and, when he did enter Kyoto in May, it was to rout the troops loyal to Kamakura and secure the city for Go-Daigo. The emperor, in the culmination of a whirlwind series of events since his escape from exile, duly arrived and took up his place in the palace so recently occupied by Kōgon. Takauji had thrown the dice at this crucial moment of his career, turned against the Hōjō, and joined what he must have seen as an exciting new start for the country. Nothing like this had happened before; the ship of state and everyone in it had been steered into uncharted waters: the Kemmu Restoration had begun.

Kawase suggests, in another interesting wrinkle, that when Takauji was passing through Koshu he may, through the mediation of the Hosokawa family, have had a meeting with Soseki. If this is so, it seems likely that their relationship dates from this time.[2] It would be fascinating to know what transpired at this meeting, but one thing that did happen was that someone, whether Takauji or someone else, passed on a message from Go-Daigo inviting Soseki to come to Kyoto and take over at Nanzenji again. Even in the relative seclusion of Erinji, Soseki could not avoid being swept up in the momentous events of 1333, and the fact that he subsequently founded a temple at Seihakuji for Takauji suggests the visit did take place and indicates that Soseki had also seen the inevitability of the Hōjō collapse and was ready to pin the future hopes of Zen and the *Gozan* movement on the success of the new forces at work in Kyoto. Certainly the fact that Takauji felt it necessary to meet Soseki confirms the latter's influential position at this time, a person above the immediate fray, whose opinion was sought and whose approval could prove vital.

Seihakuji, founded in an area with strong associations with Soseki's father, stands on another interesting site. The records of Kai note that the temple originally had much more land than it does today and that a series of old burial mounds and old *stupa* were located on this larger plot. Thus, we have a third site, following Taiko-an and Zuisenji, where Soseki founded a temple. Again, he chose a place that had associations with burial grounds, and thus with the spiritual world. At this time he also restored the temple at Kochōzenji—like Seihakuji not far from Erinji and with strong connections to his family—which now contains a "very skillfully" built garden that Kawase ascribes to Soseki.[3] The period he had spent at Erinji and in the surrounding area thus marks something very important. In a very short space of time, starting with Erinji, he had founded or restored three important temples, all closely associated with his family, and he had built four gardens, five if we count Zuisenji. As we will see in the next chapter, they all appear to mark a development in his emerging sense of style and content.

In August, three months after his Restoration began, Go-Daigo used Takauji to invite Soseki to Kyoto, this time not to head up a major temple, but rather to take over a smaller, unfinished temple at Rinsenji, from which he could teach and conduct the affairs of his lineage. Once in power, Go-Daigo determinedly promoted the *Gozan* monasteries and sought to bring Soseki to Kyoto as a part of this effort. He had, of course, his own reasons, and his patronage of Soseki was a "politically motivated compromise" in which he also kept his options open by installing his sons in the powerful Tendai temples of Mt. Hiei. The latter were to prove useful allies for him, when in times of crisis he could call on their large armies of soldier-monks. In addition to this, he continued to promote and be interested in everything Chinese and studied under monks who had recently arrived from China. He appointed one of them, Tung-ming Mui-Jih, abbot of Kenninji. When Soseki arrived, apparently feeling that the circumstances were right, Go-Daigo became his pupil and, in another gesture that recalled the traditions of Song China, made him a "National Teacher" or *Kokushi*, the same title that had been conferred on Nan'yo. From this time on he was known by the name of Musō Kokushi, and the fact that this title was rarely bestowed on those still living reflects the position that he and Bukkoku's lineage had reached.

The title had originated in China in the early twelfth century as the Chinese were trying to come to terms with the loss of the whole northern half of the empire to the Mongols. In the national reconstruction that had followed, monks, government officials, literati, artists, in fact anyone with something to contribute, were looked upon to work on recreating something of the old spiritual and cultural unity. As part of this effort they were awarded ranks and titles in recognition of their significant contribution. One of these was the title *Kokushi* (in Japanese). A "national teacher" therefore was someone who had contributed positively to the rebuilding and development of the nation's culture, someone good enough at what they did to make a real difference, whether in the arts, government, or religion. The system was subsequently adopted in Japan where titles were awarded to those who either directly taught members of the imperial family, or who were so outstanding in their field that they raised it to new levels of achievement, or who did both. There were numerous ranks within each title, and the highest rank of *Kokushi* that one could attain was that of *Nana-cho*, implying that it had been bestowed by seven emperors. This was the rank Soseki was to achieve.

The temple that Soseki took on when he returned to Kyoto was to be his base on and off for the rest of his life and the place where he chose to be buried. Rinsenji (Temple Overlooking the River) had been originally founded by Soseki's old friend Gen'nō Hongen under the patronage of one of Go-Daigo's sons, Prince Sera Shinno, but the subsequent death of both of them meant that the Zen temple was never completed. On the prince's death, Go-Daigo offered it to Soseki as a memorial to his son, and at this point it became a "closed" monastery, restricted in perpetuity to disciples of Soseki's lineage.

On arriving there Soseki set about substantially rebuilding the temple, and he added the San'e-in, a subtemple that was to act as the focal point for the affairs of his lineage. *San'e* refers to the third part of the Sutra of Maitreya, the Buddha of the future, which is concerned with the world once Maitreya reappears. In thus naming his new subtemple, Soseki seems to be using it as a way to encourage his lineage to look forward, to encourage his disciples to be concerned with their future, to look beyond his personality and leadership to what lay ahead. In Collcutt's words, "He established the San'e-in to provide cohesion and continuity after his death. . . . the subtemple consisting of three main chambers, the central chamber containing an image of Maitreya."

All this confirms that Soseki saw these times and the immediate future as uncertain, and potentially very difficult for even his well-established lineage. Today not much of the original temple survives, but at one time it was clearly a major foundation, as Collcutt points out: "Maps of Rinsenji made prior to the Ōnin War [1467–77] show a large scale, independent monastery spreading along the banks of the Oi River."[4] The temple survives now on a greatly reduced site, the only view of the river being down a narrow

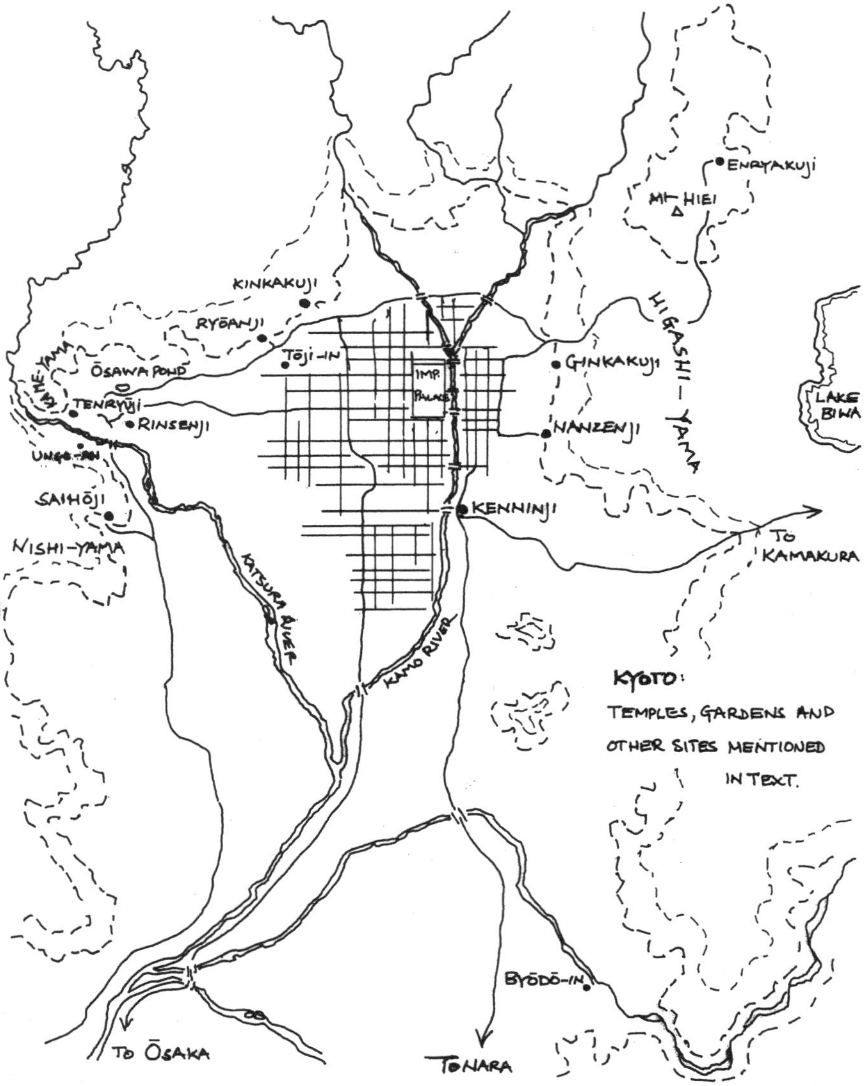

Figure 3. Map of Kyoto and its environs.

path from the gate. None of the original garden still exists, except perhaps a small bamboo grove, but Soseki and Maitreya still look out from the Main Hall across the graveled forecourt, and Soseki's grave is visible through slatted windows under the rear of the building.

Fortunately for all, the rest of 1333 passed without fresh incident. The Hōjō were evidently not in a position to attempt retaking Kyoto, and, in the wake of Takauji's defection, they needed time to reorganize their forces. In June of 1334, however, Go-Daigo, now settled into his role as the restored emperor, invited Soseki to take over the abbacy of Nanzenji and with it the leadership of the *Gozan* monasteries. Soseki was now fifty-nine and possibly not in the best of health, since initially he refused to take the post on these grounds, but it seems he was eventually persuaded, and in October he returned to the big teaching temple. It seems likely that even if he had been in bad health, he realized that this was a critical moment for the *Gozan* system and Zen itself. If he was going to have any influence on the way things were going to develop in the country, now that the balance of power had been so radically altered, he was going to have to take on a role at the heart of the new structures. For him, this meant becoming a high-profile advisor to those who had assumed power and taking an administrative role in the national monastic system, all of which he could do as abbot of Nanzenji. There is no question that Soseki's willingness at this critical moment to take his "place in the world" ensured that Zen continued to flourish, in spite of its temporary loss of patrons in Kamakura and the uncertainty of the times. His decision became even more important given the events of the following year. The fact that from this time until his death, seventeen years later, he did not leave Kyoto indicates just how important for Zen he saw these times to be.

The lull in events during late 1333 and 1334 soon proved to be just that, and hopes for a real peace were rapidly dashed when fighting on an unprecedented scale broke out in 1335. It had been a period of assessment when everyone was trying to understand what had happened and what the true ramifications and nature of Go-Daigo's restoration were going to be. In particular, it was a time when the emperor and his new ally Takauji began to discover the true nature of each other's intentions. Their initial relationship had been based on the fact that they needed each other if they were to defeat the Hōjō, but now that this had been largely accomplished, only time would tell if there was room for both of them at the top of the new administration. Unfortunately for everyone, the relationship forged of necessity in the urgency of war proved to have no foundation in mutual understanding, trust, or ambition and rapidly fell apart as the forces they had unleashed together quickly spun out of control. The results were to prove disastrous for the country.

As 1335 got under way, events began to happen quickly. The remnants of *bakufu* forces that made their way back to Kamakura from the fighting in Kyoto and Yoshino now rallied round Hōjō Takatoki and reformed as an army. Takauji, eager to set out and finally finish off this threat, first sought the title of shogun from Go-Daigo in recognition of his position and, when this was refused, took events into his own hands. This soon became necessary when, as Go-Daigo and Takauji became increasingly estranged, one of Takauji's main rivals, Nitta Yoshisada, seizing the opportunity to make his own bid for power, raised an army and stormed Kamakura, destroying the town and the remains of the government. In the face of this catastrophe, Hōjō Takatoki and his family all commited suicide, creating a sudden and dangerous power vacuum. Takauji, now seriouly at odds with Go-Daigo, could not allow Yoshida to consolidate his position in Kamakura, and he set out immediately, without imperial permission, to defeat this new threat to his power. Faced with these sudden developments and seeing in them the chance to break Takauji's hold on military power, Go-Daigo broke with his former ally and supported Yoshida. The tensions and suspicions of the past year overwhelmed the fragile alliances that had formed to break Hōjō power, and a new round of warfare broke out.

In open revolt against the emperor and with nothing to lose, Takauji unleashed a ferocious attack on Kamakura, scattering Yoshida's forces and the imperial troops sent to support him. He then turned around immediately and started fighting his way back to Kyoto. As 1336 began, Go-Daigo bowed to the inevitable and vacated the capital, retreating to his stronghold of support in Yoshino, as Takauji's swiftly moving army retook the capital. It soon became clear, however, that neither side could muster enough strength or support to force a showdown and win a clear victory. The country had been effectively split down the middle, and for the moment, until other factors came into play that altered the balance of power, a stalemate had been reached. Thus began the Nambokuchō period, lasting some sixty years, when Go-Daigo's line ruled over the Southern Court in Yoshino, and, reinstated by Takauji, Kōgon and his successors ruled over the Northern Court in Kyoto. In this strange and unsatisfactory way the political situation found some resolution, but it was by no means the end of the fighting. This continued unabated as both sides fought for local advantage through intermittent campaigns across the countryside, in the course of which Kyoto itself changed hands several times.

It was an outcome that few could have foreseen and one which created much confusion and uncertainty. It is hard to believe that Takauji could have put together a sufficiently powerful coalition of support to create an alternative court in Kyoto unless there had been extreme dissatisfaction with Go-Daigo among the warrior families. As we saw at the beginning of the chapter, it seems that, worldly though he undoubtedly was, Go-Daigo misread the mood of the nation, mistaking a general tiredness with the Hōjō Regency for a desire to see the reimposition of direct imperial rule. He seems also to have failed to understand that real power now lay not with the court nobility, whose families had traditionally held all the high offices, but with the more recently emergent warrior families and, further, that the court could not count on their unquestioning loyalty. During his short reign he had singularly failed to reward these people for their support, promoting and awarding lands to those noble families traditionally associated with the court instead. Many of these warriors came from Kamakura families who had not only lost out when the Hōjō were unable to reward them after repulsing the Mongol invasion fleets, but who now saw lands and titles taken from the Hōjō and their supporters going to noble families who had played little or no part in the fighting then or now. His other serious mistake was the assumption that those who were still loyal to the figure of the emperor would also automatically be loyal to the institutions and officers of a full-blown restoration of the court. This was clearly never going to be the case. Too much power had devolved from the court for too long, and the reinstatement of the privileged sinecures that many of the court positions represented was never going to be acceptable to these down-to-earth people who had fought hard for everything they had. In this atmosphere, resentment grew to the point where, given a choice between Go-Daigo's imperious restoration and the emperors instated by the *bakufu*, who knew exactly where the power lay, large numbers threw in their lot with Takauji and Kōgon.

Perhaps Go-Daigo's single biggest miscalculation, however, was his belief that he could afford to ignore Takauji and distribute power and positions as he pleased. This is clearly illustrated when on refusing Takauji the post of shogun, effectively the top military job, he gave it instead to one of his sons, an empty gesture that totally ignored the realities of the day. No doubt there were many at court who resented Takauji's position and who counseled Go-Daigo not to consolidate his position which such a powerful office, but it was nevertheless a fatal decision for everything he hoped to achieve.

Temporarily in control of Kyoto, Takauji and his brother Tadayoshi set about establishing themselves and the Northern Court inherited from the Hōjō *bakufu* as the central government. The emperor Kōmyō replaces Kōgon, who is no doubt quite happy to retire given the excitement and uncertainties of his reign, and the Ashikaga family rebuilds Tōjiji as their family temple. Soseki's close friend Kosen Ingen is made abbot and the temple becomes, with Rinsenji, a major center of Soseki's lineage. Soseki himself takes the opportunity to leave Nanzenji, and, returning to the relative calm of Rinsenji, he officially takes on Takauji as a student.

We do not know anything of how Soseki viewed these rapid changes of fortune or how he felt about the risks to the *Gozan* monasteries and to himself personally, because he was so closely involved with the Ashikaga cause. To an extent it was unavoidable, given their control over Kyoto and Kamakura, and the location of all the main temples, but from events and Soseki's survival over the next few chaotic years, it would appear that his actions were not seen as a personal intervention in national affairs or as necessarily implying commitment to one side against the other, but rather as inevitable given his dedication to the continuation of the "work"; Soseki's eminence as a Zen monk seems to have set him above the immediacies of the ongoing struggles, but this did not make these difficult times any easier for him. As he wrote in a poem at the time: "Now the splendor of the Patriarch's Garden / is smudged with the rising / dust of war . . .,"[5] and he would need all his courage and wisdom to prevent that splendor being lost forever. Faced with this he had to make a number of decisions to ensure that the Zen temples thrived in such adverse conditions, since, however popular they might be with individuals, one of their main prerequisites for survival was strong patronage and access to lands and income. Throughout this period he had to play his cards very carefully, balancing the need to take care of those with whom he was involved, but assiduously avoiding taking sides, and, above all, he had to ensure that he, and the institutions he represented, remained "morally autonomous from political authority."

It is important, however, not to confuse his ambitions for the Zen school and the *Gozan* system with a personal ambition. His repeated disclaimers of "greatness," his discomfort at even being compared to the famous figures of Zen, his care in avoiding even the appearance of impropriety in monastic management and his determinedly frugal life, all point to the exact opposite of a personally ambitious person. Equally, one cannot believe that unless his motives were entirely genuine he would have gone on attracting such numbers of students. Everyone, including the powerful people of the day from all sides, were drawn to him by the charismatic power of his enlightenment. For him the issues were simple. To thrive, Zen required a calm and stable society within which to operate, and to achieve this Soseki's efforts were to be directed toward encouraging peace and promoting the reunification of the country. His mixed reputation among historians is largely to do with his connections to Takauji and to the latter's role in opposing the restoration, and Go-Daigo's eventual death in exile. This view, as we have seen, was particularly widespread during the years from the Meiji Restoration to the end of the Second World War, when the emperors were again lifted back to sacredness in an equally anachronistic and ultimately disastrous attempt to return to the past. Rather than being purely opportunistic, Soseki seems to have taken on Takauji as a student, at this time, in response to what he saw as his genuine desire both to learn and come to terms with his karma. Under Soseki's guidance, Takauji undoubtedly underwent a deeply religious conversion. He seems to have been increasingly bothered by all the carnage and mayhem that had occurred and to have had a sincere desire to come to an understanding of what had happened.

For Soseki's part, the events of this period appeared as an opportunity to be taken; not just for himself or Zen, but for the entire country, an opportunity to embrace the new energies sweeping through it and move forward. He makes this very clear in one section of the *Muchū Mondō:*

> It is a characteristic tendency of human beings to indulge in emotions such as happiness, grief or anger in response to present conditions, failing to balance these feelings with the awareness that present conditions are results of past causes. It is illogical to face the present only as an object of enjoyment or tolerance, neglecting to use it as the opportunity to create the future.[6]

Behind Soseki's understanding of the potential of the situation we can sense the influence of such figures as Nan'yo Echu. At one time this reclusive monk had hidden himself away in the mountains, taking no active role in the fortunes or future of the Zen school in China. Once summoned to court and unavoidably a part of current events, however, Nan'yo embraced those aspects of the Zen teaching that encouraged social responsibility and interaction with the world beyond the temple walls. For the Zen school, using the present as an "opportunity to create the future" was part of its activist outlook, or, as one writer has put it, "While the Zen experience does not imply any specific course of action, it turns unhesitatingly to anything that presents itself to be done."[7] In addition to this, monks such as Nan'yo believed in the ability of Zen, through the purity and accessibility of its vision, the straightforwardness of its practice, and the influence of its artistic output, to improve, reinvigorate and redefine an ailing culture. Using the authority and influence that his position at court gave him, Nan'yo set about organizing the Zen temples into a network that would in turn act as a mechanism that enabled Zen to become widely active in contemporary society. Like Nan'yo, Soseki saw the positive potential in the fluid situation that arose following the collapse of strong central authority, and he intended to use the *Gozan* system in Japan to promote the position of Zen and influence whatever form of government developed in its place.

In 1336, however, there was to be little respite from the fighting, and in March the drama enters one of its most intense periods. After regrouping in their mountainous stronghold, the Southern Court armies once again marched northward and after heavy fighting retook Kyoto. Takauji, facing uprisings in Go-Daigo's cause in many parts of the country, was forced to flee, making his way eventually all the way to Kyūshū. Go-Daigo reenters the capital in triumph, and the Northern emperor retreats out of reach. Over the next few months Takauji reassembled his armies, put down several local families loyal to Go-Daigo in Kyūshū, and started to make his way back east. In July his armies met those sent from Kyoto to intercept him, and, after a major battle, he won a decisive enough victory to be able to carry on and retake Kyoto; Go-Daigo left once more for Yoshino. Throughout the summer there was continued fighting in and around Kyoto as Takauji attempted to drive away the undefeated parts of the Southern armies long enough to reinstate the Northern Court, something he finally managed to do in October.

Takauji's eventual recapture of Kyoto marked the beginning of a lull in the fighting. The campaigns of the past two years seemed to have exhausted everyone, and fighting for the next ten years or so was limited to small-scale incursions and localized power struggles. It is not until the 1350s that Kyoto was again under attack, but, by that time, Go-Daigo had died and the struggle had lost much of its focus. For his efforts in reinstating the Northern Court, however, Takauji was ultimately awarded the position of shogun, and this, in addition to the influence of his studies under Soseki, seemed to mark the start of a new phase in his life. Certainly he remained a ruthless and uncompromising warrior until the end of his life, but from this period on he worked with Soseki, for whom he appeared to have had a very high personal regard, on at least two major projects aimed at national reconciliation. One was the active promotion of the "Taihei," or Great Peace, through the Ankokuji temple project, which commenced immediately; the other, in 1339, was the construction of Tenryūji temple as a place to remember and honor the life of Go-Daigo. Both projects indicate that Takauji was aware of the effects his campaigns had had on the nation, and, if they do not suggest he was actually remorseful, they seem to show that he saw the need for compassionate action. Soseki seems to have recognized this, and from this point until his death they maintained a close relationship, both as student and master and as partners in their joint projects.

Although he had been thinking about it for some time, it was not until now that Soseki was able to start work on his great project to spread peace and reunify the country. For Soseki, his return to Kyoto in 1325 as abbot of Nanzenji had mirrored Nan'yo's experience of being summoned by the emperor to reenter public life, and Soseki's renaming of the temple as Taiheikuokoku Nanzen-ji at this time suggests that he saw this project as one of the key responsibilities of his new position and as the means by which the influence of Zen would be spread. For some ten years the circumstances of the times had provided little opportunity for him to move forward, but now, finding willing partners in the Ashikaga brothers, he began construction of the Ankokuji temples and Rishōtō Pagoda projects in 1337; these were to be "Temples for the Peace of the Realm," and with their accompanying pagodas they were to be built all over the country where their presence would help heal the nation and bring it together under the new order. At these temples "prayers would be offered to the spirits of all the warriors who had fallen in the battles of the recent civil wars and for a lasting peace." Collcutt goes on to indicate that by 1350 the temples had been established in every province of Japan with the possible exception of Yamato, stronghold of the Southern Court forces.[8] How much these temples were able to help in bringing the war-torn country together again is hard to quantify, but there is little doubt that they helped ensure the spread of Zen and with it the influence of the Ashikaga right across the country, an important consideration for all concerned.

In 1338 Takauji continued to work on settling his demons, and as part of this he moved the family temple Tōjiji from central to western Kyoto, a quieter, more meditative area, refounding it at Tōji-in, not just for the ancestral spirits of the Ashikaga, but also for the spirits of all dead soldiers. Kawase also indicates that Takauji used this new, much more private temple for prayers as part of his personal dialogue of reconciliation with Go-Daigo's spirit. Soseki is recorded as being the first abbot of the new temple and as the designer of the small pond gardens that nestle between the buildings. Although the garden is much changed and now focuses very much on the forms of the clipped shrubs, Kawase believes that at least a hint of Soseki's work remains in the rock groups in the pond.[9] In a poem written around this time, Soseki gives us some idea of the qualities he found in his controversial student, and, beyond the formalities of its language and images, the poem seems to provide a very straightforward assessment of the man behind his warrior persona. The title, Lover of Mountains, is a reference to Takauji's *dharma* name Ninzan,

> Your compassionate mind
> soars like a summit
>   there is your true effortless nature
> some places smooth and gentle
> some places rugged and
>   unapproachable
> The mountain has
> no wish to be

looked up to
It is only people
who look up
in wonder.[10]

I am sure that in the wording of this poem we can see what the basis of their relationship was. Throughout his life Soseki showed interest in those people he considered to be serious about coming to terms with their karma, and moving on through the processes of enlightenment. And he saw the fundamental quality of compassion as essential to these processes, without which nothing of real or lasting importance could ever be achieved. This is reflected in the continuing importance of the figure of Kannon in his life as a reference point he could always return to. It is not, therefore, a word he would use lightly, and it is significant that he should open the poem by associating Takauji with it. The poem then goes on to acknowledge the different sides of Takauji's character, "smooth and gentle," but at the same time "rugged and unapproachable," but concludes that here was someone ultimately uncomfortable with the position he found himself in and aware of what needed to be done to square his actions with his conscience. Unlike Go-Daigo, Hōjō Takatoki, or Takauji's brother Tadayoshi, people with whom he had many dealings and who were also his students (but with whom he does not appear to have had a close relationship), Soseki seems to have had respect for Takauji. This respect went beyond his importance to the future of Zen and the *Gozan* temples and touched on the qualities that he felt were essential for the reunification and future growth of the nation.

Certainly, Soseki had now reentered the world with a vengeance and found himself as a senior advisor to the bustling new administration in Kyoto as it struggled to form a vision for the future of the country. Collcutt describes his role at this time and its lasting influence as follows, "Musō was spiritual mentor, social conscience, and political intermediary in negotiations with the Southern Court for Takauji. This bond between [Takauji] and Musō was respected by the later Ashikaga who used the leading disciples of Musō and monks of his lineage as their closest confidants."[11] The emerging partnership between Takauji and the *Gozan* monasteries looked forward for inspiration, taking the present "as an opportunity to create the future," not back as Go-Daigo's restoration had to a status quo that had existed and failed some three hundred and fifty years before. Soseki's role in this was to position Zen and its associated culture at the very heart of this new vision, something which meant that from 1339 onward, more than ever, he needed to find some place, at hand, to which he could retreat for his personal meditation practice. The year 1339 was in fact pivotal for him in this search, the point from which we can start to follow two distinct threads running through his life and activities, one connected to his public role as advisor, abbot, and teacher, and the other to his private search for the forms and content of the place where he could unite his physical and spiritual worlds. In his promulgation of the monastic rules for Rinsenji, we see the very public aspects of his activities that year, while in his taking over of a small, run down, temple further up in the hills to the west of Kyoto, we see the start of an intensely private quest begun with a few of his closest disciples.

At Rinsenji things had been developing very fast, and Soseki now found it necessary to decide on the kind of monastery he wanted to preside over and the kind of people he wanted to see coming into the lineage. Large numbers of potential students had been arriving, and with the present lull in the fighting even more were likely to find their way there. From the tone of his official statements at the time, and maybe again because his health was not good, Soseki was clearly becoming concerned with the organization of the school after he dies, and the kind of legacy he was going to leave. Thus, over the course of that year he released two very important documents: first, the *Rinsen Kakun*, the Rules for Rinsenji, and, second, the *San'e-in Yukai*, the Last Teachings of the San'e-in. In his discussion of the thirty-two articles of the *Rinsen Kakun*, Collcutt concludes that Soseki took these very seriously and that he saw them as a way of measuring a student's commitment to the monastery. Life should not be too free and easy since this would never weed out those who were there for the wrong reasons. The articles that resulted covered three main areas, the monastery, the community, and monastic life, and Collcutt suggests that they will have been promulgated as the need arose, in response to specific problems, and then put together, rather than all written at one time.

Overall, the rules cover very little of what monks were supposed to do. Soseki assumed that this was obvious; rather, they warn about what should not happen, and we have to suppose that the practices he feels obliged to forbid would otherwise, or had already, occurred. For example, when discussing the kind of monastery Rinsenji should be, Article 12 states,

> It is much better for abbots [and other officers of the monastery] to do *zazen* with the other monks, participating in an unrelenting life-or-death Zen. . . . the abbot should sit squarely in his own quarters and instruct those who visit him there.

In short it should not be a place of special privileges, special buildings, or special quarters. It should be a stripped down, basic establishment where everybody lives and works together. This is reenforced by Article 2, which states specifically,

> The living quarters of many monasteries nowadays are equipped with individual kitchen-sitting rooms. . . . This tendency does not follow the basic principles of monastic life and should be stringently checked. Monks should be satisfied with simplicity, not seekers after ease and conviviality. . . . Guests should share the frugality.

Soseki was looking back here to the strict life he had led in the Kamakura temples of the Chinese Zen masters who saw the softer life in the traditional Japanese monasteries as the greatest possible obstacle to attaining enlightenment and the greatest threat to the health of the Zen school. Life should be simple, as should the monastic ceremonies: "Everything concerning the installation of a new abbot should be done simply . . . [there should not be] a gaudy show" (Article 31).

As for the basic framework of practice within the monastery, the most important single aspect of this should be the regular sessions of *zazen*. There was no excuse for missing these, and there were no good reasons for this regime to be relaxed, as Article 4 makes clear, "Four daily sessions of *zazen* must be held. . . . there must be no cessation. Those born in later ages still dislike the four daily sessions and sometimes wish to reduce them. . . . What could be more regrettable and shameful than this."

Many of the other articles contain admonitions of this sort as Soseki tried to create the kind of monastic organization he wanted to perpetuate at a time when he saw the enthusiasm and dedication that he witnessed as a young man in Kamakura becoming steadily less intense. He considered that many monasteries became home to large numbers of people whose commitment was at best suspect, who saw the monastic life as an easy alternative to the uncertain and difficult life outside, and he saw this attitude as a serious threat to the integrity of the lineage. He was determined to fight this trend and in particular the privileged and corrupt monastic lifestyle that he saw many of his contemporaries living. He was quite specific about avoiding even the suspicion of these things,

"The abbot and monks responsible for administration should not decide the disposal of revenue on their own initiative. This will only serve to invite suspicions on the part of the other members of the community" (Article 8).

On a slightly lighter note, two articles in particular give us a very interesting insight into the kind of everyday problems that Soseki had to deal with and which he considered worthy of his attention. The first invites an image of the august abbot coming home at night from his practice or dealing with the affairs of the *Gozan* and, hearing laughter, coming across a party going on: "It is very bad for monks who have gathered in the abbot's or monk's rooms for religious purposes to end the day eating cakes, sipping tea, and indulging in frivolous conversation . . ." (Article 16). We can be sure that that did not happen again. The second provides an intriguing glimpse of the interior life of these monasteries, and of the excitement of these still rather chaotic times when the Japanese were adapting the Chinese originals to suit their own style. In addition, one cannot help but sympathize with Soseki's tone of somewhat tired exasperation as he tries to deal with this unexpected problem. "Apart from the above buildings, do not build private retreats within the monastery grounds or in the vegetable garden. I am afraid that someone may lay out a landscape garden to the east of the San'e-in, invading the vegetable garden. Buy a piece of land nearby and use it for the purpose" (Article 22).[12] We can only hope, given the tone of this article, that there were no invaded vegetable patches in his past.

Overall, however, the complete articles show Soseki's determination to keep tight control over participation in *zazen* and prayer and the carrying out of duties, the style and practices of management, and the type of life the monks would be permitted to lead. Beyond the immediate concerns of the community at Rinsenji, we can also see these articles as being a reflection of Soseki's lifelong seriousness of practice and the way he would like to see the *Gozan* monasteries develop in the future.

In itself the *Rinsen Kakun* is a straightforward set of rules similar to those at most monasteries, but when taken together with the *San'e-in Yukai*, which he also put out this year, they combine to make an unusually powerful statement of Soseki's beliefs. In fact, they can be seen as almost an appeal from Soseki to those he knew would understand never to lose their vigilance concerning the correct practice of Zen; they were faced with a unique opportunity to establish Zen permanently at the heart of Japanese culture, and it was up to them to ensure its quality and vitality, so that it should always be an "unrelenting life-or-death Zen." If it sounds from this and the content of the *Yukai* itself as though Soseki was expecting soon to die and was worrying that the community had not yet developed the qualities he wished for, it is hardly surprising, since the normal function of a *Yukai* is as a death poem, a statement in which the dying master passes on his last piece of wisdom. Certainly the name of the piece, *San'e-in Yukai*, translates as "The Last Teachings," and so we can be sure that Soseki intended this meaning for it. Yet there is a puzzle here since he was evidently not dying and, indeed, did not do so for another thirteen years. We will be looking for the possible explanation for this in the last chapter of the book and, for the moment, we need to look at the text of this remarkable document and its impact in 1339.

Known now as "Musō's Admonition" it indicates for us just how seriously he took the problems of maintaining the quality of practice in his lineage and the quality of those wishing to join it. Ultimately it tells us that although he was concerned throughout his life with the diffusion of the Zen monastic system and the culture that went with it, he also believed passionately that it would all be worthless if the Zen practice at the center of it was anything but the highest quality. He was acutely aware of the compromises that he and Zen would have to make if they were to become generally accepted, and he clearly felt that many of these were worth making. In doing this he brought on himself constant criticism from those within the Zen movement who felt that he had become too compromised by dealings with worldly matters. But he always felt he could risk this provided that the base from which he worked, his Zen practice, remained untouched, unsullied by the "dust" of the world. He seems worried at this point that amid all the distractions and confusion of events over the last few years, the monks in Rinsenji's community were in danger of losing track of what should always be the one supremely important thing in their lives, the pursuit of true enlightenment through meditation practice.

There is a distant, almost chilling tone about the original that gets substantially lost in translation, but which indicates to us his determination that these words should be heeded, and such has been their impact that they are still recited as an exhortation in Zen temples today. The cut down language, free of all the usual classical references and examples from antiquity, gets straight to the point: "I have three sorts of disciples. The best are those who resolutely give up all worldly relationships and devote themselves wholly to seeking and realizing their own true natures. The middle group is not really earnest in Zen practice, and in order to find distraction from it prefers to read about it in books. The lowest are those who eclipse the light of their self-nature and do nothing but lick up the Buddha's spit." He is willing to accept that different people will approach their practices in different ways, so although he was not altogether happy with the second and third sorts of disciples, he toleratee them providing they actively aspired to devoting themselves wholly to seeking their true natures. Unfortunately, however, there are those seeking admission who are even lower than those licking up Buddha's spit: "As for those students who care about nothing but non-Buddhist books and their own literary reputations, they are nothing more than lay people with shaven heads. They are lower than the lowest. And lower still are those who spend their time doing nothing but eating and sleeping. Do they even deserve to be called black-robed monks? . . . [They are] 'robe-hangers' and 'rice-bags.'"

Of these people he says: "They are not monks at all, and I will not let them come and go in the temple and subtemples calling themselves my disciples. I will not even put them up for a visit and certainly would not let them stay to become followers of mine." There is a tone here of barely contained anger at the kind of people he sees as threatening the potency and value, not just of Zen practice but also his entire lineage. These people are not worthy of being his students, or of being associated with a line that has descended from Bukkō Zenji and Bokkoku Zenji, and they must be weeded out. It is an unusual outburst from a man who up to this point, in spite of all the frustrations and problems he has dealt with, had only managed mild exasperation. Determined to maintain the quality of the community, he is making it quite plain, for those who will be responsible, who can stay and who should go. In Yanagida's gloss on the Admonition, he suggests that Soseki's particular displeasure is focused on those people whom he sees as looking for material gain from association with his name. He sees Soseki as saying: "If, after I pass, there are priests or lay priests who call themselves teachers acknowledged as such by me and who look for worldly rewards, money, position or power, let it be known now that they are not my disciples, and I will have nothing to do with them. No one should use my name or teachings for material gain."[13]

The Admonition concludes very much in the tone of a *yukai*, the final instructions from a master to his pupils, and is a plain statement of the kind of behavior he expects from those connected with him. Couched in more conciliatory, almost apologetic, tones, we get a glimpse of the Soseki we have come to know: "This is the will left by this old monk. Don't blame me for not extending mercy and love to everyone. My one wish is for all students to see and correct their shortcomings and become worthy of the seeds and trees of the Way of the Patriarchs."[14]

Together these two sets of instructions must have shaken up the community at Rinsenji. In addition to these two, Soseki also released a set of instructions aimed at ensuring a smooth succession when he was gone with specific orders that he be given a simple monk's burial. It all seems rather premature, but as we will see later, it was all intricately linked with what was developing in the personal side of his life.

The second thread that we can pick up in 1339 has much to do with the foregoing and began with a critical moment when a new student, Nakahara no Chikahide, invited Soseki to take over an old family temple in Nishi-yama (West Mountains) not far from Arashi-yama where Rinsenji stood beside the river. The temple, Saihōji, had had a long and tortuous history, one of occupation followed by periods of neglect and abandonment, and it was now in a state of serious disrepair, the buildings patched up and the gardens largely overgrown. It occupied a site where the hillside above was dotted with old *kofun* burial tombs, beside the Saihōji River as it tumbled down from the mountains through its narrow valley and out onto the Kyoto Plain. Although it was not far from the city, it was nevertheless much more isolated than Rinsenji, the range of hills at whose foot it lay cutting it off from the remoter western suburbs of Kyoto. Soseki took to the run-down temple immediately; here, after all, was a place that included so many of the criteria he had used to choose the sites for his temples and hermitages in the past. Above all, perhaps, was a direct connection it had with the world and life of Ryo Zassu, since the old monk had also lived in a landscape called the West Mountains. Soseki was delighted; finally, at the age of sixty-four, he seemed to have found the place he had been looking for since his travels ended in 1325. In addition, he was aware that a number of other people before him seem also to have recognized it as being a special place.

One of these had been the founder of his lineage, Bukkō Zenji, who, on a spring visit there some time earlier, toward the end of the previous century, had been deeply moved as he sat contemplating the flowering cherry trees for which the temple had been well known for centuries. Some of these trees grew in front of the Amida Buddha Hall built by Hōnen Shonin (1133–1212) that was known as the Sairai-dō ("Coming from the West" Hall). Sixty or seventy years had passed since the hall was originally built, and, as the temple fell into disuse, its dilapidated state must have contrasted with, and commented on, the ephemeral brilliance of the cherry blossoms. A poem Bukkō wrote that day has come down to us and records one of those spine-tingling moments when, caught unawares, we sense the apparent reality of our world suddenly opening up and we catch a glimpse of something beyond; a moment when the barriers between the worlds are fleetingly thin enough for us to see across,

> Blossom-covered trees, aflame high and low.
> Sudden scattering of crimson
> As both kimono sleeves fill with the spring breeze,
> A glimpse of the world in the West:
> One blossom flies to the West, one to the East.[15]

With this poem the space at Saihōji is sharply defined as *MA* as *hashi*, which represented a threshold between this world and that of Amida's paradise in the west; the spiritual world beyond the moment of death is suddenly, intuitively glimpsed as his kimono sleeve is ruffled by the breeze. This sense was to exert a crucial influence on how Soseki saw and developed his new temple, which became in time the center of an intensely private world where he was finally able to bring his understanding to bear on finding that place where his spiritual world could become one with the physical world in which he existed; where he could finally vanish into the landscape as Ryo Zassu had done on his leaf-covered rock in the soft mountain rain. How he did this is the subject of the final chapters of this book, but from early 1339 onward, when he was first offered the site, he worked steadily on this project, fitting it in among all the other demands that were being made on him at this time.

Not the least of these occurred in June of that year when, on waking from a dream in which he had seen Go-Daigo, dressed as a monk, walking in Kame-yama hills above Arashi-yama, he was given the news of the Southern emperor's death in exile in Yoshino. At fifty-one it was a sad death for a man who had seen his dream of a Japan resurrected by a brilliant imperial court turn to dust, and whose legacy, which could have been so glorious, was a bitterly divided country whose towns, villages, temples, shrines, and palaces were instead burned black by war.

Takauji's reaction to this news was to immediately ask Soseki to found a temple to be dedicated to the spirit and memory of Go-Daigo, a major and important foundation in Kyoto where those left behind could offer prayers to him and where his spirit could find comfort and sustenance. This gesture of reconciliation was accompanied by another, the large-scale release of prisoners, both those taken on the field of battle and those who had been imprisoned for "political" crimes. For Takauji, the temple was to be a center for carrying on the work of Zen and the culture he had been so drawn to, a major teaching temple that would carry his legacy into the future. A site was found in the same Kame-yama hills Soseki had seen in his dream, just above the point where the river comes rushing out of its deep gorges to flow out past Rinsenji toward Kyoto. In October Soseki is instructed by the emperor Kōmyō to conduct ceremonies for the repose of Go-Daigo's spirit and, as part of these, to start work on the new temple, which was to be known as Tenryūji, the Dragon of Heaven Temple. Soseki entered into this big public work with enthusiasm, having actively encouraged its foundation, since it represented not only a major new center for his lineage of Zen, certainly not an opportunity to be missed, but also because it went a long way toward his goal of promoting peace and reconciliation between the Southern and Northern Courts—if not between Go-Daigo and Takauji, then at least between their successors.

There seems to be no doubt that, in spite of everything that had happened, Go-Daigo remained liked and respected, even among those who had felt compelled to resist his vision for the future. It is almost as though the Kemmu Restoration could have succeeded had calmer and wiser heads prevailed. No one could look at the events of the past few years and feel satisfied that they had "won," or that "good" had somehow prevailed. Instead, there was a sense of opportunities missed and mistakes made, above all perhaps, because of mutual misunderstanding between the major players. Certainly Go-Daigo had made mistakes. In the 1320s the Hōjō were a waning power, and weak individuals at the center were rapidly losing the support of those warrior families who had supported them for so long. For a more patient man than Go-Daigo, a real measure of power could have been his had he not so directly challenged Kamakura's authority, compelling them to take a stand, forcing them, and indeed those disaffected with them, to make choices that gave them no room to maneuver. Having precipitated a confrontation, he then failed to recognize those who had really made his initial success possible or subsequently to reward them in any meaningful way. These misjudgments were to prove fatal, but it is not immediately clear how much this was directly his fault or how much he was a victim of bad advice and the atmosphere of the court culture. His continuing popularity and the compassion people showed him after his death would seem to suggest the latter, creating an image of a man caught up in circumstances to an extent beyond his control.

This is certainly Soseki's verdict. In a sermon he delivered in 1351, when he resumed the abbacy of Tenryūji, he spoke with quite remarkable frankness about the roles of Go-Daigo and Takauji in the wars between 1331 and 1339, particularly since Takauji was in the audience. He began by outlining the Buddhist line: "Peace and disorder in the world, the distinction between friend and foe in human relationships, follow upon one another as illusion begets delusion. A man of spiritual insight will immediately recognize what is wrong . . . but a shallow-minded man will be ensnared by his own blindness. . . . In such a case one's true friend may seem a foe and one's implacable foe may appear a friend. Enmity and friendship have no permanent character; both of them are illusions." Having said this he makes no more direct comments about it; his listeners were invited to make up their own minds based on their experience of the situation. He then goes on to talk directly about the events of the recent past: "During the disorders of the Genko era [1331–34] the shogun [as Takauji was to become], acting promptly on the imperial command, swiftly subdued the foes of the state [the Hōjō regents], as a result of which he rose higher in the ranks of government day by day and his growing prestige brought a change in the attitude of others toward him. Ere long slander and defamation sprang up with the violence of a tiger, and this unavoidably drew upon him the imperial displeasure. [This happened because] he performed a meritorious task with such dispatch and to the entire satisfaction of his sovereign." The inevitable result of this, Soseki went on, was that "intimacy invited enmity. That is what it was. Thereupon amity and good will were scattered to the winds

. . .," and he concluded this part of the sermon by hoping that Go-Daigo has now understood: "I pray therefore that our late emperor will turn away from his past confusions and free himself from bondage of illusion. . . . Thus he may pass safely beyond the dark crossroad of differences between friend and foe, and attain that spiritual region wherein the identity of confusion and clear insight may be seen."

Alongside this assessment of Go-Daigo's role in the defeat of his own dreams by listening to the slanders and defamation, Soseki also presents us with his view of Takauji's behavior both during the problems and after Go-Daigo's death. He reports Takauji's reaction to the court's attitude as follows: "With a great sigh the Military Governor lamented, 'Alas, due to slander and flattery by those close to the Throne, I am consigned to the fate of an ignominious rebel without a chance to explain my innocence.' Indeed his grief was no perfunctory display, but without nurturing any bitterness in his heart he devoutly gave himself over to spiritual reflection and pious works, fervently praying for the enlightenment of the emperor and eventually constructing [in the name of the emperor] this great monastery for the practice of Buddhism." Soseki ended the sermon by hoping that through this temple Go-Daigo would "extend an invisible hand to protect the teachings, so that with his spirit ever-present in this monastery of Kame-yama his blessings may extend to all mankind." This, he said, was "the wish of the Military Governor, and so we have reason to believe that the imperial wrath will be appeased. Such a worthy intention [on the part of Takauji] is no trifling thing, and the Buddhas in their profound compassion are certain to bestow their unseen favor and protection on us."[16]

Soseki was looking ahead and seems relieved that some good, or at least the potential for good, had come out of the terrible events they had all witnessed; but even while he worked hard in Kyoto on his twin projects at Saihōji and Tenryūji, attempting to bring some peace and harmony to both his own life and that of the country, the deadly stalemate between the two courts continued. In the country at large, the dislocation of central authority meant that local disputes and rivalries were being fought between the various warrior families as they staked their claims on land and power. In addition to this, the failure of the Ashikaga family to impose their regime across the country became increasingly corrosive to their unity as the individuals, especially Takauji's brother Tadayoshi, pursued their own ambitions. This quickly led to vicious infighting that dogged them for the next ten years or so and increased the instability of the country. Some indication of just how destructive these wars had been, even to rural areas distant from the cities, can be found in one contemporary diary that gives a particularly desolate account of a trip to Ise.

The trip was made in 1342 by the priest Saka Jubutsu, and he recounts arriving at the Great Shrine: "After I passed the purification hall on the Kushida River, it became apparent how terribly the southern part of this province has been devastated since the country fell into disorder . . . one could see on approaching no houses . . . but many withered stumps along the way. When I asked a man I chanced to meet about the place, he answered that this is what had happened to neglected rice fields. His words made me feel all the sadder that the world should have changed so much." Things became even worse, however, when he realized that neglect and lack of funding meant that even the sequential rebuilding of the shrines had stopped and that dereliction was setting in: "I arrived at the residence of the High Priestess. There were what looked like the remains of old earthen walls, and here and there were tall bushes and trees. The *torii* had fallen over and the pillars lying across the road were so completely rotted that, if a person did not actually know what they were, he would pass them by without a second glance, supposing they were merely fallen trees." As he approached the shrines themselves he was devastated by what he saw: "The time for rebuilding having passed, the roof tiles were broken, and the rains dripped to the base of the oak pillars. The eaves sagged, and storm winds swept the pines that in summer gave shade. I had lamented that the warfare in the land had caused a decline in the good government of the country, but at the thought that disturbances in the world had brought about even the ruin of this holy shrine, the tears flowed, too many for my sleeves to absorb." When he turned to a nearby temple for some comfort, things only became worse. The light seemed to have gone from the world, and a spiritual winter had arrived: "No torches were lit on this cold night . . . the frost-coated bell did not stir . . . Not one flower, not one stick of incense had been offered. . . . I thought that the neglect of the images of the Buddha was a result of the falling off of human beings, and, mingled with my tears for the sadness of the world, tears for my journey spilled over copiously."[17]

Against this background a general peace was to hold for the next ten years or so, and in this time Soseki, eager to lift some of this sadness from the world, was able to complete his new building projects, establish the *Gozan* monasteries as the dominant cultural force in the country, organize the smooth running of his school at Rinsenji, and spend an increasing amount of time in his retreat at Saihōji. This was particularly true after the large-scale building at Tenryūji was completed. This took a number of years, between the erection of all the buildings and the laying out of extensive and detailed gardens, and, when funds threatened to run short, he had been able to organize a trading ship, the "Tenryūji-bune," to China in 1341 to ensure that the building project was completed and that it would be endowed for the future. Almost everything about his twin building projects at this time was different, serving very different purposes both for him and the Zen community, and as a result the gardens he produced were, as we will see later, in marked contrast to each other.

The years 1341 to 1351, the last ten years of his life, marked a period of concentrated output for Soseki, not just in temple and garden, but also in terms of teaching, poetry, and texts, as he identified more clearly the active role that he felt the Zen monks should play and as he sought to encourage the cultural output of the monasteries and his individual students. At Rinsenji his disciple Shun'oku Myōha reissued an old text called the *Engo Shinyo* and initiated the long tradition of *Gozan* publishing. A number of other texts were to follow, not least the next year, 1342, when Soseki's *Muchū Mondō* (Dream Conversations) were published in three volumes. Also that year the retired emperor, Kōgon, began his studies, having received his disciple's robes at Saihōji. Soseki conducted a series of ceremonies for the peace of the spirits of all who had died since the wars began, enemies and allies, at Hokanji to the east of Kyoto.

The fact that the *Muchū Mondō* was published in his lifetime reflects not only the interest that there was in his teachings, but also Soseki's eagerness to ensure that the Zen school did not miss what he saw as a unique historical opportunity to integrate Zen into the basic fabric of Japanese life. He therefore authorized the publication partly because he was, as usual, overwhelmed with students and, at this time of "the falling off of human beings," he wanted to make the teachings available to as many people as possible. It was also an important opportunity for him to define clearly the role the monks could play in contemporary events. The material that made up the *Muchū Mondō* appeared in the form of dialogues he had held with Ashikaga Tadayoshi, in which Soseki answered specific questions about Zen and ruminated along the way on a number of related matters.[18]

Yanagida considers that the *Muchū Mondō* should be seen basically as an outline guide to the "mission" of the Zen monks, and this seems right since, rather than reiterating the basic tenets of Zen Buddhism, it concentrates on guiding monks in their interaction with contemporary society, on how to conduct themselves and make the most of their opportunities to teach.[19] In it Soseki reminds them that in difficult times such as the present it is easy for people to lose sight of what is actually happening, what can and cannot be changed. "What causes mental suffering is not the environment itself but the mind itself," and, given this, monks must strive to help people understand that it is not the cycles of circumstances that surround them that are important but rather how they react to them. For monks to effectively offer this help they must work hard at forming sincere, interactive relationships with the secular world, and at this crucial time they cannot afford to occupy only the illusory worlds of Zen culture, "People commonly assume that it is the aspiration for enlightenment to abandon worldly ambitions and go live in a hermitage in the mountains and to clear the mind with the sound of waterfalls and the wind in the pines." But, as a scripture says "Those who live in seclusion in the mountains and forests and think they are thus better than others cannot even attain happiness, let alone Buddhahood."

In another section he emphasizes the importance of teaching in these relationships but reminds the monks that they must be open to any opportunity to connect and not to rely solely on doctrine: "Zen teachings are not doctrines kept in mind by the teachers. They are produced spontaneously at the interface between teacher and student. One should not try to freeze momentary teachings into fixed doctrines. If Zen teachers are enlightened, their teaching may effectively take any form." It is clear that Soseki took very seriously the idea that Zen monks needed to take an active role in contemporary society. Positive engagement was the only way that Zen was going to be able to establish itself and help promote the idea of the "Great Peace" to which he had dedicated himself and the *Gozan* movement. To these ends, finding ways to connect in this critical period of history was more important than some esoteric notion of the Zen "Way." Thus, he could go on to say, building firmly on his own experiences: "For Zen teachers, knowledge . . . should not be limited to the methods of Zen schools only but should extend to the devices of other Buddhist teachings and even to other philosophies and secular sciences."

While Soseki uses parts of the *Muchū Mondō* to establish what he perceives the "mission" of the monks to be, he also emphasizes the role he sees for the *Gozan* monasteries and their extensive cultural activities in helping to achieve this. Discussing the Zen *kōan,* an important teaching device in the Zen tradition, he says, "The *kōan* is not absolutely essential in Zen; it is also just an expedient means used to transcend the bounds of the conditioned mind"; in short, the important thing is not the device itself but anything, or any means, that will help people to break free of the "conditioned mind" and start to see things for what they really are. Other means to do this were to be found in the wide-ranging artistic endeavors of the *Gozan* communities with their dynamic combinations of religious and secular people and ideas. Use all of these endeavors as "expedient means," he says, but as ever, be careful because "whether the [arts] are beneficial or harmful depends on the attitude of the individual. The original purpose of the arts is to tune and refine the mind. Once they become objects of personal attachment, however, their refining action is lost and they turn into occasions for perversion and corruption." Similarly, in landscape, his own preferred vehicle of expression, it is always important to remember what it is you expect your garden or painting to achieve: "It is not necessarily bad to like landscape, and it is not necessarily good. There is no plus or minus in landscape itself; gain or loss are in people's attitudes."

Taken as a whole the *Muchū Mondō* appears as a broad and wide-ranging brief, whose purpose as much as anything was to exhort the Zen monks to make sure that they take care of their meditation practice, to ensure and continually deepen the qualities of their enlightenment, but then, having done this, also to make sure that they get up from their mats, stride out through the temple gates, and make that enlightenment count in the secular world. Its appearance at this time makes it firmly a part of Soseki's ongoing efforts to establish the circumstances that could generate and then spread the ideas and enlightened energies that would regenerate the country through the "Great Peace," and help it battle with the demons that will beset it and those involved with it. He is particularly at pains in one section to warn of the many forms in which these will appear as the monks become involved with the secular world. For Soseki, demons are anything that can obstruct the potential for true understanding. First, he lists the obvious ones: "greed, hatred, conceit, opinionated views." Then come a group that relate generally to his experience and monastic training: "addiction to meditation states, pride in knowledge, anxious haste to attain enlightenment, indulging in passions and fearing passions." Finally, there are some very specific ones: "sentimental compassion, idolizing teachers, and rejecting teachers because of finding fault with teacher's external behavior." It is interesting to note that warnings about "sentimental compassion" appear three or four times throughout the *Muchū Mondō,* and this seems to indicate that Soseki, who consistently insists on the importance of compassion, saw its sentimentalization as a primary obstruction to understanding. To help the monks deal with these many demons, Soseki quotes the following advice: "A meditation master told his disciples, 'A celestial demon had been coming here to bother me, but no matter what appearances it created, I dealt with it by not looking or listening. The demon's manifestations had an end, but my not looking and not listening have no end."

While the contents of the *Muchū Mondō* seem to reflect a close and candid relationship between Soseki and Tadayoshi, there are those who so questioned the latter's motives for engaging in the dialogue and saw them as the kind of threat to his position and reputation that Soseki had to be wary of during these dangerous times. Tadayoshi, unlike his brother, did not become Soseki's pupil at this time, and the exact nature of their relationship remains unclear, but subsequent events and his behavior, especially during the campaigns around Kamakura in 1335, show him to have been an unscrupulous man of ruthless ambition, who was resentful of his brother's position and authority. Although in the early days a common ambition to raise the fortunes of their family had given the brothers a shared purpose, their inability to gain control over the country as a whole and their differences of opinion over what should be done soon started to disrupt this unity.

Tadayoshi had always preferred taking instruction from the Chinese monks and seemed to respond to their hard line Song Zen, so it is not immediately clear why he should have engaged Soseki in the questions and answers of the *Muchū Mondō*. Collcutt quotes Professor Tamamura Takeji, who has suggested that through their question and answer sessions "Tadayoshi was deliberately exposing the didactic nature of Musō's Zen."[20] We can never know if this was the case, or, if it was, that Soseki was not aware of Tadayoshi's aims and used the opportunity anyway as a chance to further the work, but it is by no means inconceivable that Tadayoshi should have had ulterior motives and that he welcomed the chance to undermine his brother's close friend and ally. It could also be the case, however, that Soseki found in Tadayoshi's straightforward and penetrating questioning the most expedient method by which to get his message across.

There were many, however, for whom the tone and content of the conversations appeared as a serious betrayal of the traditional forms of Zen, and who would have agreed with Tadayoshi's actions had he been attempting to weaken Soseki's position and marginalize his ideas. There is no doubt that Soseki's rise to prominence had had a lot to do with his continual insistence that the teachings of his school should be accessible to everyone. People should not only have the opportunity to hear them, they should also be able to relate them to their lives and experiences. Thus, when writing and teaching, he did not simply refer to Chinese or esoteric texts but also mixed in the everyday, and anecdotes about his own life and times. In addition to this he was attempting to issue a broad based appeal to action, something that always runs the risk of alienating one or another shade of opinion.

The inclusiveness of the vision expressed in the text and his close involvement with both the *Gozan* administration and those who ran the country left him particularly vulnerable to attack from purists and, as soon as the *Muchū Mondō* was published, a rebuttal of Soseki's teachings was written by a monk of the Pure Land Sect. The main criticism contained in this centered on his "excessive worldliness" and thus, by implication, his lack of spiritual depth and commitment. There was also a number of people who saw his power and influence as a threat, or at least a hindrance, to their own and who were ready to repeat and magnify this criticism, one of the few areas where his reputation seemed assailable, and it is quite possible that Tadayoshi, in directing Soseki's answers through close questioning, may have been seeking to provide them with additional material.

Soseki for his part was unmoved by this criticism and immediately replied with the *Kōkyo-shu*, a detailed eighteen-part answer. In this he emphasized his belief that Buddhism was capable of allowing for all levels of learning and literacy and that true teaching should be able to make allowances for all of these. Teaching within the monasteries was one thing, but their tasks as teachers of the "Way" demanded that they go out beyond this closed world and reach as many people as possible. Throughout his reply he underlined his determination that no one should be excluded and that he should actively seek to teach all those he could possibly reach, making his teaching accessible to all, even if this left him open to charges of worldliness and didacticism. He saw no danger to the potency of Zen, or Buddhism generally, in making it widely available; indeed, he believed that a strong future for the country lay in its embrace of Zen understanding and the culture that flowed from it.[21]

For much of the next few years political events remained stable, allowing life to get back to some kind of normality in the capital. Soseki's time was taken up with teaching, the administration of the *Gozan* monasteries, and his two big building and garden projects at Saihōji and Tenryūji. As these developed it became increasingly clear just how different the two temples were to be and how different their roles in Soseki's life were. Saihōji from the start was to be a small, intimate foundation where he could retreat with a few close disciples for long periods of meditation. We already know that he felt it had deep associations with Ryo Zassu and that he saw it as a place where he could "hide" away in the West Mountains and maintain the quality of his personal meditation time. Saihōji's garden as it developed became an interior place, somewhere for individual sitters to practice their meditation in a focused closed-in world. His *Saihōji Ikun* (Last Instructions from Saihōji), written in 1345, make it clear that this was always intended to be a small foundation and may never in fact have had more than twenty residents at a time. In addition to this, and also underlining Saihōji's special nature, he specified that "the abbot should be selected for his devotion to meditation, that he should not hold a joint abbacy with some other monastery, and that, once appointed, he should remain at Saihōji until his death."[22]

Tenryūji, on the other hand, was from the outset designed to be a major teaching temple, its doors open to all comers and all occasions, a public celebration of Go-Daigo's life and his interest in the teachings of Zen. In fact, Soseki celebrated here not just the teachings of Japanese Zen, but also the mainland influences on it that had shaped so much of its culture. Here the large sprawl of temple buildings looked out over a wide garden in which references to the places of Chinese Zen were set firmly in a Japanese context—that of the Kame-yama hills, which were carefully "borrowed" to provide the background. Here were the grand entranceway, the wide-viewing verandas, the long views and open skies that Saihōji determinedly lacked, the two gardens representing the two very different agendas that Soseki was following during the last ten or so years of his life. In 1345 the Main Hall at Tenryūji was officially opened in combination with a ceremony to mark the seventh anniversary of Go-Daigo's death, and the following year Soseki wrote a series of Chinese poems in which he makes clear its role as an inclusive center for teaching and practice, a suitable place to act as the focal point for the mission he had set for the Zen monks.

The poems are all formal in tone and refer to places within the temple precincts, tying them by reference to places and people from Zen's early days in China, and their general tone is one of instruction, pointing out what can be learned here, and the difficulties and rewards of learning. One, entitled Hall of the Guardian God, is specific in its message of inclusiveness:

> Inside the temple enclosure
>   a place was set aside
>   for a Shintō shrine . . .

Another relates the pond in the garden, with its Song-style rockwork, to that which stood beside the hut of Hui-neng, the Sixth Patriarch, and through this to the nature of Zen understanding:

> The Dharma spring of the Sixth Patriarch
>   has never run dry
>   it is flowing even now
> a single drop
>   has fallen and spread
>   far and deep
> Don't be caught
>   by the decorations at the edge
>   and the wall around it
> In the dead of night
>   the moonlight strikes
>   the middle of the pond.

The poem Turtle Head Stupa, referring to a feature in the garden, explicitly tells the students that everything they need to understand is right here, right now, that through careful practice, enlightenment and all its rewards will come to them:

A pine tree
with long needles
has grown behind it
On top of the tower
there is a Buddha image
of eternal happiness
Now the doors and windows
are all open
and nothing inside is hidden
Dharma worlds
beyond number
are there for you to see.[23]

With the dedication and official opening of Tenryūji completed, Soseki then left the running of this big temple to others, appointing his disciple Mugoku Shigen (1282–1359) as abbot, retiring as its head and retreating to the relative peace of Rinsenji and the absolute peace of Saihōji. Before retiring, however, his work at Tenryūji was recognized when the emperor bestowed on him the title of *Shōgaku Kokushi*, raising him in rank to a National Teacher of the True Enlightenment.

In addition to living at Rinsenji and Saihōji, he founded a small hermitage, also in Arashi-yama and looking across to the Kame-yama hills, at Ungo-an (Dwelling in Clouds Hut). The site and garden are interesting for us because, although now largely derelict, the hermitage was located just to the south of an old imperial burial mound and was to be the last garden that Soseki created. Whatever may have been left of this garden by the late nineteenth century was largely laid waste by the fighting that accompanied the Meiji Restoration, and, as Kawase points out, it is a major loss to us as the last site Soseki chose to build a garden. The Unko-an garden, along with Saihōji and Tenryūji, repesents the last of a trio of gardens that had finally given expression to his understanding of not just his place within the landscape, but also how anyone else could create their own; here were the blueprints for those willing to take the time to study them.

During 1348 and 1349 Soseki was kept busy as in the previous few years with teaching and administrative work, but he did not take on any more building projects, either temples or gardens. It was the first time in many years that he was not engaged in one or another of his large-scale projects or the founding of new temples at the request of others, and he seems to have steadily cut down on his commitments and activities, perhaps finally tired out by his long active life. In 1348 we get a sense of history moving on beyond Soseki's immediate life as, first, Ashikaga Yoshiakira (1330–67),

Takauji's son and immediate successor, became his student. Then in October of that year he held ceremonies to commemorate the thirty-third anniversary of Bukkoku Zenji's death. No doubt as he did so he would have keenly missed the company of his fellow students who had also become close friends, Gen'nō Hongen, Taihei Myōjun, and Tengan Ekō, all of whom he had by now long outlived; that generation of the lineage was slowly passing away. But, equally, a new one was beginning, since in this year Zekkai Chūshin (1336–1405) became Soseki's student at Saihōji, joining Gidō Shūshin, who had become a disciple a few years before. These two were to become leading figures of the lineage, both as artists and poets within the *Gozan* cultural milieu and also as advisors to Yoshiakira's successors as shogun, Ashikaga Yoshimitsu (1358–1408) and Yoshimochi (1386–1428).

In a piece of calligraphy Soseki wrote that year at Rinsenji, we get a sense very much of a man coming to terms with his old age and feeling that he had done what he could and that it was time to pass the responsibility on:

> Drooping willows line the banks
> casting their shadows on the clear current
> But the rushing waters can be heard
> in a voice that doesn't rest.
> Of all the 80,000 *gathas*
> the ear gathers but a few;
> The spring breezes have already passed through
> the topmost branches of the trees.

He sees the autumn of his life; the spring breezes, lightly touching the high branches, have long blown away, and now he is firmly on the ground, still and hunched like the drooping willows. He personally cannot carry on gathering the *gathas*, but there are many who can and who will hear the rushing waters and respond, and through them the teaching will carry on. For Soseki, however, the shadows are gathering and the clear current is increasingly difficult to see.

But the tone of regret here is not simply for himself. After dedicating so much of his life to an attempt to bring peace and unity back to the country, now, during 1350 as he grew old and sick, he had to watch as the tenuous relationship between the Ashikaga brothers fell apart and the country once again plunged into war. In the spring of that year he had sat at Saihōji with the two brothers exchanging poems as they admired the cherry blossoms, and one of Soseki's *waka* written that day seems, read now, to carry two levels of meaning. Its traditional poetic meaning reminds us that something you can see all the time is not rare and unusual: the beauty of the flowers lies in their transience and in the period of time between when they fall and next year when they blossom again. Yet on another level it reads like an appeal to the Ashikaga brothers to look beyond their immediate situation and toward the future before it is too late. They are not to be led by the emotions of the moment but to see beyond them.

> We always look
> at the flowers
> in blossom
> But their true nature
> is only revealed
> once they have fallen.[24]

By the end of that year, however, Tadayoshi had forced the issue and was at war with his brother.

The problems began with a serious clash between troops of Tadayoshi and Kō Moronao, who had been Takauji's right-hand man for many years and was the "manager" of his household. Following the clash, Takauji reacted quickly, removing his brother from all his positions and from the command of any troops. Tadayoshi, after first becoming Soseki's student, left Kyoto and transferred his allegiance to the Southern Court, urging the then emperor Go-Murakami to attack Kyoto immediately. Fighting once more engulfed the capital in the early months of 1351. Moronao was killed and the war spread rapidly as the Southern Court, taking advantage of this rift between the Ashikaga, made an all-out bid to regain Kyoto. The continued existence throughout the country of Northern and Southern Court sympathizers meant that the fighting could be quickly reignited, and the next few decades, in fact, saw the country at the mercy of countless local feuds and skirmishes. These were often vendettas or rivalries between individuals or families, fought nominally in the name of one or the other court but in reality a struggle to the death for land and power during a period of redistribution of both following the collapse of the Hōjō. It was an ongoing struggle that dominated life during this period, and as Soseki approached the end of his life there was little reason to hope for an early resolution of the conflict. There seemed no end in sight.

In Kyoto the fighting soon became serious enough for Takauji to have to retreat to Harima, and for a brief period Southern Court troops reoccupied the city. The Northern emperor Kōmyō fled with his court to Ojima, and the capital changed hands several times before Takauji was finally able to regain the upper hand and drive out the Southern Court armies in 1353. This final surge of war effectively saw the end of the Southern Court's challenge to the Ashikaga. Tadayoshi was killed, and, following Takauji's death in 1358, his successors put in place an administration that, although never able to completely dominate the country, at least provided a central mechanism for government that lasted until the late sixteenth century.

By the middle of 1351, however, much of the capital had been burnt down, many people had been displaced, and the countryside had been reduced to the kind of desolation recorded by our visitor to Ise in 1342. Soseki recorded his feelings about all of this in "Lamenting the Civil War," a long poem that records not only his sadness about the current state of affairs after so much hard work, but also, in spite of everything, his optimism that the possibility of a great peace still existed if people could see the opportunity and take it.

So many times since antiquity
　the human world
　has barely escaped destruction
yet ten thousand fortunes
　and a thousand misfortunes
　and in one void after all
Puppets squabbling
　back and forth
　across the stage
People brawling
　over a snail's horn
　winning or losing;
The ferocity
　of a snipe and a clam
　glaring at each other
only to arrive after death
　before the tribunal
　of Yama, the Judge of Hell.
When will the horses of war
　be turned loose
　on Flower Mountain?
It would be best
　to throw their bits away
　to the east of the Buddha's Palace.[25]

Soseki acknowledges first that whatever happens, fortune and misfortune, life will go on and ultimate destruction will be avoided, but he then goes on to question the point of all of this if, in the meantime, the quality of that life is destroyed by the meaningless squabbles that occupy so much of our time and attention. The puppets, the quarrels over territory on the horns of a snail and the snipe and the clam are all stories taken from classical Chinese literature, stories used to illustrate the time, energy, and people that we waste in battle over the illusions of position, power, and ownership. Life may go on, but it is always in danger of becoming no more than a void, empty of the essentials of understanding and enlightenment. He fears this happening in contemporary Japan. A chance to create a lasting peace that will provide the space for a national enlightenment is being frittered away, the potential of the *Gozan* culture is being lost, and people's minds are closed to meditation and the pursuit of understanding by the constant distractions of short-sighted military campaigns for short-term advantages that meanwhile dominate and ruin lives.

But, while acknowledging all this, he has a clear vision of how these cycles can be broken. He firmly believes that the world of *Taihei*, the Great Peace, can and does exist in spite of these constant wars and squabbles. Flower Mountain is one of a number of poetic images from Chinese literature used to summon up a vision of an ideal place and time where wisdom and understanding rule benignly over an industrious population living at peace. In this situation, each individual is enabled in his or her own way to pursue and achieve an understanding of the illusive nature of life and thereby rise above mere existence to a place where there was some real point to life. Soseki believed that you must trust in the existence of this place, that the negative and fatalistic alternatives rob the miracles of life and consciousness of any purpose, and that the crucial first step toward accessing it is to "loose the horses of war," trust in the hope of peace and disarm, and "throw their bits away," as a sign of that trust.

In his gloss on this poem, Yanagida goes on to elaborate Soseki's position, showing that behind the words of the text lies the belief that you must act with the conviction that you are right, intervening no matter how bad things look. Peace cannot be made by war, but by the nurturing of the opportunities that arise when the rigid controls and patterns of this or that system are in flux, when anything is possible, particularly the potential for change. Soseki saw this period of Japan's history very much in this light. The stifling domination of the Hōjō Regency was broken, new and innovative systems of government were possible, new and innovative forms of culture were available, and opportunities were there if only the nation could rise above the immediacy of the squabbles. Now, even as Kyoto burned for the fifth or sixth time, he fervently believed in this potential.[26]

At seventy-six Soseki was still as determined and conscious of the work ahead as ever, but as 1351 opened, the years were beginning to catch up with him. Early in the year he gathered his closest disciples around him and told them bluntly, "In this year I am going to leave you." And by late summer it became very clear that his health was failing fast. In July, at the height of the renewed fighting, he resumed the abbacy of Tenryūji, a move which appears to have reassured a good many people at this tense and critical time, and he used the occasion to deliver his judgment on the relations between Go-Daigo and Takauji in the speech we have already noted. Soseki had always seen the course of his life, and the problems he encountered in it, as the karmic consequences of previous lives. His consistent aim was to fulfill these karmic debts, dealing with whatever he had to deal with. This attitude also lay behind his dealings with other people, their worth depending on how he read their reaction to their own karma. Kawase believes that it is this criterion that we see reflected in the judgments he makes in this speech. Because of his illness, the long speech is recorded as having weakened him considerably, and in spite of any risks to his lineage that might be incurred by such frankness, he clearly felt that the one thing he could use his unique position to do in the cause of peace was to give his view on what had happened, clear up some misunderstandings and, perhaps by so doing, change the atmosphere of the times and introduce the possibility of reconciliation and compromise.

In the speech he seems in the end to see Takauji, despite all his considerable faults and the brutality with which he conducted his wars, to be, nevertheless, an important agent of change. He was someone who had done what he felt was necessary, in the only way he knew how, but he was also one who crucially believed in the need for compassion as the basis for moving on, and who, because of this concern, was open to the compromises and opportunities that the times offered. Go-Daigo, on the other hand, Soseki sees as someone blinded to the importance of these things by an obsession with the chimera of imperial restoration. He sees Go-Daigo as someone who failed to recognize the potential of the times to create a new and vigorous nation and who therefore missed all the opportunities. Instead, he saw Takauji as a threat to achieve his anachronistic restoration rather than as an energizing force who could be used to help create something forward-looking, unique, and new. In a crucial passage in the speech, Soseki sums up the futility of pursuing illusory concepts as an end in themselves and of obsessing over the results and actions taken during that pursuit in the past. He offers instead a vision of a world where an enlightened understanding is not only given primacy and but also the authority to create the forms and relationships of government and society: "What I have stated above [concerning Go-Daigo and Takauji] is all a dream within a dream. Even if it were true, there is no use finding fault with what is past and done—how much less with what has happened in a dream! We must realize that the Throne, the highest position among men, is itself but something cherished in a dream. . . . That is why Shākyamuni gave up his royal rank and took up a solitary life of religious discipline . . . to teach all men that the Sovereign of Enlightenment is far superior to the highest position among men."[27]

It was a long speech and, no doubt, a long and tiring day for Soseki, but he was clearly determined to make this additional effort to aid the cause of peace, and the unusually blunt terms in which he couched his message reflects the fact that he had neither the time nor strength to be any more diplomatic; he must also have concluded that neither he nor the *Gozan* system had anything to lose. Soon after the speech was delivered, an additional two and a half thousand people arrived at Tenryūji seeking admission as students, and the duties of the abbacy quickly overwhelmed Soseki. Turning the position over to Tōryō Eiko, a monk recently arrived from China, he retired once more to the quieter world of Rinsenji where, during August, he was visited twice at the San'e-in by the retired emperors Kōgon and Kōmyō. In the course of one of these visits the emperors conferred on him additional ranks as National Teacher, making him *Shōkaku Shin-shu Kokushi*, the "Supremely Enlightened Teacher."

Meanwhile attacks on Kyoto by forces of the Southern Court intensified, and some of the first things to go were the temple buildings at Tenryūji; far from seeing any prospect of peace before he died, Soseki's last weeks were spent encircled by the flames that destroyed the great temple he had worked so hard to create, flames that will have been visible from the temple precinct at Rinsenji.

On September 1, his illness worsened, and, after attending a meeting in the assembly hall where he told the monks that he was leaving them and that if anyone had anything they wanted to say, now was the time, he returned to the San'e-in. Over the next few days he repeatedly refused medicines and offers of medical help from the palace, and the only outside visitors he saw were Kōgon and Kōmyō, who visited in spite of the ongoing fighting. Many other people were in fact unable to visit Rinsenji at this important time due to the fighting, and many felt that this situation boded ill for the future. This sense was intensified a few days later when two earthquakes were felt in Kyoto in quick succession, during which the grounds and buildings at Saihōji were damaged. On September 27, Soseki formally handed over control of the heavily damaged Tenryūji to Tōryō Eiko and issued his last instructions to his disciples at Rinsenji. Shun'noku Myōha, as his most senior disciple, was entrusted with the work of publishing the volumes of biography and sermons. Although never formally given the title, he also appears to have assumed the mantle of senior monk in the lineage. The San'e-in and care of his grave he entrusted to Mugoku Shigen who, although he had not joined Soseki until later in his life, had enjoyed a particularly close relationship with him. Yanagida feels that Soseki's activity during these last days of his life was directed mainly toward ensuring that his disciples "return to the source" for their future instruction, return, that is, to the inspiration of the life and words of Buddha, Bodhidharma, and the Patriarchs of Zen and to the revelation of the Truth through their practice of meditation as a basis for their search for enlightenment. His message at this time is summed up in these words from an earlier poem: "Each of you be sure / to find the deepest truth / in yourself."[28]

Above all he seems to have been concerned to prevent his life and teachings from becoming an end in themselves, to prevent the formation of a personality cult from arising around his memory, something he saw as a real threat to the strength and value of the lineage. He was the leader of one of the biggest religious organizations of his time, but he sought to play down his "footsteps," his legacy, which he not only felt was open to misuse, but which he also firmly believed was in itself of no importance, an additional distraction at a time when there were already far too many of these. The way ahead for his disciples existed independently from him personally, the Path stretched ahead but they should not look for him to accompany them any further along it.[29]

On September 29 he wrote his final poem, a direct instruction to all his students to take up the work themselves and a reaffirmation of Bukkoku's message which had proved so pivotal in his own search for enlightenment and his place in the enlightened world.

Nothing divides
    the pure worlds
No need to wait
    to meet again
Even the assembly from Vulture's Peak
    is present here today
Who beyond yourselves will
    uphold the Law
Everyone can be found on
    the One Path.[30]

Having completed the poem, he told those around him, "Tomorrow I will go."

Soseki had spent the last eighteen years of his life deeply involved in the public and administrative life of a senior *Gozan* priest. He had put all his energies into creating a strong temple system around which he hoped the cultural life of the nation would thrive when peace eventually came to the battered country. Events had made it impossible for him to retire to a quiet meditative life as Bukkoku had done, and, even as his health failed, he was called on until the end to perform the tasks of abbot, teacher, statesman, diplomat, and advisor. By the beginning of autumn 1351, however, his energies had run out, and on September 30 he refused his daily rice, called his disciples from Saihōji and Tenryūji to join those with him at Rinsenji, bade them farewell, and, attended only by those closest to him, with a smile on his face, died quietly.

He was buried at Rinsenji, and his grave is visible, if unapproachable, today beneath the rear of the temple's main hall. On top of the grave is an arrangement of rocks, said when seen from above to form the shape of a lotus flower. It is not now possible to see them from that angle but, seen now by peering in from the side through the lattice windows, the rocks are spread across the grave like a sprawling, broken mountain range, and Soseki can finally be seen to have found his place among the folds of the West Mountains.

Figure 4. Drawing of Soseki's grave at Rinsenji. The grave is beneath the main hall and visible through the slatted windows.

During those last remarkable eighteen years, however, before the burdens of his public life began to catch up with him, he also found time to create a remarkable series of gardens, places where he was increasingly able to retreat from his public life and reconnect with the private meditative world that he had last been able to occupy at Hakusen-an and Taiko-an hermitages. In these later gardens he developed ways of creating spaces that could act as a physical context for his consciousness as his life became increasingly enmeshed in a dislocated and urban world. These were spaces that he could occupy and within which he could lose himself in the greater forms of Life all around him; they were his place in the landscape. In the next two chapters we will be looking at how he achieved this and, in particular, at the garden at Saihōji where this idea was most completely expressed.

NOTES

1. Donald Keene, *Travelers of a Hundred Ages* (New York: H. Hold and Co., 1989), pp. 163–73. A vivid account of these times can be found here in the "Account of the Takemuki Palace," the diary of a court lady, Hino Nako, who was caught in the midst of the drama and tragedy of Kyoto court life.

2. Kawase Kazuma, *Musō Kokushi: Zen to teien* (Musō Kokushi: Zen and Gardens) (Tokyo: Kōdansha, 1968), p. 172.

3. Ibid., for a description of Kochōzenji and the information from the Kai Records.

4. Martin Collcutt. *Five Mountains* (Cambridge, Mass.: Harvard University Press, 1981), pp. 150, 151.

5. Musō Soseki, *Sun at Midnight: Poems and Sermons,* trans. W. S. Merwin and Sōiku Shigematsu (San Francisco: North Point Press, 1989), poem # 80, p. 87.

6. Musō Kokushi, *Dream Conversations on Buddhism and Zen,* trans. and ed. Thomas Cleary (Boston: Shambhala 1994), p. 2.

7. Maggie Keswick, *The Chinese Garden* (London: Academy Editions, 1978), p. 199.

8. Collcutt, *Five Mountains,* p. 294.

9. Kawase, *Musō Kokushi,* p. 182.

10. Musō Soseki, *Sun at Midnight,* poem # 75, p. 82.

11. Collcutt, *Five Mountains,* p. 98.

12. Ibid., pp. 150–63.

13. Yanagida Seizan, "Musō Soseki," *NHK "Reading the Heart" Series* (Tokyo: Japan Broadcasting Publishing Association, 1992), p. 148.

14. Musō Soseki, *Sun at Midnight,* p. 166, for translation of the text of the Admonition.

15. Kawase, *Musō Kokushi,* p. 179.

16. Tsunoda Ryūsaku, Wm. Theodore de Bary, and Donald Keene, comp., *Sources of Japanese Tradition,* vol.1 (New York: Columbia University Press, 1958), pp. 250–52.

17. Keene, *Travelers of a Hundred Ages,* p. 178.

18. Musō Kokushi, *Dream Conversations on Buddhism and Zen.* Translated

extracts quoted here taken from pp. 34, 32, 50, 27, 58, 57, and 7.

19. Yanagida, "Musō Soseki," p. 94.

20. Collcutt, *Five Mountains*, p. 102.

21. Kawase, *Musō Kokushi*, p. 133. This summary of Soseki's reply to the criticism is based on Kawase's account. For a more detailed discussion of the criticism and his reply see Kawase, *Musō Kokushi*, p. 133 and following.

22. Collcutt, *Five Mountains*, p. 150.

23. Musō Soseki, *Sun at Midnight*, poems # 101, 102, 108, p. 111, 112, 118.

24. Ken'ichi Kamigaito, "Japan and Chinese Culture in the Middle Ages" (in Japanese), *Shin'ika* (November 1992). Translated by Sharon Nakazato.

25. Musō Soseki, *Sun at Midnight*, poem #130, p. 140.

26. Yanagida, "Musō Soseki," pp. 99, 100.

27. Tsunodqa, de Bary, and Keene, *Sources of Japanese Tradition*, vol 1, p. 252.

28. Musō Soseki, *Sun at Midnight*, poem # 63, p. 70.

29. Yanagida, "Musō Soseki," p. 149.

30. Kawase, *Musō Kokushi*, p. 205.

CHAPTER FIVE

Mountains and Rivers without End: Developing the Gardens

Throughout this book the landscapes Soseki visited and the gardens he built have made brief appearances before the narratives of his search for enlightenment, and before his life "in the world," swept on. It is now time to look at these in detail and tell the story of how the gardens developed in response to the changing circumstances of his life. I have tried to discover who he was and what his motives and ambitions were; now I want to follow the development of his gardens and explain what he was trying to do and why.

By the time Soseki came to construct his first landscapes, "garden design" had existed in Japan for some seven hundred years. It had passed through a number of important phases, absorbed a number of important influences, and become one of the defining arts of Japanese culture. As such it performed a number of functions, carrying a number of meanings and messages for the Japanese, and these were as much a part of Soseki's make-up as an artist as the sources of creative expression that we looked at in chapter 2. Tracing the history of these gardens will provide us with some understanding of what these functions and meanings were.

The earliest landscaping, or the manipulation of ground forms to a pre-set design, in Japan, as in many other countries, was concerned with agriculture, the defense of the agricultural communities, and the settings for their communal ritual and burial. Once millet and rice had become staple parts of the Japanese diet, by around 500 B.C., a great deal of landscaping had to follow to facilitate the farming of these crops, and a majority of this work had to do with the collection and delivery of irrigation water. Equally, landscaping was also concerned with the creation of sacred and ritual sites to serve the growing communities, particularly those connected with the burial of the dead. During the prehistoric Jōmon period in Japan there is some evidence for the layout and construction of ritual or burial sites, typically the "sundial" sites we looked at in an earlier chapter, but it was with the Kofun tomb culture (A.D. 250–552) that full-scale ritual landscapes started to be created. These tombs, consisting of stone-lined chambers and entrance passages covered in substantial earth mounds, were of considerable size and surrounded by the "spirit-fences" of the *haniwa* figures and often, in the case of the biggest ones, by a moat or pond. The layout also included upright marker stones indicating the nature of the site. Thus, by approximately A.D. 500 and the formation of the Yamato state, many of the components that would be used in later gardens were already established: canals for carrying water, ponds, mounds built up in association with water, and stones and statues integrated with the other elements. These components were then co-opted, under the influence of Chinese garden building, to create the landscapes that expressed Taoist and Buddhist visions in the tradition we now understand to be "Japanese" gardening.

By the late sixth century entries in the *Nihongi* indicate that full-size hunting parks were being built for the imperial family, and that these had taken on the role of recreational landscapes on the Chinese model. At the same time, this period also marks the introduction of Buddhist images and artifacts into Japan via Korea. One particularly important form of Buddhist image introduced at this time was the *Shumisen-seki*, stone models of Mt. Sumeru, which became the central theme around which the mountain and water landscapes were to develop.

One of these stone "landscapes" was dug up in 1902 in Asuka (Nara Prefecture) and is described in detail by Irmtraud Schaarschmidt-Richter. It consisted of "three pieces of carved stone set on top of each other, covered with sculptured motifs . . . on the middle stone silhouettes of tiers of mountains in sculptured relief can be seen . . . very similar to the depiction of hills on grey clay tiles from the Korean Kingdom of Paekche dating from the seventh century. The bottom stone also carries landscape motifs, while the upper stone is rounded and decorated and has an aperture. All three stones are hollowed out like pipes. It must have been filled with water and worked like a spring."[1]

The *Shumisen* is in fact a very interesting artifact since the next *Nihongi* entry of interest in this context comes in Empress Suiko's reign and tells us that "this year [A.D. 612] a man emigrated from Paekche," and it turns out that he had "a small talent" for making "the figures of hills and mountains . . . Accordingly he was made to draw the figures of Mt. Sumi [Mt. Sumeru] and of the Bridge of Wu . . . The people called him Michikono Takumi."[2] It is not clear from this description whether he built a *Shumisen-seki* as described above, or whether he actually built an earth hill, dug a pond, and built a bridge. Either could have been possible since there are records, on the one hand, that a *Shumisen-seki* was erected for the empress in 613, and, on the other hand, that her "Southern Garden" contained a *Shumisen* and a bridge, suggesting that a real landscape was created. Either way, it seems clear that gardens in the full sense of the word were being created at this time and that these were seen as models or "figures" of "mountains and water" that illustrated important aspects of Buddhist cosmology. Interestingly enough, it should be noted that it was a Korean who was used to create this landscape, early confirmation of the tradition in Japan that it was "outsiders" or *kawaramono* people who were delegated to deal with the dead or to work with the things of the spirit world. In earlier times these were the people who had built the landscapes around the *kofun* tombs, and now, even though these were part of the new Buddhist cosmology, these were the people who were to build the new style "gardens." It was a tradition that continued right through Soseki's time and beyond.

While these models of mountains and water were being built for the imperial household, it did not take long for those noblemen who surrounded the court in the early capital at Asuka, and who had sufficient finances and authority, also to show an interest in this new phenomenon. One such was Soga-no-Umako, one of the few people in a position to follow the imperial example. It is recorded in the *Nihongi* in an entry dated A.D. 626 that he "had a small pond dug in a courtyard of his house, and there was a little island in the middle of the pond."[3] Whatever the exact details of the garden, it must have been a considerable undertaking and was unusual enough to earn Soga-no-Umako the nickname of "princeling of islands." This name is interesting for us because although the word *niwa* was used to describe open spaces other than those used for agriculture, it appears that at this time the word *shima*, or island, was currently being used to describe this specific kind of landscaped garden; "island" in this sense was any small mound built up in a flat place.[4] Thus, the change in wording reflects the changing perception of what a garden was, focusing now on what the space contained rather than on the "space" itself.

The court and aristocracy continued to enhance their palaces and villas around Asuka with increasingly elaborate "models" of mountains, ponds, streams, bridges, and pavilions. From the language used to describe them we can be pretty sure that these mountains were "piled-up" in much the same way as those in China and that the Japanese had not yet started to develop their own styles. A description of one of these Asuka era gardens, following excavations by Osamu Mori, indicates that, although increasingly elaborate, these early gardens were still very much in a beginning phase with few of the aesthetic sensibilities we normally associate with Japanese gardens.[5] A photograph of Mori's excavation of a very early pool at the site of the Charuda Palace near Asuka shows a small pool, approximately three meters by two, with a gently winding, shallow ditch running from one side. Both pool and ditch are lined with carefully installed flat rocks to prevent erosion, placed upright along the edges and laid flat to cover the sloping bottoms. From what remains, at least, there is no indication of any creative or artistic placement of rocks or of any artistic style that had begun to emerge; one could well be looking at a drainage or irrigation system.

With the establishment of the capital at Nara in A.D. 672, however, while the Japanese created public and private buildings under the influence of the Chinese urban architectural system, important differences also emerged, particularly in the treatment of the landscape around these buildings. While they did adopt the Chinese use of gravel to cover the ground immediately between buildings such as temples and shrines, they seem to have embraced rather than shunned the wider setting of these and domestic complexes. Instead of altering the forests or fields that fell within the views of the windows or verandas, or attempting to shut them out, as the Chinese tended to do, with high, solid walls, they were content to see them for what they were, content to let them, as much as the buildings, form the setting for their everyday lives. This seems to reflect their longstanding comfort with the landscape around them and their ancient and unthreatening relationship with the forces of the natural world, an attitude that was to be the determining factor as to how their landscape art developed.

Within this framework, Mori's excavations at Nara and his descriptions of the remains of the garden show developments that reflect a growing concentration on the art and details of the rockwork around them rather than the water features themselves. While the same careful attention to edging and lining the ponds and streams seems to continue, once garden building in Nara began in earnest important changes become noticeable. Mori's description of his excavation of the To'in garden at the Heijō Palace provides a good example of this change in emphasis.[6] Here a shallow, irregularly shaped pond was discovered with both a pebble beach and a central island. A small ditch-shaped depression running into the pond appears to indicate the path of a meandering brook that was spanned by a small bridge, the foundations of which are still visible. In addition to these remarkable details, on a small mound at the edge of the pond there appears to be the remains of a rock arrangement, using rocks up to one and a half meters long. What remains of this arrangement is pretty chaotic, but it is definitely a grouping of natural, "found" rocks and not an elaborate piece of pond edging or a cut-stone assembly. This seems to indicate that right at the beginning of the eighth century the Japanese were "designing" landscapes that, while they may have been stylized, were nevertheless fully artistic, emphasizing aesthetic rather than functional qualities.

That this was the case is confirmed by two other discoveries at this site. First, the excavators found that the stream widened out at certain points to form small pools and that a series of small rock groups had been placed at intervals along the banks and around these pools. These groups of flat-topped rocks are particularly interesting because they had been positioned on bends in the stream and on the downstream sides of curves in the pool banks. They are clearly based on patterns suggested by the relationships of rock and water in a natural watercourse and indicate that the setting was designed to look like a natural stream. As such, they appear to mark the beginning of a conscious effort to develop gardens that featured natural layouts and rock groupings rather than architectural or symbolic ones. The second discovery was that Mori's team was able to determine that the pond and stream were laid out to conform with the existing topography of the site, the design fitted into the natural landscape rather than being imposed upon it. These may seem small enough matters, but they clearly indicate that during the first decade of the eighth century, and probably from a little earlier still, Japanese sensibilities were already causing them to break radically with the received traditions of Chinese garden design to create a unique style of their own. In A.D. 794 the court left Nara and, taking most of the aristocratic establishment with it, moved to the site that became Kyoto, initiating the Heian period (794–1185) and some major changes in the world of landscaping.

If the street plan of the new capital still followed the grid system used in Nara and borrowed from China, its siting on the floodplain of the Kamo River and the wide views that were available led to a radical change in style around this time for private buildings. This was particularly true for those of scholars, merchants, and aristocrats who could afford detached villas because the new style better reflected the Japanese climate and the way of life that began to emerge during these times. Known as the *shinden* (hall) style, these new houses were based on a main building connected by covered walkways to various auxiliary ones, a style that had its roots in the traditional Shintō shrines.

While the new site of the capital clearly influenced the development of the gardens, so too did the continuing introduction of new schools of Buddhism, the Tendai School being introduced in A.D. 805 by Saichō, the Shingon School following in 806 when Kūkai returned from China, and the Pure Land School introduced in the mid-twelfth century; in addition to the new teachings, with each one came a different cultural tradition, artistic approach, and set of images. For the development of gardens, perhaps the most important of these new influences was the Shingon concept of the mandala, which provided additional dimensions to the idea of space. The Chinese convention of raising standing stones actually went all the way back to an Indian tradition where references to the "stones of both worlds" meant the worlds of the Diamond and the Womb mandalas. Raising stones was a technique for "fixing space" in the landscape in the same way as a mandala fixed space in a diagrammatic painting (see ch. 2). It was seen as an extension of the same process. This meant that the raising of standing stones became a means of laying out a landscape that had psychological as well as physical dimensions. Once these boundaries of the space had been established, marking the area within as one of special meaning, then any garden components placed within it—rocks, paths, pools, plants, and so on—were charged with Buddhist associations and meaning, based mainly on images taken from Buddhist and Taoist mythology.

A third factor then arose, one that hastened the move toward a distinctly Japanese form of landscaping, and this was the emergence during this period of new groups of people, mostly amateurs in the sense that they also had other jobs or callings, who were interested in garden building and who began to establish a new relationship with existing professional garden designers. An important part of this new group were the aristocrats and noblemen who had the means and leisure to build extensive new *shinden* style residences and to then oversee the creation of their landscape setting. These gardens, viewed either from various rooms or verandas or from boats on the lakes, became the elaborate backdrops for the cultivated life of the new capital: a life of entertaining and participation with one's friends in the art of poetry, conversation, and appreciation of the refinements of the garden.

Alongside these people there also emerged a number of semiprofessional priest gardeners, known as *ishitate-sō* or "monks who arrange rocks,"[7] whose particular aptitudes meant that as part of their daily round of prayer, meditation, and work, they were singled out to create the landscapes within the temple precincts. Their numbers included a few professional painters who were called upon to use their knowledge of the content, use of perspective, and the layouts of Chinese painting to create gardens that reflected the mainland traditions. Whatever their exact status, noblemen, priests, or artists, Kawase indicates that contemporary records tell us that by this time there were a number of different people, perhaps experts, in charge of different aspects of garden construction: those who erected standing stones, those who built waterfalls, and so on. It had become a sophisticated business.[8]

On the other hand, working in partnership with these new groups of designers, those who seemed to make it all happen were the professional garden builders drawn from the ranks of the *kawaramono* people. We have already noted in this chapter that the people used to create the early landscapes were Korean immigrants, and they were just some of those who became part of the large "untouchable" class known as the *kawaramono* or "river thing." This name refers to the fact that they lived a precarious existence along the riverbanks, places prone to floods and erosion that were avoided by others, in ghettos that were considered to be outside government jurisdiction. This "class" of people has existed throughout the historic period and, although it was abolished, officially at least, in 1868, those who were part of it still very much exist and live in discernible communities. Living apart, they never intermarried or mixed socially with the Japanese, and generally did the jobs that others would not touch or that were considered unsuitable for genteel people. Thus the *kawaramono* included everyone from entertainers and singers to sewage collectors, but the most important jobs were those considered "impure" through their connection with death. These jobs included butchery and leather working, executions, burying the dead, both people and animals, and cemetery watchmen to name a few. This connection with death, however, rather than simply relegating them to a menial subclass, also gave them a unique and potent status, since their dealings with the spirit world in the course of much of this work placed them on a par with aspects of the roles played by priests, monks, and shamen. In spite of their position outside society, this status meant they played a crucial role in the development and construction of the medieval gardens.

Aston believes that it is people from the *kawaramono* who are being referred to in the following passage from the *Nihongi:* "and so he added his name to the misasagi [*Kofun*] guardians." Each tomb was known to have at least five of these guardians, individuals who were seen as being in the service of the dead.[9] These aspects of their work are reflected in another name given to them, that of *hi-nin*, or "non" or "spirit" people. This carries the implication that because they were in the service of the dead and worked, as it were, in the other world, they were not quite human. There is a sense of "untouchableness," of separation from them, because they were spiritually charged, that is, so involved in the sacred mysteries that they should not mingle with "normal" people.

In these ways the background of those people put them in a unique position to influence and, to some degree, control the development of garden building since their traditional role as intermediaries with the spirit world through constructing and landscaping the tombs gave them an unusual authority in these matters. Further, their access to the riverbeds near their homes enabled them to choose, collect, and supply the prized water-worn rocks that became the key materials for the emerging designs. Certainly by the Heian period trading in rocks had become an important business, and those who conducted it became sought after and, sometimes, wealthy. An indication of just how important these people became is provided by the discovery at Ryōanji, the famous gravel and rock garden built in 1499, of the names of "the riverbed workmen" Kotaro and Seijiro carved on the back of one of the fifteen rocks. For this to have happened indicates that these were clearly not simply workmen but people with some authority and standing.

These, then, were the people who provided the muscle, the expertise, and the materials for landscaping projects. They were the expert families who had made a living, sometimes for several generations, taking on the landscaping of "untouchable" sites such as the imperial tombs, graveyards, and the sacred precincts of temples and shrines. These were the experts who knew how to fill in or clean out Kyoto's swampy landscape, survey new garden sites, lay out, dig, and line new ponds and streambeds; who could find, transport, and set up the rocks needed for the "piled-up" arrangements; who found or made the stone bowls, lanterns, and statuary, built the *stupa*, and all the other components that complemented these rocks; and who provided the plants, labor, management, and tools to create the gardens, whether they did the designing themselves or worked with others. But they were much more than simply "landscape contractors" as we understand that profession today; they were more than skilled managers, artisans, and laborers, since their presence on a garden site removed it from the everyday, secular world and gave it the other-worldly dimension that, even today in some places, is part of the special experience of Japanese gardens.

Remains of the gardens built during the Heian period by these partnerships are few and far between, and where possible examples do exist, they are notoriously hard to date. At the Kyoto Imperial Palace and at Rokujo-kawara-no-in, off Kyoto's Kawaramachi Street, there are fragments of gardens that are thought to be parts of Heian originals, but more useful for us are the firmly dated remains at Ōsawa Pond and the Byōdō-in at Uji, on the western and southern outskirts of Kyoto, respectively, and at Mōtsuji in Yamagata Prefecture. Taken together these three give us a very interesting glimpse of the makeup of the Heian pond garden. Ōsawa Pond represents the remains of the emperor Saga's country estate, built during his reign 809–23, and a considerable pond can still be seen today. It lies now beside a busy road and has densely overgrown, reedy shores, but one islet of rocks still breaks the water. Evidently this was once part of a chain of five islets, the others having collapsed and become submerged, but it is enough to make it still an evocative site on a summer evening when the traffic dies down and a degree of peace returns to it. Excavations of the site have confirmed the existence of the other islets and of one other particularly intriguing detail, the possible inclusion of a dry waterfall. One writer reports that excavation has found evidence of the "existence of a cascade built into the hillside on the north bank of the pond. It is believed to have been built as a dry cascade, the style used when there was no source of flowing water. Until this example was discovered it was not realized that Japan used this technique so early."[10]

More extensive, however, are the remains of the garden at Mōtsuji.

Here the components of a very large Heian pond garden can be seen, with most of the pond and some of the rock placements still intact. Built by the powerful Fujiwara family within the area of their rural power base, the garden must have rivaled anything built in Kyoto at the time and doubtless survived because of its very distance from the capital. Photographs of the garden clearly show the "island" stones out in the water and a number of other rocks forming small promontories and other details along the shoreline. Those out in the pond stand upright following the traditional Chinese style of the Islands of the Immortals, while others along the shore have been laid down and grouped in a more "naturalistic" style, giving us a strong indication of the combination of styles, both those imported and those developed in Japan, that formed the basis of many of these early gardens. The other firmly dated garden from this period is that of the Byōdō-in, completed originally in 1053. Built, again, for the Fujiwara family, it was an outstanding example of the Chinese style Paradise garden, a gorgeous palace set among a carefully designed pond garden, a place for the family to rejoice in the splendors of their earthly achievements and to ponder immortality spent in a heavenly paradise such as this. The buildings one can see today are careful reproductions, fire having claimed the originals, but the pond garden is thought to be essentially undisturbed, and together they represent a vision of paradise taken directly from Buddhist art from China.

Between 850–1150, however, Japan's borders were closed. No travel in or out was allowed, and the flow of new ideas stopped, eventually causing a kind of stagnation of ideas to set in. Perhaps illustrative of what happened to garden design during the long years of isolation is the story of the *Sakutei-ki*, or "Notes on Garden Making," compiled and published by Tachibana Toshitsuna in the mid-eleventh century, and its subsequent elevation to the role of being the definitive guide to Japanese landscaping techniques. Tachibana and his father turned to garden design out of frustration at not being able to find good designers for their Kyoto estates. His father pinpointed the problems of contemporary design work, as he saw it, as follows. "Following what I have heard from tradition, you just put the rock in; there is nothing to tell you what is a good or bad setting," and he goes on, "in fact, recently no one knows about these things in detail, they simply copy what has already been done."[11] In short, at this time the Japanese were running into the "artistic" problem. Rocks were "put in" in a certain way in accordance with the traditions of the type-forms, the correctness of the setting being taken for granted. But here the guidance ran out, and the designers and clients had evidently lost the ability to make aesthetic judgments for themselves.

At a time when few seemed to understand the processes of truly creative art, the Tachibana family took matters into their own hands. The *Sakutei-ki* was the result of their determined exploration of the "art" of garden design, a distillation of their experiences and the types of form they came up with in response to their artistic sensibilities. Like the *Yuan Yeh* (Craft of Gardens) published in China in 1631, the *Sakutei-ki* relies on a standardization of garden features. To produce these "correct" landscapes it lists the various type-forms, identified as representations of different natural conditions in the Japanese landscape, with which the overall design should be built up: pond forms, stream forms, shoreline and rock forms, waterfalls, bridges, and hills. Everything was covered. These basic forms were then to be assembled in certain "styles" or expressions, based on the various categories of calligraphy: *shin* (true or honest), *sō* (grass), and *gyō* (running). In the end, the ideas the Tachibanas came up with to provide the traditions of landscaping with standards of aesthetic value to complement the practical advice became intellectual conventions as moribund as those they sought to invigorate, having more to do with discussing gardens than making them. As one writer has put it, "The classifications *shin*, *sō*, and *gyō* types . . . still haunt writers on Japanese garden subjects, although the garden makers themselves never seem to have paid much attention to them."[12]

By 1150, however, the situation in Japan began to change as pressures within the country made it inevitable that the borders should be opened again and trading relations reestablished with the mainland. Once this happened the vice-like grip of the Heian era was inexorably released as new influences and ideas began to flow in from Song China. Japan's creative imagination started to come back to life, spurred on by all this activity and in particular by the influential artistic cultures of Pure Land and, later, Zen Buddhism.

Introduced in 1175 by Hōnen Shonin, the Pure Land sect was to become as popular in Japan as it had been in China, and its clear images of Amida's Pure Land, into which believers were to be reborn, were to provide the existing paradise garden designs with invigorating new ideas. There were important differences in atmosphere and mood between the Heian paradise gardens and those that began to be built in response to these new ideas. While the earlier gardens, such as the Byōdō-in, had emphasized a bright, rich paradise, full of a worldly brilliance that reflected the style and grandeur of the imperial palaces and pavilions, the Pure Land school was subtler, more complex, and mature, reflecting the character of its founder, Hui Yüan (336–416), who had lived during the introspective years of the Eastern Chin dynasty. Living in his "Eastern Forest" monastery on Mt. Lu, his emphasis on a quiet life of meditation was extremely influential. His biography contains passages that were to stir the imaginations not only of

Chinese writers and artists but also of the Japanese garden designers hundreds of years later when they were finally exposed to them: "Inside the monastery grounds Hui Yüan developed a special grove for meditation. The mist condensed on the trees and dripped onto the paths, which were covered in moss. Every spot . . . was full of spiritual purity and majesty."[13] An invocation of atmosphere such as this, relating directly to both the physical and psychological mood of a landscape, fitted in exactly with their sense of place and their reaction to it. Drawing on their intuitive connection with the kind of place described here, the Japanese began to produce paradise gardens that were more natural and less stylistically by the book. This new approach led to a more naturalistic use of rocks and garden designs that reflected Hui Yüan's places "full of spiritual purity and majesty" rather than the technical correctness of the gardening texts.

Some twenty years after Hōnen Shonin, Eisai arrived back from his studies in China ready to establish the first Zen temple. As we have seen, introducing Zen to a wide audience was not to be an altogether straightforward process, and it was not until the Hōjō regents established their capital in Kamakura and began welcoming Chinese monks that Zen really began to make itself felt and Japanese cultural traditions began to respond to the full impact of the Song Zen culture. Both traditions were altered and invigorated by the interaction that occurred, and it was not long before the gardens of the Kamakura period (1185–1392) began to reflect a markedly new approach. The Chinese monks brought with them the Song style of "standing stones," or *sen-seki*, itself a crisp, clear refinement of older Chinese rock styles that emphasized the illusory compositional possibilities of two or three rocks rather than the "piled-up" artificial "mountains" or the symbolic features of individual rocks. On arriving in Japan, and influenced in turn by Japanese sensibilities, the Chinese began to set their rocks in increasingly natural settings that were linked to longer views and to the wider landscape setting and that began to lose much of the stylization that is so marked in the mainland originals. The garden at Tenryūji is an outstanding example of the eventual refinement of this integration of styles and is perhaps the only one that has survived sufficiently intact for us to appreciate what a rich and extraordinary artistic achievement it was.

If Tenryūji, renovated and added to by Soseki in 1339, marks a culmination of this fusion, its beginnings can be found at Tōkoji in Yamanashi. This temple garden built for Hōjō Tokiyori by Rankei Dōryū still contains the remains of the original stone garden, one of the earliest built by a Chinese Zen monk.[14] Rankei (1213–78) had been invited over to Japan by Tokiyori in 1246, and the garden at Tōkoji is one of the first that he built. Although some of the settings have been destroyed by the growth of trees on the site and by much neglect, the rest of the layout is only slightly damaged, and the overall scheme of temple and garden remains clear. The layout is based on three stages that step down from the mountain behind the temple. With the mountain as the first step, the temple sits on the second step with its back to the mountainside and looks down over the garden that slopes away in front of it. Immediately below this, a pond occupies the third and lowest level. It was on the second level, between the temple and the pond, that Kawase found what is left of the stone garden. Several groups of standing stones remain there, created in a style that he describes as "free and daring," and reflecting the refreshing and dynamic new style that Rankei had brought with him from China. Of equal interest, however, is the fact that instead of building this garden in the enclosed courtyard style of the mainland tradition, Rankei placed this out in the landscape, making use of the existing topography of the temple site and producing a garden that was recognizably Japanese rather than Chinese. This was one of the vital new beginnings that were made possible by the decision to reopen the country's borders.

It appears that Rankei was also responsible for the equally innovative rock arrangements that include the *Ryūmon no Take*, or "Dragon Gate Falls," at Tenryūji, built while he was staying there between 1261 and 1264. Adding to an already existing pond garden, Rankei placed his rock groups on the far pond bank using the slope provided by material piled up from the pond building. The waterfall itself consists of seven main rocks: a lower group of three, in which the large vertical rock of the fall is flanked by two "guest" peaks; a central group of three, halfway up the slope and marking the course of the water down from the peak above; which, in turn, is marked by a large triangular shaped rock that sits on the crest of the slope. In the water, a lovely group of four or five rocks forms an island composition, its largest rock forming a rising spire above the water, while a bridge composition forms three low spans across the outflow of the fall. The falls take their name from an old Chinese story concerning a king of the semilegendary Hsia Dynasty (ca. 2000 B.C.), which is recounted in the seventeenth-century Japanese anthology the *Zenrin-Kushu* as follows: "In ancient times King Yu of the Hsia Dynasty cut a three-tiered sluice through the Lung-men mountains on the border between Shensi and Shansi provinces to open up a passage for the Yellow River. This was known as the Gate of Yu or the Dragon Gate. There is an old legend that on the third day of the third month, when the peach trees are in flower, vigorous carp that could scale this three-tiered waterfall would become dragons and rise into the sky."[15] In the Zen context this story and the falls became associated with the difficulties of following the Way and achieving enlightenment. The garden acted as a focal point for contemplation for those seated on the veranda of the Hōjō looking across the pond. Interestingly, the site at Tenryūji is, like that at Tōkoji, very much defined by the surrounding mountains, and, like the earlier site, this places the Chinese rockwork firmly in a Japanese context. This was to be very much the pattern of development over the next few decades as Song Zen became increasingly integrated with its new surroundings.

No doubt numerous other gardens built in and around Kamakura and Kyoto (now lost) form the immediate background against which Soseki's garden building developed. However, to understand the form and content of the gardens he started to build after 1313, we need to go back and follow his search for experience and understanding in the landscapes in which he was brought up, through which he later repeatedly traveled, and from which he developed the gardens.

We have already seen that he was born in the mountainous terrain of Mei Prefecture and, after the age of three, was brought up on the Kofu Plain in Yamanashi Prefecture, which was surrounded by the sharply defined mountain ranges over which, to the south, rose the snowcapped cone of Mt. Fuji, and, to the north, the peak of Mt. Gentoku. During the years he then spent at Heienji, between 1284 and 1292, his life became thoroughly immersed in this landscape, and the temple became the base from which he set out on trips into the foothills of Mt. Gentoku. He opened himself up to the full influence of the shapes and forms of this world and firmly grounded his practice of Buddhism in it. In addition to this, the site of Heienji itself was the first in a long line of places in which he stayed where there was a strong association between the temple, and the landscape around it, and the spirit world of the ancestors. These were places where his immediate environment was intimately shared with another dimension of existence that lay just beyond the immediate reality of his everyday life. The temple itself was dedicated to the ancestors of the local Takeda family, and the grounds contained numerous Takeda graves. The mounds, grave stones, and other markers were all integrated into the surrounding landscape, and, perhaps most importantly, one of these graves seems to have been that of his mother, making his relationship to the place a very direct and personal one.

Following his stay at Heienji, Soseki spent the next five or six years at a number of Zen temples both in Kyoto and Kamakura. At those in Kamakura in particular, which were mostly built by Chinese Zen masters, he would have been exposed to the very latest ideas from China concerning temple architecture and garden building, and especially to the way in which the Chinese Zen masters "saw" the illusory world that was revealed to the Awakened Eye. When enlightenment finally came to him in 1305, he had also undertaken his two journeys to the north, during the course of which he had been exposed to a wide range of new experiences of landscape. Most importantly, he had experienced the garden designed by his teacher Bukkoku Zenji at Unganji, a place that was to prove a seminal influence on how he developed his own relationship with the natural world.

During the first trip, 1300–1301, he traveled widely through present-day Fukushima, Miyagi, Iwate, and Yamagata Prefectures and visited areas known both for their natural beauty and for their associations with the practices of the *yamabushi* priests. He made a point of visiting the coastal landscape at Matsushima, which consists of some 260 pine-covered rocky islands and chains of islets, the tuffs and sandstones eroded into wonderful shapes topped by twisted, wind-battered trees. Many of the islands have caves that have been used as hermitages from ancient times. The seventeenth-century poet Bashō, on his long trek through the "deep north," described the scene at Matsushima as follows: "All sorts of islands gathered here, steep ones pointing to the sky, others creeping upon the waves. Or some piled double on each other, or even triple, and some divided at one end and overlapping at the other. Some bear others on their backs; some seem to embrace them, as if caressing their offspring. Green of the pines deep, needles and branches mauled by the salt winds—though contorted by nature—look artificially trained. The feeling: one of intense beauty . . . who with brush or speech can hope to describe the work of heaven and the earth's divinity?"[16] No doubt Soseki found this place equally inspiring and learned, from the quality of unreality that it seems to have possessed, something of the illusionary reality that is seen by the Awakened Eye.

After touring the far north, Soseki eventually made his way back down via the Ōkita River valley to Unganji, where he hoped to meet Bukkoku. He had clearly felt drawn back to the Ōkita River, as he had been to the Fuefuki River when younger, but now it was for another reason; this time he was searching for something slightly different. Unlike the Fuefuki, a big, severe crashing river with a large watershed, its big tumbled rocks showing the effects of powerful spring runoff and winter storms, the Ōkita was smaller and more delicate, its rounded river rocks having a worn rather than pounded feel, as it fell over a series of secluded "flying falls." Kawase notes that the area has a very pronounced mountain valley feel as the river tumbles down through the forests and out onto the plain below, and Soseki may well have been drawn by this detailed intimacy which was in sharp contrast to the wider landscapes that he had seen in the far north along the Kitagawa River. During his visit to Uchi-no-kusa, Soseki spent time at Usuba, an open site on a gently sloping mountainside above which were a number of caves that had been used for burials and by hermits in ancient times. Tradition has it that he used some of these caves for meditation during this time, and from the mouth of one of them, where there is also a *stupa* dedicated to him, the surrounding hills frame a view of the Pacific Ocean. This is exactly the kind of spot to which he was increasingly drawn, where a wide view opened up in front of him. He spent about a year in these surroundings before heading back to Kamakura. It was, of course, on this return journey in 1305 that he experienced enlightenment one evening in Jōshu, the months he spent in the Usuba clearly having had a lasting effect on him.

Following his enlightenment and a brief period spent in Kamakura with Bukkoku, Soseki soon set out again on his travels, this time heading back to the Kofu Plain where he had been brought up, for the first time in some thirteen years. He stayed initially at Heienji once more, and then, moving up into the foothills of Mt. Gentoku, he founded Jōkyoji, where he stayed between 1309–11. Although only a few, mostly ruinous, buildings remain, the nameplate for the temple survives, and, written in Soseki's calligraphy, it reads, "Great Waterfall Mountain."

On his visit to Jōkyoji, having explored the area around the temple buildings, Kawase set off up the mountain and recorded the setting above the temple as follows: "Up a steep path behind the buildings a flat area opens up, surrounded by the hills on three sides but open on the fourth." From here there are very long, unrestricted views east across the wide plain below toward the mountains. From the temple itself, on the other hand, the view looks out across the steep valley below toward tightly intertwined mountain ridges that run right across the view, dividing it in half: sky above, mountains below, the view framed on either side by the enclosing forest. Clearly the temple site was picked for its interesting variety of views, which provided Soseki with a choice of places to sit, but the upper site seems to represent an interesting change in pattern. Up to now, when he has stayed anywhere for any length of time, he has chosen places to stay like the lower site, where the view is focused, closed in on the sides and open at the front, the situation that applied at Unganji and Usuba; the wide open views from the higher site were a new departure.

Adding further interest to the site at Jōkyoji is the small stream that tumbles down beside the path leading up from the temple. The water accompanies the path down the hill, appearing and disappearing among the fractured plates of rock, and, half way down, falls over a low tumble of broken rocks into two uneven streams, one slightly larger than the other, which Kawase labels the "male and female" falls. He believes that this was exactly the kind of place that Soseki was particularly drawn to and that he certainly would have "sat" there in front of the falls, as well as at those places that overlooked the different views.

Jōkyoji altogether represents an interesting and diverse place with grand uninterrupted views on the one hand and the intense, tiny details of the streambed and falls on the other. It provides us with some insight into Soseki's life in the hills. In addition, his choice of name for the temple "Great Waterfall Mountain" illustrates for us the process going on below the surface whereby the landscapes he lived among became at the same time a part of a parallel world, an illusory world in which things took on a significance and scale of their own unrelated to immediate "reality." Hence, as in the traditions of art, a small waterfall tumbling down the hillside becomes a "Great Waterfall," its importance as the focal point of meditative thought raising it in size and status. It became a part of the material removed from the context of its everyday existence and made available for artistic expression, as the mountains of the Miura Peninsula had been. Slowly, however, life at Jōkyoji became busier and busier and, in time, Soseki retreated with a few close disciples further up into the remote foothills around Mt. Gentoku, where he built a small hut, the Ryōzan-an, the "Dragon Mountain Hermitage," in which he stayed between 1311–13.

Discussing this period in the *Musō Nempu*, Soseki tells us that "in Kawaura on the Fuefuki River I went 30 *li* into the mountains. I came across interesting rocks in a mysterious place, and here I established a hermitage." It is interesting to note that he chose a place for the hermitage where the unusual rocks on the forested slopes of the mountain created a "mysterious" place, a place where the shapes or positions of the rocks among the steep terrain, the ancient trees, a moss- covered fallen log, or a combination of all these things took him out of the everyday and drew him into a frame of mind and consciousness that recognized this mysterious place as being part of the illusory world of Zen landscape. Equally, as far as one can tell, this place did not include either views over the wider landscape or water, whether a river gorge, tumbling stream, or pool. For the first time we can imagine Soseki sitting and looking out over a shaded landscape, with groups of rocks dotted between the twisting trunks of the old mountain trees, a few hardy shrubs and plants breaking up the ground. And over everything there was the moss, spreading out in front of him, smoothing out all the shapes and surfaces as the snow would in winter, and just as it would do some thirty years later at Saihōji as he looked out from his pavilion at the rocks of the Kō-inzan. His move to this remote place seems to have been successful since he was able to spend almost a year and a half in relative seclusion before large numbers of people discovered the hermitage and their huts started filling the forest around his. In the end the number of new arrivals destroyed the mystery of the place, and once again he left, slipping away at night, initially back to Jōkyoji, but then vanishing beyond Mt. Fuji.

The poems and stories from his time at the Ryōzan-an deal almost exclusively with the experience of the winters that settled around the huts, and rather than scrambling along darting mountain streambeds seeking waterfalls, or searching out places of long views, Soseki seems to have been content to concentrate on life at the hut, carrying out his daily chores, teaching, reciting texts, and meditating with his companions. Above all, he enjoyed sitting and watching the winter arrive and quietly occupy the landscape: the piles of blown leaves settling deeper in their tucked away places, the first brief, light frosts, "settling flowers of ice" as he called them, forming in the evening shadows and melting away as the sun found them next day, until one morning the weakened, withdrawing rays could only glance across the surface, bringing the frost to brief, sparkling life but unable to warm it. And then the snow started to fall, giving new shapes to the rocks around him, soundlessly folding all the details of the landscape into a smooth, unbroken carpet of frozen white light. On short walks in this transformed world not even his shadow was carried away down the mountain as he stepped across the frozen stream. He was adrift in an illusory place "with no family but the ice on the snow mountain."[17] Today, sadly, no traces are left of the Ryōzan-an, nor is there any way of identifying the "mysterious place" where it stood nor the "interesting rocks" it looked out over. All we know is that it was somewhere on the slopes of Mt. Gentoku along the upper reaches of the Fuefuki River.

After their stealthy departure from the Ryōzan-an and then Jōkyoji, Soseki and a core group of disciples headed south across the Kofu Plain and into the foothills around Mt. Fuji. As he later described it, they were "doing nothing" on this trip, but it is quite clear that throughout it they were actively seeking out new experiences of the landscape. Their journey crossing several mountain ranges into the immediate landscape around Mt. Fuji was for Soseki "like entering another realm, crossing a boundary into the place where the gods and the immortals live,"[18] and I think we should see this as an explicit description of the sense in which the right people at the right time could slip out of the everyday world and into the spiritual world beyond. In this new frame of mind they stopped off at West Lake, one of the five lakes that ring Mt. Fuji from the northwest to the northeast, engaging a fisherman to row them around "from inlet to inlet." Soseki's description of what happened next, which forms part of an answer in the *Muchū Mondō*, gives us a valuable insight into his new awareness of landscape: "One time I went with seven or eight monks to West Lake, at the foot of Mt. Fuji." He reports that the fisherman who rowed them around, having lived there all his life, became increasingly amazed at how excited they became on seeing the different views, "exclaiming and clapping the sides of the boat with their hands," and was unable to understand what they were so excited about. "We are admiring the beauty of this landscape, the views of this mountain and this lake," they told him, but he still did not understand. Soseki's comment on this situation is instructive and warrants quoting in full: "I said to the monks, 'If this old man asks us to explain to him what there is about this place that moves us, how can we tell him? If we point to the landscape of mountains and rivers and say to him that what moves us is just that, the old man will say that he has seen that for years and that there is nothing remarkable about it. On the other hand, if we try to change his mind by telling him that we are moved by something besides what he sees in front of him, he will think that what he sees is not what we care for at all, and that there is a further splendor beyond the West Lake.'"

There is not a "further splendor beyond the West Lake," but there is "something besides what he [or anyone] sees in front of him"; there is, in short, nothing other to be seen beyond the landscape in front of them, but the "something besides" is that landscape removed by the enlightened eye from its immediate context and placed within a personal, illusory vision, a removal that enables it to become more than simply the physical world in which we exist and part of our spiritual world as well, part of that place where our worlds meet and interact.

Between this incident on the lake and the eventual end of the journey at Eihōji, Soseki and his group visited a number of places, the most important of which seems to have been Dōgashima on the mountainous and picturesque Izu Peninsula. Here there is a temple that has records of Soseki having built a *muhoto* there, and a *zazen-seki* still stands by a thatched hall. When Kawase visited he located a place nearby, called the "retreat of Musō," where two waterfalls seem to have been the focal points of his meditation practice. At one of these, the "Waterfall of Melodies," a beautiful, streaming fall of water over the ledges and rounded shoulders of a steep, buttressed cliff, Soseki's hut was located looking back across the river as it turned at the foot of the fall. The other site, on a stream a little farther up the mountain, was located at what was the "White Thread Falls." Here Kawase reports that although there is no longer any flow over these rocks, you can see, above where the falls used to be, the remains of a small meditation cave. He also reports that "sitting in the mouth of the cave above the fall, you can look down into the river gorge below toward the 'Waterfall of Melodies.'" Clearly this was a very special site, very typical of the kind of place Soseki particularly liked, and one that Kawase believes he would have known about from his years in Kamakura. Unfortunately for the modern visitor, Kawase also reports that since the construction of a large hotel, views of the "Waterfall of Melodies" have been blocked, and the connection between the falls broken.

In addition to the huts or small temple that Soseki may have occupied at this inland site, he seems also to have founded a temple, now known as Ryōunji, on high ground above the inlet at Dōgashima, from which one can look down over the island of Awashima "floating" in the bay. If he did alternate between these two sites, it marks an interesting departure from his usual practice, one which shows him beginning to seek out the contrasting landscapes of mountain and water. Dōgashima, however, was only one of a number of stops their party made as they continued their leisurely journey, and soon they moved on, making their way toward Mino. Once there, Soseki went on to found Eihōji, and, after becoming once again overwhelmed by the arrivals of those seeking to become his students, he slipped away to the seclusion of Myōrakuji. When he was exploring the location of this temple, Kawase found a cave in the hillside some distance above the present-day temple that stands almost on the valley floor. Looking more closely at this site, he noticed an area below the cave where the hillside flattens out, creating an open space, and it is here that he believes Soseki's dwelling would have stood, a building that later became a temple. This seems to be confirmed by the fact that the site, bounded at the back by the mountain ridge, also contains a large rock, known as "Musō's *zazen-seki*" and the remains of what Kawase describes as a "carefully built wall" that still surrounds a spring close by. The setup is reminiscent of that at Unganji, with the mountains sweeping around the cave up behind the temple, while the wide views in front reminded Kawase of those at Jōkyoji.

It is clearly the kind of site Soseki had been consistently seeking out, sites that contained both a cave that provided a location for his meditative practice and a certain kind of framed view that provided the focal point. Putting the details of these views together, one starts to see a pattern emerge in the places where he chose to live. In the first place, they were all elevated above the middle distance and were carefully framed to focus on a distant landscape. This usually consisted of a ridge of mountains running across the skyline, close enough for the larger details to be visible but also far enough away to become a generalized, nonspecific overall shape. Above these distant ranges spread huge skies, broken only, in the earlier days in Kofu, by the snow-capped cone of Mt. Fuji, an image released from this world by the clouds that obscured its lower slopes. Interestingly, the views from both Jōkyoji and Myōrakuji focus on a section of the distant ridge that rises clear of the rest in a cap or dome that reminds one of Mt. Fuji, and the visible ridge lines below these fall away in a manner that suggests something of a mirror image of the shape above. Perhaps these formed reference or focal points for Soseki during meditation.

In the choice of these sites I think we are seeing the process by which Soseki slowly came to be able to perceive the physical world around him as part of the illusory world that his enlightened understanding recognized as the true nature of reality. He is consistently framing and composing the landscapes in front of him as one would a painting, using the low middle distance as a blank space to break immediate physical connections with the mountains in the distance, removing them from their "real" context and setting them up to be "played" in by the meditating consciousness. Thus, the mountains of Japan came to form as important a part in Soseki's consciousness of an illusory world beyond the immediate as the mountains of China, the landscapes of which the great Zen masters had roamed, and were thus able to increasingly take over as the location for his consciousness. If they were to mean anything, his gardens had to reflect his native landscape, not those of China that he had come to know through the writings, poems, and paintings that made up the body of Zen culture.

After Myōrakuji, Soseki moved on to a site now known as Tōkoji a little further round the hills surrounding the Kiso River. The buildings from that time are now gone, but a *zazen-seki* and a spring indicate the approximate location of his temple on the mountainside. The grounds of the temple stand in the foothills at the "entrance" to the Hida mountain range, above the valley of the Hida River as it flows out of the surrounding heights and down to join the Kiso River flowing toward Gifu and Nagoya. Also associated with the site are two shrines attributed to Soseki that he dedicated to local Shintō deities. Kawase feels that vague references to exile in a poem written about Tōkoji suggest that this was where Soseki spent the bulk of his time after leaving Eihōji, since it was both higher and more remote than Myōrakuji, and thus offered more interesting views and a better chance of providing Soseki with peace and privacy.

When he investigated the site at Tōkoji, Kawase noticed that a flat area beside the still flowing, but silted up, spring was in the sun all day, and he suggested that this may well have been the site of Soseki's hut. Walking up the steep path behind this through the dense forest of pine trees and shrubs, Kawase eventually came to the cliffs crowning the ridge, and on top of these he found a spot with exceptional, panoramic views that reminded him strongly of those from the top of Mt. Gentoku. This he believes is the spot where Soseki would have sat, looking out over a view "toward the Hida River as it flows toward Gifu and out across the plains of Mino to the mountains of Ise and Suzuka in the far distance." After climbing there on a cold day of "blown snow" in mid-February, Kawase, in some of his most evocative phrases, describes the mountains as "spreading away in overlapping, rounded triangles," opening up like a folding screen. He notes: "In spite of the exposure of the place, I found myself lost in contemplation of the silent deeps."[19] One has a particularly strong sense here of Soseki choosing sites where his place of meditation could act as a bridging point for him to cross between his physical location and the illusory, spiritual world beyond, places where he could "gaze into nature."

Clearly Soseki's time at Tōkoji produced results since by the time he was ready to move on, his contemplation of nature took a dramatic turn. Leaving the world of the mountains, he started a period of practice centered on water, both rivers and the sea, which was to last for the next six years. His next stop, at Shōrinji, marks the beginning of this phase, and this temple was situated not in the mountains but rather down beside the Kiso River as it wound across its wide floodplain. A slight rise close to the riverbank, covered now in pine trees, marks the spot where Soseki's hut stood, and, apart from ensuring that the hut was not subject to seasonal flooding, this position also opened up the views sufficiently for him to see wide views across the river and out over the plain, out toward the distant mountains. Kawase reports that the site is close to where the Kiso River emerges from the mountains to flow out across the Mino Plain, and he notes that the waters of the river are still fresh, very cold and energized from their descent through the steep valleys. This, plus the unusually wide views, make it in his opinion a particularly unique and unusual place.

When Kawase found the site he was struck by just how long the views were for such a low-lying place, and he noticed in particular that, even though they appeared at some distance, the low-lying mountain range following the far side of the river plain had a very detailed outline, a finely drawn saw blade of numerous small peaks. This consistent dark band forms part of a horizontal layered pattern that stretches away from the viewer: the long foreground shore of the river; the flow of the river itself, which in Soseki's day, still free from the concrete flood-control dykes, would have spread in broken channels across the plain; the far shore; the long low line of the mountains; and finally the big, broad skies. These stacked layers, compressed beneath the expanse of sky, alternating the details of shoreline, the movement of water, the details of the plain with its expanses of reeds and grasses nodding in the wind, the rising and falling lines of the serrated mountains, and the movement of the changing skies, were all in one view, were all distinct yet deeply interconnected. Laid out before the viewer was the full range of those polarities between which the dynamic energies flow and the places where the processes of their interaction animate Life in the physical world. Here the hard rock of the mountains lay in compressed contact with the flows of water, weather, and wind in the river, skies, and bending reed beds, and the results of all this erosive interaction were laid out in the fine sands and pebbles of the shoreline. It is a place where one can watch Process at work in the potent crucible defined by the point where the mountains and waters meet.

After spending time in Tosa at the Kyūko-an and then traveling to

Kamakura, Soseki's next stop was down on the Miura Peninsula. Here at his new retreat, the Hakusen-an hermitage, he was able to pursue the contemplation of intersections between the mountains and waters as he had at Shōrinji and the Kyūko-an, but, this time, with one crucial difference. Unable to leave the world and live a hermit's life in the mountains, he settled on the outskirts of the fishing communities of Yokosuka and began a process, which we can follow in the poems that he wrote, by which he was to internalize his surroundings through meditation and transfer them from the immediate world into an illusory one. His intent was to be a part of the other realm without leaving this one, as the old Chinese hermits had done with their idea of "distant mind." Alongside this, the poems that he wrote at the time also help us follow how he came to define his place in this illusory, intuitive world. In one he wrote,

> The vast expanse of sky
>   becomes the roof of my hut
> I make the mountains my thatch
>   and the sea my garden . . .

while in another he tells us,

> I have gathered the infinite worlds
>   and made them my hut.
> There are none save me alone
>   in all directions above and below
> Yet the essential spirit is present
>   and all that is sacred is here.[20]

With the phrases "vast expanse of sky" and "the infinite worlds," Soseki is explaining to us how he "sees" the location of his existence here; far from being a monk sitting in a small hut, he perceives an "essential spirit" set loose from the conventional world into the limitless, undifferentiated spaces of enlightened understanding. The hut is an illusion; it has become a contact point as much in "another realm," and this is why it is so pointless for people to pursue him here seeking answers for their questions. There is nobody here, just the mountains and the sea. Lines from three other poems help to fill this picture in,

> I don't go out
> to wander around
> I stay home here in Miura
> while time flows
> on through

the unbounded world
In the awakened eye
mountains and rivers
completely disappear . . .

Cradled on the breast of this mountain
I have forgotten
    its original wildness...
    a quail's nest is where I live
    here by the sea
It's all so cramped and huddled . . .
    and yet a simple bubble
    contains the whole
    limitless sky.[21]

Thus, stringing these images together, a sense of reality as Soseki saw it emerges: "In the awakened eye, mountains and rivers disappear," that is to say, the conventional images of what is "real" and the poet's conventional relationship to these disappear. In place of the image of the hut set in the wider landscape of the mountains, with all the detail that one would expect in this setting, something else has been identified. Soseki sees himself "cradled in the breast of this mountain" overlooking the sea, in that exact spot, the size of "a quail's nest," cramped into the point where the vertical and horizontal meet, his back to the mountains looking out over the sea, where life on the islands took root and from which his consciousness stems. This is not a place for those tied to the materialism of the physical world but one where, for the right person, "a single bubble contains the whole limitless sky."

The images in these poems can be seen almost as blueprints for the gardens he was to build. They represent an explanation of how he saw the components he used in the gardens and, equally important, of how we should approach them if we are to understand them—like the hut at Hakusen-an, we must see them as elements of the unbounded and limitless worlds. The atmosphere surrounding his life at Hakusen-an reduced the "real" world to a shifting mirage of glimpsed views, the undefined mass and textures of ocean, clouds, mist, and haze, the ephemeral "reality" of a sand beach drying as the tide steadily recedes. This is the key shift in consciousness that he had been able to make during his years of traveling and which we must try to make if we are to follow.

With the exception of Eihōji, where he had built a garden as early as 1314, it was only after his departure from the Taiko-an in 1325, at the age of fifty, that Soseki began building the series of gardens for which he became so well known. The first of these followed two years later in 1327 when he set about converting the grounds at Zuisenji to create a garden that expressed his new understanding of landscape. To get a clear picture of all this, however, of how this understanding had changed and developed in the intervening ten or so years, we need first to go back and look in more detail at what he created at Eihōji.

It was in 1313 that Soseki initially founded the Kokei temple, now known as Eihōji, in Nagase. The area is now a part of Tajimi City, yet to this day the site, tucked among the cliffs beside the Tōki River as it flows through its gorge below Mt. Nagase, manages to retain some of the sense of isolation that attracted him to it. In an introduction to one of his poems of the time, he notes with some satisfaction: "When I lived in the middle of the mountains at Kokei in Mino, there was not a single well-defined path."

As we have already seen, Soseki seems to have immediately felt that there was an especial affinity between this place and the settings of many of the old stories of Zen hermits in T'ang China, and in particular to "Tiger Mountain" (Kokei in Japanese), one of the peaks of Mt. Lu in Kiang-si. This mountain range had been home to a number of well-known monks, including Hui-yüan, the founder and first Patriarch of the Pure Land School, whose "Eastern Forest" monastery on the mountain included the serene, mist-shrouded and moss-covered meditation grove described earlier in this chapter. Soseki originally called the site Kokei (Old Deep Mountain Valley) but soon changed the *Ko* character to read Tiger, giving it the name Tiger Deep Mountain Valley, and associating it with the deep mountain gorges of Mt. Lu and, therefore, with the characters and tales that were associated with the place. All this makes the site particularly interesting since it was here that he went on to build one of his first major gardens.

Running down to and along the river for a short distance, the lane down from the village ends at the temple gates. Most of the present temple buildings date from a restoration project in the nineteenth century, and, once inside the gates, the path at first leads between these more recent structures. Past these, the grounds and buildings of Soseki's time open up, spread across the area between the river on the left and the cliff on the right. The cliff face drops straight down into the water of the "Sleeping Dragon Pond," which occupies most of the area in front of it. Toward the far side a wooded island breaks up the pond, creating a complex edge that contrasts strongly with the clean sweep of the cliff behind. Beyond the far shore, the tree-covered, tumbled landscape obscures the line of cliffs until they run out into the gorge where, away to the left, the river can be seen as it chops and swirls its way round the bend and out of sight.

When looking over this scene, however, these details form only a background impression because a graceful, curving bridge that arches across

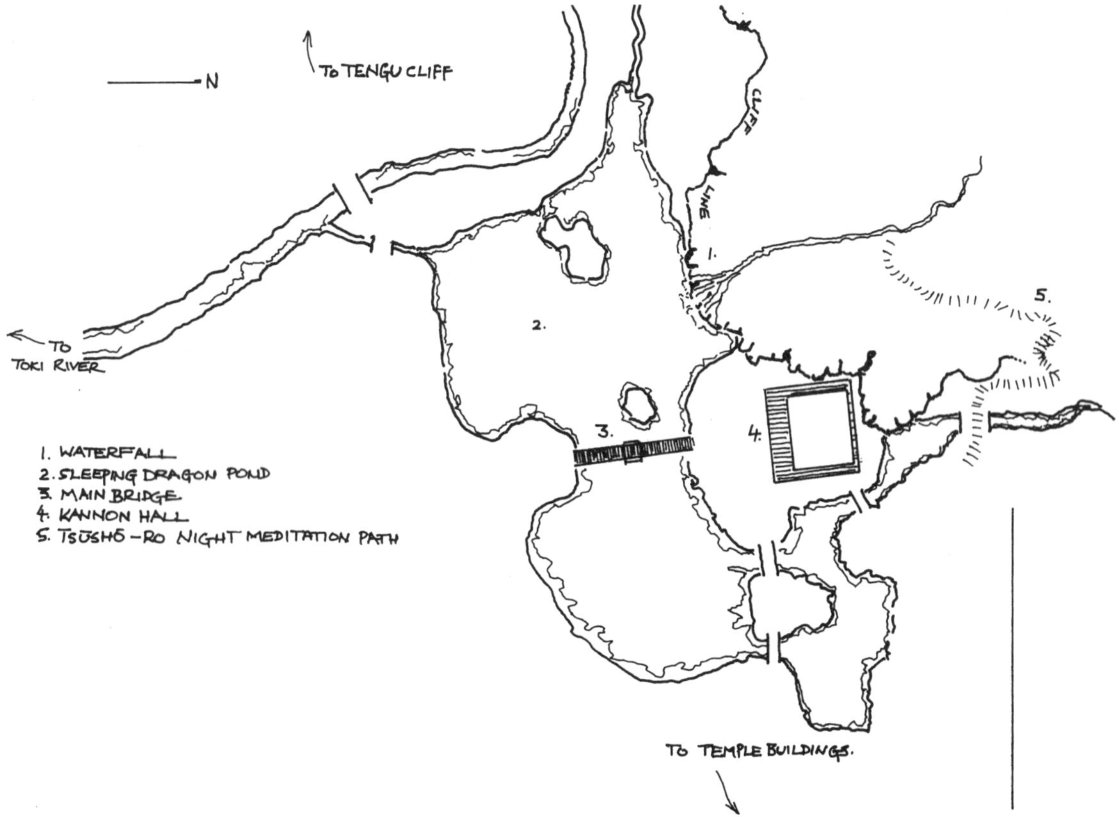

Figure 5. Plan of Eihōji. Based on the plan by Shigemori Mirei and Shigemori Kanto.

the water dominates the pond from this angle. Beyond the highpoint of the arch is a small, low island, and behind this again the cliff rises up out of the pond; flashes and streams of water down its face indicate the location of the waterfall. The island, cliff, and fall all lie on the far side of the bridge, and for the moment they take second place as the eye is led along the curving line of the bridge that drops gently onto the right-hand bank of the pond. From here it is immediately reengaged by the sharp pointed roof curves of a building set among the trees. This building, Soseki's Kannon Hall, is perhaps the greatest treasure at Eihōji, since it is not just one of the two or three of his buildings that have remained intact, but it also, perhaps uniquely, has retained at least some of its original contents. Looked at closely, this building alone gives us more insight into the complexities of Soseki's spiritual world than any other single thing, and understanding it is essential if we are to unravel his vision of his place in the landscape as it is expressed in this garden.

At the foot of the waterfall cliff, as it curves around to the right away from the pond, the Kannon Hall stands, as it has for some six hundred years, on a small level piece of land. The pond sweeps around in front of it, splits into narrow channels around another island, and leads up behind the hall as a wide stream to the foot of the cliff. The hall is thus cut off from the rest of the main garden, being accessible only by bridge; there is the central, curving bridge, two smaller ones across the narrow channels and another small bridge across the stream before it rejoins the cliff. The hall, which together with the line of the bridge approaching it lies just east of a north-south alignment, is a strange, exotically elegant building, with a heavy and dense upper roof of cedar that plunges down to the four corners from the light line of the ridge tiles in huge sweeping curves that turn sharply up at the ends. Immediately below this a second roof emerges from the shadows and stretches out beyond the one above in longer, shallower curves. There are no other visible details, no projecting beams, no carved eaves, and no fancy ridge tiles. The uniformity of the dark and dense cedar thatching throws the sculpted, clear lines of the roofs into razor sharp profile. Below the roofs, shadowed by the deep eaves, is a low, single story wooden building, surrounded by an open veranda, accessed by sliding doors in the front but otherwise totally featureless. Visitors today can no longer see into the hall, but plans show the interior to be a single room, and in the middle toward the back stands the Kannon altar.

Both the hall itself and the high, arched design of the bridge in front, complete with its open pavilion at the top of the curve, display heavy influences from Song China and alert us immediately to their Chinese connection that Soseki had felt on arrival here and had emphasized in his choice of a

Figure 6. The main bridge and Kannon Hall at Eihōji. The main bridge sweeps over the pond and leads to the Kannon Hall nestled among the trees. The building is one of only two or three to survive from Soseki's day. The waterfall cliff is visible beyond. Photo by the author.

Figure 7. The roofs of Kannon Hall at Eihōji. The roofs of Soseki's Kannon Hall lift up from the cliff as one climbs the Tsūshō-ro to the upper garden. Views like this illustrate the illusive, slightly "other-worldly" setting of the temple and its grounds, something that is still evident today in spite of all the time that has passed and all the development that has occurred. Photo by the author.

name. Inside the hall, however, is something that, as we will see a little later, takes us in another direction altogether.

Behind the Kannon Hall, a path crosses the stream and starts to ascend a set of steps that lead up across the cliff, passing close to the roof of the hall, and leading out onto the top. Part of the function of these steps had to do with the Tsūshō-ro, or "night meditation path," and they were included on the route taken by the monks during nightly walks that provided variation for their meditation practice. On the top of the cliff a stream runs through a small garden on its way to the top of the waterfall, and tradition has it that a large, flat stone, thought to be Soseki's *zazen-seki,* was located in this garden. From this position he could have looked out over the pond to the river, with the cliffs of the gorge visible through the trees on the right, while to the left the distant mountains could be seen over the temple roofs. The stream courses through the middle of the garden space, and, once over the top of the cliff, the water falls in a series of steps down over the uneven ledges of the rock face. Two concentrated streams at the top, they rapidly break up on the way down to splash and slide in a succession of delicate fans and trickles into the "Sleeping Dragon Pond" below. The Sleeping Dragon in Taoist mythology is one that is still down on earth, curled up below the surface; it is slowly and steadily building up its strength, waiting to burst free and rise up into the clouds. The Chinese likened this image to a person of great acknowledged potential who has yet fully to realize it.

One other feature of note completes the setting at Eihōji. Among the broken rocks and trees at the far end of the pond, where numerous ravines and gullies lead down to the river, there is a unique, isolated tower of rock that stands free of the jumble around it. Known as the "Tengu Cliff," Kawase quotes temple records indicating that on top of this there was a flat rock known as "Musō's *zazen-seki.*" More than any other part of the site, this setting reminds one of the wild, remote landscapes of T'ang China and the hermits who sat on just such pinnacles during their practice.

But the heart of Eihōji lies in the shadows within the Kannon Hall, remote from the changing landscape outside. It is as powerful and vital as the day it was completed; in here, in the dark obscurity where sleeping dragons lie, Soseki takes us not out into the wider world of Zen traditions and into the places where these were formed, but rather inward to the personal places and interior landscapes from which his individual consciousness arose.

That inward place is focused on the Kannon altar, the Kannon image, and the strange and unique setting in which it has been placed. Sitting in *zazen* position on a seat of lotus leaves, the Kannon image is surrounded by a grotto or cave built up of rough pieces of rock, small chunks and slabs, piled up and arching over its head. Tree roots and other pieces of wood seem to snake in and out among the stones, which are set tightly packed on end, swirling up and over in dense, sinuous curves that at once suggest the strata of bedrock, the flow of water, draughts of air, tongues of flame, or the passage of energy. Here are multiple meanings; they can be the physical elements of our world, or the dark, hollow places that the spirits of our world occupy, or the mountain caves of the hermits and *yamabushi* monks. In various forms, all are the ancient locations of spiritual power and practice that lie at the heart of the consciousness into which Soseki was born, the contact points between our physical and spiritual worlds. As if to confirm this inclusiveness, in front of Kannon is a small Shintō-style mirror, standing in its frame as it would in a shrine, and beside and behind the figure are the phoenixes, flaring up in feathers and flame, and other apparel of Buddhist image and practice. Even the mirror itself carries multiple references. As one of the central objects of Shintō, Shingon, and wider Buddhist ritual, it is a manifestation of the Sun Goddess Ama-terasu no Oho-kami, the "moon of the deep mountains," the full moon of enlightenment, and the pure space of the undifferentiated Oneness of existence. In addition to all this, there is a connection in the approximate north-south alignment of the bridge and the Kannon Hall to the *kofun* tombs, the bridge at Eihōji playing the same liminal access role to the "cave" within the Hall as the entrance passages did to the stone tomb chambers, bringing to bear on the garden at Eihōji the full weight of association with the world of ancestors who have gone before and provide access to the world they occupy.

In short, built into this extraordinary setting are the full complexities that made up Soseki's spiritual world and his consciousness of where this fit into his physical existence. Almost shocking in its primitive, raw power, it is redolent of the swirling, dangerous energies battled by the hermit shamans of old in their rituals of contact and passage between worlds, the *yamabushi* at the places of power in the mountain landscapes, and the Shingon priests in their "fixed" places in front of the Buddha altars. And yet from its center radiates the utter calm of Soseki's enlightened understanding and the serenity of Kannon's compassionate patience. Once one becomes aware of this dynamic engine powering the heart of this garden, the whole setting comes to life, and it takes on an illusionary reality into which one can enter, the encroachment of Tajimi City and modern life notwithstanding, and with it the sense that close at hand, close enough to touch, was the parallel and timeless world of enlightened existence. Here, as though one can actually see him, sits Soseki meditating in his cave, at the foot of a cliff, beside a waterfall, just as he had done first at Unganji and then so many other places since.

Unlike the Chinese elements he incorporated later into the garden

Figure 8. Drawing of the Kannon altar at Eihōji.

at Tenryūji, which were to be specific and easily identifiable, those discernible at Eihōji are very different. They are unspecific; they have to do with atmosphere, suggestions scattered here and there in the words of a poem or the associations of a name or the upturned corners of a roof; and through them Soseki is moving the site from its immediate setting and associating it with one far distant in space and time. And in the ethereal, uplifted lines of the Kannon Hall, we have a building that, while not exactly Chinese, is determinedly not Japanese either, its rising roofs and associations with the spirit world of the tombs lifting it clear of this world altogether. In short, I believe that we have an experiment in invoking the free-roaming unfettered world of the enlightened soul, not existing anywhere recognizable or anywhere in particular, a place beyond immediate definition. At the center of this place, Soseki / Kannon sits in meditation, outside the everyday world.

This garden was in many ways a very personal endeavor, too personal in some ways for the situation he was in. After leaving Eihōji, he did not found another temple for some ten years or so, preferring instead to travel. During these travels, when he did stop, it was only to found a small hermitage, and this pattern continued until he reached Zuisenji. Up until Eihōji, he had been content to set his hut in the middle of the "mysterious" forms of the natural world, but in the Eihōji garden he would attempt to assemble the forms around it himself. For success in any endeavor of this kind two aspects of perception need to be highly developed: one's memory and one's imagination. The degree to which either of these can achieve this development depends on the length and quality of their exposure to the experience of the landscape. How successful he considered Eihōji to be we can never know, but the fact that he did not build another garden on this scale for such a long time, and that, in the meantime, he sought out such a variety of landscape, suggests that he may have felt that he needed more of this kind of experience before he could fully achieve what he was looking for.

At Eihōji, Soseki had used associations with the landscapes of China as the setting for the garden, choosing a place in Japan that played into these associations. When eventually he was ready to build again, however, the garden that developed was set firmly in the landscapes of Japan, to the extent that it was based around two different views of Mt. Fuji, the most explicit icon of Japaneseness available. This would seem to indicate that one of the results of the intervening years of experience of landscape was the sharp refocusing of his perception around the physical and cultural traditions of Japan, those, in short, which lay at the heart of his consciousness. The new garden, at Zuisenji, the "Miraculous Spring Temple," was started in 1327, the first of the series of gardens that eventually led to Saihōji, and all of them share this refocused perception, each one settling deeper into this fertile matrix.

Soseki was at Zuisenji between August 1327 and 1329, again briefly in September 1330, and finally between the spring of 1331 and early 1332, starting the garden right away and adding to it as the opportunity arose. From the beginning this was a very different place from Eihōji since, as Kawase tells us, it "does not appear to have been conceived primarily as a hermitage . . . but rather as a gathering place that could act as a catalyst to interaction"; it was to be somewhere where Soseki could meet not just with his disciples and students, but also with the Chinese Zen masters based in Kamakura. Together they needed to discuss the deteriorating situation in the country and ensure the survival of the *Gozan* system in these difficult times, working out the best rules and regulations for the monasteries to help ensure this, as well as to participate in the conventions of *Gozan* culture, tea-drinking and exchanges of poetry.

Zuisenji was located northeast of Kamakura in the ring of mountains that surrounded the town on three sides. The temple sat on the mountainside up against a steep cliff below the top of the ridge. Set in the cliff was one of the numerous caves found around Kamakura, many of which had been used early on for burials and, more recently, as retreats for monks and hermits. The gardens started behind the Kannon Hall and were focused in an area in front of the cave mouth at the foot of the cliff. Here Soseki dug a small pond, and beside the cave entrance he built a simple hut. The setting was completed by a waterfall feeding water into the pond. From the main buildings a path led past the cave and hut before twisting its way up the mountain in a series of steep steps all the way to the top of the ridge. The path was cut out of the bedrock of the cliff and "according to poems written by monks at the time, the path up the hill at Zuisenji was a Tsūshō-ro, or Night Meditation Path, used for meditative walking practice throughout the night and similar to that at Eihōji.[22] On the top of the ridge Soseki built a small pavilion, the Ichiran-tei (The Whole-World Viewing Pavilion), a building that was clearly intended as a focal point for both public and private occasions and from which there were wide panoramic views as far as Mt. Fuji. This building and the Kannon Hall were among the first things that Soseki built upon arriving there in the summer of 1327, and this gives us a good idea of where his priorities for this garden lay. Kawase does not believe that much of the detail remains from Soseki's day, but the pond, cave, and path are still there and give a pretty good idea of how things were.

Perhaps more important than these details, however, are the two views of Mt. Fuji from the garden, and the marked differences between them, all of which helps us to fill in more details of the image of place that Soseki was searching to express. As we have already noted, Mt. Fuji was a ubiquitous presence in the distant views from the landscapes in which Soseki grew up, it was there when he first started to meditate on the nature of the world around him, and Kawase points out its continuing importance when he describes it as the "central natural pillar within Musō's heart." One of these views of Mt. Fuji is visible from the Ichiran-tei, set on the top of the ridge. The site of the pavilion offers spectacularly long and wide-ranging views in every direction across the tops of the neighboring ridges, and in particular to the snow-capped cone of Mt. Fuji in the west. As we will see, the Ichiran-tei was significant to Soseki for several reasons, but placing his meeting hut here, with this view, was a deliberate public celebration of the place the mountain occupied at the center of their natural world, at the center of nature itself, and, therefore, at the center of his perception of that natural world.

The other view of Fuji from the garden serves to emphasize this, but this time in a more personal, almost private, way. The quiet intimacy of this experience makes it all the more powerful and explicit. This view is from the mouth of the cave above the pond and from the door of the hut that Soseki built next to it. The nature of this view seems to confirm that this was the spot where Soseki spent the bulk of his time meditating while he was able to stay at Zuisenji. Looking west from the mouth of the cave, Soseki would see a special view of the top, snow-covered part of Fuji's cone framed by a perfectly positioned notch in the mountain ridge in the foreground. Nothing else beyond the ridge is visible and, perhaps because of the low angle of vision and lack of other features to provide scale, the cone appears to be much larger and closer than it does from above at the Ichiran-tei. Kawase was particularly struck when he saw this, commenting that he had not realized that such a view was possible from such a relatively low place in Kamakura. He goes on, in some of the most personal writing in his book, to describe the effect that seeing this had on him when he visited on a snowy evening in February. Sitting in the cave entrance and seeing the top of Fuji framed almost at eye-level, looming so close that it appears to have suddenly popped up, he writes that this in itself is enough to "waken the eye," to enlighten the viewer, but there was more to come. While he was there, as the winter evening closed in around him and the snow gradually stopped falling, Fuji appeared, "this shape piercing the sky in the sudden cold of the evening." He was astonished at what he saw, an image of such clear and vivid beauty that he would never forget it. "To tell the truth," he goes on to say, "when I saw this view of Mt. Fuji at Zuisenji I completely revised my view of Musō." He felt that he suddenly understood the true depth and range of Soseki's understanding. On that solitary, cold evening Kawase felt a flash of enlightenment as he momentarily shared Soseki's vision of the world.[23]

Although he had not built a garden for some time before Zuisenji, once he started again, several followed. The most important of these came soon after the Zuisenji garden during his return to the Koshu area. Here he founded Erinji, the Forest of Wisdom Temple, with the patronage of a local branch of the Takeda family. Two things are interesting about the names he gave this temple. First, the "mountain" name he chose was not that of the nearest mountain but that of one it looked out toward, Mt. Gentoku, and by so doing he brought to the temple all the associations of his childhood, his early search for understanding, and all the people who helped him at that time. Second, the characters he chose to make up the word Erinji give very explicit meaning to the name: *E* meaning, first, to give to, to take pity on or provide assistance and, second, compassion, benevolence, while *rin* has the meaning of a forest. From this, the purpose he had in mind for the temple is clear, and we can be sure that what he did here in terms of the position, buildings, and gardens was done with this in mind. He wanted it to be an accessible place that would be widely influential, and in a later poem about Erinji, he wrote, "the Forest of Wisdom / will grow dense / and cover the world." It was to be a place where people could both find help and where they could help themselves. As we look at the gardens that he built here we need to keep these considerations in mind, since it is in the light of these that we can make the most sense of the landscapes he built and understand the role they played in the development of his garden style.

A poem from the time indicates his mood as he started work at Erinji, and this also provides important background to his garden building,

> All worries and troubles
> have gone from my breast
> and I play joyfully
> far from the world . . .[24]

Once we see that key word "play," we can be sure that something has changed for Soseki. It indicates that he is no longer concentrating purely on the quest for deeper enlightenment and further experience but feels that he now has the tools at his disposal to create an environment in which the pursuit of Zen activities can take place. Thus, what he went on to build at Erinji is of great importance to us since up to this point the gardens that he had built, including Eihōji, were in a sense still part of his search. Now he felt confident of being able to build a "small hut" that contained "worlds without number" in which he could "play."

The subtly changing views of Mt. Gentoku are the first thing to notice about the layout of Erinji. To start with, as Kawase points out, there is a view just of the peak as you look north through the "Middle Gate," but gradually more of the mountain is revealed as you climb the slope behind the temple, and, finally, when you reach the "Musō Fields," a wide, open area above the temple, a full view of the mountain opens up, set in its huge landscape. This may be seen as the key "bridging point," the moment at which you lose the view below, the farms and tracks and houses and temple, all the things of the everyday, and you look instead into the wide-open voids of the skies and mountains. It is the place where you enter "all the infinite worlds."

Back down at the temple complex, between the Middle Gate and the temple buildings, there is a "Hoshō-no-ike" (Lake for Releasing Living Things), a standard component in many temple gardens, the place where extra merit was accumulated by releasing animals, particularly turtles, from captivity at special ceremonies during the year. Kawase reports that this pond is now abandoned, but he says that it clearly dates from the original temple building and uses water fed from the main gardens at the back of the temple.

These gardens focus on a pond that stretches back from the temple buildings. The ground rises up to its left and right, while directly behind it, where the forest thins, there is a limited view of the mountains beyond. In the back left-hand corner of the pond, framed by carefully placed rocks, a small waterfall is tucked into the bank. Leading away from this, around the pond individual rocks and groups of rocks line the edges and define a small central island. On the right-hand side of the pond a small stream brings water in from another section of the garden, which, in turn, focuses on a smaller, and much more hidden, waterfall. This fall and its stream are also carefully edged with rocks, and the banks, as they lift up away from the water, feature a number of groups of small rocks and plants. The water is fed to the garden from the Fuefuki River, which also appears to have been the source of at least some of the rocks in the garden, a good portion of which are very pale grey to white in color and smoothed by the action of water. While these clearly come from the river, other rocks in the garden, darker, more angular, and showing no signs of water smoothing, most likely come from the mountain slopes around the temple. The main pond is visible from the temple buildings, but the smaller fall and its associated landscape are designed to be seen from a covered walkway that leads out from the main buildings to a secondary building on the right. Though clearly part of the same overall scheme, the two parts of the garden are not laid out to be fully visible from any one place. Kawase tells us that another view opens up from the walkway if one looks to the right, away from the garden. By looking this way, the more distant mountains are clearly visible, framed by the forest trees on either side. He also reports that eroded soil had been removed from another part of the garden to reveal a group of white rocks, from the river, designed in the Chinese standing-stone style. Perhaps they are those Soseki mentions in his poem when he talks of his offering being "these white stones." It is interesting to note at this point that Kawase believes this to have been the first of the gardens that Soseki used *kawaramono* people to help build, no doubt valuing their experience and knowledge given the importance of the project. If this is so, then they will almost certainly also have provided the rocks from the river.

From these descriptions it seems that Soseki carefully structured the gardens around a series of opposites, using the energy within the garden generated by the tensions between these, to draw in the viewers' attention and animate their thoughts as they contemplated the composition. These pairs of opposites include water / rock, white rock / dark rock, the twinned waterfalls, open / hidden, male / female, the left and right sides of the garden, one side featuring a pond, the other a stream, one view from the temple, and one from the walkway, open views on one side / garden on the other. And then, within the rockwork itself, there are the endless variations and contrasts in shapes and sizes. All these are components that were first articulated in this garden and that were to feature in those that followed.

When the imperial summons finally came in 1333 asking Soseki to take up a position in Kyoto, he was fifty-eight and entering the most influential and high-profile part of his life. After this move he never again left the area in and around the capital, never returned to Kamakura, and never returned to the landscapes around Mt. Gentoku, which for so long had provided him with sanctuary and inspiration. He was also in the full swing of his garden-building activities, which, after a slow and uncertain start, had blossomed to become one of his major preoccupations. The gardens that followed Erinji, all tightly bunched, with the exception of Nanzenji, in the western suburbs of Kyoto, demonstrate that in fact Soseki had no need to revisit the remote mountain areas again. He had gained the experience necessary for his memory and imagination to provide him with the ability to create the various gardens for his teaching temples and, in the end, to create the place where he could slip into the landscape and disappear, as Ryo Zassu had done before him.

With his move to Kyoto, Soseki entered the period of his garden building for which he is most remembered. He built Rinsenji and Nanzenji between 1333–34 and Tenryūji and Saihōji between 1339–45. Unfortunately, very little survives of the buildings at Rinsenji from Soseki's time, and the wide central garden he built now lies buried beneath the clean sweep of the modern gravel garden that owes more to the garden at Ryōanji and designs of the late fifteenth century than to Soseki's work.

At Rinsenji the garden area in front of the main hall is dominated on three sides by the wide, open skies of the Kyoto Plain, while on the fourth, the Kame-yama hills above Tenryūji rise up to fill the horizon. Facing away from the hills one can still sense, with a little effort, the presence of the river and its once marshy plain stretching away in front of the temple gates. Today, however, as at Shōrinji, the river finds itself much diminished, its true character and vitality extinguished by the concrete sluices and channels of modern flood controls. Most of that wildness has been lost, and now an orderly path leads from the concrete embankment that carries the main road from central Kyoto along the riverbank, up to the temple gates, which in turn open up onto the chill white and grey sterility of the gravel garden, its scattered rocks, and the swooping slate roofs of the new temple buildings. All the rich, nurturing detail of Soseki's enlightened vision has gone, and yet with the mountains behind and the river in front, the place has a strong sense of familiarity. One can imagine that Soseki felt very much at home here, and it seems appropriate that he should be buried at a place where everything has been stripped down to the fundamental elements, the vertical and the horizontal, mountain and water.

Fortunately his gravesite remains intact; peering into the gloom beneath the Buddha Hall, we can still share a moment of quiet intimacy in a small place among the boundless worlds above. It would be fascinating to know what kind of a garden Soseki built in this place, and our frustration at the loss is only added to by Kawase's reporting of the suggestion that Soseki's garden, complete with the rockwork, still lies largely intact below the rocks and gravel of the present one. Equally fascinating is his reference to a record dating from 1730, during the Edo period, which reports that "a hill behind the Main Hall at Rinsenji" was created by Soseki, and that the original name of the temple meant "Looking Down on the River" rather than "Riverside" Temple.[25] This suggests at least that the landscape that Soseki created here was much more complex and detailed than that which survives. All this may have gone now, but at least one can still visit Rinsenji and, before making one's way around the back of the buildings to visit the grave, stand in front of the open doors of the main hall to spend a few minutes in the calm presence of his statue (see frontispiece). Tucked away on the left, deep in the quiet gloom, Soseki sits, his hands on his lap, as reassuring today as he must have been to those who knew him all those years ago.

Nanzenji, the second temple garden that dates from this initial period of building, is situated on the opposite side of Kyoto on the slopes of Higashi-yama, the low hills that run down the eastern side of the city. The site began life as an imperial palace, and, surrounded by forested ridges at a point where a mountainside spring bubbles to the surface, it must have provided members of the imperial family with a welcome retreat from the heat and humidity of the summer months in Kyoto. It became the country retreat of the retired emperor Kame-yama, and in 1291 he gave the site and buildings to his Zen teacher, Fumon, to be converted into a Zen monastery and a place where they could study together. Fumon died soon after, but, perhaps

Figure 9. General view of Rinsenji. The hills of Kame-yama dominate the modern gravel garden in front of the Main Hall. It has been suggested that Soseki's original garden lies more or less intact underneath this new layout. The San'e-in, the focal point of Soseki's Zen lineage, lies at the far end, on the right. Photo by the author.

Figure 10. The rear of the Main Hall at Rinsenji. Soseki's grave can be glimpsed through the slats of the wooden screen seen at the far end of the building. Nothing else remains from Soseki's time. Photo by the author.

because of its imperial patronage and the importance of Fumon's school, Nanzenji rose to become the most important of the Kyoto *Gozan* monasteries, a large and busy teaching center that, in time, became one of the important creative centers of the *Gozan* arts. It is also known to have had gardens among the buildings, and certainly Soseki added to or altered these during his second stay in 1334.

Subsequent to its initial construction, the temple was substantially rebuilt and enlarged on a number of occasions, particularly in 1703, and the gardens were developed by several designers, notably Koboori Enshū (1579–1647), to whom the existing rock and gravel gardens are attributed. It is thus difficult to know just what Soseki built during his relatively brief stay there, or how much of what he built can still be discerned. Certainly the pond garden set into the hillside has a very familiar feel and a sense of unchanged age about it that suggest that it has retained some of its original layout and rockwork. The garden centers on a small pond fed by a spring whose waters emerge from slightly higher on the hillside and flow down over a carefully built fall and streambed into the pond. The forest trees press in around the garden and pond giving it an intimate, secluded feel, a place of quiet dappled light enlivened by the play of shadows and the whispers of flowing water. Kawase feels that the pond preserves its original form, even if some of the bank details have changed, and that the general view of the garden from the buildings is basically unaltered.

Of interest here, however, is the design and execution of the watercourse down from the spring to the pond. Parts are known to have been rebuilt during the Edo period, so we have to be very careful, but there are elements in its positioning—the rocks associated with the waterfall, the path crossing the stream by a small bridge placed just below the fall, and the rocks placed on the pond edges where the stream enters into it— that have similarities to the layouts at Erinji and parts of what he inherited at Tenryūji. Erinji, Nanzenji, and Tenryūji all have gardens with water features that in one form or another repeat this relationship of elements, and at Nanzenji it is particularly clear. Here water flows from the carefully constructed group of fall rocks, down under a bridging point and out into the pond. Looking at this from across the pond, just to the right of the point where the water enters the pond from the fall, a large, pointed rock, roughly triangular in shape, is located on the bank overlooking the water. A rock of very similar shape is located in the same place just to the right of the fall as part of the left-hand fall group at Erinji, while another sits to the right of the fall and bridge group as one looks across the pond at Tenryūji (see figure 12). These rocks stand out from most of the others used in the compositions they complement, both in their pointed shapes and in being set upright in the ground on their sides. Like the Kannon Hall at Eihōji, they provide the focal point from which the other elements of the composition radiate out; in the increasingly illusory nature of his designs, these rocks seem to provide a location for Soseki, or indeed for us, in these landscapes. He occupies them much as the Kannon statue occupies the stone grotto hidden away at the heart of the garden at Eihōji, and while these rocks may provide his location, the waterfalls have come to provide a glimpse of the "Way" he has been following, his steep and difficult path toward enlightenment that he first identified when he changed his name to Soseki, the isolated, rocky landscape he would have to journey through.

Following Nanzenji, it was to be another five years before he started his next garden, when in 1339 two opportunities came at once, one at Tenryūji and one at Saihōji. Although Tenryūji was to become the biggest of the public teaching temples that Soseki built and was thus firmly grounded in the everyday realities of religious life, its origins lie in the troubled dream world of a nation torn apart by protracted and complex civil strife, something to bear in mind as we examine the garden Soseki built there.

The origins of Tenryūji's foundation as a Zen temple and the type of place it became lie specifically in two dreams. The first, as we have seen in an earlier chapter, came to Soseki on the night of June 24, 1339, the night, it turned out, that the emperor Go-Daigo died, exiled from the capital and unreconciled with all those who had opposed him. His was an unquiet spirit, one that needed careful attention if it was to settle and let the nation move on. When he heard of Soseki's dream and of Go-Daigo's death, Ashikaga Takauji, uneasy at having waged war against Go-Daigo and forcing him into exile, immediately decided to found a temple specifically for the emperor's spirit and took the location of Soseki's dream as an indication that this was the appropriate place. As these decisions were made, Tadayoshi, Takauji's brother, also had a dream in which he saw a "golden dragon" appear in the "river of the southern heavens," the Milky Way. From this auspicious image the name of the temple was taken, becoming "Tenryū-shisho zenji," (literally, the Miraculous Revelation of the Heavenly Dragon Temple) or The Dragon of Heaven Temple. These were the strange, almost otherworldly, circumstances in which this important project was conceived, and they were to heavily influence the way in which Soseki developed the garden there.

Given the role that Tenryūji was created to play, the gardens were always going to have to make a strong statement; this was not the place for small, private spaces suited to individual contemplation. This garden had to provide a suitable setting for a grand complex of buildings and also grab the attention of those viewing it, bringing them face to face with the world of Zen in all its complexity. As we have looked at the gardens that Soseki built, we have seen the landscapes of Zen, and his perception of them, lurking in the background and providing both a creative palette and a source of image and inspiration. Now at Tenryūji we see them emerge as the subject of the garden itself, their dreamlike, illusory qualities being particularly suited to the circumstances surrounding the founding of the temple. Here they would be asked to take on a central importance in the bid to provide those visiting the temple with the full experience of the nature of Zen consciousness. But the garden actually goes one important step further than this, since Soseki made sure that this expression of consciousness was firmly rooted in the Japanese context, in a way that the garden at Eihōji had not been. Here the world of Zen would not be seen as an exotic import, but rather as something that arose directly out of the Japanese context and that spoke directly to the Japanese experience.

To achieve this, the gardens were built to be looked out over, to be seen as a whole from the central verandas of the Hōjō, and this applied not just to the pond and waterfall but to the whole setting of the gardens, including the hills that surround it. As Kawase put it, "one looks out from the veranda, a very public, central place, over the wide pond and up to the *shakkei* background of the Kame-yama hills."[26] Once out in the garden the various areas in it could be visited by wide strolling paths that took the visitor up behind the pond and onto the lower slopes of the hills beyond. It was an open, laid-out garden that called on the hills around to provide the setting. *Shakkei*, or the "capturing alive" of a view or landscape and "borrowing" it to form an important element in the garden, had been a part of landscape design since the Heian period and is discussed at length in the *Sakutei-ki*. However, as with most elements of design at that time, its effects were looked upon as a way of increasing the aesthetic quality of a garden rather than as something that could bear spiritual content. The use of the *shakkei* views at Tenryūji, however, come complete in the designer's mind with a full set of references to the Japanese spiritual consciousness: the mountain repositories of communal wisdom, the home of the shamans, hermits, *yamabushi*, and monks who shared these places with the spirits of the ancestors in their world of the dead and with all the *kami* that occupy the places of the natural world. In capturing these views for his garden, Soseki wanted it understood that the spirit of the Chinese Zen masters, and the world they occupied, was now firmly placed in a Japanese context. In using *shakkei* views in this way, the garden at Tenryūji gave this old technique a whole new life and purpose and a fresh relevance in the new cultural milieu of the *Gozan* arts.

Within this wider context, however, he was interested only in the world of Zen, giving his garden an authority that was built up using mul-

Figure 11. General view of Tenryūji. The Song-style rockwork of the waterfall, bridge, and islands on the far side of the pond is set emphatically among the landscape of the Kame-yama hills. It was very important to Soseki that this temple and its garden, a grand celebration of the Zen school, with all its Chinese antecedents, be seen as deeply embedded in the Japanese context. Photo by the author.

Figure 12. View across the pond from the veranda of the Hōjō at Tenryūji. The delicate spires of the island rocks, the three slabs of the bridge at the foot of the dry fall, and the solid bulk of the fall composition stepping up the hillside are all thought to be the work of the Chinese émigré monk Rankei Doryou and, if so, represent one of the few remaining examples of Song-style Zen rockwork still extant in Japan. On the far right of the composition, sitting just above the waterline, is one example of the large, individual triangular rocks that we see featured in just such a position in a number of Soseki's gardens, a marker, perhaps, of his own, or the Zen School's, place in the landscape. Photo by the author.

tiple references to the matter of Zen: the names, stories, ideas, techniques, people, and places that made up people's perception of what it was. As the central core of this garden he was happy to call on what may be the only piece of Song Chinese rockwork that has survived intact in Japan, Rankei Dōryū's Dragon Gate Falls, a piece of Zen imagery that could not have been more authentic or more representative of the illusive world that he wanted to capture. The importance of this composition lies in its references to China and in the subtly exotic feeling of illusion that it brings to the center of the garden, a feeling that brings to mind a line in a speech that Soseki made at Tenryūji in 1351, just before his death. The occasion was the thirteenth anniversary of Go-Daigo's death, and at one point in the speech Soseki says, "What I have stated above is all a dream within a dream." Calling up the circumstances under which his temple at Tenryūji came into being, following his dream of Go-Daigo walking in the hills and Tadayoshi's dream of a dragon rising to the heavens, he refers here to the dream that exists within these, the all-encompassing dream or illusion, the True Nature of Reality, and this is what he chose to build into the garden.

To conjure this up, Soseki used references within the garden that brought in the important places of Chinese Zen and the people who occupied them. The soaring spirit-filled mountains, their steep cliffs and deep ravines, their rocks and waterfalls all joined in one landscape dotted with the huts, hermitages, monasteries, ponds, peaks, and bridges. The masters, disciples, monks, and hermits, scuttling back and forth, animated the scene and made the legends. At Tenryūji, in fact, Soseki seems to have been concentrating on the life and reputation of the Sixth Patriarch Hui-neng by invoking his life and example through seeking to create an unbroken connection with the old master, and by introducing his presence directly into the lives of people in the middle of the fourteenth century. It was a span of time, interestingly enough, which is very similar to the one that now separates us from Soseki.

To understand this garden it is therefore necessary to register this span of time he was aiming to bridge, and, second, to understand the limitless worlds of "endless space" that he saw present here. It was to be his biggest expansion into these illusory places, and clearly this was not in any way an internal garden; rather, it was a celebration of Zen. Apart from the specific references contained in the waterfall composition at the center of the garden, Soseki introduced a number of others through the place-names he gave to the various areas within it, and he left no doubt about their purpose by leaving ten poems to accompany them, the *Kizan Jikyō*, which we looked at briefly in the last chapter. The poems not only underline Tenryūji's role as a center for teaching and practice; they also provide us with a kind of road map of the Zen world spread out in front of those who sit in contemplation on the veranda of the Hōjō. Although many of the original locations are now lost, the pond and waterfall are two that are not: the poems are each named after the place to which they refer and start at the Fumyō-kaku, "Gate of Universal Light," the gate, or threshold place, that leads through to the universal light or the great "emptiness" that spreads out beyond it. For us the gate is the space, or pause, that indicates the location of this great emptiness, and with practice we can pass through this,

> . . . When your eyelids
> have fallen across
> the whole of the empty world
> The gate will open
> at the snap of a finger . . .

Once again we are firmly in the world of *MA*, its meanings and forms providing access to worlds beyond our immediate reality, but, once again, we must do the hard work ourselves, for these things only become apparent with time, practice, and experience. Once through the gate and into the garden, the paths lead past a number of places, each with its own point to make, question to raise, or thought to provoke.

The second poem is called Zesshō-kei, and the title can be read "Incomparable Verse Valley" or "Narrow Valley Stream," the incomparable verse, the sounds of the stream, being the guiding way of Zen.

> The wondrous voices
> of the swift running brook.
> Deep conversations
> 80,000 *gatha* chanted day and night
> But not one word
> is spoken.

Not only is this the world of Zen set firmly within the context of the Kameyama landscape and linked firmly with Japan's geography and cultural traditions; it is also given the protection of the ancestral guardian spirits, the very ones that had saved and protected the nation from Mongol invasion back when Soseki had been a child. As the poem Reihi-byō, "Hall of the Ancestral Guardian Spirit," tells us, "Inside the temple enclosure / a place was set aside / for a Shintō shrine" at which you should,

> . . . Wish with your whole self
> for the divine wind
> to help the Way of the Patriarchs

Thus, Soseki's garden was not simply to provide a background for the practice of Zen; it was to protect and actively intervene to nurture and promote it and, in turn, be strengthened and burnished by the process.

The next three poems all speak of the unbroken "flow" of the Buddha's legacy, the sermons and teaching traditions of the Zen masters, and the direct connection of both to those using this garden: "The *Dharma* spring of the Sixth Patriarch / has never run dry / it is flowing even now . . ." (from Sōgen no Ike, "Hui-neng's Pond"), ". . . Look: the fragrant seedlings / have been handed all the way down / to the present . . ." (from Nenge-rei, "Peak of the Held Up Flower"), and "It arches like a rainbow / dividing the stream / joining the shores . . ." (from Tōgetsu-kyo, "The Bridge the Moon Crosses").

The seventh poem, Sankyū-gan ("Three Step Waterfall") refers to the central composition in the garden and gives us a careful warning as to what the ascent of the difficult path to enlightenment is really like in practice.

> All kinds of dangers
> awesome ledges
> three barriers . . .
> So many fish
> have fallen back
> foreheads stamped with failure . . .

An alternative reading of the title gives us "Three Grades of Cliffs," in which the emphasis is neatly switched from the waters of the "sermons" to the route they come splashing down.

The next two poems, Manshō-dō, "Cave of the 10,000 Pines," and Ryūmon-tei, "Dragon Gate Pavilion," are both concerned with the boundless worlds of Zen reality that are contained and accessed through the points of contact occupied by those practicing the Way: the huts, caves, forest groves, mountain sides, islands, all the locations dotted across the topography of the illusive Zen world. In the last poem, the struggles are finally over, the goal has been reached, and the Kichō-tō, "Turtle Head Stupa," is there before you.

> . . . nothing inside is hidden
> *Dharma* worlds
> beyond number
> are there for you to see.[27]

To understand the full implications of the layout of this garden and the way in which this pathway and the places along it were understood by those using it, we should remember that many of these pathways were specifically designed for meditative walking. They were routes that guided the monks deep in meditation along journeys through the garden that reflected the patterns of a "journey" through a mandala, or the mountain trails that led through the *shin'iki* or sacred land. Some of these, such as the "Womb-Diamond Trail" along the Great Ridge of Mt. Ōmine near Yoshino,[28] are arduous, long-distance trails, while others, like the Tsūshō-ro, began and ended within the garden or temple compound and were designed to be used as part of meditative practice at night.

Thus, in its layout and aims Tenryūji was a public celebration of the world of Zen and, in particular, of Soseki's lineage, which, following its initial introduction by Bukkō Zenji, had been in the hands of Bukkoku Zenji and then himself, neither of whom had ever traveled to China, and which was by now firmly rooted in the Japanese context. As such the garden stands as a perfect complement to that at Saihōji, a garden that represented an entirely different aspect of Soseki's life and character. At Tenryūji, Soseki took part in wide-ranging public discussions and debates about everything to do with Zen and its role in the life of the country. At Saihōji, on the other hand, he retreated into a private world in which his everyday existence could merge with his spiritual consciousness and from which he drew his strength and wisdom.

NOTES

1. Irmtraud Schaarschmidt-Richter, *Japanese Gardens,* essay by Osamu Mori, trans. Janet Seligman (New York: Morrow and Co., 1979), p. 25.

2. W. G. Aston, trans., *Nihongi: Chronicles of Japan from the Earliest Times to A.D. 697* (London: G. Allen and Unwin, 1956), book 2, p. 144.

3. Ibid., book 2, p. 154.

4. See Kawase Kazuma, *Musō Kokushi: Zen to teien* (Musō Kokushi: Zen and Gardens) (Tokyo: Kōdansha, 1968), p. 106, for further discussion of the possible meanings of *shima* at this time.

5. See Schaarschmidt-Richter, *Japanese Gardens,* p. 279, for the invaluable description of the research and excavation work carried out by Mori in both Asuka and Nara.

6. Ibid.

7. Teiji Itoh, *Space and Illusion in the Japanese Garden,* trans. Ralph Friedrich and Masajiro Shimamura (New York: Weatherhill, 1973), p. 49.

8. Kawase, *Musō Kokushi,* p. 108. His source here is the *Shūgaisho,* a collection of notes and essays from the Momoyama period of the late sixteenth century.

9. Aston, *Nihongi,* book 1, p. 388.

10. Loraine Kuck, *The World of the Japanese Garden: From Chinese Origins to Modern Landscape Art* (New York: Walker / Weatherhill, 1968), p. 81.

11. Kawase, *Musō Kokushi,* p. 110.

12.Kuck, *The World of the Japanese Garden*, p. 240.

13. Ibid., p. 54.

14. Kawase, *Musō Kokushi*. Descriptions of this garden and the one at Unganji to follow are taken from Kawase's accounts of his visits to the gardens, and I pass on his interpretations of the remains that he found.

15. From the *Zenrin-Koshu* published in 1688 by Ijushi. English translation in Sōiku Shigematsu, comp. and trans., *A Zen Forest, Saying of the Masters* (New York: Weatherhill, 1981).

16. Matsuo Bashō, *Back Roads to Far Towns: Bashō's Oku-no-hosomichi*, trans. and notes by Cid Corman and Kamaike Susumu (Fredonia, N.Y.: White Pine Press, 1986), section 25.

17. Musō Soseki, *Sun at Midnight: Poems and Sermons*, trans. W. S. Merwin and Sōiku Shigematsu (San Francisco: North Point Press, 1989), poem #3, p. 7.

18. Kawase, *Musō Kokushi*, p. 148; extract from the *Muchū Mondo*.

19. Ibid., p. 155.

20. Ibid., p. 160. Translation by Sharon Nakazato. These are difficult poems to translate since the choice of readings and associations connected to the characters used give the poems a wider field of meaning. To make sense of the poems in English, one is required to make choices within these fields and, inevitably, lead the meanings in a certain direction. Similarly, the translation of the first poem here is slightly different from the version used in chapter 3, which was taken from the translation by Merwin and Shigematsu in *Sun at Midnight*, because in this context this interpretation seems more appropriate and explanatory.

21. Musō Soseki, *Sun at Midnight*, poems #7, p. 11, #8, p. 12, and #9, p. 13.

22. Yoshikawa Motome, *Karesansui no niwa* (Karesansui Gardens), Nihon no Bijutsu 61 (Tokyo: Shibundo, 1960), p. 35.

23. Kawase, *Musō Kokushi*, p. 166.

24. Musō Soseki, *Sun at Midnight*, poem #53, p. 60.

25. Kawase, *Musō Kokushi*, p. 178.

26. Ibid., p. 180.

27.The second and eighth poems were translated by Sharon Nakazato. The others are from Musō Soseki, *Sun at Midnight*, poems #99–108, p. 109–18.

28. Gary Snyder, *The Gary Snyder Reader: Prose, Poetry and Translations* (Washington, D.C.: Counterpoint, 1999), p. 371, for an excellent description of this trail as it can be found today.

CHAPTER SIX

A Place in the Landscape: Saihōji

The site upon which Saihōji was built was one of ancient significance, being set in Kyoto's Nishi-yama (West Mountains), the center of a large concentration of tumulus burial mounds. Remains on the hillside in the upper part of the present garden indicate that it was the site of a group of *kofun* tombs built and in use sometime between A.D. 250–552, or just before the formation of the Yamato state. In the lower section, between the hillside and the river, records indicate that the area had at one time been used as a burial ground for commoners. In later years—it is not clear at what stage this happened—the upper part of the site containing the *kofun* tombs became known as Edōji (Temple of the Defiled Ground, "defiled" having the sense of the Land of the Dead) and was seen as entirely separate from the area below. Nothing is known of the buildings at Edōji, and it could be that right up to Soseki's day the succession of temples we will be looking at were limited to the lower section below the slope of the hill. If Soseki were the first person to include the upper region in his temple designs, that might explain one strange event specifically associated with his garden building among the *kofun* tombs, which we will look at later.

Some sources state that during the Asuka period (538–671) the site was developed as a retreat for Prince Shōtoku, regent during the reign of Empress Suiko.[1] But the first recorded temple at the Saihōji site was founded by the monk Gyōki Bosatsu (668–749), who, as part of his vision of reaching out and taking religious practice out of the temples and into people's lives, advocated the idea that the existing divinities and spirits of Shintō belief and the ancestral spirits of the dead were manifestations of those that made up the Buddhist cosmology. In line with this belief, he often chose sites for his temples where connections with the old places of power were particularly strong, and of particular power were those places which "in pre-Buddhist times were believed to be the world of the dead or dwelling places of numina"[2]; they were places where the tombs and burial grounds were located. When Soseki started work at Saihōji, it was the second time that he had occupied a site that Gyōki had also used—the first being at the

Figure 13. Kasumi-jima and the pond at Saihōji. The delicate, moss-covered bridge linking Kasumi-jima (Mist Island) with the shoreline of the Ōgon Ike (Golden Pond) sums up the ethereal beauty of Saihōji's Lower Garden as we can see it today. In the background, on the left-hand side, the steep banks of the Asahi-jima (Island of the Morning Sun) rise from the clear water, while to the right, the path leads off to the Tanhoku-tei pavilion. The garden is not as dark and lush as when Kawase Kazuma first saw it in the 1920s, but, still, the rocks lining the edge of the Mist Island carry a deep layer of mosses. A considerable degree of peace and quite has returned to the garden since restrictions were placed on the number of visitors in the mid-1970s. Photo by the author.

Kyūko-an hermitage site on Shikoku Island. Undoubtedly, part of the reason that Soseki was so drawn to Saihōji was the connection with Gyōki and the site's long history as a threshold to the spiritual world.

According to the official temple history of Saihōji, the *Saihōji Chitei Engi*,[3] Gyōki built a hall in which he enshrined a triad of Buddhas with Amida in the center flanked by Kannon and Seishi, both of whom were also revered for their compassion. This triad was later redecorated by Hōnen and is still at the temple to this day. The other, somewhat more tentative, link to Gyōki at the site is the large willow tree standing by the western gate that temple legend maintains is a descendant of one planted by him. The *engi* goes on to say that Kūkai, founder of Shingon Buddhism in Japan, spent time at Saihōji, sometime after returning to Japan in 806. It narrates that, while there, he created the first pond on the site in order to hold a "Hōjō-e" ceremony, the release of captive animals, particularly fish and turtles, which were to be sold as food, as an act of compassion emphasizing the importance of all forms of life. Following Kūkai's visit, the temple was handed on to prince Shinnyo Shinno, the son of Emperor Heizei (r. 806–9) and a pupil of Kūkai's, as his place of practice. Although his poems make clear that he was very fond of the temple, he was not to occupy it for very long. A devout Buddhist, he soon left on an extraordinary pilgrimage, having set his heart on visiting India but, unfortunately, after traveling through T'ang China, he died on the journey and thus never returned to the temple to enjoy the cherry trees he had planted.

The temple was then abandoned for some two to three hundred years until the 1190s, when Hōnen Shonin was invited to build a hall there for the Amida Buddha. Hōnen had founded the Jōdo-shū, "School of the Pure Land," in 1175, but he was to die in 1212, exiled from the capital. His populist approach had made him many powerful enemies in the entrenched religious establishment in Kyoto. It is with Hōnen's foundation, however, that we get an idea of what existed at the Saihōji site. Whether or not there were any buildings or garden features still existing from earlier times when he arrived is unknown, but Hōnen himself established an Amida Buddha Hall facing onto the pond that he called the "Sairai-dō," the "Coming from the West Hall," a reference to the direction from which Amida will arise to guide those who are lost and struggling to find his western paradise. We know too that sometime between 1257 and 1259, or just after his retirement from the regency, Hōjō Tokiyori built the O-dō (Cherry Blossom Hall) somewhere by the lake close to where the stream flowed in from the Diamond Pond, so that he and his friends could come and enjoy the glorious display of the flowering cherries, drink, talk, and exchange poems.

There seems to be no record of where the O-dō stood, but plans of Saihōji during Soseki's time there suggest that the Sairai-dō stood with its back to the hillside, looking down, past the cherry trees, over the pond. The *Musō Nempu* mentions that Saihōji had by Hōnen's time become famous above all for the beauty of the cherry trees that Prince Shinnyo had planted and that during this time "one great cherry tree in particular stood in front of the hall, and in spring the flowers were strewn in deep drifts across the path."[4] Hōnen's other lasting legacy to the site was that it was he who first gave it the name Saihōji, meaning "Western Direction Temple," thus relating it to Amida's paradise.

Over the next fifty years or so the temple suffered from the effects of fire and neglect, as the fashion for visiting it came and went, and its fortunes declined. Although few people may have been there to see it, however, the crimson scatter of blossoms will still have drifted across the garden and been blown gently into the deepening folds of the green carpets of moss. With dilapidation came another kind of beauty.

This period in Saihōji's history continued until 1339 when a fortuitous visit, guided by a whim, led to its revival by Soseki and to its place in history. That year Nakahara Chikahide, the Shrine Priest of Matsuo-Taisha, the local shrine under whose jurisdiction Saihōji then was, visited the neglected property and, for one reason or another, decided to stay overnight. During the night he had a visionary dream of the temple's future, and on waking in the morning, he was determined to revive and rebuild it. When approached soon after this event by Chikahide, who may well have been his student, Soseki immediately agreed to take on the temple: the speed of his decision, in fact, seemed to suggest that he knew all about the site and was already drawn by its nature and its associations with the places of Ryo Zassu's life. The *Musō Nempu* gives a glimpse of his excitement: "for years I have been searching for the mood of Ryo Zassu's world in the mountains, and now I too have a Western Mountain (Nishi-yama) Dwelling. How could I not be delighted?"[5] Thus, at the age of sixty-five and at one of the busiest points of his life, he took on the project that was to represent the culmination of his personal search to understand the true context of his enlightenment: that place of connection between his enlightened spirit and the physical world in which he existed. Few temple sites in Japan can claim such an illustrious pedigree as Saihōji, which had, in Gyōki Bosatsu, Kūkai, Hōnen Shonin, and now Soseki, attracted some of the most important and influential religious figures of their times, who were monks whose understanding of Buddhism took them out of elite society and into the world of the lost and forgotten, those for whom hope was a long lost memory. These were the kind of priests who brought a human warmth to the cold, clear eye of the Buddhist vision, who softened its necessarily pessimistic expectations of what life could and could not offer. The fact that these people were drawn to the site at Saihōji should alert us to the fact that it must have had some special quality of atmosphere, tradition, or landscape that has been lost, without trace, but which was nevertheless a powerful ingredient in its appeal.

Soseki, already captivated by the site, with all its connections and history, and the coincidence of names and places associated with Ryo Zassu, appears to have immediately decided that the place should become a small foundation, a community limited in numbers and access. Essentially, he envisaged a hermitage where he could concentrate on the more private, meditative side of his life, a balance to the busy public world of the Zen School at Tenryūji and the large community of his lineage at Rinsenji. His determination to keep this a small temple is reflected in the *Saihō-yuiken*, the rules and regulations he left for its administration. In these, he fixed the number of priests living there at sixteen and stipulated that whoever was chosen to oversee the running of the temple should not have ambitions for further promotions in larger temples.

Looking at the plans of Soseki's garden at Saihōji reveals it was visualized in two sections. The larger of these is the Lower Pond garden next to the Saihōji River, which is separated from the more modern temple buildings by a series of hedges and walls. The other section of the garden, the "Upper Garden," appears to be much smaller. Bunched up along the lower slopes of the hill above, tucked up behind the large mass of the Kannon Hall and the *kuri*, or monks' quarters, it appears as an entirely separate, almost incidental space. It is based around a single building, and, thus, its paths and the rock groups are invisible from below, hidden deep in the dense bamboo and forest of the mountain. In fact, this apparent disparity in size is illusory and stems from the fact that few plans of the site now include the mountain behind, but show only the immediate garden on the lower slopes. In fact, this upper garden originally included the whole mountain, with pathways leading up it to a pavilion on the top, as at Jōkyoji, Zuisenji, and Tenryūji. When viewed in this context, we understand the overall gardens as two distinct and balanced worlds, very different from each other but linked by the pivotal bridging threshold of the Kōjō-kan, the "Upward Bound Gate."

The speed with which this design was executed, pretty much within the next year, suggests not only that Soseki already had much of the plan in mind, and the materials at hand, but also that he modified existing ponds and waterways rather than starting the whole Lower Pond garden from scratch. Fujita and Omichi, in their book on Saihōji, include two stories about the construction of the garden that give us a priceless glimpse of what went on during this busy time. First, they refer to an early story—not one, incidentally, included as an entry in the *Saihōji Chitei Engi*—that tells of Soseki

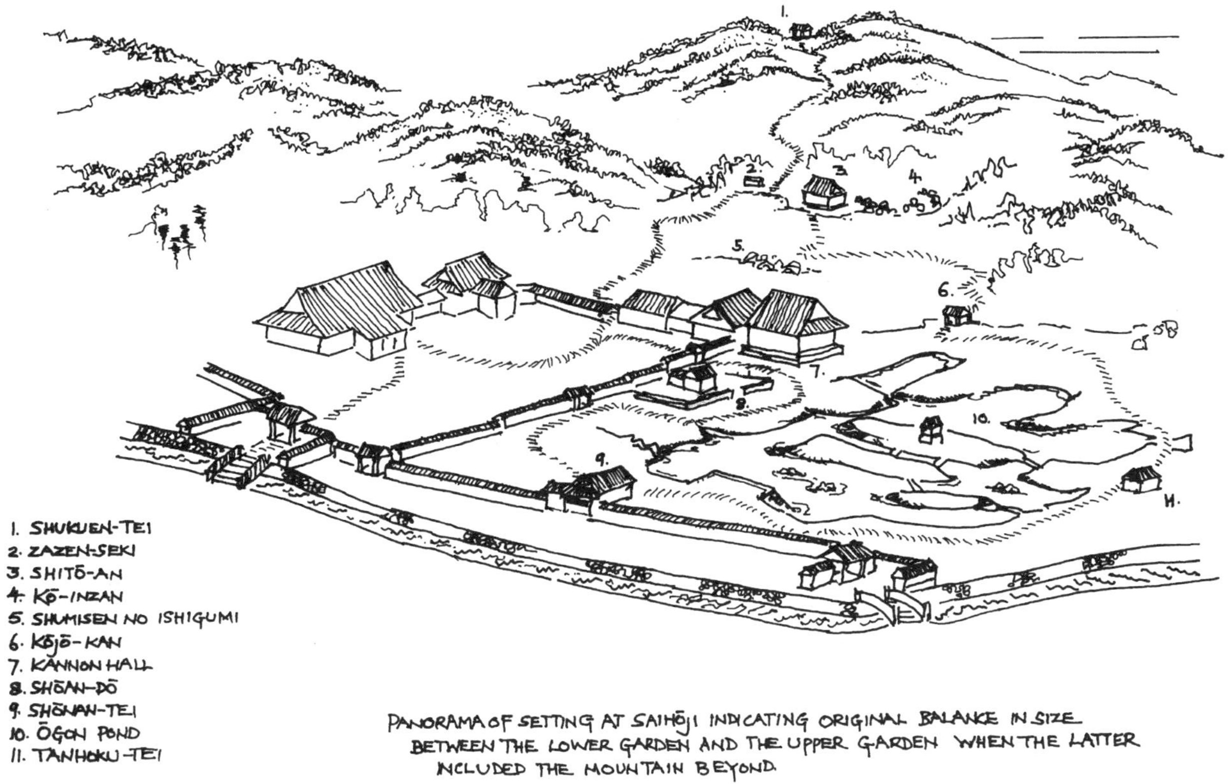

Figure 14. Panoramic impression of Saihōji and the surrounding mountains.

"sweating profusely" during the construction of the garden and clearly very involved with what was going on. The second story, this from the *engi*, tells a slightly more puzzling tale but one that adds to Saihōji's reputation as a place deeply connected to the spirit world and that may indicate that it was Soseki who first used the upper sections of the site as part of the garden.

This second story tells of one particularly big and strong laborer, one of the "stone builders," whose strength in lifting large rocks and carrying them up the hill and whose single-minded dedication to the project had soon caught Soseki's attention. One day this man approached Soseki, held out his long wooden staff, and offered it in exchange for Soseki's *kesa*, a patchwork bib that was an important part of a Zen monk's ceremonial clothing. Much to the surprise of those around him, far from being taken aback, Soseki immediately agreed, and the exchange was made, leaving everyone puzzled and curious as to why he should have done so. That evening, to find out more about this mysterious laborer, one of the temple servants followed the big man as he left after the day's work wearing the *kesa*, and, although he nearly lost him in the busy streets of the Shijō area of Kyoto, he was just in time to see him disappear into the doorway of a small roadside hostel known as a Jizō-in, after the bodhisattva Jizō, the protector of travelers. When the servant hurried to the spot and peeped inside the open door, however, there was nobody there. All he could see inside was a statue of Jizō, wearing, he noticed immediately, the *kesa* Soseki had exchanged that afternoon. Were the man and the statue one and the same?

The meaning of this strange tale perhaps becomes a little clearer when we appreciate that the original *sanskrit* version of Jizō's name was Kshitigarbha, or "womb of the earth," and that he was a central figure in folk belief as a savior of spirits from the torments of hell. It seems to me that what we have here at the very least is the ornamentation of an event whereby Soseki, someone who was always extremely sensitive to the spirits of folk traditions, held a ceremony during which he formally offered the guardian spirits of the tombs and burials that preexisted at Saihōji some recognition of their continuing place and importance at the site. If so, it serves to illustrate just how aware Soseki was of the site's earlier history and just how important this was to him as a part of the place he was building. Yet the events of this story could also, as suggested earlier, relate to something more significant. If, as seems quite possible, the upper area containing the tombs (and known perhaps as Edōji) had remained a separate entity throughout its long and varied history, the story concerning the Jizō figure could well mark the moment at which this old site was finally amalgamated with the temple below, allowing Soseki to expand his gardens up the mountain and realize his ambitious building program. One thing that can be said is that even after

Soseki took over the temple, his new arrangements meant that the upper garden remained out of bounds to all except his special group of monks, maintaining to a large degree its esoteric nature. Whatever the case may be, a statue of Jizō, complete with *kesa,* is still enshrined at Shijō-Teramachi in modern Kyoto, while the staff can be found at the Jizō-in just to the south of Saihōji. For now anyway, there it must rest.

The division of the garden at Saihōji into two parts confirms the central importance of the stories of Ryo Zassu and Nan'yo Echu. In the Lower Pond area we have the water, ponds, streams, and springs of a *sansui* garden. It is an orderly landscape of level ground and wide strolling paths linking the pavilions and communal halls, which are full of details with direct associations to the story of Nan'yo, all of which is laid out in the area that was once a place of communal public burial. In the Upper Garden, on the other hand, we have a steep hillside site that encompasses the whole wild landscape of the mountain: a *karesansui*, or dry setting of rocks, the private worlds of the hermitage building, and *zazen-seki* linked by narrow winding paths, all of which belong to the world of Ryo Zassu's mountain place, set among the ruined individual graves of the *kofun* tombs.

We will begin our exploration of these twin worlds at Saihōji in the Lower Garden, but, before doing so, we need to remind ourselves of the poem that was written by Nan'yo's disciple for the emperor Su-tsung. The emperor had asked Nan'yo what he could offer in return for Nan'yo having left his mountain retreat to come to the capital and become his teacher. Nan'yo had replied that he should build a "seamless tower" for him and ensure that it was maintained into the future. Uncertain as to what this tower should look like the emperor asked for more details and received the poem in reply,

> South of Shō, north of T'an;
> In between there's a land filled with gold.
> Beneath the shadowless tree there is a ferryboat,
> Within the crystal palace there is no one who knows.

There are two things associated with this story that are of great interest to us here. First, there is the seamless tower itself, which, in one sense, was to be seen as a *stupa*. *Stupa* had originally been built in India as places to house the mortal remains of the historical Buddha, the *sharira* (meaning, literally, body or husk), and then the concept developed over the years to signify a more generalized symbol of the Buddha, his life and his works. Their external shape seemed to act as a reminder of the awakened state of mind. Thus, the *stupa* can be seen as a kind of memorial of wide-ranging significance, meaning different things to different people right across the Buddhist world, but also as a reminder of the on-going importance of the Buddha's message. It was not simply something that commemorated a past event and those involved in it, but rather it suggested the continuing presence of the vital spirit or message, accessible, at hand and ready to help. The *stupa* was not simply an empty reminder of someone or something long gone; rather, it was something charged with energy and the potential for action now, in the present, and for the future.

It is in this sense that the *stupa* came also to take on the role of *muhoto*, and it is in the light of this meaning that we should look to understand Nan'yo's seamless tower. The *muhoto* were generally some form of a *stupa* or a small pagoda in which the spirit of an enlightened person could reside, and thus they were a type of memorial, but the idea of *muhoto* also crucially includes the concept of *jyuto*, a "grave" or space built during a person's lifetime into which their spirit can retreat whenever the need arises. It can therefore be seen as the location of an enlightened person following the great "death" of the moment of enlightenment. Beyond this, and equally importantly, it is the place where the spirit can be contacted.

On another level, however, the poem is clearly concerned with a much wider definition of space than that related to an individual memorial. "South of Shō, north of T'an" concerns places that represent the northern and southern limits of T'ang era China. The land between these is China itself, and it is a land, as the second line points out, that is "full of gold," or in other words, a place that possesses the means to sustain its population and create a stable, lasting civilization. In the third line the "shadowless tree" is that which can only be perceived by those who have achieved enlightenment. Of those carried along on the current by the ferryboat beneath the trees, some will be able to see but many will not. Many will not because it had been a long time since anyone in the emperor's "crystal" palace could see the shadowless trees, since anyone there knew, or realized, the importance of Buddhism to the lasting health and prosperity of the state. In short, Nan'yo is telling the emperor that the best way he could repay him and the best way to ensure the stability of his empire was by becoming enlightened himself, and by doing everything in his power to ensure the survival of the Law of Buddha. In this sense, the empire in its entirety could become a *muhoto*, a living memorial to the spirit of the Buddha, carrying it safely into the future.

As we have seen earlier, Soseki identified very closely with Nan'yo and, as the pattern of his life started to follow closely that of the old T'ang master, he sought to learn from Nan'yo's experience and example. Thus, when he came to build his most personal garden, not only was he seeking to create his own *muhoto*, a place where he could be "dead" in life, but also, in the "public" areas of the Lower Garden, he drew heavily on this story, encouraging his contemporaries in power, those who had a chance to create a better future for Japan, to recover something good from the destruction of the ongoing wars, to look to the enlightened understanding of Zen Buddhism to provide the means by which they could do it.

It is clear that the spring-fed pond already existed, and it seems likely that Soseki immediately started the job of cleaning it out, recutting and shaping the banks, and reforming two large islands, the Asahi-jima (Island of the Morning Sun, or more literally, "dawn") and the Yuhi-jima (Island of the Evening Sun, or "dusk"). On the latter he refurbished the Chinju-dō, or Inari (Fox) shrine, which had almost certainly stood there for many hundreds of years and which may also have related back to the days when the site was a burial ground. It was an ancient and still potent contact point with the *kami* and one that Soseki would have been anxious to preserve. The work on the pond, which became known as the Ōgon Ike, or "Golden Pond," would have opened it up and stabilized its water sources by cleaning out the Asahi no Shimuzu, the "Morning Sun Spring," which flowed directly into the southwest corner of the pond, and by cleaning out the stream from the Yuhi no Shimuzu, "Evening Sun Spring," which flowed into the pond from the temple compound to the west of the garden. Additional islands were also created, some rocky islets, like the Hakuo-tō (White Cherry Island) with its "Tortoise" cliff rock, and others more substantial, like the wonderfully ethereal Kasumi-jima (Mist Island) with its trees and moss-enveloped rocks and bridges. Whether or not the small pond now known as the Diamond Pond existed as a separate entity before this time is not clear, but it now has a distinct identity of its own, complete with some twenty rocks forming orderly rows across the surface. Known as Yahaku-seki ("Evening Mooring Stones"), arrangements like these were used to suggest lines of fishing boats tied up after a long days work, with the further suggestion of peaceful calm following the turmoil and battles of life. Although the *Saihōji engi* informs us that these stones were taken from the broken *kofun* tombs, no one directly attributes this arrangement of rocks to Soseki, so it may date from a later period.

Once the work on the ponds was done, Soseki started to implement his vision for the garden by building the Shariden pavilion on the west bank of the Golden Pond. This structure, now sadly gone, was a two-storied building, the lower of which he called the Ruriden (the Lapis Lazuli or Crystal Pavilion), while the upper formed the Shari-dō (the Relics Hut or *muhoto*). Here then was the very heart of his plan: a building that on one level stood for the Crystal Palace, the imperial palaces of the Chinese and Japanese emperors and which, by extension, represented the temporal and

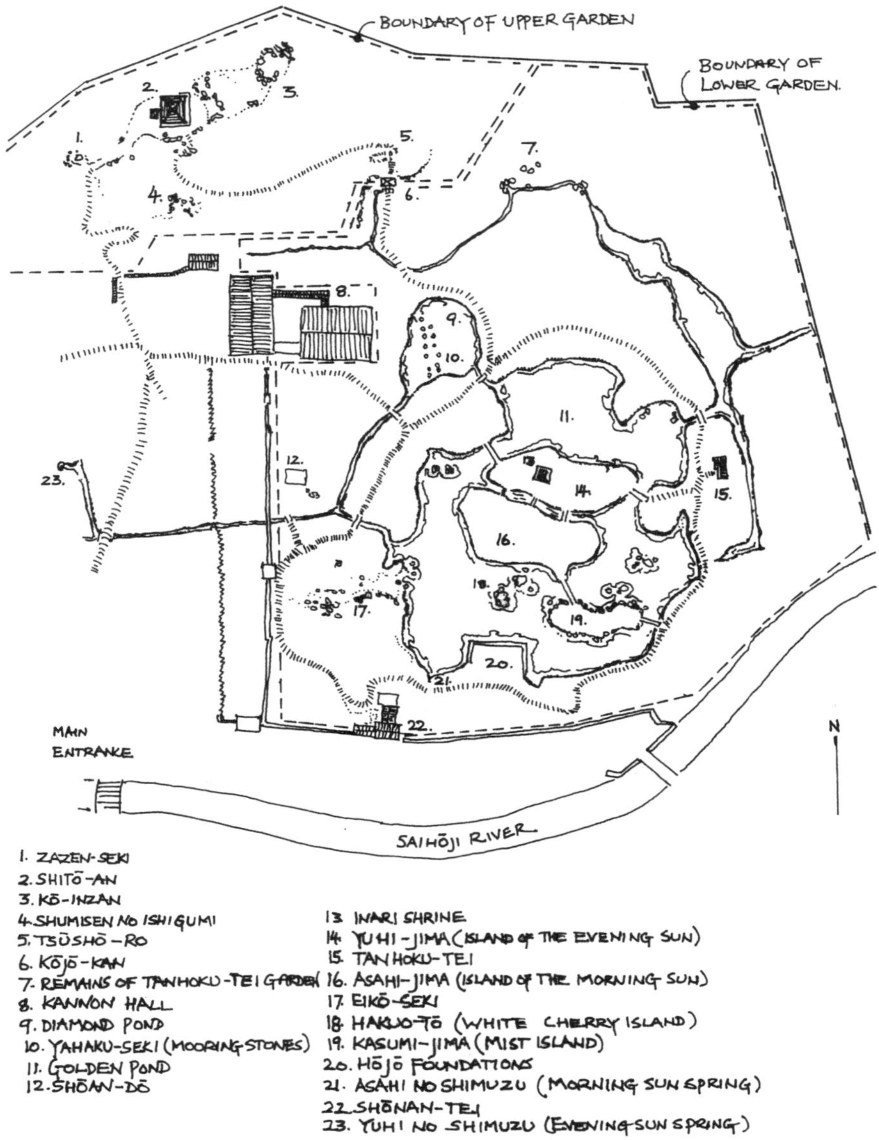

Figure 15. Plan of Saihōji today. Based on Shigemori Mirei and Shigemori Kanto.

physical worlds of these nations and all their peoples and cultures. On another level, it provided a resting place for the wandering spirit of Go-Daigo and of Soseki himself in his official role as master, teacher, and leader of his lineage. Thus, it fulfills the role of Nan'yo's seamless tower in providing a focal point from which the Law of Buddha could then be disseminated throughout the country.

Soseki then completed the "geography" of the garden by constructing two more pavilions, one, the Tanhoku-tei, to the north of the Shariden, and the other, the Shōnan-tei, to the south, using the names of "Tan" and "Shō" to identify this space as the nation itself. In so doing, he linked this garden to the world of Nan'yo, a time when the Zen Buddhism brought to China by Bodhidharma had helped to heal a nation torn apart by war and insurrection, just as Soseki saw the same occurring in the Japan of his time. Following the construction of these two pavilions, Soseki then sited his Hōjō or Abbot's Hall on foundations that dropped straight into the water's edge on the southern bank of the pond, an ideal spot for gatherings of people to sit and lookout over the pond and the intricacies of its islands and rocks, to the Shariden on the left, to the old Sairai-dō beyond, and up into the forested mountain rising calmly behind.

Once the garden was finished it became once again a popular place for the elite of Kyoto to come and visit, drawn partly by Soseki's reputation and partly by that of the cherry blossoms, which were still particularly fine. Accounts survive of the parties that were held there, as do the poems that were written while they were taking place, and with guests including everyone from the emperor and Ashikaga brothers on down, with their palanquins all lined up on the road outside.[6]

An important point to bear in mind about this garden is that the single path that today runs round the perimeter of the Ōgon Ike, through the Kōjō-kan, into the Upper Garden and out into the temple precincts again almost certainly does not reflect the original layout of the path system. It is not clear who chose the present layout and determined the direction visitors are now required to take, but it is unlikely that it reflects the situation in Soseki's day, not least because the gates are in different places. What the original path layout was is equally unclear, but one can imagine, given Soseki's lifelong interest and belief in Shingon / Kannon ritual, that progress through the garden would have been much more convoluted, perhaps reflecting the twisting and turning route involved in a journey through the mandala, or the "actualization of the mandala" traced out in the movement of the *yamabushi* through the Womb mandala of the mountains. Were this the case the pathways no doubt included passing back and forth between the islands using the, otherwise unnecessary, large number of bridges. In short, passing through the garden may have involved a meditative journey, a "mandalizing" of the Lower Garden similar to the process that during the early fourteenth century was being applied to whole areas of Japan such as the Kii Peninsula from Yoshino to Kumano.[7]

Apart from these possible differences in the path system, there are other aspects of this popular and public garden that cannot be seen today since the Hōjō, the Shariden, and the Sairai-dō are all long gone and only the sharply defined foundations of the former still rise somewhat mysteriously from the green waters of the pond. In addition to this, the original Tanhoku-tei has gone, and there is some question as to whether the still surviving Shōnan-tei is in its original position. The Tanhoku-tei originally occupied a site north of the Golden Pond at the foot of the hillside in what are now known as the Northern Gardens of the Tanhoku-tei, while the present Tanhoku-tei in its position on the east bank of the pond is a modern building erected as a teahouse by the twentieth-century ceramicist Mashimizu Zoroku. Running along the bank of the stream, the site of the Northern Gardens still contains the ruins of a number of rock groups, but they now lie off the path and are difficult to make out.

The existing Shōnan-tei now also serves as a teahouse and is especially revered since it is one of only two buildings that have survived in any of the gardens Soseki built, the other being the Kannon Hall at Eihōji. Today the Shōnan-tei stands beside the path around the pond just inside the southern wall of the garden, and this may well have been its original position. Certainly this would fit in with its apparent function of defining the limits of the space running between it and the Tanhoku-tei in the north, but there is some question as to whether or not it originally stood on the more southerly of the two large islands, the Asahi-jima, just across the water from the old Hōjō. If this were indeed the case, it would mean that the whole scheme would have been laid out in front of a viewer sitting on the veranda of the Hōjō, and this may well have been what Soseki intended. The exact history of the Shōnan-tei is thus something of a mystery, but the surviving building with its moon-viewing veranda overlooking the Ōgon Ike is particularly beautiful and evocative, its ephemeral, gentle presence seeming to reflect that of Sen no Rikkyū as the great tea master spent a few of his last tragic days there before committing *seppuku* in 1591.

Existing buildings in the Lower Garden are completed by the Shōan-dō (Small Hut), a tea ceremony house built in 1925. It is dedicated to Shōan (also referred to as Sen Dōan), Sen no Rikyū's son, who seems to have repaired the dilapidated Shōnan-tei after his father's death and who has thus retained a connection with the garden. Whether the site or the small garden that now surrounds the Shōan-dō was built in Soseki's day remains unclear.

Other than these buildings the Lower Garden contains a number of complex rock groups and waterways, many of which show signs of much disturbance and alteration, which make it difficult to relate them to Soseki's time or to comment on their possible roles in his scheme for the garden. Two streams enter the pond from the west, one flowing in under the garden walls from the Yuhi no Shimizu spring, while the other makes its way from below Gyōki's willow tree by the west gate, through an area of chaotic, tumbled rocks which may once have been a carefully designed streambed and waterfall, and out to the pond, passing a solitary standing rock known as the Eikō-seki (Descending Spirit Rock) on its way. The name of this stone carries a number of interesting associations, and it could also be translated something like "Altar Stone for Descending Spirits," referring particularly to those great spiritual figures of the past. The suggestion here is of the manifestation of a supernatural being, the fleeting glimpse of a shadow, something powerful sensed rather than seen, and this seems to bring us firmly into the ancient realms of the shamans. It would appear as though this small stone next to the flowing spring waters may mark one of the oldest sacred places in the garden, a place perhaps that was the center of activity when the *kofun* tombs were erected, or even before. Whatever the case, the stone's survival suggests powerful traditions protected it, allowing it to play a crucial role in the story of the garden, since it was on this rock that the local god Matsuo Myo-jin was sitting when he appeared in Nakahara Chikahide's revelatory dream that night in 1339. In the dream, the spirit lamented the state of the temple, saying, "From the beginning I have made my appearance in this place [made himself accessible], but now this seems to have been forgotten. There is no one caring for my shrine." The next day Chikahide went in search of the rock, perhaps he had to clear away the overgrown garden to find it, and when he found it he noticed it had been freshly wrapped with a *shimenawa*, the sacred rope of the *kami*. Since this time, in remembrance of the occasion, a new rope is tied around the rock at the New Year.[8]

To the east of the pond just beside the Tanhoku-tei, a stream enters the pond having flowed all the way around the northern sweep of the garden from a source behind buildings of the Kannon Hall and Kuri, picking up water from various trickles coming off the hillside along its route. As this stream wends its way round the northeastern corner of the garden, it passes through the tumbled rocks, some of them of considerable size, which were clearly once part of the gardens of the Tanhoku-tei. Having passed this point, it flows through a now abandoned and shapeless part of the gardens until it eventually turns and flows into the Golden Pond. Like the disturbed rock groupings, the original course and shape of this streambed is now indiscernible and lost.

Figure16. The Eikō-seki at Saihōji. Tucked away amid the scattered remains of a stream setting beside the Golden Pond, the Eikō-seki (Descending Spirit Rock) is just visible wrapped in a new shimenawa in the right-hand middle distance. This rock was one of the focal points of ancient spiritual power on this site. It drew Soseki to it and linked his endeavors here to Japan's traditional spiritual consciousness. Photo by the author.

Having mapped the garden that Soseki built, two surviving descriptions of it help us to understand what it looked like. Kawase quotes part of one such description, from the *Nempu*: "The shallow water flowed across the stones, until they appeared polished like jewels glittering below the surface." It goes on to talk about the white gravel, the pine trees of fantastic shapes, the groves of trees, and the "eccentric" boulders, all surrounded by deep forest. It mentions "a boat tied up to the pavilion which in turn is reflected in the water" and concludes that it was a unique and wonderful place that "could not have been made simply by the hand of man."[9]

The other eyewitness account of the garden comes seventy years after Soseki completed it, by which time some changes must have occurred but before the depredations of the brutal Ōnin Wars (1467–77), which left so much of Kyoto and its temples and gardens in ruins. The short account comes from the *Rosho do Nihon Goroku*, the diary of the Korean official Sokikan, and it records that of all the gardens he saw in Kyoto Saihōji was his favorite. Here he saw a garden focused on a pond that had three islands. One of the islands was made of white sand and stones and had a pine tree and a *tei*, or small rectangular building, on it. The other two islands had small *ro*, round Chinese-style buildings, on them, and on three sides of the pond there were dense clumps of flowering trees pruned "on two levels." What Sokikan saw was not the moss-covered, natural-looking, garden of today, but a tightly organized layout dominated by Chinese design. Nevertheless, as Kamagaito's commentary goes on to point out, while Soseki on the one hand seems to have borrowed freely from the Chinese-influenced Jōdo gardens around the ponds, he also created a series of austere rock groupings that drew on different traditions and that represented something unique. Sokikan comments on this austerity and goes on to note that the hillsides above the garden were so heavily planted with pines, bamboo, and flowering shrubs that the whole garden felt dark. In spite of the unexpected austerity and dark feel of the garden, Sokikan notes that in bringing to life the "gentleness of *sansui*" Soseki had shown the "true heart or essence of a garden designer."[10]

As at Tenryūji this part of the garden comes with a list of ten areas or special places. An attempt to interpret their connotations helps us, I think, to get a better feel of what effect Soseki intended it to have:

10 Areas around the Ōgon Ike.

Eikō-seki:	Descending Spirit Rock (extant)
Hakuo-tō:	White Cherry Island (extant)
Suichiku-sho:	Green Bamboo Islands
Godo-tei:	Meeting hut
Yogetsu-ko:	Moon Viewing Bridge (extant)
Shōnan-tei:	Name taken from poem (extant)

Tanhoku-tei:	Name taken from poem (extant)
Sairai-dō:	Coming from the West Hall
Ruriden:	Lapis Lazuli Hall
Chōsei-kaku:	Spirit Polishing Pavilion

Many of these, "White Cherry Island," "Meeting Hut," and so on, are straightforward place-names used in identifying parts of the garden or in providing inspiration for those sitting and writing poetry, and the Eikō-seki, as we have noted, brings to our attention the presence of those who have gone before, making us conscious of Gyōki, Hōnen, and Kūkai and, in a wider sense, of Nan'yo, and sets the whole tone for the experience of the garden. Equally important, as we prepare to leave the garden, we would have come across the Chōsei-kaku or "Spirit Polishing Pavilion," and in this case we are to understand the word *spirit* to also contain the sense of *ch'i*, or the animating flows of energy that swirl through everything.[11] Judging from the use of the word *kaku*, this particular pavilion actually appears to have been a small tower-like building that functioned something like a spiritual whetstone, providing a place to stop and pause, to concentrate our energies and focus the mind on what the path has just led us through and what is coming next. Interestingly, Yoshikawa also quotes from the introduction to one of Soseki's *waka* poems, in which he tells us specifically that the reason he "plays around with *sansui*" is in order to polish up the luster of the spirit. In Soseki's time, reaching this point was the end of the garden experience for most visitors, but for him and his students it was a place to prepare to ascend to the Upper Garden. As we too prepare to ascend, it is our loss that the pavilion no longer exists, but there is some confusion as to where it actually stood: the lists of place-names include it in the Lower Garden, while some research has suggested that it in fact stood in the Upper Garden, just before we reach the Shitō-an, and that the extant Shumisen no Ishigumi rock group is built around the original foundation stone of this hall. Either way, Soseki meant it as a place to help clear the mind and sharpen the focus of practice.

Just as the position of the Chōsei-kaku is uncertain, the descriptions of the Lower Garden that we have looked at suggest that it was evidently very different from today. This means that, when attempting to unravel the complexities of Soseki's design, we have to be very careful not to assume too much from what we see today, especially when, as Kawase's experience of the garden shows, it is clear just how fast the garden can change.

Kawase recounts first visiting the garden in the mid 1920s and then again in the 1960s. His first visit was on a hot summer's day, and, having walked a considerable distance from the train station at Uzumasa, he was delighted to find that descriptions he had heard of the deep, shady lushness

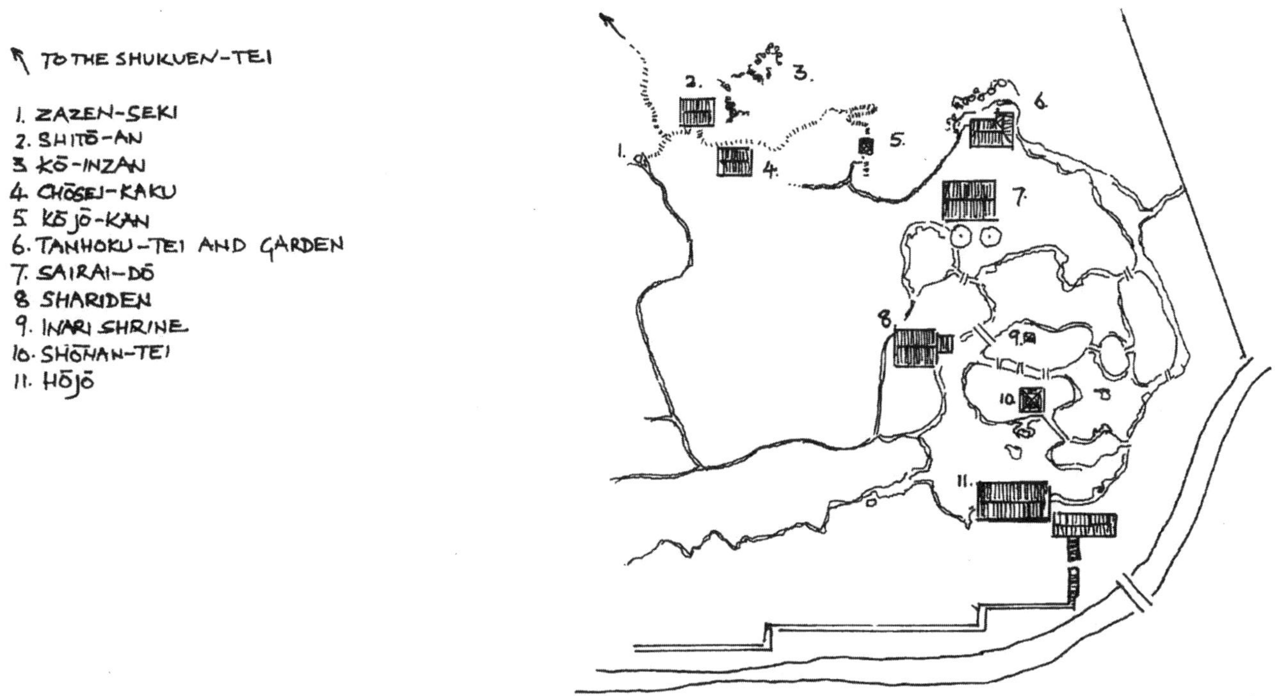

Figure 17. Plan of Saihōji in Soseki's day. Taken from a plan by Nishizawa Fumitaka.

of the garden were true. After crossing the Saihōji River he entered the main gate. When he stepped into the temple grounds, out of the bright sunlight and into the shade of the tree canopy overhead, the dense vibrancy of the moss took him aback. The shades and textures were so deep that he felt, as he describes it, "enveloped in color," the whole experience far surpassing everyone's descriptions. And he had yet to enter the moss garden itself. In the years between this visit and his next, however, things had changed considerably, mostly as a result of the devastation wrought on the trees and moss during a major typhoon in 1935. Whereas before he could only make out the sky in the clearing above the pond, on returning in the 1960s, he found the canopy drastically thinned, the dense shade gone, and the moss fading and degraded. It was still a wonderful garden to visit, but something of the magic that circumstances had given rise to at the beginning of the twentieth century had gone.[12] Now, at the beginning of the twenty-first century, and the garden's seventh, trees that were regrowing during the 1960s are fuller and more mature, and some of that deep shade is beginning to close in again. This pattern of change serves to warn us regarding the ebbs and flows of various aspects of the garden.

An interesting question that this raises, however, is, Was the carpeting of moss in the garden there when Soseki took it over, or was it introduced by Soseki, or did it creep in of its own accord during one of the many long periods when the garden subsequently fell into neglect? Given the nature of the site, it seems most likely that the answer lies in a combination of all of the above. It seems likely that moss has always covered the damp floor of the forest, that Soseki carefully cultivated it, encouraging it to play its part in aging and unifying the designs he built, and that it came back with a vengeance whenever human activity slackened off. If this is so, it probably means that we will never see it again as Kawase saw it in the 1920s since the pressures on the moss from visitors and pollution are too overwhelming for it ever to regain that kind of vigor.

Having followed the path around the Golden Pond, we leave the Lower Garden and, climbing a few steps, cross the stream to approach the Kōjō-kan. At one time the gate marked the end of the public gardens, and its sturdy form provided the garden and hillsides above with a sense of deep, impenetrable privacy that is impossible to imagine today. But it was, nevertheless, a gate; it was always meant to open, and we must try to understand the function that it had since it was not simply a barrier but also the link that provided access from the lower to the upper gardens. As such it is one of the most important elements in the garden, something very easy to miss today since it is now rarely, if ever, closed, so we no longer have to pause to open it on our way up the hill. This means that our experience today of this crucial transition point has lost the momentary break in progress that might cause us to stop and reflect on the gate and its purpose.

It was not meant, however, to be something that, when shut, bars access to the mountainside above, but rather something that, when opened, makes us aware that we are passing from one place to another, from one state of mind to another. Even though it is well over six hundred years old and for many of us sits on the other side of the world, it still has the ability to draw us in and provide this experience with a degree of intimacy and a sense of enchantment that have become truly rare in our modern world. I know of very few places outside the natural world, whether they are in a garden or not, about which this can be said.

There are three aspects of Soseki's Kōjō-kan and its setting that immediately make it special. First, there is its name, the Kōjō-kan or "Upward Bound Gate," which should alert us to the fact that this is more than just a gate as barrier. Certainly it will have acted as this, but since it is not flanked by walls or even fences of any length or substance, security was clearly not its primary aim. Indeed, its name suggests movement rather than obstruction, and the flight of steps visible immediately behind it confirm that this is what is being implied. But the idea of a barrier that is not a barrier, the barrier that encourages movement through it, takes us immediately into the world of the Zen *kōan*, since it is a direct reference to the "Gateless Gate" (*Mumon-kan*), the title of an important collection of *kōans* published in China in1229. The *kōans* were used by Zen masters to point out some aspect of the true nature of reality, and, set as a puzzle, their comprehension required the student to make a leap to a higher level of understanding. Thus, we see another aspect of the Kōjō-kan revealed as we realize that the upward movement associated with it has a spiritual as well as a physical dimension, an idea that another phrase using the characters for *kojo* seems to confirm. This is *kojo no ichiro* where the meaning is a path leading upward, or, in other words, the path or "way" of totally dedicated practice. The gate, then, is telling us something; it is inviting us forward into an experience that has the potential to take us to a higher level, up the twisting mountain path that leads to understanding.

The second point of interest here is the gate itself, which is a small, unassuming structure on a small site. It is not known how many times this structure has been replaced or how it originally looked, but it seems pretty clear that this was never a grand or decorated building, but rather one that echoed the quiet, muted appearance of the forest above. The final aspect that makes this gate so special, and perhaps the most intriguing of all, however, is its setting, a careful integration of the structure among a number of other components, which has all the signs of being original. Looking at the plan,

Figure 18. The Kōjō-kan at Saihōji. The Kōjō-kan (Upward Bound Gate) is the pivotal point in one's journey through these gardens. Although a simple structure, this gate nevertheless marks the crucial threshold between the Lower and Upper Gardens at Saihōji. This is the point where Soseki wanted the visitor to be aware of stepping through subtle boundaries into a higher state of consciousness, and ultimately into enlightenment. The rising steps of the Tsūshō-ro (Night Meditation Path) can be seen rising up the wooded slope behind, leading to the Upper Garden. Photo by the author.

Figure 19. Closeup view of the Kōjō-kan at Saihōji. The carefully engineered introduction of water right in front of the gate and the bridge crossing the water indicate just how important this place was to Soseki as an expression of *MA* as *Hashi*, a bridging point between worlds. Here, we leave the everyday world and enter the illusive world of enlightened consciousness. Photo by the author.

two things about how and where the gate is sited are immediately clear. First, it sits exactly at the point where the descending slope of the mountain meets the horizontal level of the garden area, that special spot or matrix formed by the meeting of the vertical and the horizontal that we have seen Soseki choose again and again as the site for his place of meditation. This brings into play not just the immediate visible context of the gate but also the entire matter of Japanese myth and consciousness, giving the site a particular importance. In addition to this, the second thing to notice is that the gate and the approach to it are aligned closely enough to the north-south line for us to speculate that this was deliberate, echoing the approach to the Kannon Hall at Eihōji, and this in turn brings into play associations with the *kofun* tombs. Soseki has thus constructed an entrance to his Upper Garden that has associations with some of the most important aspects of Japanese consciousness, that place where their lives are perceived to be lived and where the relationship of those lives with the spirit world of the dead exists.

Perhaps the most interesting aspect of the setting, however, is the carefully engineered addition of water and what this adds to its impact and the associations attached to it. A quick look at the plan will show that considerable care was taken to bring water right to the threshold of the gate. A small channel leading off the nearby streambed was built alongside the path approaching the gate to feed water into the small pool positioned exactly in front of the it and from which its plinth rises. The pool is the same width as the gate, and the short watercourse ends right there. This arrangement was specifically built to include water in the setting, and this means, in turn, that the gate is actually entered from a narrow stone bridge rather than the path itself. Apart from aesthetic considerations, I believe that this piece of design is a crucial prompt from Soseki to help us to understand just how important this gate is. It unmistakably tells us that this is *MA* as *Hashi*, as the bridging threshold between one world and another, one of those critical points where the boundaries between the spiritual and physical worlds are thin enough to be crossed and where interaction between the two can take place. The bridge is itself a kind of intermission, a pause or space between the banks; passing over it, one has an opportunity to prepare for the other side. It is one of Soseki's great achievements that the Kōjō-kan should be so unobtrusive and ordinary even while it is manifestly something of great significance.

It is quite clear that the experience of the Kōjō-kan was carefully engineered to ensure that those passing through it had a vivid awareness that they were on the threshold of another realm both in a physical and a spiritual sense, that they were moving through one of those special places where the shift was possible from ordinary, everyday consciousness to something beyond. Specifically, this shift was into that ancient mountain world of the shamans, hermits, *yamabushi*, and Zen masters where a purity of self and vision, impossible in the world of dust below, gave access to the great stores of wisdom and knowledge that had for so long been hidden away and protected up there. Soseki was providing access to this as seen through the clear eye of Zen enlightenment, for himself, but also for those able to follow the markers he left in his illusory landscape. Passing through the gate and starting the upward journey by ascending the steps immediately behind, we are aware that Soseki expects us also to move up into a higher spiritual plane, but what were the markers to this higher plane that he left for us in his own search for his place in the landscape?

First, there are the ten areas of the Upper Garden to help set the tone and guide us along:

Kōjō-kan:	Upward Leading Gate (extant)
Tsūshō-ro:	Night Meditation Path (extant)
Shukuen-tei:	Distance Shrinking Pavilion
Bifu-ten:	Shop for Selling the Wind
Shitō-an:	Pointing East Hut (extant)
Ryoga-kutsu:	Ryoga Grotto
Kiun-dō:	Returning Clouds Cave
Ryū-ensui:	Deep Dragon Pool or Spring (extant)
Macho-matsu:	Wearing Down Head Pines
Kinjaku-an:	Fishing for Silence Hut

Very different from the names used in the Lower Garden, these are all references to the world of Zen practice and the process of meditation. As we have seen, the first of these relates to the world of *MA*, the gate as *hashi*, forming the threshold and providing access into this very different world. The second, the steps of the Night Meditation Path, relates to *MA* as *michiyuki*, pacing the visitors progress and setting a rhythm for the upward journey ahead, all the way up to the Shukuen-tei, where everything is pulled together into sharp relief and interrelated. On the way up, the path passes markers that focus the mind on the processes of meditation: "Selling the Wind," "Returning Clouds," "Wearing Down Head," and "Fishing for Silence," and in the middle of it all, the "Pointing East Hut" bringing the story and life of Ryo Zassu into the forefront of consciousness. Interestingly enough, the list also includes two caves, about which absolutely nothing is known, their significance and location lost, but it is tempting to think that these might well be in someway associated with the collapsed spaces of the *kofun* tombs that also occupy this mountainside. Fujita and Omichi are emphatic that all these named places relate in one way or another directly to the ruined tombs, but the only one that I think can be identified today is that which plays a central role in the layout of the Kō-inzan, about which we will say more later. Also of interest at this point is the Ryō-ensui, the small spring that to this day bubbles up next to the *zazen-seki* to the west of the Shitō-an. The connotations of the pure spring water, its life-giving properties, its function as the key agent of purification in traditional Shintō beliefs, as well as its associations in Buddhist thought to the sermons of the Buddha, combined with the idea of the awakening dragon that we have see repeated in the Ryūmon no Take waterfalls, produce a mix of references that provide a potent "spiritual" setting for the *zazen-seki* to complement the power of its physical location.

The Tsūshō-ro, or "Night Meditation Path," leads from the Kōjō-kan and winds its way up the steep zig-zag set of steps and out across the wooded hillside. Eventually it leads all the way to the top of the mountain, where Soseki erected the Shukuen-tei, "The Shrunken Distance Pavilion." On the way up it passes the Shitō-an, a small hermitage building, and the *zazen-seki* with its accompanying spring. And all around, the dense bamboo groves, the trunks of the forest trees with their shady canopy, and the moss-covered landscape beneath them create a world of small sudden views as the path turns and a clearing opens up. It is an intense, inward-looking place, full of small corners and angles of rock and tree trunk, with dark shadows surrounding the shafts of light that pick out the steeply rising bank of the hillside, a set of steps, a group of rocks, or the lichen on a twisted tree branch; and here and there, dotted along the slope, are the tumbled remains of the *kofun* tombs, ancient places that had once been potent passageways to the spirit world. Much more than from the look and feel of the Lower Garden, we can be sure that this was how the Upper Garden would have appeared in Soseki's day, something seemingly confirmed by an entry in the *Nempu* that describes the building of the Shukuen-tei. This entry describes how Soseki and his garden builders cut back the trees and built a path, now lost, for bringing up the logs for the building. The path, incorporating forty-nine steps, was "dangerous and winding, slippery with moss, shrouded in the clinging mist and pressed in on by the thousands of trees of the dense, dimly lit forest," the sloping floor of which was covered in moss that "lay densely packed like a covering."[13] Of the Shukuen-tei itself there is apparently no trace; the really important part of this garden, however, lies not at the top of the mountain but rather in the complex of components that are associated with the Shitō-an hermitage, components laid out in an area that was once the sacred space of Edōji, within landforms originally built around the *kofun* tombs and that reuse stones taken from their collapsed structures. Of the Shitō-an Soseki says, "About halfway up the mountain there is a separate hermitage that I have named the 'Shitō-an' and to which I have made direct reference in the story of Yushu-sai meeting Ryo Zassu."

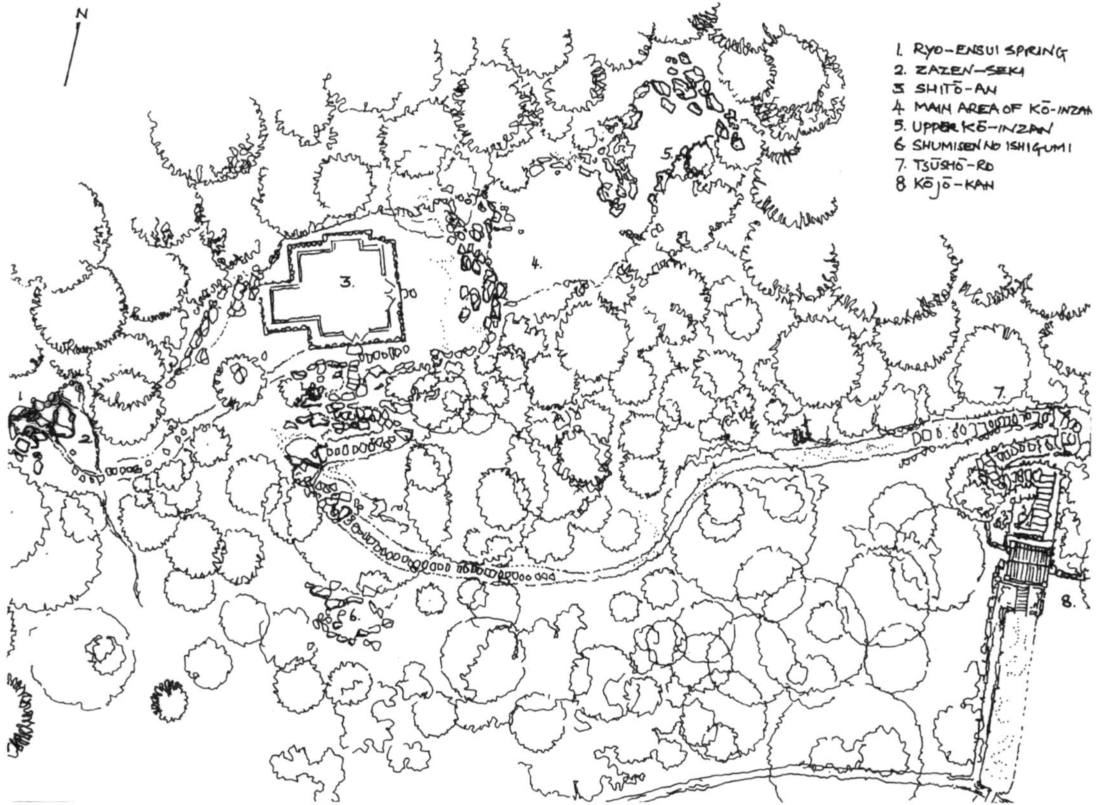

Figure 20. Plan of the Upper Garden at Saihōji. Based on Shigemori Mirei and Shigemori Kanto.

1. Shitō-an: The hermitage that Soseki established halfway up the mountain marks the center of the whole Upper Garden layout and focal point between the *zazen-seki* immediately to the west and the Kō-inzan rock group stretching away to the east. The name means literally Pointing East Hut, and this places it firmly in the story of Yushu-sai's meeting with Ryo Zassu at the point where the old monk rises from amid his pile of leaves and, in answer to the traveler's question, "Ryo Zassu, is it you?" points to the east and vanishes, leaving only his warm dry rock as evidence he was there. It is not clear exactly how old the existing building is (it is certainly not the original), but it is now a striking building, its clean lines and bright white walls standing out in the subdued light of the forest. It has two doorways, one facing south and the other east, which open up into a small, uncluttered room. All it contains now are commemorative plaques for all the "ancestors" of Saihōji, from Gyōki onward, and, in alcoves, wooden statues of Soseki looking east out of the open door up to the Kō-inzan, and Nakahara Chikahide and his wife sitting next to each other, looking south out over the temple complex they had so much to do with establishing.

It is the experience of approaching the Shitō-an from below that first alerts one to the thresholds of rock that are built into this part of the garden. The first is formed by the rocks through which the steps to the Shitō-an pass. They serve to separate the building from the slopes below, visually setting it on a different plane. It is not an overwhelming structure, but in the back of one's mind the closely packed rock composition creates an awareness that this building is up on a level above, reminding us of the sense of upward movement established at the Kōjō-kan. Once we are up on the level of the Shitō-an, two more rising thresholds of rock become apparent in the structure of the Kō-inzan rock groupings, thresholds that are also provided with steps and that have the potential to take us up into the illusory world of Zen enlightenment.

Turning back to the Shitō-an for the moment, even if this particular building bears little resemblance to that which existed in Soseki's time, its function in the garden is still clear; it represents the location in which Soseki placed himself among the components that he saw as making up his place in the landscape. This was where he sat, folded into his surroundings, and able to bring together all that went to make up his consciousness of self, all that came with who he was, and all that had come to him through his Buddhist practice. Around him were the things that made up this consciousness, his *zazen-seki*, connecting him to all those enlightened souls who had passed before and would pass in the future; the mountain rising behind, connecting him not just to the ancient locations of wisdom and knowledge of the shamans and hermits of Japan but also to those of China and India, and the

Figure 21. The Shitō-an from below. Climbing through the Upper Garden, the visitor finds the Shitō-an (Pointing East Hut) sitting above the barriers of rock through which those seeking enlightenment must find a path. Once there, today's visitor enters the illusive world of Zen enlightenmentg, the place where Soseki, following the example of Ryo Zassu so many years before, could take his place in the landscape and unite his spiritual and secular lives. The Kō-inzan rock group lies to the right of the building, while the *zazen-seki* is to the left. Photo by Mahalo Wilbury.

landscape stretching away in front of him, to where, for the awakened eye, "the mountains and rivers / completely disappear." The important thing to realize about this design is that, unlike all the others, the Lower Garden included, this was not a garden that was meant to be looked *over*, from a particular viewing point like, for example, the veranda of the Hōjō. Instead, the entire composition represented the viewing point itself; it was designed to be looked out *from*, out over further, distant places. It was the contact point where he and the greater reality became One and differentiation ended.

Thus, the critical element of this building was the east-facing open door that provided the link with the world of the Kō-inzan, which was designed to be seen from a sitting position and framed by the posts of this doorway, the space created by these being the pause that is defined by *MA*. This pause provides the threshold from one world to the next: *MA* as *hashi* provides the bridge, and *MA* as *himorogi* defines the sacred space beyond, into which one moves. The enlightened consciousness that can see this bridge and the space beyond is freed from the world of intellectual convention and can move out into nirvana, the extinction beyond differentiation. For a seated person, the viewing point formed by the doorway creates the correct distance and low angle from which the Kō-inzan should be seen. From this distance, with the "non-looking" eye of meditation, neither focusing on nor registering any particular rock or area, the rocks of the composition form up in peripheral vision, creating an unspecific illusionary world that has a similar volume to those he had spent his life looking at, from Mt. Gentoku onward. Yanagida's comment on this extraordinary place sums up what was so new and important about it: "[Soseki] was a unique artist who converted the traditions and forms of Ch'an Chinese style into something accessible and valid for the Japanese."[14]

2. Shumisen no Ishigumi: There is very little one can say about this group of rocks that lies on the hillside below the Shitō-an. There is a real problem about its origins, subsequent history, name, and nature. If the foundation stone of the original Chōsei Hall lies in their midst, then the group is a composition that should not concern us. If, however, it is indeed a *Shumisen* group and it stood either to the side of the Chōsei Hall, or on its own (if the real location of the hall was in the Lower Garden), then it obviously has significance in that it expands enormously the volumes of the illusive worlds visible from the Shitō-an. But if, as some commentators believe, it is a turtle island group, then it would seem to be strangely out of keeping with the sophistication of the rest of this garden and would seem to be a later addition, or at least a rearrangement of whatever Soseki put there. So much uncertainty makes any other comment rather futile.

3. *Zazen-seki*: As the present-day path leads on west, past the Shitō-

an, it rises slowly before coming to a set of steps, at the top of which it turns left, to head downhill again and eventually out of the garden. As it reaches the top of the steps, however, it passes one of the biggest single rocks in the garden sitting up to the right, a big rectangular block of rock about 1 m high, 1 m wide and 1.5 m long, its grey flat sides speckled with moss and lichens, its broad flat top warm and dry. This is Soseki's *zazen-seki*, the place he sat for long hours of meditation, the place in the Nishi-yama where as he sat through the long seasons as the leaves slowly built up around him. Were we to approach him today and ask, "Soseki, is that you?" if, as he stood up and pointed east, we followed his gaze, we would be looking across into the Kō-inzan, into "the worlds beyond number" of enlightened consciousness. Is this what Yushu-sai saw when he looked east following Ryo Zassu's gaze?

The rock is actually part of a careful setting. Just behind it, tucked in among the rocks, a spring fills a small pool from which the water overflows and runs out into a narrow rill, which, in turn, passes beside the *zazen-seki* before coming together below the path with another rill that flows along the other side of the rock and runs off down the hill. You have to listen very carefully to hear any activity from the spring, but it is there, and the rills are most active after rain. The spring is not featured in any way; in fact, rocks placed between the path where it turns and the spring itself make the spring hard to see, and this seems to suggest that it was the presence, and perhaps the sound, of water that was important to Soseki here, thus completing the set of elements that we have identified again and again at the places he chose for his outdoor practice from Unganji onward. The *zazen-seki* here represents the culmination of this long succession and, of all the places in this garden, it is perhaps this one that could be said to represent the heart of this place that Soseki, as a student himself and then a teacher, had finally been able to create. The enlightened eye, the hard-won experience, and the location all came together for him at this rock. And as he sat there, with him were all the Zen masters who had in one way or another helped him along to this point, all of them from Bodhidharma himself, to Hui-neng, Ma Tsu, Ryo Zassu, and Nan'yo during the T'ang, to Chung-feng Ming-pen and Rankei Dōryū, to Bukkō Zenji, Issan, and, last but not least, Bukkoku Zenji. All of these were with him, as well as all the Zen poets and painters who had shown the way through their art. All these people sat shoulder to shoulder with Soseki on this rock and gazed out into the world.

> Among mist-wrapped vines and rocky caves
> Here in the wilderness I am completely free,
> . . . On a bed of stone I sit alone in the night,
> While the round moon climbs up Cold Mountain.[15]

Figure 22. The *zazen-seki* at Saihōji. Soseki's big, square *zazen-seki* looms large above the Ryō-ensui spring behind it. Photo by Mahalo Wilbury.

Thus, on one level, the *zazen-seki* drew on old traditions that defined the hollows in rocks, trees, and so on that were periodically occupied by the returning spirits. In this way the stone could be sensed to be the location where the unbroken chain of consciousness that was represented by all these enlightened people was focused and could then be contacted and drawn on. By creating this location, the *zazen-seki* thus represents one-half of the equation of time and place that provides the means for accessing that chain of consciousness as a step toward enlightenment. The other half is not so easily explained because the closest Zen understanding comes to a recognition of "time" is the identification of something that might be called the "continuity of process." The problem that Zen has with the idea of "time" is that it carries with it the fixed and differentiated concepts of a past, a present, and a future, where all it recognizes is a single undifferentiated "now," a moment of sensation that in itself contains the experience of everything that has gone before and the potential for everything that will come after. Thus, the only thing that is real is "now." As we have seen, *MA* sees the onward movement of Process as a series of intervals or pauses, and it is perhaps in this way that we can see the *zazen-seki* as marking the passage of time within the Zen sense of Now.

To do this we need to imagine, for a moment, a person standing on a level piece of ground who then throws a stone up into the air in front of him or her. The stone will travel up and away from the person in an arc, reaching a high point and then falling away to land on the ground again. There is a sense, in the vertical plane, in which that stone is actually in the same place because it has fallen back to the same level it left, but there is also a sense, in the horizontal plane, in which an interval was created and that, although it appears to be in the same place, movement has occurred; it is further away on the far side of the pause caused by its flight. Process has moved on, and the "same place," or "now," has changed. The stone and the level are the same; in other words, all that existed before is still present, but they are present in a new "now," not left behind in isolation. Equally, the potential for it all to change again is there, part of it now, not existing separately in a future. In this scenario, then, the *zazen-seki*, as a stone filled with the consciousness of everything and everybody from the past and the potential of the future, marks the spot where the descending vertical line meets the continuous horizontal line, delineating an interval and creating the moment and place of "now."

In its role of marking this point of intersection, the *zazen-seki* also becomes a critical contact point between the spiritual consciousness it contains and its place now in the physical world. In this context it represents *MA* as *himorogi*, the location of the space into which the spirits descend and are manifested, and thus carries a particular responsibility as that dimension of a place that makes it special, or sacred, rather than just a place. Crucial also to its function as an effective place of contact is the fact that it is a natural, uncut, and unshaped piece of rock, a part of the natural world into which the enlightened spirit can blend. Here is some explanation of Soseki's remark that only a moss-covered rock can act as a *zazen-seki.*

The *zazen-seki* was thus a very important and complex component of this garden. On the one hand, its practical everyday use was to provide the location for Soseki's long hours of meditation, a practice that continued unbroken through those busy times of garden building. On the other hand, it was also the connection not just to the wider world of Zen beyond its walls, but also to the whole thread of Soseki's life. When sitting in the Shitō-an looking east into the Kō-inzan, Soseki would have been fully conscious of the *zazen-seki* at his back, just behind the hermitage, marking that place he had sought so consistently in the landscapes of his travels: the meeting point between the vertical and the horizontal, the mountains rising up behind him and the view stretching out in front, the point where the mountains met the sea and life found a foothold, where, in meditation, his consciousness had seamlessly intertwined with that of the world around him.

4. Kō-inzan: Laid out to the east of the Shitō-an across a flatter piece of the hillside, this was, as we have noted, designed to be seen from a seated position inside the Shitō-an. Stretching out for some 25 m, and, at its widest, about 4 m across, the composition steps up in three main levels, each rising about 1 m, the last of which turns to the left, back into the hillside. In all, the painstaking and beautiful plans measured and drawn up by Mirei and Kanto Shigemori in 1976 show that the layout contains some eighty rocks of various sizes, the largest, up in the back, being about 1.7 m high. These are not large rocks, but the sharp edges, points, and irregularities that characterize them suggest strongly that we are looking at the broken remains of much bigger pieces that once formed the structures of the *kofun* tombs. These are definitely not river rocks but rather pieces of mountain outcroppings that have been chosen specifically because their crisp outlines and grey denseness powerfully express the hard resilience and vibrant strength of the mountain world.

The relationship of the rocks to the landform around them has altered to some extent after six hundred years of weather, and after ardent sweeping by the gardeners has in some places eroded up to 30 cm of soil from around their bases. For example, the second step of rocks now stands quite a bit higher in relation to the flat area in front of it, and the small chinking pieces used to support and level up the front row of these rocks are clearly visible. The rocks have thus become more prominent, a situation that has slightly altered the balance of elements that lay at the heart of this piece of design and that made it so extraordinary. Looking at the composition of rocks visible from the Shitō-an, one is immediately struck by the fact that the eye passes over it in unbroken sweeps; there are no featured rocks, nothing that stands out as a focal point, everything has been set at heights and angles that ensure the individual units merge into one. Apart from this one distortion of the original composition by the process of erosion, however, the homogeneity and understated completeness of what we see today seem to support the unanimous opinion of the commentators that Soseki's original work has survived in a way that it has not in the Lower Garden. It was informed by all the traditions that had gone before, those of the Heian gardens and those introduced from Song China, but this rockwork was something new and individualized. It grew out of the tumbled ruins of the *kofun* tombs, but it was also a work of deep personal experience of the landscape and takes us all the way back through Soseki's travels, back past all the places he stayed and meditated, past the mysterious rocks on the slopes of Mt. Gentoku, to the landscapes of his childhood. The intensity that this rock setting expresses as a result reflects the something of the qualities that drew followers to him then, especially the hard-bitten samurai, and it is an aspect of it that draws us now. That these rocks survived is perhaps due simply to chance, but I would not be surprised to find that, at least until the secularization that accompanied the drive to modernize the country toward the end of the nineteenth century, these rocks, and indeed the whole area that occupied the "defiled grounds" that had once been Edōji, had been protected by powerful taboo, as they were in Soseki's day, and that people rarely visited this domain of the *hi-nin*.

Although we are going to look at the composition of the Kō-inzan in some detail, so that the reader has a clear idea of what is actually there, this is not, I believe, how it was meant to be viewed. As I have mentioned in the discussion of the Shitō-an, I believe that the compositional elements only make any sense if they are not "looked at," but rather allowed to form the peripheral shapes in our vision as we look away toward the middle distance above the second step of rocks. This way, helped by the homogeneity of the arrangements, they form part of where we are looking "from," out toward the infinite worlds, and part of the threshold space, so that the differentiation between viewer and view disappears. Looked at in this way, the rock groupings take on forms and scale not possible if looked at directly, and the viewer's perception of what is out there alters radically.

The first two levels of the Kō-inzan sit on a wide, basically flat "bench" on the hillside, the hill rising steeply up on the left from the edge of the rock groups while, on the right, after a slight roll in the ground that

Figure 23. The Kō-inzan from the east side of the Shitō-an. The rocks and spaces of the Kō-inzan lead the eye out and away from its immediate surrounding. The sunken, upper section of the composition lies to the left, the top halves of its rocks visible at the back of the setting. Note also the massive presence of the central rock in the lower section, gathering the entire composition and lifting it toward the middle distance. Photo by Mahalo Wilbury.

Figure 24. The Kō-inzan from sitting level in the Shiō-an. The Kō-inzan rocks serve not as a view to be looked *at* but as part of the place *from* which one is looking out into the distant world beyond. In this photograph it is possible to see the long-term effects of erosion that have removed a considerable amount of soil from the flat, central area. This is evidenced by the clear exposure of the small supporting rocks beneath thr rock on the right-hand side in the background. The main result of erosion is that the rocks in the foreground are in sharper relief, and therefore more prominent, than they would have been when Soseki laid out this composition. Photo by the author.

rises just high enough to frame the edge of the setting, the land falls steeply away to the slope below and to the path winding up from the Kōjō-kan. The setting alters radically after the second step of rocks. At this point the composition angles to the left, entering a clearly defined, almost rectangular space cut back into the rising hillside, the sides lifting sharply up with the slope on either side. This space is obscured from below, tucked away from view, and at the back of it, built into the bank, perhaps 2 m in height, are the big rocks of the dry Ryūmon no Take composition, the hidden heart of the composition: but more about these rocks a little later. First, we need to understand the nature of the space in which they are set. Two things are immediately apparent about this shadowy place. First, it was at some time dug out of the hillside; second, it faces roughly southeast, well within the range of directions found not just in the *kofun* and key-hole tombs of Japan, but also those of Korea.[16] This would all seem to suggest that this rock grouping has not only been built of rock from the ruined *kofun* tombs but has also been built reusing the tomb space itself, providing this part of the garden with a particular set of associations and giving it a gravity and importance all of which we need to bear in mind when we come to interpret it.

With the upper section obscured from view, it is the two lower bands of rocks and the flat area between them that dominate the area to the east of the Shitō-an. The lowest band of rocks sits on a clear, mossy slope of the ground rising gently up from the graveled path that runs around from the front face on the southern side, and this path provides the viewpoint for visitors today. Into this band is set a small flight of five steps that lead up to the large flat area beyond. Placed to either side of these is a series of rocks and rock groupings that rise and fall along a line of sharp-pointed summits, gathering up toward a central peak that leads the eye away across the slope, an arrangement that is contrasted with the generally flat tops of the rocks behind which is a tightly composed group of square shapes and rising flat tops. Between the two, the composition is given depth by the flat, mossy, open space and the angled rocks that point back along its left-hand side. With the space of the upper section largely out of sight, the second band of rocks and the tops of the Ryūmon no Take rocks meld into the hillside and the gathering tree trunks of the forest beyond. From a seated position inside the doorway of the Shitō-an, this place becomes focused within a long, thin line of sight, a carefully balanced juxtaposition that concentrates on the relationship between the vertical and the horizontal elements. Soseki knew all about the power of this place,

Looming up
  rough and steep—
  what force

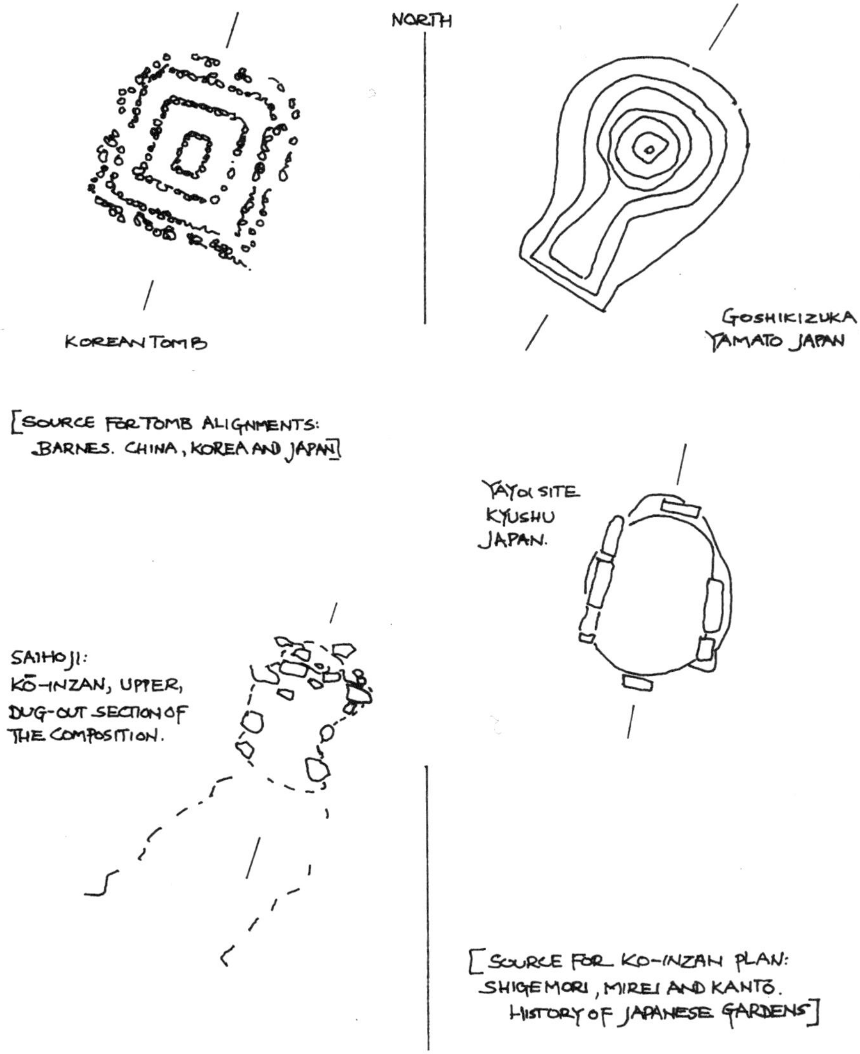

Figure 25. Relative alignments of old tombs and the Kō-inzan composition.

Figure 26. The rocks of the Ryūmon no Take (Dragon Gate Falls). These rocks of the dry waterfall lie at the heart of the Kō-inzan's upper section. The composition sits in a space originally dug out to hold one of the *kofun* tombs that dot this hillside, and like the rest of the garden's rock settings, it reuses rocks from those tombs. Photo by Mahalo Wilbury.

The trees look like works of magic
and all of the stones
are possessed of powers
Once you climb the peak
your eyes
will start from your head
but until then
it stands veiled in unbroken
fog and mist.[17]

The *karesansui* or "dry garden" of the Kō-inzan is formed by stones and moss. Shadows move across it, and the light picks out a detail here and there. As we stand on the path beside the Shitō-an, we gaze across it, looking for images, trying to at least say, "I know what's there." It is described by many visitors and writers as a dry waterfall, partly because the name that became attached to this style of Zen garden, *karesansui,* translates as "dry mountains and water" (*sansui* or "mountains and water" being a Chinese term for a garden), and partly because, looking at it, one has a strong sense of a mountain streambed, the water tumbling down through the constricting rocks and then flowing gently on through a series of wide, slow, eddy-filled pools and over the next falls. Equally there are people who see it as a section of the long, difficult uphill path taken by those seeking enlightenment. Twisting up the mountainside, up short flights of steps, turning away into the unknown, the path is not one lightly embarked upon, nor is it clear where or when, if ever, the end will be reached. Then, in the back of the one's mind is an awareness of the specific names and references that are attached to this place. The name Kō-inzan applies to the whole area in which the composition sits and refers to the "Mountain of Seclusion," with the additional sense of meaning specifically a secluded refuge, while the name given to Soseki's poem about it is *Rinsenkochi,* or "Forest Spring Reaching Heights of Accomplishment." It is also referred to in the one widely available translation into English as *Poem on Dry Mountain (A Zen Garden).*[18]

All this is telling us something: first, as I have already indicated, this should not be looked at in a focused, analytical manner, and, second, following on from this, it is not a monolithic composition. As was apparent when we looked in detail at the components of the composition, it is made up of a number of elements, not all visible from below and not all relating directly to each other. While it all falls within a strikingly cohesive whole with the individuality of the details carefully muted, it is nevertheless a complex combination of ideas. Something of the complexities within this composition can been glimpsed in the word Soseki used to describe the process of making it. Rather than using the standard word *tsukuru,* "to make," which is used of the garden as a whole, for creating the rockwork he uses the word *kumu*, to make as in "design and create." But more than this, the characters that make up the written word carry the sense of bringing things together and interlocking them. They contain the radical for "thread" and thus the sense of creating something by interweaving, the process of taking disparate elements and fusing them together. This sense of interaction is then extended to the relationship between the elements and the maker and then, further, to the finished object and the viewer.[19] It is clear, then, that far from being a closed and completed work, complete and explicable within itself, the rockwork is an open-ended proposition that depends on viewers interweaving their perceptions with it, as much on what they bring to it as to what they actually see.

Before going further with this we need to look again at Soseki's poem to remind ourselves of what he had to say about this garden. He refers to a "forest spring" in the title of the poem, but, from the start, it is clear that this is not one that we should expect to see as we would the Asahi no Shimuzu or the Yuhi no Shimuzu of the Lower Garden.

Without a speck of dust
a high peak rises,
Without a drop of water
a loud waterfall plunges.
On one or two evenings
the wind and the full moon
have enabled the right person
to create and play within the scene.

It is a strange description of a garden, but it makes very clear what Soseki was trying to achieve: Mountains tower up, roaring waterfalls tumble below, but to an enlightened understanding it is clear that there is actually no differentiation. Neither "mountains" nor "waterfalls" exist but are in fact, like everything else, just momentary manifestations of process, and occasionally, given the right circumstances, a person who is ready will suddenly understand this while "playing," rather than consciously searching, in this garden. The idea of the "right person at the right time" is one that he refers to a number of times in his writings, emphasizing the fact that even a teacher with knowledge and experience "will not be able to benefit everyone until he has found the right person and the right circumstances."[20] This is an illusory landscape, bringing Soseki's world into the mainstream of Zen culture and aligning it with the mist-shrouded, hermit-filled mountains of China, a garden that will reveal itself and to which people will react depending on what context they can put it into, not a place where empirical answers should be sought. This garden was not to be taken as literal reality, but rather as an indication of where the true nature of reality lay—in its impermanence.

It slowly becomes clear just how radical a departure this garden was from the Pure Land gardens that came before and even from the pond garden that Soseki had built below. As Yoshikawa puts it, the builder of this garden was no longer satisfied with reproducing an idealized paradise in this world; he sought to explore the "deepest and most demanding principles of Buddhist thought." Sometimes mistakenly discussed in terms of the descriptions of *karesansui* in the *Sakutei-ki*, the treatise on garden making that was by now over three hundred years old, this garden is clearly from a different age and should be seen within the context of its own period. It was a time when Song Zen was not only firmly established in Japan but also the driving force behind contemporary culture. Far from being concerned with the aesthetics of pleasure gardens, Soseki's had an intensely serious purpose as a telling remark concerning his garden at Zuisen-ji indicates. It appears in the diary of the Chinese Zen monk Seisetsu Shōchō, who was involved in the reorganization of the Kamakura *Gozan* monasteries around 1315. After visiting Soseki at Zuisenji and sitting with him in the Ichiran-tei pavilion, he noted, "This garden was not built as a place to simply enjoy oneself."[21] This recognition of the seriousness of purpose behind the Kō-inzan is emphasized by Soseki himself in part of a poem he wrote on completing Saihōji:

> . . . Make no mistake
>   when this humble man
> plays about in
>   the mountains and water
> It is purely to further
>   polish his enlightened spirit.[22]

As to what others might stand to gain by "playing in the mountains and water," Soseki is quite specific in one section of the *Muchū Mondō*: "One cannot say categorically that a liking for mountains and rivers is a bad thing or a good thing. There is neither gain nor loss in the mountains and the river. Gain or loss exist only in the human mind." In short, he can only create a landscape in light of what his long years of experience and his understanding tell him. Whether anyone else gets anything from it depends entirely on what they bring to it, whether they are the right person at the right time. He goes on to specify, "Whether there is profit or loss depends on the heart of the person."[23]

We have gathered, then, that the *karesansui* garden is inextricably bound up with the elusive world of Zen enlightenment, but, more than this, it was involved with the relationship the Zen monks saw as existing between themselves and this landscape. For Parker this is expressed very clearly in the arts of the *Gozan* monasteries from this and the following periods, and he sees it as based on the monks' insistence on the "non-duality of illusion and truth" as they applied this not just to the art they produced, but to themselves and each other. In so doing "we can see that [they] understood the landscape not only as a realm to be explored in free moments from their administrative duties . . . but also as something crucial to their own identities in a fundamental way," and thus "they used the landscape to understand their own sense of self and self-image." Crucially, in doing this, they were able to "seamlessly integrate themselves with not just the 'landscape,' but with a carefully selected 'illusory' individual landscape that mirrored their nature and into which they fitted."[24]

Seen in this light it is clear that the arrangement on the hillside, the Kōjō-kan, the *zazen-seki,* and the Kō-inzan on either side of the Shitō-an, and the careful integration of the Kō-inzan rock groups into the site of the ancient *kofun* tomb, also served another vital purpose for Soseki. It was one that he had been working toward ever since Bukkoku had warned him that if he "made the slightest distinction between the secular and the priestly world, *satori* will remain unattainable."[25] Most specifically, the location of "self" in this composition for Soseki lay in the Ryūmon no Take, the same waterfall group that we have seen at Nanzenji and Tenryūji.

Located within the space originally dug out to form the tomb chamber, the rocks that make up this fall are big square blocks, some of the biggest in the garden, and one can see that, in a different configuration, they might originally have formed the sides or end of the *kofun* tomb. Two large central ones form the first section, while three slightly smaller ones stack up above them forming the top of the fall. Two or three extra form the cliffs to either side. In the center of the composition, one low rock sits down in front of the big ones, while between them a long, thin rock is placed upright, suggesting the struggle upward. Here again are Tenryūji's "Three Grades of Cliff" that Soseki feels he still has to climb to achieve his goals, with the way ahead marked out for him in the vertical faces and twisting route up the falls. Here his spiritual consciousness and physical location combine seamlessly into one, identified not so much by himself as by his pursuit of the Way. In placing himself here, in the ancient space of the tomb, we see Soseki completing the construction and occupation of his *jyuto*, the location where he could be "dead in life."

If aware, we would have been prepared for this aspect of the Kō-inzan from the moment we passed the Kōjō-kan, that carefully constructed entrance to the Upper Garden. Two important Buddhist references come into play as we cross to the small bridge and enter the gateway. The first of them is the image from art and writings of the *hōkyō*, the "dharma bridge," the term in which Buddhism is "compared to the bridge that permits you to cross the river of life and death."[26] The second is, in Buddhist terminology, "arriving at the Other Shore," or at the opposite shore; this means one has lived through one's useful life. The rising arc of its upward flight, powered by internal energies, has stalled and the downward arc, powered by other forces, has begun; at this point it is time to let go of the persona who achieved upward flight and find the new one suited to the next phase: as process moves on, so must we. Thus, on passing through the gate we are aware that the terms of reference for this garden are different, and, with everything the Kōjō-kan is telling us, we can sense something of the ancient, liminal purpose of this site, a place where the entrances and tunnels of the *kofun* tombs provided a threshold to the world of spirits beyond. Once we register this, it becomes clear why Soseki could have written his *yukai*, or "death poem," in 1339, the year he built the garden, but some twelve years before he became ill and eventually died. It was a strange thing to do and remains a puzzle until, as Yanagida points out, we realize that it clearly had something to do with the building of the garden. Once the Upper Garden was built and he had "hidden" himself in it, he considered himself to be "dead in life." He had arrived at the opposite shore and withdrawn, a "temporary master of heaven and a temporary master of the real world,"[27] able to move back and forth, crossing the barriers and pulling his life together, with all distinctions gone.

The convention of the *jyuto* was essentially a "grave" you make for yourself before you die, a memorial or a legacy, a prearranged acknowledgment or retrospective of your life, which took many forms, including the *yukai*. In both China and Japan, aspects of this "retirement" had a long tradition as a form of sanctuary used particularly by those on the defeated side of a power struggle. The convention of retiring into your *jyuto* was respected by those coming into power as confirmation that they need not pursue you further since you had agreed, by retiring, not to participate any more in public life. Soseki's situation and motives were slightly different; after writing his death poem so that everyone understood what he was doing, he constructed his *jyuto* and vanished inside it. His immediate circumstances meant that he had to remain in public life, but he ensured that he retained his private life by retiring to his *jyuto*, and "achieved his serene composure, life without intent by being dead while being alive."[28]

D.T. Suzuki has described this idea of death in life as "the unconscious breaking into the field of the conscious when consciousness loses itself, abandoning itself to the dictates of the unconscious." This is a state closely allied with great "death" of the conscious self that occurs at the moment of enlightenment, and the Zen poets often refer to the life of an enlightened person as "living as a dead man":

> While living
> be a dead man,
> Be thoroughly dead—
> And behave as you like
> And all is well.[29]

These examples are a part of the meaning of what it meant for Soseki to enter his *jyuto,* and, in this sense, this part of the garden at Saihōji was the most important thing that Soseki built. It provided him with that crucial place where his consciousness could slip into the unconscious and return at will, enabling him to maintain control over his life; he had finally found the place where his enlightened soul fitted into the greater matrix of the life of the physical world in which it existed.

There is one further aspect of this association between the garden and the history of the site that is interesting, and this perhaps goes some way toward explaining the degree to which Soseki involved the *kawaramono* people in the construction process. In the *Saihō-yuiken,* in stating the rules and regulations for Saihōji, Soseki stipulates that there were to be three kinds of laymen allowed at the temple. First, there are the *sansui bungyō* or garden managers, second, the Masters of the Baths, and, third, the Masters of the Temples and Stupa of the Defiled Grounds. The rules go on to state that people should be chosen for these posts solely by ability, and that there were no restrictions on the length of their stay. These were, in short, permanent posts, the only proviso being that if someone did not want to work they would not be allowed in. The creation of the third category indicates that not only were the grounds of the upper garden still considered special but that special people would be needed for the garden to be built there.

It is clear that well before Saihōji, Soseki's garden-building activities were cooperative efforts between him and his *kawaramono* helpers, but the project at Saihōji marked something rather more than this, and understanding the garden requires an appreciation of the special relationship that developed here. Yanagida refers to them as Soseki's "hands and feet" but tells us that he also became very involved in their lives and welfare, pointing out that there is much written evidence concerning Soseki's unorthodox relationship with these people and of the criticism he received for working so closely with them in the business of garden building. Manual labor of this sort was considered to be beneath the dignity of a religious figure. It seems, however, that Soseki was willing to go beyond the bounds of conventional behavior to create this garden, and to risk criticism of himself and his Zen lineage. During such uncertain times this cannot have been done lightly, and it was necessary, perhaps, because the *kawaramono* were the only people who would have been able to take over a place so powerfully connected with the "other" world and realign its spiritual associations.

If these were some of the reasons why the *kawaramono* people were so central to the process of the garden building, Parker suggests another when he discusses the extent to which the sense of illusion permeated the art of the *Gozan*. He quotes from the diary of Soseki's key disciple Gidō Shūshin, where he describes a garden as having been "conjured up": "He skillfully built up an artificial mountain for me in a tiny space . . . conjuring up the appearance of a thousand precipices and ten thousand canyons." Parker goes on to point out that the Japanese word translated here as "conjuring up" literally means "produced in an illusory manner."[30] If this description applies to the way the Kō-inzan was created, it suggests that "conjurers," people who, with special esoteric knowledge, can produce magic effects using natural means, were needed to produce this vision of an illusory world. Thus, it was only these people who, because of what they did, were not quite of this world; it was only they who could have produced this landscape. Right here, we are firmly back in the wider understanding of who the *kawaramono*, or *hi-nin*, the nonpeople, were. Soseki could have known what he wanted, drawn the pictures, and chosen the sites and materials, but only these people could have realized it. Only they could have translated the blueprint, laid out in his poem of the Kō-inzan, into the *karesansui* garden.

The details of the three positions for lay people that Soseki created for Saihōji are instructive in understanding how this relationship may have worked. As Kawase points out, these positions were specializations not seen in other temples, and two of them concern the way the garden was constructed and built. It seems that Soseki created the post of *sansui bungyō* specifically for Saihōji, indicating not only how special the project was but also how special these garden managers were. Kawase indicates that their responsibilities included not just overseeing the construction of the garden, organizing and directing the crews, creating the landforms, and placing the rocks and planting the trees, but also maintaining the garden after completion. Change comes inevitably to gardens, and the managers' key responsibility after completion was to carry out whatever care and development was necessary, while ensuring that the spirit of the designer continued to live and be expressed through it, that its special individuality should not be lost. It seems that Soseki created this post to recognize the importance of these people, and Kawase even suggests that he may have lent these managers to the emperor or the shōgun to oversee the building of their own gardens.[31]

We can never know the full details of this working relationship between Soseki and his "managers," but it was a partnership he had used many times before and with which he was clearly thoroughly comfortable. This would require a situation where the concept, the detail of plans developed from it, and decisions concerning the relative importance of these plans within it—and therefore the allocation of the best and indifferent rocks—were necessarily Soseki's responsibility, since this was his search for place. The interpretation of these details and the job of installing the rocks and of making it all work as a finished piece of garden lay with the gardeners. This is a difficult relationship to pursue and one which, to be successful, requires a lot of time and understanding, the ability to articulate and pool experience, as well as a mutual trust and respect which allows ego and all its defense mechanisms to be laid aside. It is a tall order and one that suggests that Soseki may well have been using the same key people through the series of gardens leading up to Saihōji.

Many people visited Saihōji during and after Soseki's time, from members of the imperial and Ashikaga families, important nobles and their samurai, government officials, abbots, priests, monks, and lay people of all kinds. All who saw it, however superficially they took it in, were exposed to "the path of the teacher" whether they knew it or not. As Kawase puts it, all those who visit and come into contact with Soseki's experience and aesthetics as expressed by his garden also come into contact with him, his character, his consciousness, and a method of teaching that placed great emphasis on the role of the garden. Unlike the more elitist literati in China, or even of contemporary Japan, Soseki proposed that Zen could provide a much more broad-based way of reintegrating the human and natural worlds and thus provide a new basis for society. This is clear right down to the makeup of his disciple body, a mixed bag of people from all strata of society. Through this garden innumerable people have been exposed to the path of Zen, and in it we see not just his place in the landscape but also his method for pointing out how others might find theirs. Indeed, he left nothing for the kind of garden design manual often written by the priest gardeners. He preferred instead to indicate a way that would allow the forms of new gardens to emerge from the experience of those who were capable of seeing, through an understanding of their individual consciousness, "the mountain, the river, the earth, the grass, the tree, the tile, the pebble, as their own essential nature."[32] In this way he helped ensure that the Zen gardening tradition did not become frozen into set forms and content, as happened with the ideas in the Sakutei-ki garden manual; the tradition thus was continually able to change and adapt as long as the Zen understanding behind it remained pure and vital.

The Saihōji that Soseki left behind him was not to last long. Although his immediate followers kept it up as a vibrant and important center for the spirit of his Zen, lesser people followed them, and by the time the Ōnin Wars destroyed much of it, the will and ability to resurrect it one more time was no longer there. Despite late attempts by Ashikaga Yoshimasa (1436–90) to rebuild it, during the Warring States period from 1534–1615, the temple fell into a long period of disuse. On top of this, two serious floods swept through the unprotected Lower Garden during the Edo period (between 1603–1868), and, then, as part of the Meiji emperor's efforts to rein in the power of the Buddhist temples, much of the land around the temple was confiscated, never to be returned. Inside what remained, Yoshimasa's buildings slowly collapsed, and the moss and trees reclaimed the garden.

Then, during the earlier part of the last century, the temple began to rise again, when two successive head priests were appointed to restore enough of the buildings to restart a working temple; but the person most responsible for its appearance today was the head priest Kaikatsu, who in the 1970s rebuilt the Sairai-dō in its present position. In this new building, in response to a dream, he enshrined the Gyōki Buddha triad, and then went on to build the three-storied tower known as the *Sanju-nokyoto*, "Sutra Offering Pagoda," which comes closest to replacing the lost Shariden and thus Soseki's *muhoto*. Finally, and perhaps this was his biggest task, Kaikatsu had to find a way of coping with the demands of modern tourism, a problem no one before him had been faced with, and which came to pose as much of a threat to the temple and its gardens as any it had faced before. This was done in the end by firmly regulating access, which meant in 1978 closing the gates to general admission and putting in place a system whereby visits must be booked in advance. This now means that once a day a limited number of people are allowed to visit, and some degree of calm has returned to the garden.

In spite of all the activity and problems that arose during the last six years of his life, Soseki did find time in 1345 to found one more hermitage, the Ungo-an, in the hills just above Arashi-yama. It was considerably closer to both Rinsenji and Tenryūji than Saihōji, and perhaps he used it when his presence was required at either of these two big temples, but he was reluctant to be too accessible to large numbers of people. The site is now occupied by the temple Shōgenji, which sits on a bluff looking down over Arashi-yama with the river running through it, a position that gives it long views out over the plain, now almost entirely filled with the city and suburbs of Kyoto, and away to the surrounding mountains beyond. All that remains from Soseki's time is the semi-derelict garden, the site having been the location of a major battle during the Meiji Restoration. Kawase believes, however, that it is an important garden, not simply because it was Soseki's last, but also because, in spite of the gardens he had just built at Rinsenji, Saihōji, and Tenryūji, it is clear that he still had new ideas that he wanted to express, aspects of our relationship with the natural world that he wanted people to contemplate.

The site he chose confirms the pattern that we have already noted in that not only did it command a fine view, but the hermitage was also built next to an old imperial grave mound. Clearly this association had become a central part of his sense of his place in the landscape, an important connection for him to the deeper roots of the Japanese people and culture and, as at Saihōji, to the spirit world beyond the liminal structures of the tombs. In turn, the name he gave the hermitage also provides some more clues as to the ideas that Soseki was looking to express through the new garden. Ungo-an was named for the T'ang Zen priest Ungo Dōyō (Yun-chu Tao-ying, d. 902), who had been an important master of the Caodong School, which arrived in Japan in 1227 when the Japanese monk Dōgen returned from studying in China to found what became the Sōtō school of Zen.

It seems that Soseki, through choosing to name the hermitage after Ungo, was seeking to emphasize Ungo's reputation for the clarity of his understanding of nonduality, and that the garden here was to convey the idea that beyond Ungo, beyond himself indeed, the important thing to recognize is the form that is revealed once the body and mind have fallen away. That form is the great Oneness that exists beyond individuals and personal consciousness, beyond the dualities of intellectual convention. In his determination to "hide his footsteps" and prevent a cult of personality building up around his legacy, in his final garden Soseki is redirecting everyone's attention to the world of nature beyond our immediate concerns.

Kawase's account of Ungo-an seems to confirm that this is where the emphasis lay. He refers to a drawing that appeared in the *Book of Famous Places*, published in the1820s, some forty years before the garden was largely destroyed during the fighting associated with the Meiji Restoration, which shows the hermitage just to the south of the burial mound and the garden looking out toward the Kame-yama hills above Tenryūji with a wide panorama of mountains leading off beyond Arashi-yama in the background. In the garden itself the drawing shows an arrangement of stones beside a pond with a central island, all done in low profile and opening out to the wide views beyond. Today, what is left of the pond appears in the foreground, while an arrangement of rocks on the far side leads the eye out into the distant view beyond, and this "stacking of planes of perspective gives a sense of multiple resonances, near, mid, and far echoing back and forth." The pond serves as a "collection point for these deep resonances," presenting them in a focused concentration to the viewer. Kawase considers that, although damaged and only a shadow of its former self, the garden still suggests what Soseki intended for it. He thinks it is very significant that Soseki should have chosen this to be the setting for his last garden and believes that Soseki was aiming to emphasize the "ever widening abundance and omnipresence of Nature."[33] What a loss this garden is, since it was not the private world of Saihōji, but rather a final attempt to point the way forward for all those who had joined his school because of his reputation, to enable them to forget him and immerse themselves in the real work of hiding their own bodies and allowing their real form to be revealed.

NOTES

1. Fujita Shūgaku and Ōmichi Jiichi, *Saihōji,* Old Temples of Kyoto, no. 6 (Kyoto: Tankōsha, 1995).

2. Carmen Blacker, *The Catalpa Bow: A Study of Shamanistic Practices in Japan*, 2nd ed. (London: G. Allen and Unwin, 1986), p. 166.

3. *Engi* are the records of origins that every temple keeps, and they are a mixture of hard facts of the temple's foundation—dates, patrons, and founding abbots—and the more poetic semi-legendary stories that give some indication of the founder's intentions and the "feel" of their particular Buddhist consciousness.

4. Fujita and Omichi, *Saihōji.*

5. Yoshikawa Motome, *Karesansui no niwa* (Karesansui Gardens), Nihon no Bijutsu 61 (Tokyo: Shibundo, 1960), p. 32.

6. See especially Fujita and Omichi

7. Allen G. Grapard, "Flying Mountains and Walkers of Emptiness: Toward a Definition of Sacred Space in Japanese Religions," *History of Religions*, vol. 20, no.3 (February 1982): 212, 213, and 215.

8 . Fujita and Omichi, *Saihōji.*

9. Kawase Kazuma, *Musō Kokushi: Zen to teien* (Musō Kokushi: Zen and Gardens) (Tokyo: Kōdansha, 1968), p. 179.

10. Kamagaito Ken'ichi, "Japan and Chinese Culture in the Middle Ages" (in Japanese), *Shin'ika* (November 1992). The account of Sokikan's description of the garden that I have given here borrows heavily from Kamagaito's commentary on it, and I am much indebted to him for bringing it to my attention and offering me his thoughts on this and a number of other aspects of Soseki's work.

11. Yoshikawa, *Karesansui no niwa*, p. 33.

12. Kawase, *Musō Kokushi,* p. 180.

13. Ibid. and Yoshikawa, *Karesansui no niwa,* p. 32.

14. Yanagida Seizan, "Musō Soseki," *NHK "Reading the Heart" Series*, October-November (Tokyo: Japan Broadcasting Publishing Association, 1992), p. 70.

15. Burton Watson, trans., *Cold Mountain: Poems by Han-shan* (New York: Columbia University Press, 1970), poem #49, p. 67.

16. Alignments taken from Gina L. Barnes, *China, Korea and Japan: The Rise of Civilization in East Asia* (London: Thames and Hudson, 1993).

17. Musō Soseki, *Sun at Midnight: Poems and Sermons*, trans. W. S. Merwin and Sōiku Shigematsu (San Francisco: North Point Press, 1989), poem #27, p. 31.

18. Ibid., poem #28, p. 32. See p. 92, n. 44 for an explanation of the use of "Dry" instead of "Artificial" in this translation of the title of this poem.

19. Kawase, *Musō Kokushi*, p. 179.

20. Musō Soseki, *Sun at Midnight*, p. 144.

21. Yoshikawa, *Karesansui no niwa*, pp. 32, 31.

22. Kawase, *Musō Kokushi*, p. 126.

23. Musō Soseki, *Sun at Midnight*, p. 163.

24. Joseph D. Parker, *Zen Buddhist Landscape Arts of Early Muromachi Japan (1336–1573)* (Albany, N.Y.: SUNY Press, 1999), pp. 180, 181.

25. Musō Soseki, *Sun at Midnight*, p. 149.

26. Stephan Schumacher and Gert Woerner, eds., *Shambhala Dictionary of Buddhism and Zen* (Boston: Shambhala, 1991), p. 86.

27. Yanagida, "Musō Soseki," p. 75.

28. Ibid., p. 82.

29. D.T. Suzuki, *Zen and Japanese Culture*, 2nd ed. rev. and enlarged (New York: Pantheon Books, 1959), p. 102.

30. Parker, *Zen Buddhist Landscape Arts of Early Muromachi Japan*, pp. 156, 157.

31. Kawase, *Musō Kokushi*, p. 178.

32. Musō Soseki, *Sun at Midnight*, p. 163.

33. Kawase, *Musō Kokushi*, pp. 180, 181.

CONCLUSION

"Thick Green Moss, All Pure and Sunny Warm"

Saihōji represented something unique, something never done before. It was one of the things that grew out of the dynamic interaction between Chinese Zen and Japanese sensibilities, and, as direct precursor and major source of inspiration for the *roji*, the teahouse gardens of the Muromachi period, it had a profound effect on artists, poets, designers, and crafts people. Equally importantly, it affected the way their patrons saw the world around them and, therefore, the aesthetics of what they built and created to express this vision.

The immediate influence of Soseki's work, the actual forms of the Saihōji gardens, lasted for some 150 years, during which two gardens were built that drew directly on the design at Saihōji, the Kinkakuji, or "Golden Pavilion," built in 1397, and the Ginkakuji, "Silver Pavilion," built as late as 1482. Both gardens were modeled consciously on Saihōji by their respective builders, the Ashikaga shoguns Yoshimitsu and Yoshimasa, who, during difficult times, sought to restore to the faltering Ashikaga dynasty some of the cultural luster of the days of Takauji. Both were serious students of Zen and, believing in the restorative power of *Gozan* art and culture, collected around them the best artists, poets, calligraphers, noh actors, and tea masters of their times.

The layout of both gardens features a two-storied pavilion overlooking a pond dotted with islands of rock groups and pine trees, while on the slopes above, *karesansui* gardens like the Kō-inzan were built. Both pond gardens have survived, giving us a very useful glimpse of how Saihōji's Golden Pond may have looked, particularly that at Kinkakuji which was built only fifty-two years after Saihōji, but both *karesansui* gardens are in ruins and can add nothing to the story. At Kinkakuji the pavilion was originally called the Shari-den, or Reliquary Hall as at Saihōji, but after the walls, doors, posts, and veranda railings were all gilded, it became known as the Golden Pavilion. Amazingly, this beautiful building survived until a fire in the 1950s. Most of the garden had been destroyed in the Ōnin Wars, but it was rebuilt. Freshly gilded in 1988, it shimmers to this day floating on the edge of the pond, lighting up the whole garden. While the pavilion is focused on the pond garden, the slope behind it was originally the site of a rock garden, all traces of which, unfortunately, are long gone. Although one can see plenty of places where the rocks may have been set, all that remains is a modern gravel "streambed." What has survived, however, is the Ryūmon no Take at the foot of the slope, just behind the pavilion. More explicit than anything Soseki built, the water from this fall drops, in a stream, from large plates onto a thin vertical rock set in the pool below, which immediately gives us the image of the carp leaping free of the swirling water as it tries again and again to jump the falls. This fall, as much as the pines and rocks of the islands in the pond, the shoals of lotus plants floating between them, and the *shakkei* views that framed it all, would have been the focus of the many parties, discussions, and exchanges of poetry that Yoshimitsu hosted in his gardens for the leading *Gozan* monks and artists of his time.

At Ginkakuji the connections with Saihōji are even more explicit since its builder, Yoshimasa, is known to have been particularly fond of Saihōji and to have visited it regularly, even making sure, during his military campaigns, that he got away long enough to spend a hurried day or two there. He seems to have particularly enjoyed visiting the garden when it was raining, and he took on the responsibility of ensuring that the buildings and gardens remained in good repair. By Yoshimasa's time, the Ashikaga shogunate was almost a spent force, worn down by ten years of relentless attrition during the Ōnin Wars and by internal mistrust that dated all the way back to the days of Takauji and Tadayoshi. But Yoshimasa looked back to those days, to the achievements of Takauji, Soseki, and the *Gozan* monastries, as a golden era, when they had attempted to bring the "great peace" to a troubled country through the establishment of Zen at the heart of elite society and the promotion of *Gozan* culture as a vehicle for achieving this. Although no longer wielding the same political power as Takauji, and even while the fighting continued, Yoshimasa determined to create at Ginkakuji a center of Gozan culture that would rival Saihōji during its heyday, and make it a place from which the country could again draw inspiration for a cultural renaissance.

Supervising the work himself, Yoshimasa created a pond garden that was viewed from the Kannon Hall, a building that became known as the "Silver Pavilion" even though the silver decoration was never actually added. Seated on the verandas, his guests looked out over the small islands and connecting bridges toward the rising slopes of Higashi-yama behind. At the foot of the slope a stream coming off the mountain flows into the pond over an exquisite waterfall, the water jumping free in a single fragile

Figure 27. The Ryūmon no Take at Kinkakuji. Behind the Golden Pavilion, the Dragon Gate Falls is tucked away into the hillside. The dynamic, rising lines of its main rocks help to lift the leaping fish up and over the obstacle. Photo by the author.

Figure 28. The waterfall at Ginkakuji. The exquisite delicateness of this waterfall at the back of the main garden, and the quiet, moss-covered details of its setting, indicate how the spirit of Soseki's garden at Saihōji was carried forward into the *roji* teahouse gardens that were developed to create the right atmosphere and setting for conducting the tea ceremony, and that were to become so influential in the development of Japanese aesthetics and culture. Photo by the author.

stream as it emerges from the moss at the foot of an old tree, falling past dark, moss- and fern-covered rocks, until it breaks up in a fine spray on a rock some 2 m below. Beyond this a path leads up the slope to a point where the ground flattens out, creating a bowl in the mountainside. Here can be seen the remains of a rock setting, today no more than a jumble of shapes in the long grass on the open hillside, but which, given the quality of work that went into the waterfall, may at one time have been an important composition. There is no indication now of how extensive this composition was or how thickly forested the site was in the fifteenth century, but given Yoshimasa's attachment to Saihōji, one cannot help but believe that this may have been a composition and setting that was, in its way, as interesting as the Kō-inzan.

If, in the basic layout of the garden, Yoshimasa was looking back for inspiration to Soseki and Takauji's time, other aspects of it broke new ground, one of which was the small, four and a half mat room, that looked out over part of the garden and that was specially designed for conducting the tea ceremony. Cha-no-yu, or the Way of Tea, had been popular with the Zen monastic communities for many years, becoming firmly established as a mainstream part of *Gozan* culture during the Muromachi period. But this was the first time that a special room had been specifically built for tea drinking. The tea ceremony, and the teahouses and gardens that provided a context for it, was to become one of the defining arts of Japanese culture, and the sense of design and aesthetics that grew up around it became an important influence on cultures all around the world. Another innovative aspect of the garden was the inclusion of an area of raked gravel surrounding a cone of white sand, used as a focus for moon-viewing parties, a clear emptiness that was soon to be taken up as a major design element.

Yoshimasa's Ginkakuji was thus a thriving center of activity, as Saihōji had been in its day, where traditional artistic pursuits such as poetry writing and ink painting were carried on, and new ones, Noh theater and the tea ceremony, were practiced and developed. Its garden, like that at Kinkakuji some time before, was full of resonances and ideas taken from Saihōji's gardens. There was, however, one big difference between them and Saihōji. These were both multi-faceted places, where Zen practice and the arts were actively promoted, but they were also essentially secular foundations. Although both became Zen temples after the death of their founders, these were not initially temples; they were retreats where members of the Muromachi elite created a cultured and comfortable world for themselves. The severe and uncompromising world of Song Zen practice, which had provided the setting in which Soseki and his contemporaries sought to develop Zen culture, was largely gone, dissipated by time and circumstances.

It was not until the late fifteenth century that, through the efforts of reforming monks such as Ikkyū Sōjun (1394–1481), that some of that spirit returned to *Gozan* practice and culture, turning its back on the pleasure gardens of the dilettante elite.

One of the last outstandingly innovative gardens to be built in Japan, the successor in this sense to Saihōji, was at Ryōanji, a Zen temple not far from Tenryūji. Built in 1499, this garden grew out of the same urge to regain the brilliant sharp clarity of Song Zen that motivated Ikkyū, and its stark, uncompromising rock and gravel landscape indicates just how much had changed in the country. A fierce new aesthetic austerity had developed in response to the continuing decline of the country in the wake of the ten years of war and lawlessness that had swirled around the end of the Ashikaga shogunate. Soseki's approach to Zen, like many other aspects of *Gozan* culture, was seen as too elitist, altogether too soft and compromised by the influences of esoteric Buddhism and traditional beliefs. Now, as Kamagaito remarks, the contemplation of the ephemeral natural world, its seasons and moods, its plants and flowers, was seen as too ordinary and compromisingly intimate; only the hard, unforgiving, burnished forms of the rocks themselves and the spaces in which they existed could help with the search for enlightenment: "By this time, the non-sentient nature of the rocks was seen as the key to understanding, the living plants had no part; the universe is not composed of a gathering of lives but of an all-excluding, transparent nothingness. This strict philosophical spirit put no value on the tremulous lives and fleeting presence of the cherry blossoms."[1] It is important to note, however, that until the twentieth century, the Ryōanji garden also included a *shakkei* view, the composition of the "low wall and the pine grove beyond combining to capture Mt. Otoko, 16 km to the south."[2] This view is now completely lost, and the garden today, turned in on itself by the boundary walls and trees behind, has an even more pronounced sense of alienation from the world; but it seems that the original was, perhaps, not quite such a radical departure from what went before as it now seems.

In spite of the new directions represented by the innovative garden at Ryōanji, which were to alter both the style and our perception of Zen gardens forever, Saihōji remained the seminal influence on the development of the teahouse gardens that became the most important gardens of the sixteenth and seventeenth centuries in Japan and, perhaps, the most influential worldwide of all the styles that developed there.

The use of green tea in monasteries, as a method of staying awake during extended hours of meditation, had a long history in China before it was introduced into Japan by returning monks and the arrival of the Chinese masters in the thirteenth century. Once established as part of the ritual surrounding meditation in the Zen monasteries, drinking tea together seems then to have become a common practice as part of the monastic day. Soseki is known to have conducted tea ceremonies, but it was not until 1339 that these became formalized occasions. The first *daisu*, or stand for holding tea utensils, had been brought back from a Chinese Zen temple in 1286, and the ceremony for drinking tea was created around this. In 1339 this *daisu* was given to Soseki, and he began holding tea ceremonies in the garden at Saihōji. It seems that during this period he was the arbiter of tea taste and handed down a set of rules concerning how the *daisu* should be used.[3] The same *daisu* was subsequently passed down to Yoshimasa, who used it as the focus for the tea ceremonies he held at Ginkakuji. What is interesting here is that the subdued and tranquil moss-covered garden that Soseki created at Saihōji, the illusory world of remote mountain landscapes, thus became the prototype for the first teahouse garden.

Cha-no-yu also felt the influence of the Zen reformers like Ikkyū, and it was with the emergence of a new type of tea master in the mid-sixteenth century that it began to steadily establish itself at the very heart of Japanese aesthetics, deeply influencing the development of every branch of art, craft, and design from architecture to pottery glazes, water bowls to garden gates. The most outstanding of all these figures was Sen no Rikyū (1521–91), who defined forever the "Way of Tea," creating a new style of teahouse and garden in reaction to what he saw as the excessive luxury of the Muromachi style that had developed from the sensual beauty of Yoshimitsu's Kinkakuji. Rikyu's teahouses and tea utensils emphasized the simple, unadorned, and rustic. Things were valued for their imperfections, their roughness, and their humble appearance. Small tea huts of bare wood, chipped tea bowls, an undecorated iron kettle, the simplest bamboo spoons and dippers—these were the things of Rikyū's tea. Further, to create the right setting for his guests as they approached the hut, there was a small garden that suggested a remote mountain path far removed from the everyday world. These gardens were known as *roji*, or Dewy Path, and were seen as the essential place of preparation for the experience of tea that was to follow. When asked to describe the feeling these gardens should provoke in the visitor, Rikkyū said that it was a feeling of "thick green moss, all pure and sunny warm." Unfortunately, influential though he was, the great tea master eventually fell foul of Toyotomi Hideyoshi, the last shogun of the Ashikaga era, and, on being ordered to commit suicide, he spent his last few days at Saihōji, preparing to leave this world in that special place where the next had been brought so close. But perhaps he was also paying a final homage to the garden whose mysterious mossy spaces beyond the Kōjō-kan had, through Yoshimasa and those who followed, provided the inspiration for the *roji* and the whole aesthetic that accompanies the Way of Tea to this day.

"The Kamakura (1185–1338) and the Ashikaga (1338–1568) periods are generally considered the dark ages of Japanese history; the fact is, they are far otherwise. During those times, the Zen monks were active in bringing Chinese culture into Japan and preparing the way for its assimilation later on. Indeed, what we now regard as particularly Japanese was in the process of hatching during those periods."[4] From what we have seen of Soseki's life and work, it is clear that he was at the forefront of this move to assimilate the practices and culture of Chinese Zen, a prime figure in the establishment of the *Gozan* culture at the heart of Japan's, in spite of all the difficulties of the times in which he lived. Yet it is also clear that he was much more than simply a Zen monk seeking to promote Zen culture. Here was a person deeply in touch with his country, its landscapes, culture, and spiritual traditions, whose family influences led him to a sensitive and compassionate outlook on life, someone who, even as the great shrines at Ise lay in desolate ruin, could see a future for everybody.

His Zen enlightenment, when it finally came, was of a depth and quality that surprised even his teachers, and it led to a view of the world based on an encompassing compassion that ensured his teaching methods included everybody from the emperor to the "nonpeople" who worked in the graveyards. But compassion, as personified by his lifelong companion Kannon, was something a person had to work at, to go out and promote actively; it was not enough for it simply to exist, and we see much of Soseki's energies being put into the promotion of the "great peace," bringing renewal out of the experiences of wars, and taking care of all the uneasy spirits through the Ankokuji and Tenryūji projects so that society could move on.

To achieve his own enlightenment he had used his own resources; drawing on his heritage and personal experience, he had battled the difficulties and frustrations until, on his own one evening, far from the monasteries and teachers of Kamakura, he fell over backward and understood. From then on he based his method of teaching on that experience, and the way it had been gained, since his deep, meditative understanding of his personal experiences had led him to that critical union of self and place, joined seamlessly, which he recognized as vital for everyone. Once understood, he then searched tirelessly for the ways in which this could be expressed, avoiding all responsibilities of office until he was ready.

Once ready, he did all he could to show others the way, and, not least, this involved ensuring that the Zen school was as strong and as influential as possible. If it needed patrons to provide lands and incomes, he found them; if it required him to participate in the dangerous world of court and politics, he would; and if it required his temples to be strictly regulated places of dedicated practice and few comforts, they would be. Though compassionate by conviction, Soseki was a nonsentimental, hard-edged teacher, determined that people had to go through the same experiences and processes that he had, and adamant that his personality and teachings should not become a substitute for personal search and experience. Yet elusive as he was during his travels, demanding though he was as a teacher, and as complex as his motives and activities on the political stage may have seemed, he was enormously popular and influential throughout his life; his "way" was clearly very successful.

Apart from what we can never know, the specific insights that flashed before him at the moment of his enlightenment, for example, it is possible, having looked at his life and work, to understand a few of the crucial things on which his "way," or method of teaching, was based. For us these are important since they remain universally valid and offer, at the very least, a starting point for those people today who are seeking this unity of self and place in their lives.

The first of these, I think, is the understanding that he left us of the relationship between life and death, the physical and spiritual worlds, or the intuitive and intellectual forms of insight that we see expressed through his interest in the spaces outside the immediate world. These places included, as well as the caves and tombs, the pauses of *MA* in the processes of life all around us, the *muhoto* and the "distant mind" of the hermits, and Ryo Zassu in particular. Here are the places of the landscape and the mind that can act as the contact points, the bridging points, between states of consciousness that enable us to roam beyond our immediate existence. Recognition of these places on a personal level is an essential prerequisite if one is searching to express "something beyond what one sees."

Following this I believe that Soseki's work shows us how, once contact has been made, "something beyond" can be expressed. As we have seen, artistic pursuits for these monks were of primary importance. They were as important to them as all the other activities that made up their everyday lives, the practice of meditation and the daily chores, something to be pursued with a similar seriousness and dedication. They were not seen as pastimes, or hobbies, or as providing the trappings for elite lifestyles, but rather they were the essential balance to everyday existence, the key to bringing physical and spiritual existence together. Thus, the pursuit and development of the *Gozan* arts was a deadly serious business; it was intimately concerned with expressing their identification of self, the very nature of right here, right now: the place of the enlightened Self within the landscape. Soseki, like all the others, expressed himself in as many forms as he intuitively understood. The primary instrument of artistic expression in both China and Japan has always been the brush, and while it does not appear that he painted, he did use this extensively to practice the art of calligraphy and, leading naturally on from this, composing and writing poems. In both of these disciplines he is recognized now as having been talented, if not exceptional, and his lasting reputation is based firmly on something altogether more tactile and more directly related to the actual elements of the natural world, his landscaping. Through this, and in particular at Saihōji, he left us a succession of pointers as to how he understood artistic endeavor to be able to express that something beyond, and, given who he was, these pointers are inclusive and universal for everyone and anyone who is willing to take the time to understand them and how they relate to themselves.

At Saihōji we can understand what Soseki meant when he told his students about his trip to the liminal world around Mt. Fuji, and how, while there is no "further splendor beyond the West Lake," no heavens or paradises more splendid than the landscape we inhabit now, there is "something besides what [the fisherman] sees in front of him." It is the landscape removed by hard won experience and understanding from its immediate, everyday context and placed in a personal, illusory context, where it can be approached and used. Such a removal enables it to become more than simply the physical world in which we exist and pursue our lives; it becomes also a part of our spiritual existence as well, the place where our worlds can meet and interact. This removal was achieved by Soseki and his fellow monks by means of intense and prolonged meditation on their experiences of the physical world, something unlikely to occur outside their culture. Yet I have seen it achieved in the West by other, no less difficult means. Part of these is a dogged and unrelenting examination of, first, the landscape as it exists, finding out both what it is and the effects its different forms and cycles have on one's consciousness, and, second, the processes of design and construction by which the insights gained can be transformed into a physical reality. With this, however, there must be a determination to approach "art" and "design," and the work of artists and designers, as things that can and should be both informed and improved by the insights, experience, and knowledge of others involved in the process. There must also be a willingness to repeat the processes of design and, if necessary, construction until the results are manifestly "right." Above all, however, there must be a willingness to place the whole endeavor into realms of serious importance that in the West are usually reserved exclusively for business and commerce rather than art and culture. Without this it will never be given sufficient time or urgent concentration.

Soseki had forced himself on to a deeper and better understanding of the nature of reality and his relationship to it, and in spite of being shaken as a young monk by the death of his teacher, he was rewarded with a peaceful death. He had done what he could and had slipped into that place he had identified and built where he was at one with everything around him. Nevertheless, he left many pointers for us to follow, to help us, if we need it, to find our own places in the landscape and in the end be able to reply as this Chinese monk could at the end of the twentieth century, and mean it:[5]

> "Do you get lonely?"
> "No, not as long as I have the wind and the moon, the water and the mountains for my companions."

NOTES

1. Kamagaito Ken'ichi, "Japan and Chinese Culture in the Middle Ages" (in Japanese), *Shin'ika* (November 1992).

2. Itoh Teiji, *Space and Illusion in the Japanese Garden*, trans. Ralph Friedrich and Masajiro Shimamura (New York: Weatherhill, 1973), p. 36.

3. A. L. Sadler, *Cha-no-yu: The Japanese Tea Ceremony* (London: K. Paul, Trench, Trubner & Co., Ltd., 1934), p. 2.

4. D. T. Suzuki, *Zen and Japanese Culture*, 2nd ed. rev. and enlarged (New York: Pantheon Books, 1959), p. 41.

5. Bill Porter, *Road to Heaven: Encounters with Chinese Hermits* (San Francisco: Mercury House, 1993), p. 138.

BIBLIOGRAPHY

Aston, W. G., trans. *Nihongi: Chronicles of Japan from the Earliest Times to A.D. 697.* London: G. Allen and Unwin, 1956.

Barnes, Gina L. *China, Korea and Japan: The Rise of Civilization in East Asia*. London: Thames and Hudson, 1993.

Barrie, Thomas. *Spiritual Path, Sacred Place. Myth, Ritual, and Meaning in Architecture.* Boston: Shambhala, 1996.

Blacker, Carmen. *The Catalpa Bow: A Study of Shamanistic Practices in Japan*. 2nd ed. London: G. Allen and Unwin, 1986.

Cleary, Thomas, and J. C. Cleary, trans. *The Blue Cliff Record*. Foreword by Taizan Maezumi Roshi. Boulder, Colo.: Shambhala, 1977.

Collcutt, Martin. *Five Mountains.* Cambridge, Mass.: Harvard University Press, 1981.

Collcutt, Martin, Marius Jansen, and Isao Kumakura. *Cultural Atlas of Japan*. Oxford: Phaidon, 1988.

Davidson, A. Keir. *The Art of Zen Gardens*. Los Angeles: J. P. Tarcher, 1983.

De Bary, William. *The Buddhist Tradition in India, China and Japan*. New York: Modern Library, 1969.

Dobbins, James C. "Buddhism in Japan." In *A Thousand Cranes: Treasures of Japanese Art*. Seattle: SeattleArt Museum; San Francisco: Chronicle Books, 1987.

Dōgen. *Moon in a Dewdrop: Writings of Zen Master Dōgen*. Edited by Kazuaki Tanahashi. Translated by Robert Aitken. San Francisco: North Point Press, 1985.

Ebersole, Gary L. *Ritual Poetry, and the Politics of Death in Early Japan*. Princeton: Princeton University Press, 1989.

Engel, Heinrich. *The Japanese House: A Tradition for Contemporary Architecture.* Rutland, Vt.: Charles E. Tuttle Co., 1964.

Feng Gia-Fu, and Jane English, trans. *Tao Te Ching: Lao Tzu*. New York: Vintage Books, 1972.

Fujita Shugaku, and Omichi Jiichi. *Saihōji*. Old Temples of Kyoto, no. 6. Kyoto: Tankōsha, 1995.

Grapard, Allen G. "Flying Mountains and Walkers of Emptiness: Toward a Definition of Sacred Space in Japanese Religions." *History of Religions,* vol. 20, no.3 (February 1982).

Grousset, René. *The Rise and Splendor of the Chinese Empire*. Berkeley: University of California Press, 1953.

Hall, Edward T. *The Hidden Dimension*. Garden City, N.Y.: Doubleday, 1966.

Hallendy, Norman. *Inuksuit: Silent Messengers of the Arctic*. Vancouver: Douglas & McIntyre; Seattle: University of Washington Press, 2000.

Hansen, Valerie. *Changing Gods in Medieval China: 1127-1276*. Princeton: Princeton University Press, 1990.

Hayakawa Masao. *The Garden Art of Japan*. New York: Weatherhill, 1973.

Henricks, Robert G., trans. *Lao- Tzu: Te-Tao Ching*. New York: Ballantine Books, 1989.

Hisamatsu Shin'ichi. *Zen and the Fine Arts*. Translated by Gishin Tokiwa. Tokyo and New York: Kodansha International, 1982.

Isozaki Arata. *Space and Time in Japan—MA*. Exhibition Catalog. New York: Cooper-Hewitt Museum, 1979.

Itoh Teiji. *Space and Illusion in the Japanese Garden*. Translated by Ralph Friedrich and Masajiro Shimamura. New York: Weatherhill, 1973.

Kamigaito Ken'ichi. "Japan and Chinese Culture in the Middle Ages" (in Japanese). *Shin'ika* (November 1992).

Kawase Kazuma. *Musō Kokushi: Zen to teien* (Musō Kokushi: Zen and Gardens). Tokyo: Kōdansha, 1968.

Keene, Donald. *Travelers of a Hundred Ages*. New York: H. Hold and Co., 1989.

Keswick, Maggie. *The Chinese Garden*. London: Academy Editions, 1978.

Kuck, Loraine. *The World of the Japanese Garden: From Chinese Origins to Modern Landscape Art*. New York: Walker / Weatherhill, 1968.

Lin, Shuen-Fu. *The Transformation of the Chinese Lyrical Tradition*. Princeton: Princeton University Press, 1978.

Matsuo Bashō. *Back Roads to Far Towns: Bashō's Oku-no-hosomichi*. Translation and notes by Cid Corman and Kamaike Susumu. Fredonia, N.Y.: White Pine Press, 1986.

_____. *The Narrow Road to the Deep North, and Other Travel Sketches*. Translated from the Japanese with an introduction by Nobuyuki Yuasa. Harmondsworth: Penguin Classics, 1966.

Morton, W. Scott. *Japan: Its History and Culture*. New York: McGraw-Hill, 1994.

Musō Kokushi [Soseki]. *Dream Conversations: On Buddhism and Zen*. Translated and edited by Thomas Cleary. Boston: Shambhala, 1994.

Musō Soseki. *Sun at Midnight: Poems and Sermons*. Translated by W. S. Merwin and Sōiku Shigematsu. San Francisco: North Point Press, 1989.

Nakamura Bunpo, and Inoue Hakudo. *Musō Kokushi no fuko* (The Artistic Sensibility of Musō Kokushi). Tokyo: Shunjūsha, 1998.

Parker, Joseph D. *Zen Buddhist Landscape Arts of Early Muromachi Japan (1336–1573)*. Albany, N.Y.: SUNY Press, 1999.

Polosmak, Natalya. "Siberian Mummy Unearthed." *National Geographic*, vol. 186, no. 4 (October 1994).

Porter, Bill. *Road to Heaven: Encounters with Chinese Hermits*. San Francisco: Mercury House, 1993.

Ross, Nancy Wilson. *The World of Zen*. New York: Vintage Books, 1960.

Sadler, A. L. Cha-no-yu: *The Japanese Tea Ceremony*. London: K. Paul, Trench, Trubner & Co., Ltd., 1934.

Sato, Hiroaki, and Burton Watson, eds. and trans. *From the Country of Eight Islands: An Anthology of Japanese Poetry*. New York: Columbia University Press, 1986.

Schaarschmidt-Richter, Irmtraud. *Japanese Gardens*. Essay by Osamu Mori. Translated by Janet Seligman. New York: Morrow and Co., 1979.

Schumacher, Stephan, and Gert Woerner, eds. *Shambhala Dictionary of Buddhism and Zen*. Boston: Shambhala, 1991.

Shibata Masumi. *Les Mâitres du Zen au Japon.* Paris: Maisonneuve & Laros, 1969.

Shibayama Zenki. *Zen Comments on the Mumonkan.* New York: Harper & Row, 1974.

Shigematsu, Sōiku, comp. and trans. *A Zen Forest, Saying of the Masters.* New York: Weatherhill, 1981.

Shigemori Mirei, and Shigemori Kanto. *Nihon teienshi taikei* (History of Japanese Gardens). Vol. 3: *Gardens of the Kamakura Period.* Tokyo: Shakai Shisosha, 1976.

Slawson, David. A. *Secret Teachings in the Art of Japanese Gardens.* New York: Kodansha, 1987.

Smith, Kidder, Jr., et al. *Sung Dynasty Uses of the I-Ching.* Princeton: Princeton University Press, 1990.

Smithsonian Institute. *Dream Window: Reflections on the Japanese Garden.* VHS video.

Snyder, Gary. *The Gary Snyder Reader: Prose, Poetry and Translations.* Washington, D.C.: Counterpoint, 1999.

Stryk, Lucien. *The Penguin Book of Zen Poetry.* London: A. Lane, 1977.

_____, and Takashi Ikemoto, trans. *The Crane's Bill: Zen Poems of China and Japan.* New York: Grove Press, 1973.

Sutherland, Mary, and Dorothy Britton. *National Parks of Japan.* Tokyo and New York: Kodansha International, 1980.

Suzuki, D. T. *Zen and Japanese Culture.* 2nd ed. rev. and enlarged. New York: Pantheon Books, 1959.

Takahashi Kyōichi. *Sites Associated with Musō Soseki* (in Japanese).

Tamamura Takeiji. *Saihō-ji and Musō Soseki.* Nihon Zenshushi Ronshu. Tokyo: Shibunkuka, 1976.

Tanizaki Jun'ichirō. *In Praise of Shadows.* Translated by Thomas J. Harper and Edward G. Seidenstickerf. New Haven, Conn.: Leete's Island Books, 1977.

Tsunoda, Ryūsaku, Wm. Theodore de Bary, and Donald Keene, comp. *Sources of Japanese Tradition.* 2 vols. New York: Columbia University Press, 1958.

Von Franz, Marie-Luise. *Time: Rhythm and Repose.* New York: Thames and Hudson, 1978.

Watson, Burton, trans. *Cold Mountain: Poems by Han-shan.* New York: Columbia University Press, 1970.

_____, trans. *Complete works of Chuang Tzu.* New York: Columbia University Press, 1968.

Watts, Alan. *The Way of Zen.* New York: Pantheon, 1957.

Yanagida Seizan, ed. *Musō. Nihon no Goroku* (Japanese Zen Sayings and Records), vol. 7. Tokyo: Kōdansha, 1977.

_____. "Musō Soseki." *NHK "Reading the Heart" Series*, October-November. Tokyo: Japan Broadcasting Publishing Association, 1992.

Yoshikawa Motome. *Karesansui no niwa* (Karesansui Gardens). Nihon no Bijutsu 61. Tokyo: Shibundo, 1960.

INDEX

ABOUT THE AUTHOR

Keir Davidson, a landscape gardener for many years, has published three previous books on the planning and construction of gardens and on Zen gardening: *Simple Garden Construction* (1980, with David Roberts), *Zen Gardening* (1982 [published in the U.S. as *The Art of Zen Gardens*, 1983]), and *Garden Planning and Construction* (1983, with David Roberts).